Missing Links Exam Preps

Exam Prep for

GEOLOGY: Comprehensive Exam Preparation

Cram101, 1st Edition

The MznLnx Exam Prep is your link from the texbook and lecture to your exams.
The MznLnx Exam Preps are unauthorized and comprehensive reviews of your textbooks.

All material provided by MznLnx and Rico Publications (c) 2010
Textbook publishers and textbook authors do not particpate in or contribute to these reviews.

MznLnx

Rico
Publications

Exam Prep for GEOLOGY: Comprehensive Exam Preparation
1st Edition
Cram101

Publisher: Raymond Houge
Assistant Editor: Michael Rouger
Text and Cover Designer: Lisa Buckner
Marketing Manager: Sara Swagger
Project Manager, Editorial Production: Jerry Emerson
Art Director: Vernon Lowerui

Product Manager: Dave Mason
Editorial Asistant: Rachel Guzmanji
Pedagogy: Debra Long
Cover Image: Jim Reed/Getty Images
Text and Cover Printer: City Printing, Inc.
Compositor: Media Mix, Inc.

(c) 2010 Rico Publications
ALL RIGHTS RESERVED. No part of this work
covered by the copyright may be reproduced or
used in any form or by an means--graphic, electronic,
or mechanical, including photocopying, recording,
taping, Web distribution, information storage, and
retrieval systems, or in any other manner--without the
written permission of the publisher.

For more information about our products, contact us at:
Dave.Mason@RicoPublications.com

For permission to use material from this text or
product, submit a request online to:
Dave.Mason@RicoPublications.com

Printed in the United States
ISBN:

Contents

CHAPTER 1
Test Preparation Part 1 — 1

CHAPTER 2
Test Preparation Part 2 — 21

CHAPTER 3
Test Preparation Part 3 — 38

CHAPTER 4
Test Preparation Part 4 — 59

CHAPTER 5
Test Preparation Part 5 — 81

CHAPTER 6
Test Preparation Part 6 — 102

CHAPTER 7
Test Preparation Part 7 — 115

CHAPTER 8
Test Preparation Part 8 — 136

CHAPTER 9
Test Preparation Part 9 — 155

CHAPTER 10
Test Preparation Part 10 — 175

CHAPTER 11
Test Preparation Part 11 — 196

CHAPTER 12
Test Preparation Part 12 — 213

CHAPTER 13
Test Preparation Part 13 — 237

CHAPTER 14
Test Preparation Part 14 — 255

CHAPTER 15
Test Preparation Part 15 — 271

CHAPTER 16
Test Preparation Part 16 — 284

CHAPTER 17
Test Preparation Part 17 — 304

CHAPTER 18
Test Preparation Part 18 — 323

CHAPTER 19
Test Preparation Part 19 — 332

CHAPTER 20
Test Preparation Part 20 — 337

Contents (Cont.)

CHAPTER 21
  Test Preparation Part 21 — 344
ANSWER KEY — 345

TO THE STUDENT

COMPREHENSIVE

The *MznLnx* Exam Prep series is designed to help you pass your exams. Editors at MznLnx review your textbooks and then prepare these practice exams to help you master the textbook material. Unlike study guides, workbooks, and practice tests provided by the texbook publisher and textbook authors, *MznLnx* gives you **all** of the material in each chapter in exam form, not just samples, so you can be sure to nail your exam.

MECHANICAL

The MznLnx Exam Prep series creates exams that will help you learn the subject matter as well as test you on your understanding. Each question is designed to help you master the concept. Just working through the exams, you gain an understanding of the subject--its a simple mechanical process that produces success.

INTEGRATED STUDY GUIDE AND REVIEW

MznLnx is not just a set of exams designed to test you, its also a comprehensive review of the subject content. Each exam question is also a review of the concept, making sure that you will get the answer correct without having to go to other sources of material. You learn as you go! Its the easiest way to pass an exam.

HUMOR

Studying can be tedious and dry. MznLnx's instructional design includes moderate humor within the exam questions on occassion, to break the tedium and revitalize the brain

Chapter 1. Test Preparation Part 1

1. _____ is the term used in geology for the increase in land elevation due to the deposition of sediment. _____ occurs in areas in which the supply of sediment is greater than the amount of material that the system is able to transport. The mass balance between sediment being transported and sediment in the bed is described by the Exner equation.
   a. Ostwald ripening
   b. Erosion prediction
   c. Orientation Tensor
   d. Aggradation

2. _____ are minerals of importance to agriculture and horticulture, are usually essential plant nutrients. The study of _____ is termed agrogeology, and agrogeologists are concerned with issues such as the replenishment of soil fertility in areas where _____ have been mined out or depleted by unsustainable farming methods.
   a. AL 129-1
   b. AASHTO Soil Classification System
   c. AL 333
   d. Agrominerals

3. An _____ contains aragonite and high-magnesium calcite as the primary inorganic carbonate precipitates. Therefore, the chemical conditions of the seawater must be notably high in magnesium content for a _____ to form. This is in contrast to a calcite sea in which low-magnesium calcite is the primary inorganic marine calcium carbonate precipitate.
   a. AASHTO Soil Classification System
   b. AL 129-1
   c. AL 333
   d. Aragonite sea

4. In geology _____ is the section of a floodplain where deposits of fine silts and clays settle after a flood. They usually lie behind a stream's natural levees.
   a. Salt tectonics
   b. Subfossil
   c. Sclavia craton
   d. Backswamp

5. _____ is a geologic term for a type of topography characterized by a series of separate and parallel mountain ranges with broad valleys interposed, extending over a more or less wide area. It is typified by the topography found in the Great Basin in the western United States, which is part of a larger regional topography known as the _____ Province. _____ topography results from crustal extension.
   a. Basin and Range
   b. Planar deformation features
   c. Zechstein
   d. Palynomorph

6. In machining, _____ is the process of enlarging a hole that has already been drilled (or cast), by means of a single-point cutting tool (or of a _____ head containing several such tools), for example as in _____ a cannon barrel. _____ is used to achieve greater accuracy of the diameter of a hole, and can be used to cut a tapered hole.

The term _____ is also sometimes used for drilling a hole, especially with respect to tunnels and wells in the earth.
   a. 1509 Istanbul earthquake
   b. 1700 Cascadia earthquake
   c. Boring
   d. 1703 Genroku earthquake

7. A _____ is one in which low-magnesium calcite is the primary inorganic marine calcium carbonate precipitate. An aragonite sea is the alternate seawater chemistry in which aragonite and high-magnesium calcite are the primary inorganic carbonate precipitates. The Early Paleozoic and the Middle to Late Mesozoic oceans were predominantly calcite seas, whereas the Middle Paleozoic through the Early Mesozoic and the Cenozoic (including today) are characterized by aragonite seas (Wilkinson et al., 1985; Wilkinson and Given, 1986; Morse and Mackenzie, 1990; Lowenstein et al., 2001; Palmer and Wilson, 2004.)

- a. 1509 Istanbul earthquake
- b. 1703 Genroku earthquake
- c. 1700 Cascadia earthquake
- d. Calcite sea

8. _____ are layers of distinctively textured carbonate rocks which typically form the uppermost layer of sedimentary sequences reflecting major glaciations in the geological record.

The rising temperatures, and increased oceanic surface area - due to reduced ice cover and rising sea levels - at the end of a glaciation increase the rate of precipitation.

High concentrations of greenhouse gasses such as carbon dioxide (CO_2) must build up in the atmosphere to overcome the effect of the high reflectivity (albedo) of ice and allow temperatures to rise sufficiently to begin melting.

- a. Teilzone
- b. Bediasite
- c. Cap carbonates
- d. Tidal scour

9. In chemistry, a _____ is a salt or ester of carbonic acid.

To test for the presence of the _____ anion in a salt, the addition of dilute mineral acid (e.g. hydrochloric acid) will yield carbon dioxide gas.

_____-containing salts are industrially and mineralogically ubiquitous.

- a. 1700 Cascadia earthquake
- b. 1509 Istanbul earthquake
- c. 1703 Genroku earthquake
- d. Carbonate

10. The _____ is the subsurface layer in which groundwater seeps up from a water table by capillary action to fill pores. Pores at the base of the _____ are filled with water due to tension saturation. This saturated portion of the _____ is less than total capillary rise because of the presence of a mix in pore size.

- a. 1509 Istanbul earthquake
- b. Capillary fringe
- c. Rockall
- d. Historical geology

11. _____ are surfaces of synsedimentarily cemented carbonate layers that have been exposed on the seafloor (Wilson and Palmer, 1992.) A hardground is essentially, then, a lithified seafloor. Ancient hardgrounds are found in limestone sequences and distinguished from later-lithified sediments by evidence of exposure to normal marine waters.

- a. 1509 Istanbul earthquake
- b. 1700 Cascadia earthquake
- c. 1703 Genroku earthquake
- d. Carbonate hardgrounds

12. A _____ is a sedimentary body which possesses topographic relief, and is composed of autochthonous calcareous deposits (Wilson, 1975.) Platform growth is mediated by sessile organisms whose skeletons build up the reef or by organisms (usually microbes) which induce carbonate precipitation through their metabolism. Therefore, carbonate platforms can not grow up everywhere: they are not present in places where limiting factors to the life of reef-building organisms exist.
   a. 1703 Genroku earthquake
   b. 1700 Cascadia earthquake
   c. 1509 Istanbul earthquake
   d. Carbonate platform

13. In geology, a _____ is a continental area covered by relatively flat or gently tilted, mainly sedimentary strata, which overlie a basement of consolidated igneous or metamorphic rocks of an earlier deformation. Platforms, shields and the basement rocks together constitute cratons.

It is also common practice to use the term _____ as a very general term for a sequence of shallow water carbonate _____.

   a. Platform
   b. Perched coastline
   c. Fluting
   d. Fabric

14. _____ is a weathering phenomenon of rock surface induration. It is observed commonly in: felsic alkaline rocks, such as nepheline syenite, phonolite and trachyte; pyroclastic rocks, as pyroclastic flow deposit, fine air-fall deposits and vent-filling pyroclastic deposits; sedimentary rocks, as sandstone and mudstone.
   a. Case hardening
   b. Gibraltar Arc
   c. Patterned ground
   d. Geomechanics

15. _____ is the removal of solids (sediment, soil, rock and other particles) in the natural environment. It usually occurs due to transport by wind, water, or ice; by down-slope creep of soil and other material under the force of gravity; or by living organisms, such as burrowing animals, in the case of bioerosion.

_____ is distinguished from weathering, which is the process of chemical or physical breakdown of the minerals in the rocks, although the two processes may occur concurrently.

   a. AASHTO Soil Classification System
   b. AL 333
   c. AL 129-1
   d. Erosion

16. _____ is any particulate matter that can be transported by fluid flow, and which eventually is deposited.

They are most often transported by water (fluvial processes) transported by wind (aeolian processes) and glaciers. Beach sands and river channel deposits are examples of fluvial transport and deposition, though _____ also often settles out of slow-moving or standing water in lakes and oceans.

   a. Sediment
   b. Salt glacier
   c. Bovey Beds
   d. Brickearth

17. A _____ is a practice or device designed to keep eroded soil on a construction site, so that it does not wash off and cause water pollution to a nearby stream, river, lake, or bay. Sediment controls are usually employed together with erosion controls, which are designed to prevent or minimize erosion and thus reduce the need for sediment controls.

- Check dam
- Diversion dike
- Fiber rolls
- Sand bag barrier
- Sediment basin
- Sediment trap
- Silt fence
- Storm drain inlet protection
- Straw bale barrier
- Turbidity curtain

Chemical treatment of sediment, commonly called an active treatment system, is a relatively new form of _____ for the construction industry. It is designed to reduce turbidity in nearby water bodies and involves collection of sediment-laden stormwater in a basin or tank, and adding a chemical flocculant.

a. Mitigation of seismic motion
b. Geologic preliminary investigation
c. Sediment Control
d. Riprap

18. _____ is applied to any orthopyroxene-bearing granite, composed mainly of quartz, perthite or antiperthite and orthopyroxene, as an end-member of the _____ series (Classification of Igneous Rocks, 2nd ed., 2002, by R. W. Le Maitre et al.)

The _____ suite or series is a group of igneous rocks, variably metamorphosed of wide distribution and great importance in India, Ceylon, Madagascar and Africa.

The name was given by Dr T. H. Holland from the fact that the tombstone of Job Charnock, the founder of Calcutta, is made of a block of this rock.

a. Litchfieldite
b. Great Dyke
c. Coldwell Complex
d. Charnockite

19. In stratigraphy, _____ is the native consolidated rock underlying the surface of a terrestrial planet, usually the Earth. Above the _____ is usually an area of broken and weathered unconsolidated rock in the basal subsoil. The top of the _____ is known as rockhead and identifying this, via excavations, drilling or geophysical methods, is an important task in most civil engineering projects.

a. Cyclostratigraphy
b. Polystrate
c. Sequence stratigraphy
d. Bedrock

20. A _____ is the uppermost part of a valley, or a short valley or hollow on a hill or coastline.
a. Combe
b. Diamond Head
c. Submersion
d. Compaction

21. _____ refers to the process by which a sediment progressively loses its porosity due to the effects of loading. This forms part of the process of lithification. When a layer of sediment is originally deposited, it contains an open framework of particles with the pore space being usually filled with water.
   a. Geothermal
   b. Combe
   c. Diamond Head
   d. Compaction

22. In geology the term _____ refers to the system of forces that tend to decrease the volume of or shorten rocks. Compressive strength refers to the maximum compressive stress that can be applied to a material before failure occurs. In tectonics, plates are always subjected to compressive stress.
   a. Leaverite
   b. Geodiversity
   c. Seismic to simulation
   d. Compression

23. The _____ refers to an apparent difference between modelled estimates of tropical temperatures during warm, ice-free periods of the Cretaceous and Eocene, and the colder temperatures which proxies suggested were present. The long-standing paradox was resolved when it became clear that the proxies were misleading, meaning that tropics were warmer than previously believed.

Proxy-based reconstructions of paleotemperature appeared to predict a low temperature gradient between the tropics and poles.

   a. 1700 Cascadia earthquake
   b. 1509 Istanbul earthquake
   c. 1703 Genroku earthquake
   d. Cool tropics paradox

24. _____ is a geographical term best used to describe the wearing away of small/fine particles of rock on a river/seabed by a sandpapering action called abrasion, and it collapses to form a dip in the bed. This sometimes happens at the bottom of cliffs to a slanted edge.
   a. Patterned ground
   b. Geomechanics
   c. Paralithic
   d. Corrasion

25. In geology, _____ refers to inclined sedimentary structures in a horizontal unit of rock. These tilted structures are deposits from bedforms such as ripples and dunes, and they indicate that the depositional environment contained a flowing fluid (typically, water or wind.) This is a case in geology when original depositional layering is tilted, and that the tilting is not a result of post-depositional deformation.
   a. Forebulge
   b. Fabric
   c. Cross-bedding
   d. Geometallurgy

26. In fluid dynamics, the _____ is a phenomenological equation, which relates the head loss -- or pressure loss -- due to friction along a given length of pipe to the average velocity of the fluid flow. The equation is named after Henry Darcy and Julius Weisbach.

The _____ contains a dimensionless friction factor, known as the Darcy friction factor.

Head loss can be calculated with

$$h_f = f \cdot \frac{L}{D} \cdot \frac{V^2}{2g}$$

where

- h_f is the head loss due to friction;
- L is the length of the pipe;
- D is the hydraulic diameter of the pipe (for a pipe of circular section, this equals the internal diameter of the pipe);
- V is the average velocity of the fluid flow, equal to the volumetric flow rate per unit cross-sectional wetted area;
- g is the local acceleration due to gravity;
- f is a dimensionless coefficient called the Darcy friction factor. It can be found from a Moody diagram.

a. Darcy-Weisbach equation
b. 1700 Cascadia earthquake
c. 1509 Istanbul earthquake
d. 1703 Genroku earthquake

27. The _____ is used to calculate the shear stress at the bed of an open channel containing fluid that is undergoing steady, uniform flow. It is widely used in river engineering, stream restoration, sedimentology, and fluvial geomorphology. It is the product of the water depth and the mean bed slope, along with the acceleration due to gravity and density of the fluid.
   a. 1703 Genroku earthquake
   b. Depth-slope product
   c. 1509 Istanbul earthquake
   d. 1700 Cascadia earthquake

28. _____ is a geological term used to describe particles of rock derived from pre-existing rock through processes of weathering and erosion. Thesel particles can consist of lithic fragments (particles of recognisable rock), or of monomineralic fragments (mineral grains.) These particles are often transported through sedimentary processes into depositional systems such as riverbeds, lakes or the ocean forming sedimentary successions.
   a. Leaverite
   b. Pillow lava
   c. Platform
   d. Detritus

29. A _____ or dyke in geology is a type of sheet intrusion referring to any geologic body that cuts discordantly across

- planar wall rock structures, such as bedding or foliation
- massive rock formations, like igneous/magmatic intrusions and salt diapirs.

They can therefore be either intrusive or sedimentary in origin.

An intrusive _____ is an igneous body with a very high aspect ratio, which means that its thickness is usually much smaller than the other two dimensions. Thickness can vary from sub-centimeter scale to many meters and the lateral dimensions can extend over many kilometers. A _____ is an intrusion into an opening cross-cutting fissure, shouldering aside other pre-existing layers or bodies of rock; this implies that a _____ is always younger than the rocks that contain it.

a. Pneumatolysis
b. Duricrust
c. Dike
d. Detritus

30. _____ occurs when a soil is sodic. When a sodic soil is wetted the clay particles are forced apart. This is generally a major cause of erosion.
   a. Metamorphism
   b. Type locality
   c. Honeycomb weathering
   d. Dispersion

31. In geology, _____ is transported rock debris overlying the solid bedrock. The term is also sometimes refers to organic debris so-transported. In the largest sense, it refers to the material left behind by retreating continental glaciers.
   a. Cross-bedding
   b. Geopetal
   c. Drift
   d. Riegel

32. _____ are isolated fragments of rock found within finer-grained water-deposited sedimentary rocks. They range in size from small pebbles to boulders. The critical distinguishing feature is that there is evidence that they were not transported by normal water currents, but rather dropped in vertically through the water column.
   a. 1703 Genroku earthquake
   b. 1509 Istanbul earthquake
   c. 1700 Cascadia earthquake
   d. Dropstones

33. _____ refers to a thin hard layer on or near the surface of soil, usually a few millimeters to a few centimeters thick. It is a general term (not to be confused with duripan) for a zone of chemical precipitation and hardening formed at or near the surface of sedimentary bodies through pedogenic and (or) non-pedogenic processes. It is typically formed by the accumulation of soluble minerals deposited by mineral-bearing waters that move upward, downward, or laterally by capillary action, commonly assisted in arid settings by evaporation.

   a. Slope Mass Rating
   b. Fulgurites
   c. Georeactor
   d. Duricrust

34. _____ is an earth science project using geological and geophysical techniques to explore the structure and evolution of the North American continent and to understand the processes controlling earthquakes and volcanoes. Thousands of geophysical instruments will comprise a dense grid covering the continental United States. Scientists from multiple disciplines have joined together to conduct research using the large influx of freely accessible data being produced.
   a. AL 333
   b. AL 129-1
   c. AASHTO Soil Classification System
   d. Earthscope

35. _____ is concerned with earth materials that can be utilized for economic and/or industrial purposes. These materials include precious and base metals, nonmetallic minerals, construction-grade stone, petroleum minerals, coal, and water. The term commonly refers to metallic mineral deposits and mineral resources.
   a. Ostwald ripening
   b. Economic geology
   c. Eilat stone
   d. Isostasy

36. The _____ are ancient life-forms of the Ediacaran Period, which represent the earliest known complex multicellular organisms. They appeared soon after the Earth thawed from the Cryogenian period's extensive glaciers, and largely disappeared soon before the rapid appearance of biodiversity known as the Cambrian explosion, which saw the first appearance in the fossil record of the basic patterns and body-plans that would go on to form the basis of modern animals. Little of the diversity of the _____ would be incorporated in this new scheme, with a distinct Cambrian biota arising and usurping the organisms that dominated the Ediacaran fossil record.
   a. Ediacara biota
   b. AL 129-1
   c. AL 333
   d. AASHTO Soil Classification System

37. _____ is the name for a green-blue inhomogeneous mixture of several secondary copper minerals including malachite, azurite, turquoise, pseudomalachite, chrysocolla.
   a. Eilat stone
   b. Overbank
   c. Economic geology
   d. Erosion prediction

38. _____ can mean:

   - In volcanology, particles that came out of a volcanic vent, traveled through the air or under water, and fell back on the ground surface or on the ocean floor. _____ can consist of:
     1. Juvenile particles - (fragmented magma and free crystals)
     2. Cognate or accessory particles - older volcanic rocks from the same volcano
     3. Accidental particles - derived from the rocks under the volcano.
   - In planetary geology, the debris that is ejected during the formation of an impact crater.
   - In astrophysics, material expelled in a stellar explosion.
   - In firearms ballistics, everything expelled from a gun, including the bullet, propellant, sabot, wad, etc.

   a. AASHTO Soil Classification System
   b. AL 129-1
   c. AL 333
   d. Ejecta

39. _____ is a geologic term that refers to internal processes and phenomena that occur beneath the Earth's surface - or any other celestial body. Plate tectonics, earthquakes and volcanoes are all _____ processes.

Exogenic refers to external processes and phenomena that occur on or above the Earth's surface.

   a. AL 333
   b. Endogenic
   c. AASHTO Soil Classification System
   d. AL 129-1

40. _____ refers to external processes and phenomena that occur on or above the Earth's surface. Comet and meteoroid impacts, the tidal force of the Moon and radiation from the Sun are all _____. Weathering effects and erosion are also _____ processes.
   a. AASHTO Soil Classification System
   b. AL 129-1
   c. AL 333
   d. Exogenic

41. _____, like hydrogeology, is a multidisciplinary field of applied science and is closely related to engineering geology and somewhat related to environmental geography. They all involve the study of the interaction of humans with the geologic environment including the biosphere, the lithosphere, the hydrosphere, and to some extent the atmosphere. It includes:

- managing geological and hydrogeological resources such as fossil fuels, minerals, water (surface and ground water), and land use.
- defining and mitigating exposure of natural hazards on humans
- managing industrial and domestic waste disposal and minimizing or eliminating effects of pollution, and
- performing associated activities, often involving litigation.

a. AL 129-1
b. AASHTO Soil Classification System
c. Iron catastrophe
d. Environmental geology

42. There are dozens of _____ models. Most have been developed for agricultural areas and are design to compare predicted annual rates of soil loss from broad areas under various cropland and rangeland management techniques. Some are purely statistical models, others mechanistic.

a. Orientation Tensor
b. Economic geology
c. Eilat stone
d. Erosion prediction

43. In igneous petrology, _____ is a term applicable to the layered or banded texture in some extrusive rock bodies. The layering is often caused by the compaction and flattening of glass shards and pumice fragments.

a. Eutaxitic
b. AASHTO Soil Classification System
c. AL 333
d. AL 129-1

44. The _____ of an earth (rock and regolith) material is a measure of the material to be excavated (dug) with conventional excavation equipment such as a bulldozer with rippers, backhoe, scraper and other grading equipment. Materials that cannot be excavated with conventional excavation equipment are said to be non-rippable. Such material typically requires pre-blasting or use of percussion hammers or chisels to facilitate excavation.

a. AL 129-1
b. Excavatability
c. AL 333
d. AASHTO Soil Classification System

45. The _____ is a statement of conservation of mass that applies to sediment in a fluvial system such as a river. It was developed by the Austrian meteorologist and sedimentologist Felix Maria Exner, from whom it derives its name.

The _____ describes conservation of mass between sediment in the bed of a channel and sediment that is being transported.

The equation states that the change in bed elevation, $>\eta$, over time, t, is equal to one over the grain packing density, $\boxed{\times}>$, times the negative divergence of sediment flux, q_s.

$\boxed{\times}>$

a. Economic geology
b. Isograd
c. Erosion prediction
d. Exner equation

46. In geology the term _____ describes the spatial and geometric configuration of all the elements that make up a particular rock.
   a. Perched coastline
   b. Type locality
   c. Slope Mass Rating
   d. Fabric

47. _____ is a stratum in crystalline rock, containing metallic sulfides. It may also refer to tetrahedrite.
   a. Schmidt hammer
   b. Gradualism
   c. Lake capture
   d. Fahlband

48. _____ is a process of differential weathering and erosion by which an exposed well-jointed coarse-grained rock such as granite or gneiss, develops a corrugated surface of flutes; especially the formation of small-scale ridges and depressions by wave action.

_____ in glacial geology:

- the formation by glacial action of smooth deep gutterlike channels or furrows on the stoss side of a rocky hill obstructing the

advance of a glacier; the furrows are larger than glacial grooves, and they do not extend around the hill to the lee side. Also, a furrow so formed

- lineations or streamline grooves and ridges parallel to the direction of ice movement, formed in newly deposited till or older drift. They range in height from a few centimeters to 25 meters, and in length from a few meters to more than 20 km.

_____ with respect to sedimentary action:

- the process of forming a flute by the cutting or scouring action of a current of water flowing over a muddy surface
- scalloped or rippled rock surfaces.
- flute cast

   a. Fluting
   b. Lithotope
   c. Metamorphism
   d. Paralithic

49. In geology, a _____ is a flexural bulge in front of a load on the lithosphere. This load causes the lithosphere to flex by depressing the plate beneath it. Because of the flexural rigidity of the lithosphere, the area around the load is uplifted by a height that is 4% of that of the depression under the load.
   a. Geomicrobiology
   b. Metamorphism
   c. Perched coastline
   d. Forebulge

50. _____ are the preserved remains or traces of animals, plants, and other organisms from the remote past. The totality of _____, both discovered and undiscovered, and their placement in fossiliferous rock formations and sedimentary layers (strata) is known as the fossil record. The study of _____ across geological time, how they were formed, and the evolutionary relationships between taxa (phylogeny) are some of the most important functions of the science of paleontology.

- a. 1509 Istanbul earthquake
- b. 1700 Cascadia earthquake
- c. 1703 Genroku earthquake
- d. Fossils

51. A _____ is an ancient or prehistoric beach or sea floor surface which is revealed in modern geological form. Often a _____ is discovered in urban or rural areas where a limestone quarry or strip mining operation is present. As an example, Miami, Florida which derives much of its revenues from limestone mining has _____ sites in many regions.

- a. Fossil beach
- b. Gibraltar Arc
- c. Geomechanics
- d. Type locality

52. _____ are natural hollow glass tubes formed in quartzose sand, silics, or soil by lightning strikes. They are formed when lightning with a temperature of at least 1,800 degrees Celsius instantaneously melts silica on a conductive surface and fuses grains together; the fulgurite tube is the cooled product. This process occurs over a period of around one second, and leaves evidence of the lightning path and its dispersion over the surface.

- a. Geostrophic current
- b. Geotechnics
- c. Fulgurites
- d. Honeycomb weathering

53. _____ is a methodolgy and associated software tool for 3D geologic modelling developed by Hans-Georg Sobisch over the last 16 years initially in collaboration with the Geological Survey of Lower Saxony. The software is written in Java and data is stored in extensible mark-up language XML. For the past 6 years the British Geological Survey has been acting as a test bed for the accelerated development of the system.

_____ utilizes a digital elevation model, surface geological linework and downhole borehole data to enable the geologist to construct cross sections by correlating boreholes and the outcrops to produce a geological fence diagram.

- a. 1509 Istanbul earthquake
- b. 1700 Cascadia earthquake
- c. 1703 Genroku earthquake
- d. GSI3D

54. A _____ or gem is a piece of attractive mineral, which -- when cut and polished -- is used to make jewelry or other adornments. However certain rocks, and organic materials are not minerals, but are still used for jewelry, and are therefore often considered to be gemstones as well. Most gemstones are hard, but some soft minerals are used in jewelry because of their lustre or other physical properties that have aesthetic value.

- a. 1509 Istanbul earthquake
- b. 1700 Cascadia earthquake
- c. 1703 Genroku earthquake
- d. Gemstone

55. _____ is a sub-field of archaeology which uses the techniques and subject matter of Geography, geology and other earth sciences to examine topics which inform archaeological knowledge and thought.

Geoarchaeologists study the natural physical processes that affect archaeological sites such as geomorphology, the formation of sites through geological processes and the effects on buried sites and artifacts post-deposition.

Geoarchaeologists' work frequently involves studying soil and sediments as well as other geographical concepts to contribute an archaeological study.

   a. 1703 Genroku earthquake
   b. Geoarchaeology
   c. 1509 Istanbul earthquake
   d. 1700 Cascadia earthquake

56. _____ is the variety of earth materials, forms and processes that constitute either the whole Earth or a specific region of it. Relevant materials include minerals, rocks, sediments, fossils, and soils. Forms may comprise folds, faults, landforms and other expressions of morphology or relations between units of earth material.
   a. Patterned ground
   b. Geodiversity
   c. Geostrophic current
   d. Rock mechanics

57. _____ is the science of predicting the movement of tectonic plates and the future climate, shape, and other geological elements of the planet.
   a. South American Mammal Ages
   b. 1509 Istanbul earthquake
   c. Geoforecasting
   d. 1700 Cascadia earthquake

58. A _____ is a special-purpose map made to show geological features.

The stratigraphic contour lines are drawn on the surface of a selected deep stratum, so that they can show the topographic trends of the strata under the ground. It is not always possible to properly show this when the strata are extremely fractured, mixed, in some discontinuities, or where they are otherwise disturbed.

   a. 1703 Genroku earthquake
   b. 1509 Istanbul earthquake
   c. Geologic map
   d. 1700 Cascadia earthquake

59. A _____ is a survey of the subsoil conducted by an engineering geologist in conjunction with a civil engineer. Typically, the footprint of the structure is established on the proposed building site and trenches up to fourteen feet deep are dug both outside, and more importantly, inside, the proposed footprint using the bucket-end of a backhoe. In extreme cases, a larger, more powerful tracked excavator is used.
   a. Silt fence
   b. Sediment trap
   c. Mitigation of seismic motion
   d. Geologic preliminary investigation

60. _____ describes geological events that account for the stratigraphy, petrology and structure seen in rocks or earth materials.
   a. Patagonian Ice Sheet
   b. First appearance datum
   c. Geological history
   d. Paleoseismology

61. The term _____ can be used to describe both the conduct of a survey for geological purposes and an institution holding geological information.

A _____ is the systematic investigation of the subsurface of a given piece of ground for the purpose of creating a geological map or model. A _____ employs techniques from the traditional walk-over survey, studying outcrops and landforms, to intrusive methods, such as hand augering and machine driven boreholes, to the use of geophysical techniques and remote sensing methods, such as aerial photography and satellite imagery.

a. Drift
b. Megamullion
c. Haloclasty
d. Geological survey

62. _____ is the geologic study of the behavior of soil and rock. The two main disciplines of _____ are soil mechanics and rock mechanics. The former deals with the behaviour of soil from a small scale to a landslide scale.
   a. Fulgurites
   b. Metamorphic reaction
   c. Lake capture
   d. Geomechanics

63. _____ is a subset of the scientific discipline microbiology. The field of _____ concerns the role of microbe and microbial processes in geological and geochemical processes. The field is especially important when dealing with microorganisms in aquifers and public drinking water supplies.
   a. Medical geology
   b. Type locality
   c. Geometallurgy
   d. Geomicrobiology

64. A _____ is a void or cavity that has been filled with sediments, that indicates the direction of up and horizontal deposition. This process commonly occurs with cephalopods and brachiopods.
   a. Fluting
   b. Megamullion
   c. Geopetal
   d. Mineral hydration

65. _____ is the study of interaction among living organisms on the Earth operating under the hypothesis that the Earth itself acts as a single living organism (Gaia.)

The term '_____' was popularized by James Lovelock as part of his writing about the Gaia hypothesis, but it was in fact foreshadowed by many others. James Hutton (1726-1797), the 'Father of Geology' in 1789, in a lecture presented on his behalf by Dr Black, had written 'I consider the Earth to be a super-organism and that its proper study should be by physiology.' This view that the Earth in some ways could be viewed as a superorganism was widely held in the early 19th century, and was supported even by such early biologists as Huxley (1825-1895.)

   a. 1700 Cascadia earthquake
   b. 1703 Genroku earthquake
   c. 1509 Istanbul earthquake
   d. Geophysiology

66. The _____ is a proposal by J. Marvin Herndon that a nuclear fission reactor may exist and operate at the Earth's core and serves as the energy source for the geomagnetic field. Herndon had earlier proposed the existence of fission reactors at the centers of large gaseous planets such as Jupiter and Saturn.

The _____ hypothesis modifies the widely accepted dynamo theory. The _____ hypothesis explains how convection can occur and power a dynamo, even though the solid rock of the crust insulates the core and should stop the convection.

   a. Pumice raft
   b. Detritus
   c. Georeactor
   d. Dispersion

67. _____ is the application of scientific methods and engineering principles to the acquisition, interpretation, and use of knowledge of materials of the Earth's crust and earth materials for the solution of engineering problems. It is the applied science of predicting the behavior of the Earth and its various materials towards making the Earth more habitable to human activities.

_____ embraces the fields of soil mechanics and rock mechanics, and many of the engineering aspects of geology, geophysics, hydrology, and related sciences.

- a. Geopetal
- b. Lisasion
- c. Geotechnics
- d. Gibraltar Arc

68. The _____ is a geological region corresponding to an arcuate orogen surrounding the Alboran Sea, between the Iberian Peninsula and Africa. It consists of the Betic Cordillera (south Spain), and the Rif (North Morocco.)

Maximum altitudes of the region are reached at the Mulhac>én peak (3482 m) at the Cordillera Betica.

- a. Georeactor
- b. Schmidt hammer
- c. Geodiversity
- d. Gibraltar Arc

69. A _____ is a line on a map representing the farthest advance of a glacier that has retreated. It generally refers to the extent of continental, rather than alpine, glaciers.

In the northern hemisphere, glaciers advanced from the north during the Pleistocene epoch.

- a. Glacial boundary
- b. 1509 Istanbul earthquake
- c. 1703 Genroku earthquake
- d. 1700 Cascadia earthquake

70. Sediments deposited into lakes that have come from glaciers are called _____. These lakes include ice margin lakes or other types formed from glacial erosion or deposition. Sediments in the bedload and suspended load are carried into lakes and deposited.
- a. 1509 Istanbul earthquake
- b. Bull Lake glaciation
- c. 1700 Cascadia earthquake
- d. Glaciolacustrine deposits

71. In the natural sciences, _____ is a theory which holds that profound change is the cumulative product of slow but continuous processes, often contrasted with catastrophism. The theory was proposed in 1795 by James Hutton, a Scottish geologist, and was later incorporated into Charles Lyell's theory of uniformitarianism.
- a. Pumice raft
- b. Lake capture
- c. Geomicrobiology
- d. Gradualism

72. The terms _____ and icehouse Earth refer to the prevailing global climate on a timescale of millions of years.

During a _____ Earth period, the planet's atmosphere contains sufficient _____ gases such as carbon dioxide and methane for ice to be entirely absent from the planet's surface.

During icehouse periods, glaciers are present in fluctuating amounts; variations in the Earth's orbit may result in many ice ages, glacials, and interglacials.

a. 1700 Cascadia earthquake
c. 1703 Genroku earthquake
b. 1509 Istanbul earthquake
d. Greenhouse

73. _____ is a type of physical weathering caused by the growth of salt crystals. The process is first started when saline water seeps into cracks and evaporates depositing salt crystals, when the rocks are then heated up the crystals will expand putting pressure on the surrounding rock which will over time splinter the stone in to fragments.

Salt crystallization may also take place when solutions decompose rocks (for example, limestone and chalk) to form salt solutions of sodium sulfate or sodium carbonate, of which the moisture evaporates to form their respective salt crystals.

a. Geological survey
c. Medical geology
b. Haloclasty
d. Compression

74. _____, is a type of salt weathering common on coastal and semi-arid granites, sandstones and limestones. _____ is not limited to natural settings and can be seen to develop on buildings where a rate of development can be established. This rate can be as fast as several centimeters in 100 years
a. Duricrust
c. Mineral hydration
b. Honeycomb weathering
d. Dispersion

75. A _____ is a tall thin spire of rock that protrudes from the bottom of an arid drainage basin or badland. Hoodoos are composed of soft sedimentary rock and are topped by a piece of harder, less easily-eroded stone that protects the column from the elements.

They are mainly located in the desert in dry, hot areas.

a. 1700 Cascadia earthquake
c. 1509 Istanbul earthquake
b. 1703 Genroku earthquake
d. Hoodoo

76. Inertial waves are a type of mechanical wave possible in rotating fluids. Unlike surface gravity waves commonly seen at the beach or in the bathtub, inertial waves travel through the bulk of the fluid, not at the surface. Like any other kind of wave, an _____ is caused by a restoring force and characterized by its wavelength and frequency.
a. AL 129-1
c. AASHTO Soil Classification System
b. AL 333
d. Inertial wave

77. In geology, an _____ is a plane of constant metamorphic grade in the field; it separates metamorphic zones of different metamorphic index minerals. On geologic maps focusing on metamorphic terranes (or landscapes underlain by metamorphic rocks), the boundaries between rocks of different metamorphic grade are commonly demarcated by _____ lines. The garnet _____, for example, would mark the first occurrence of garnet in the rocks.
a. Ostwald ripening
c. Espresso crema effect
b. Exner equation
d. Isograd

78. _____ is a term used in geology to refer to the state of gravitational equilibrium between the earth's lithosphere and asthenosphere such that the tectonic plates 'float' at an elevation which depends on their thickness and density. This concept is invoked to explain how different topographic heights can exist at the Earth's surface. When a certain area of lithosphere reaches the state of _____, it is said to be in isostatic equilibrium.

a. Orientation Tensor
b. Isostasy
c. Isograd
d. Economic geology

79. _____ is the term used by geologists for the sinking of large parts of the earth's crust into the asthenosphere. The sinking is caused by a heavy weight placed on the earth's surface. Often this is caused by the heavy weight of glacial ice due to continental glaciation, a process in which permanent ice places pressure on the earth's crust thereby depressing it with its weight.
   a. AASHTO Soil Classification System
   b. AL 129-1
   c. AL 333
   d. Isostatic depression

80. _____ is a geomorphic feature formed from the dissolution of carbonate bedrock where a spring emerges then the discharge abruptly disappears into a sinkhole.
   a. Karst fenster
   b. Fluting
   c. Lisasion
   d. Lake capture

81. In geology, _____ is the process of capture of the waters collected in a lake by a neighbor river basin.

The occurrence of a _____ is mainly controlled by the water balance at the lake's basin and the changes in topography due to erosion, sedimentation, and tectonism. If evaporation at the surface of a lake, plus the water loses through underground infiltration and plant evapotranspiration, are high enough to account for all precipitation water collected by the lake, then the lake becomes endorheic, closed, or internally-drained.

   a. Cross-bedding
   b. Geodiversity
   c. Seismic inversion
   d. Lake capture

82. The _____ is a key axiom based on observations of natural history that is a foundational principle of sedimentary stratigraphy and so of other geology dependent natural sciences:

The principle was first proposed in the 11th century by the Persian geologist, Avicenna , and the law was later formulated more clearly in the 17th century by the Danish scientist Nicolas Steno.

While discussing the origins of mountains in The Book of Healing in 1027, Avicenna first outlined the principle of the superposition of strata as follows:

Assuming that all rocks and minerals had once been fluid, Nicolas Steno reasoned that rock strata were formed when particles in a fluid such as water fell to the bottom. This process would leave horizontal layers.

   a. Law of superposition
   b. Geologic record
   c. Paleomagnetism
   d. Milankovitch Theory

83. _____ is a slang term used by geologists, minerologists, and amateur rock collectors to identify a specimen in the field that may look interesting but is actually not. Rocks identified as such should be left in situ, as they are not worth the hassle of transportation or deserving of a place in a respectable collection.
   a. Metamorphic reaction
   b. Lisasion
   c. Corrasion
   d. Leaverite

Chapter 1. Test Preparation Part 1   17

84. _____ is a form of erosion where the earth is eroded by intentional human action.

_____ is described by Michael John Selby in his book 'Earth's changing surface: an introduction to geomorphology' as 'the erosion of land, most commonly along rivers and coastlines, by intentional human action'. It is important to note that _____ only applies to intentional human action, whereby humans deliberately erode the landscape for reasons including for recreation, hazard management and all forms of constuction and demolition.

- a. Platform
- b. Type locality
- c. Lake capture
- d. Lisasion

85. In geology, _____ is the study of rocks, and the conditions in which they form. Lithology once was approximately synonymous with petrography, but in current usage, lithology is a subdivision of _____ focusing on macroscopic hand-sample or outcrop-scale description of rocks, while petrography is the speciality that deals with microscopic details.

In the oil industry, lithology, or more specifically mud logging, is the graphic representation of geological formations being drilled through, and drawn on a log called a mud log.

- a. Petrology
- b. Metamorphic zone
- c. Rock cycle
- d. Migmatite

86. A _____ is either an environment in which a sediment was deposited or an area of uniform sedimentation.
- a. Honeycomb weathering
- b. Lithotope
- c. Geometallurgy
- d. Geotechnics

87. A _____ develops in the direction under which it is sheltered by a headland, in an area called the shadow zone. It is characterized as a logarithmic spiral because if you look at it in plan view or aerially, it represents the same shape that is created from the logarithmic spiral function. These beaches are also commonly referred to as e;zeta cure bayse;, e;half hearte; or e;crenulatee; shaped bays, or e;headland bayse;. Logarithmic Spiral

The logarithmic spiral can be determined using the equation (written in polar coordinates):

$r = e^{\theta \cot É'}$

where:

θ = the angle of rotation, is located between two lines drawn from the origin to any two points on the spiral.

r = the ratio of the lengths between two lines that extend out from the origin.

- a. Rockall
- b. Logarithmic Spiral Beach
- c. 1509 Istanbul earthquake
- d. Historical geology

88. A _____ is the geological name given to pockets of oxygen-poor air which can be lethal to any human or animal life inside. The term comes from Swahili and means 'evil wind.' They are created when an odorless and invisible gas such as carbon dioxide accumulates in pockets low to the ground. CO_2 is heavier than air (oxygen and nitrogen) which causes it to stay close to the ground, and is also undetectable by human olfactory or most visual conditions.

a. 1509 Istanbul earthquake
b. Strainmeter
c. Mazuku
d. Seismic refraction

89. _____ is an emerging interdisciplinary scientific field consisting of those aspects of geology as they affect human, animal and plant health.

In its broadest sense, _____ studies exposure to or deficiency of trace elements and minerals; inhalation of ambient and anthropogenic mineral dusts and volcanic emissions; transportation, modification and concentration of organic compounds; and exposure to radionuclide's, microbes and pathogens. (Geotimes 2001)

Examples include:

- Lead and other heavy metal exposure resulting from dust and other particulates
- Asbestos exposure such as amphibole asbestos dusts in Libby, Montana
- Fungal infection resulting from airborne dust, such as Valley Fever or coccidioidomycosis

a. Fabric
b. Metamorphic reaction
c. SWEAT
d. Medical geology

90. A _____ is an abyssal geologic structure with an ellipsoidal, shield-like form. It is mainly made up of serpentinized ultramafic rocks of abyssal mantle and secondarily of gabbroic rocks. The positive relief is variable in size: 10 to 150 km long, 5 to 15 km wide, and 500 to 1500 m high.

a. Fluting
b. Cross-bedding
c. Megamullion
d. Type locality

91. _____ relates to the practice of combining geology or geostatistics with metallurgy, or, more specifically, extractive metallurgy, to create a spatially- or geologically-based predictive model for mineral processing plants. It is used in the hard rock mining industry for risk management and mitigation during mineral processing plant design. It is also used, to a lesser extent, for production planning in highly variable ore deposits.

a. Lake capture
b. Fabric
c. Geomechanics
d. Geometallurgy

92. _____ are exposures of deep crust exhumed in association with largely amagmatic extension. They form, and are exhumed, through relatively fast transport of middle and lower continental crust to the Earth's surface. During this process, high-grade metamorphic rocks (eclogite-, granulite- to amphibolite- facies) are exposed below low-angle detachment faults (mylonite shear zones) that show ductile deformation on the lower side (footwall) with amphibolite- to greenschist-facies syndeformational metamorphism, and ductile-brittle to brittle deformation on the upper-side (hanging-wall.)

a. Metamorphic core complexes
b. 1509 Istanbul earthquake
c. 1703 Genroku earthquake
d. 1700 Cascadia earthquake

Chapter 1. Test Preparation Part 1

93. A _____ is a chemical reaction that takes place during the geological process of metamorphism in an amalgamate of minerals that helps determine the final stable state of the resulting metamorphic rock.
   a. Type locality
   b. Metamorphic reaction
   c. Geostrophic current
   d. Lake capture

94. _____ is the solid-state recrystallization of pre-existing rocks due to changes in physical and chemical conditions, primarily heat, pressure, and the introduction of chemically active fluids. Both mineralogical, chemical and crystallographic changes can occur during this process.

Three types of _____ exist: dynamic, contact and regional.

   a. Pumice raft
   b. Metamorphism
   c. Leaverite
   d. Paralithic

95. A _____ is a multi-layered sheet of micro-organisms, mainly bacteria and archaea. They grow at interfaces between different types of material, mostly on submerged or moist surfaces but a few survive in deserts. They colonize environments ranging in altitude from 10 km above sea level to more than 20 km below the surface of the oceans and as much as 30 km below the surfaces of rocks and sediments, and in temperature from from -40>°C to +120>°C.
   a. 1703 Genroku earthquake
   b. 1700 Cascadia earthquake
   c. 1509 Istanbul earthquake
   d. Microbial mat

96. _____ is an inorganic chemical reaction where water is added to the crystal structure of a mineral, usually creating a new mineral, usually called a hydrate.

In geological terms, the process of _____ is known as metasomatism, or alteraion and is a process occurring in retrograde metamorphism. Hydration of minerals occurs generally in concert with hydrothermal circulation.

   a. Pumice raft
   b. Dispersion
   c. Lithotope
   d. Mineral hydration

97. In topography, a _____ is a point on a surface that is lower in elevation than all points immediately adjacent to it. Mathematically, a _____ is a local minima of elevation. A _____ may be the lowest point of a dry basin or depression, or the deepest point of a body of water or ice.
   a. 1509 Istanbul earthquake
   b. Nadir
   c. 1703 Genroku earthquake
   d. 1700 Cascadia earthquake

98. _____ is the study of nanoscale phenomena related to geological systems. Predominately, this is interrogated by studying environmental nanoparticles between 1-100 nanometers in size. Other applicable fields of study include studying materials with at least one dimension restricted to the nanoscale (e.g. thin films, confined fluids) and the transfer of energy, electrons, protons, and matter across environmental interfaces.
   a. 1509 Istanbul earthquake
   b. 1703 Genroku earthquake
   c. Nanogeoscience
   d. 1700 Cascadia earthquake

99. The _____ is a geological structure which stretches across south Wales from Swansea Bay northeastwards as far as Hereford in western England. It comprises both a series of faults and associated folds which were active during the mountain-building period known as the Variscan orogeny. This line of weakness probably featured in the earlier Caledonian Orogeny and perhaps reflects a more ancient line of weakness in the basement rocks.
- a. 1703 Genroku earthquake
- b. 1509 Istanbul earthquake
- c. Neath Disturbance
- d. 1700 Cascadia earthquake

100. _____ is a phenomenon that occurs when the temperature of the soil is above 0>°C and the surface temperature of the soil is below 0>°C. The subterranean moisture is brought to the surface via capillary action.
- a. 1700 Cascadia earthquake
- b. 1703 Genroku earthquake
- c. 1509 Istanbul earthquake
- d. Needle ice

101. _____ is a branch of geologic sciences which studies the formation and composition of oil shales-fine-grained sedimentary rocks containing significant amounts of kerogen, and belonging to the group of sapropel fuels. Oil shale formation takes place in a number of depositional settings and has considerable compositional variation. Oil shales can be classified by their composition (carbonate minerals such as calcite or detrital minerals such as quartz and clays) or by their depositional environment (large lakes, shallow marine, and lagoon/small lake settings.)
- a. AASHTO Soil Classification System
- b. Oil shale geology
- c. AL 333
- d. AL 129-1

Chapter 2. Test Preparation Part 2

1.

In geology, especially in the study of glacial till, eigenvectors and eigenvalues are used as a method by which a mass of information of a clast fabric's constituents' orientation and dip can be summarized in a 3-D space by six numbers. In the field, a geologist may collect such data for hundreds or thousands of clasts in a soil sample, which can only be compared graphically such as in a Tri-Plot (Sneed and Folk) diagram , , or as a Stereonet on a Wulff Net . The output for the _____ is in the three orthogonal (perpendicular) axes of space.

   a. Exner equation   b. Ostwald ripening
   c. Isostasy   d. Orientation Tensor

2. _____ is an observed phenomenon in solid (or liquid) solutions which describes the evolution of an inhomogenous structure over time. The phenomenon was first described by Wilhelm Ostwald in 1896. When a phase precipitates out of a solid, energetic factors will cause large precipitates to grow, drawing material from the smaller precipitates, which shrink.
   a. Exner equation   b. Isograd
   c. Orientation Tensor   d. Ostwald ripening

3. _____ is a geological term referring to the appearance of bedrock or superficial deposits exposed at the surface of the Earth. In most places the bedrock or superficial deposits are covered by a mantle of soil and vegetation and cannot be seen or examined closely. However in places where the overlying cover is removed through erosion, the rock may be exposed, or crop out.
   a. AL 333   b. AL 129-1
   c. AASHTO Soil Classification System   d. Outcrop

4. The term _____ describes the type of alluvial geological deposit or sediment that is deposited on the flood plain of a river. Because it occurs outside the main channel, away from faster flow, the deposit tends to be fine-grained.
   a. Overbank   b. Isograd
   c. Espresso crema effect   d. Erosion prediction

5. The term _____ is applied to a pressure difference, relative to a 'normal' or 'ambient' pressure.

- In geology: the pressure regime in a stratigraphic unit that exhibits higher-than-hydrostatic pressure in its pore structure. This phenomenon is the primary cause of 'oil gushers'.

Geological _____ in stratigraphic layers is fundamentally caused by the inability of connate pore fluids to escape as the surrounding mineral matrix compacts under the lithostatic pressure caused by overlying layers. Fluid escape may be impeded by sealing of the compacting rock by surrounding impermeable layers (such as evaporites, chalk and cemented sandstones.) Alternatively, the rate of burial of the stratigraphic layer may be so great that the efflux of fluid is not sufficiently rapid to maintain hydrostatic pressure.

Common situations where _____ may occur is; in a buried river channel filled with coarse sand that is sealed on all sides by impermeable shales, or when there is an explosion within a confined space.

   a. AASHTO Soil Classification System   b. AL 129-1
   c. AL 333   d. Overpressure

6. _____ comes from the Latin word palus or marsh. Wetlands within this category include inland marshes and swamps as well as bogs, fens, tundra and floodplains. _____ systems include any inland wetland which lacks flowing water, contains ocean derived salts in concentrations of less than 0.05%, and is nontidal.
   a. 1703 Genroku earthquake
   b. 1509 Istanbul earthquake
   c. Palustrine
   d. 1700 Cascadia earthquake

7. _____ studies examine the preservation of particulate organic matter and palynomorphs to provide information on the depositional environment of sediments and depositional palaeoenvironments of sedimentary rocks. The term _____ was introduced by the French geologist Combaz in 1964. _____ studies are often linked to investigations of the palynology and organic geochemistry of sedimentary rocks.
   a. Labyrinthodont
   b. Conodont Alteration Index
   c. Cambrian explosion
   d. Palynofacies

8. _____ is the geological term used to describe a particle of a size between five and 500 micrometres, found in rock deposits (sedimentary rocks) and composed of organic material such as chitin, pseudochitin and sporopollenin.' Palynology is the study of _____ fossils and can be considered a subdiscipline of micropaleontology or paleobotany. Expressed more simply, palynology is the study of organic microfossils.

They form a geological record of importance in determining the type of prehistoric life that existed at the time the sedimentary formation was laid down.

   a. Zechstein
   b. Fort Union Formation
   c. Salt tectonics
   d. Palynomorph

9. _____ is a weathered later of bedrock. The term comes from the Greek language words Para meaning akin to, and Lithic meaning stony.
   a. Paralithic
   b. Duricrust
   c. Karst fenster
   d. Haloclasty

10. _____ is a term used to describe the distinct, and often symmetrical geometric shapes formed by ground material in periglacial regions. Typically found in remote regions of the Arctic, Antarctica, and the Australian outback, but also found anywhere that freezing and thawing of soil alternate, the geometric shapes and patterns associated with _____ are often mistaken as artistic human creations. The nature of _____ puzzled scientists for ages.
   a. Seismic inversion
   b. Fabric
   c. Lithotope
   d. Patterned ground

11. A _____ is a fossil coastline currently above the present coastline.
   a. Perched coastline
   b. Geomicrobiology
   c. Mineral hydration
   d. Metamorphism

12. _____ are pillow-shaped structures sometimes seen in lavas and are attributed to the congealment of lava under water, or subaqeous extrusion. A pillow structure in certain extrusive igneous rock is characterized by discontinuous pillow-shaped masses, commonly up to 1 metre in diameter. _____ commonly occur at Constructive plate boundaries, forming part of a mid-ocean ridge.

a. Megamullion
b. Pillow lava
c. Detritus
d. Rock mechanics

13. In geology, a _____ is a continental area covered by relatively flat or gently tilted, mainly sedimentary strata, which overlie a basement of consolidated igneous or metamorphic rocks of an earlier deformation. Platforms, shields and the basement rocks together constitute cratons.

It is also common practice to use the term _____ as a very general term for a sequence of shallow water carbonate _____.

a. Perched coastline
b. Fluting
c. Platform
d. Fabric

14. In geology, a _____ is the sedimentary and volcanic deposits that lie on top of a craton.
a. Fluting
b. Platform cover
c. Duricrust
d. Lisasion

15. _____ is a fine-grained mixture of the minerals kamacite and taenite found in the octahedrite iron meteorites. It occurs in gaps between the larger bands of kamacite and taenite which form Widmanst>ätten patterns.

Many types of _____ exist and vary in formation mechanism and morphology.

a. 1703 Genroku earthquake
b. Plessite
c. 1509 Istanbul earthquake
d. 1700 Cascadia earthquake

16. In geology and climatology, a _____ was an extended period of abundant rainfall lasting many thousands of years. The term is especially applied to such periods during the Pleistocene Epoch. A minor, short _____ may be termed a 'subpluvial'.
a. 1703 Genroku earthquake
b. 1509 Istanbul earthquake
c. 1700 Cascadia earthquake
d. Pluvial

17. _____ is the alteration of rock or mineral crystallization effected by gaseous emanations from solidifying magma.
a. Fahlband
b. Seismic inversion
c. Gibraltar Arc
d. Pneumatolysis

18. _____ is water that has recently emerged from deep in the Earth's mantle, having been previously dissolved in magma. _____ is allegedly released by hydrothermal vents.
a. Primordial water
b. Palynomorph
c. Basin and Range
d. Tidal scour

19. The term _____ is used in materials sciences as an analogue model for superficial material alteration.

Alteration processes (e.g. weathering) can influence the physical character and chemical composition of surface-near matter areas, not affecting the source-medium beneath. Particularly due to resultant higher porosity, the light-refraction, -reflection and -scattering potential increases resulting in a brightening of the materials surface.

a. Economic geology
b. Ostwald ripening
c. Isostasy
d. Espresso crema effect

20. A _____ is a floating raft of pumice occasionally created by ocean-based volcanic activity.

Recent volcanic activity in the South Pacific near Tonga on August 12, 2006 revealed the emergence of a new island. The crew of the Maiken, a yacht that left the northern Tongan islands group of Vava'u in August, reported that they saw streaks of light, porous pumice stone floating in the water -- then 'sailed into a vast, many-miles-wide belt of densely packed pumice.'

a. Karst fenster
b. Metamorphism
c. Geopetal
d. Pumice raft

21. The _____ is a physiographic subprovince of the New England Uplands section of the New England province of the Appalachian Highlands. The prong consists of mountains comprised of crystalline metamorphic rock.

The _____ stretches from near Reading, Pennsylvania, through northern New Jersey and southern New York, reaching its northern terminus in Connecticut.

a. Seismic inversion
b. Cross-bedding
c. Corrasion
d. Reading Prong

22. In geology, the term '_____' refers to structures or minerals from a parent rock that did not undergo metamorphosis when the surrounding rock did, or to rock that survived a destructive geologic process.
a. Relict
b. 1509 Istanbul earthquake
c. 1703 Genroku earthquake
d. 1700 Cascadia earthquake

23. A _____ is a subglacially formed type of landform, that mainly occur in Fennoscandia, Scotland, Ireland and Canada. They cover large areas that have been covered by ice, and occur mostly in what is believed to be the central areas of the ice sheets.
a. 1703 Genroku earthquake
b. 1509 Istanbul earthquake
c. Rogen moraine
d. 1700 Cascadia earthquake

24. A _____ is any glacially formed accumulation of unconsolidated glacial debris (soil and rock) which can occur in currently glaciated and formerly glaciated regions, such as those areas acted upon by a past ice age. This debris may have been plucked off the valley floor as a glacier advanced or it may have fallen off the valley walls as a result of frost wedging. Moraines may be composed of silt like glacial flour to large boulders.
a. 1703 Genroku earthquake
b. 1700 Cascadia earthquake
c. 1509 Istanbul earthquake
d. Moraine

25. The _____, also known as the local magnitude (M_L) scale, assigns a single number to quantify the amount of seismic energy released by an earthquake. It is a base-10 logarithmic scale obtained by calculating the logarithm of the combined horizontal amplitude of the largest displacement from zero on a Wood-Anderson torsion seismometer output. So, for example, an earthquake that measures 5.0 on the Richter scale has a shaking amplitude 10 times larger than one that measures 4.0.

Chapter 2. Test Preparation Part 2

 a. Surface wave magnitude   b. Mercalli intensity scale
 c. Medvedev-Sponheuer-Karnik scale   d. Richter magnitude scale

26. A _____ is a German term that describes traverse ridges of bedrock that have been exposed by glacial erosion. They are also known as rock bars, thresholds, and verrous. They are found in glaciated valleys, and are often associated with waterfalls and zones of rapids when streams are present.
 a. Metamorphism   b. Drift
 c. Platform   d. Riegel

27. _____ is the theoretical and applied science of the mechanical behaviour of rock and rock masses; it is that branch of mechanics concerned with the response of rock and rock masses to the force fields of their physical environment. _____ itself forms part of the broader subject of geomechanics which is concerned with the mechanical responses of all geological materials, including soils.
 a. Geomicrobiology   b. Rock mechanics
 c. Haloclasty   d. Geometallurgy

28. The _____ is a non-dimensional number in fluid dynamics which determines how sediment will be transported in a flowing fluid. It is a ratio between the sediment fall velocity w_s and the upwards velocity on the grain as a product of the von Kármán constant κ and the shear velocity u_*.

$$\text{Rouse} = \frac{w_s}{\kappa u_*}$$

 a. 1700 Cascadia earthquake   b. 1509 Istanbul earthquake
 c. 1703 Genroku earthquake   d. Rouse number

29. _____ by Romana (1985, 1988, 1991) improving the estimate of the geologic characteristics, of the volume of the potentially unstable blocks and the underground water circulation.
 a. Geodiversity   b. Slope Mass Rating
 c. Schmidt hammer   d. Patterned ground

30. _____ stands for southwestern United States and East Antarctica, which theorizes that the southwestern United States was at one time connected to East Antarctica.

A hypothesis for a late Precambrian fit of western North America with the Australia-Antarctic shield region permits the extension of many features through Antarctica and into other parts of Gondwana, specifically, the Grenville orogen may extend around the coast of East Antarctica into India and Australia. The ophiolitic belt of the latter may extend into East Antarctica.

 a. Corrasion   b. Geomicrobiology
 c. Perched coastline   d. SWEAT

31. The _____ are a geological phenomenon found in Racetrack Playa, Death Valley. The stones are assumed move to slowly across the surface of the playa, inferred from the long tracks behind them, without human or animal intervention. They have neither been seen nor filmed in motion and are not unique to The Racetrack.

a. 1509 Istanbul earthquake
b. 1703 Genroku earthquake
c. Sailing stones
d. 1700 Cascadia earthquake

32. _____ is the movement of saline water into freshwater aquifers. Most often, it is caused by ground-water pumping from coastal wells, or from construction of navigation channels or oil field canals. The channels and canals provide conduits for salt water to be brought into fresh water marshes.

a. Porosity
b. 1509 Istanbul earthquake
c. 1700 Cascadia earthquake
d. Saltwater intrusion

33. A _____ is a device to measure the elastic properties or strength of concrete or rock. Original Schmidt Concrete Test Hammer

The hammer measures the rebound of a spring loaded mass impacting against the surface of the sample. When conducting the test the hammer should be held at right angles to the surface which in turn should be flat and smooth.

a. Schmidt hammer
b. Rock mechanics
c. Slope Mass Rating
d. Leaverite

34. _____ ($V_2Ti_3O_9$), is a vanadium, titanium oxide found in the Lasamba Hill, Kwale district in Coast Province Kenya. It is a polymorph of kyzylkumite.

The ore mineral occurs as exsolution lamellae and particles in rutile, coexisting with kyanite, sillimanite, and tourmaline in a highly metamorphosed gneiss.

a. Schreyerite
b. Slope Mass Rating
c. Platform
d. Reading Prong

35. The _____ is the representation of the changes of the sea level throughout the geological history.

The first such curve is the Vail curve or Exxon curve. The names of the curve refer to the fact that in 1977 a team of Exxon geologists from Esso Production Research headed by Peter Vail published a monograph on global eustatic sea-level changes.

a. Reading Prong
b. Metamorphism
c. Perched coastline
d. Sea-level curve

36. _____ is any particulate matter that can be transported by fluid flow, and which eventually is deposited.

They are most often transported by water (fluvial processes) transported by wind (aeolian processes) and glaciers. Beach sands and river channel deposits are examples of fluvial transport and deposition, though _____ also often settles out of slow-moving or standing water in lakes and oceans.

a. Sediment
b. Brickearth
c. Salt glacier
d. Bovey Beds

37. The phrase _____ is used to describe the movement of solid particles (sediment) and the processes that govern their motion. _____ is typically due to a combination of the force of gravity acting on the sediment, and/or the movement of the fluid in which the sediment is entrained. This is typically studied in natural systems, where the particles are clastic rocks (sand, gravel, boulders, etc.), mud, or clay; the fluid is air, water, or ice; and the force of gravity is due to the sloping surface on which the particles are resting.
   a. 1700 Cascadia earthquake
   b. 1509 Istanbul earthquake
   c. 1703 Genroku earthquake
   d. Sediment transport

38. The _____, is a geologic eon before the Proterozoic and Paleoproterozoic, before 2.5 Ga (billion years ago, or 2,500 Ma.) Instead of being based on stratigraphy, this date is defined chronometrically. The lower boundary (starting point) has not been officially recognized by the International Commission on Stratigraphy, but it is usually set to 3.8 Ga, at the end of the Hadean eon.
   a. AL 333
   b. Archean
   c. AL 129-1
   d. AASHTO Soil Classification System

39. The _____ Era, is the most recent of the three classic geological eras and covers the period from 65.5 million years ago to the present. It is marked by the Cretaceous-Tertiary extinction event at the end of the Cretaceous that saw the demise of the last non-avian dinosaurs and the end of the Mesozoic Era. The _____ era is ongoing.
   a. 1509 Istanbul earthquake
   b. Cenozoic
   c. 1700 Cascadia earthquake
   d. 1703 Genroku earthquake

40. _____ describes geological events that account for the stratigraphy, petrology and structure seen in rocks or earth materials.
   a. Patagonian Ice Sheet
   b. First appearance datum
   c. Paleoseismology
   d. Geological history

41. The _____ is the geologic eon before the Archean. It started at Earth's formation about 4.6 billion years ago (4,600 Ma), and ended roughly 3.8 billion years ago, though the latter date varies according to different sources.
   a. 1700 Cascadia earthquake
   b. Hadean
   c. 1509 Istanbul earthquake
   d. 1703 Genroku earthquake

42. The _____ Era is one of three geologic eras of the Phanerozoic eon. The division of time into eras dates back to Giovanni Arduino, in the 18th century, although his original name for the era now called the '_____' was 'Secondary' (making the modern era the 'Tertiary'.)

The _____ was a time of tectonic, climatic and evolutionary activity. The continents gradually shifted from a state of connectedness into their present configuration; the drifting provided for speciation and other important evolutionary developments.

   a. 1703 Genroku earthquake
   b. Mesozoic
   c. 1509 Istanbul earthquake
   d. 1700 Cascadia earthquake

43. The _____ is the earliest of three geologic eras of the Phanerozoic eon. The _____ spanned from roughly 542 to 251 million years ago (ICS, 2004), and is subdivided into six geologic periods; from oldest to youngest they are: the Cambrian, Ordovician, Silurian, Devonian, Carboniferous, and Permian.

The _____ covers the time from the first appearance of abundant, soft-shelled fossils to the time when the continents were beginning to be dominated by large, relatively sophisticated reptiles and modern plants. The lower (oldest) boundary was classically set at the first appearance of creatures known as trilobites and archeocyathids.

- a. 1509 Istanbul earthquake
- b. 1703 Genroku earthquake
- c. 1700 Cascadia earthquake
- d. Paleozoic

44. _____ was the supercontinent that is theorized to have existed during the Paleozoic and Mesozoic eras about 250 million years ago, before the component continents were separated into their current configuration.

The name was first used by the German originator of the continental drift theory, Alfred Wegener, in the 1920 edition of his book The Origin of Continents and Oceans, in which a postulated supercontinent _____ played a key role.

The single enormous ocean which surrounded Pangaea is known as Panthalassa.

- a. 1703 Genroku earthquake
- b. 1509 Istanbul earthquake
- c. 1700 Cascadia earthquake
- d. Pangea

45. The _____ Eon is the current eon in the geologic timescale, and the one during which abundant animal life has existed. It covers roughly 545 million years and goes back to the time when diverse hard-shelled animals first appeared.
- a. 1703 Genroku earthquake
- b. 1700 Cascadia earthquake
- c. 1509 Istanbul earthquake
- d. Phanerozoic

46. The _____ is an informal name for the supereon comprising the eons of the geologic timescale that came before the current Phanerozoic eon. It spans from the formation of Earth around 4500 Mya (million years ago) to the evolution of abundant macroscopic hard-shelled animals, which marked the beginning of the Cambrian, the first period of the first era of the Phanerozoic eon, some 542 Mya. It is named after the Roman name for Wales - Cambria - where rocks from this age were first studied.
- a. 1700 Cascadia earthquake
- b. 1509 Istanbul earthquake
- c. Precambrian
- d. 1703 Genroku earthquake

47. _____ is a coastal management erosion control technique. This is most suitable for softer or less stable cliffs. Generally speaking, the cliffs are stabilised through dewatering (drainage of excess rainwater to reduce water-logging) or anchoring (the use of terracing, planting, or wiring to hold cliffs in place.)
- a. Geogrid
- b. Geotechnical investigations
- c. High strain dynamic testing
- d. Cliff stabilization

48. _____ is a method to verify the integrity of drilled shafts and other concrete piles. This method is considered to be more accurate than sonic echo testing in the determination of soundness of concrete within the drilled shaft inside of the rebar cage. This method provides little indication of concrete soundness outside the cage.

Chapter 2. Test Preparation Part 2

a. Wave equation analysis
b. High strain dynamic testing
c. Tieback
d. Crosshole sonic logging

49. In _____ if water falls uniformly over a field such that field capacity of the soil is not exceeded, then negligible water percolates to groundwater. If instead water puddles in low lying areas, the same water volume concentrated over a smaller area may exceed field capacity and groundwater recharge.
   a. 1700 Cascadia earthquake
   b. Groundwater
   c. 1509 Istanbul earthquake
   d. Depression focused recharge

50. _____ is the removal of water from solid material or soil by wet classification, centrifugation, filtration or removal of water from a riverbed, construction site, caisson by pumping, draining, or evaporation. This is often done during the site development phase of a major construction project due to a high water table. It usually involves the use of '_____' pumps.
   a. 1703 Genroku earthquake
   b. 1509 Istanbul earthquake
   c. 1700 Cascadia earthquake
   d. Dewatering

51. _____ of piles is a fast and effective method of assessing foundation bearing capacity that requires instrumenting a deep foundation with accelerometers and strain transducers and analyzing data collected by these sensors.

The procedure is based on the case method of pile testing and is standardized by ASTM D4945-00 Standard Test Method for High Strain Dynamic Testing of Piles. It may be performed on driven piles, drilled shafts and other cast in place foundations.

   a. Slurry wall
   b. Soil nailing
   c. Shaft construction
   d. Dynamic load testing

52. _____ is the removal of solids (sediment, soil, rock and other particles) in the natural environment. It usually occurs due to transport by wind, water, or ice; by down-slope creep of soil and other material under the force of gravity; or by living organisms, such as burrowing animals, in the case of bioerosion.

_____ is distinguished from weathering, which is the process of chemical or physical breakdown of the minerals in the rocks, although the two processes may occur concurrently.

   a. AL 129-1
   b. Erosion
   c. AL 333
   d. AASHTO Soil Classification System

53. _____ is the practice of preventing or controlling wind or water erosion in agriculture, land development and construction. This usually involves the creation of some sort of physical barrier, such as vegetation or rock, to absorb some of the energy of the wind or water that is causing the erosion. Effective erosion controls are important techniques in preventing water pollution and soil loss.
   a. AASHTO Soil Classification System
   b. AL 129-1
   c. Erosion control
   d. AL 333

54. The _____ of an earth (rock and regolith) material is a measure of the material to be excavated (dug) with conventional excavation equipment such as a bulldozer with rippers, backhoe, scraper and other grading equipment. Materials that cannot be excavated with conventional excavation equipment are said to be non-rippable. Such material typically requires pre-blasting or use of percussion hammers or chisels to facilitate excavation.
   a. AL 129-1
   b. Excavatability
   c. AASHTO Soil Classification System
   d. AL 333

55. A _____ is a rough bundle of brushwood used for strengthening an earthen structure, or making a path across uneven or wet terrain. Typical uses are protecting the banks of streams from erosion, covering marshy ground and so on.
   a. 1700 Cascadia earthquake
   b. 1703 Genroku earthquake
   c. 1509 Istanbul earthquake
   d. Fascine

56. A _____ is a temporary erosion control and sediment control device used on construction sites to protect water quality in nearby streams, rivers, lakes and bays. It is made of straw, coconut fiber or similar material formed into a tubular roll. Fiber rolls are installed on slopes or at the base of slopes below the active construction area, before soil disturbance (earth moving) begins.
   a. Mitigation of seismic motion
   b. Fiber roll
   c. Silt fence
   d. Geologic preliminary investigation

57. _____ is earthy material which is used to fill in a depression or hole in the ground or create mounds or otherwise artificially change the grade or elevation of real property.

_____ is usually subsoil (soil from beneath the top soil) and underlying soil parent material which has little soil organic matter or biological activity. _____ is taken from a location where soil is being removed as a part of leveling an area for construction; it may also contain sand, rocks, and stones, as well as earth.

   a. Shaft construction
   b. Soil nailing
   c. Fill dirt
   d. Slurry wall

58. The development of methods of preparing relatively rigid polymeric materials by tensile drawing, in a sense 'cold working,' raised the possibility that such materials could be used in the reinforcement of soils for walls, steep slopes, roadway bases and foundation soils. Used as such, the major function of the resulting geogrids is in the area of reinforcement. This area, as with many other geosynthetics, is very active, with a number of different products, materials, configurations, etc., making up today's _____ market.
   a. Slurry wall
   b. Geogrid
   c. Geotechnical investigations
   d. Hydro excavation

59. _____ is the geologic study of the behavior of soil and rock. The two main disciplines of _____ are soil mechanics and rock mechanics. The former deals with the behaviour of soil from a small scale to a landslide scale.
   a. Metamorphic reaction
   b. Fulgurites
   c. Lake capture
   d. Geomechanics

60. _____ are a kind of geosynthetic material. They are impermeable membranes used widely as cut-offs and liners. Until recent years, _____ were used mostly as canal and pond liners.

a. Shaft construction
b. Nuclear Densometer Test
c. Geomembranes
d. Geotechnical investigations

61. _____ is the term used to describe a range of generally polymeric products used to solve civil engineering problems. The term is generally regarded to encompass six main product categories: geotextiles, geogrids, geonets, geomembranes, geosynthetic clay liners, geofoam and geocomposites. The polymeric nature of the products make them suitable for use in the ground where high levels of durability are required.
   a. Geosynthetics
   b. Shaft construction
   c. Rock bolt
   d. Geogrid

62. A _____ is a woven fabric like material primarily used for the lining of landfills. It is a kind of geomembrane and geosynthetic which incorporates a bentonite or other clay, which has a very low hydraulic conductivity. The resulting lower permeability slows the rate of seepage out of the landfill.
   a. Fill dirt
   b. Rubble trench foundation
   c. Geosynthetic clay liner
   d. Dynamic load testing

63. _____ is a naturally occurring material composed primarily of fine-grained minerals, which show plasticity through a variable range of water content, and which can be hardened when dried and/or fired. _____ deposits are mostly composed of _____ minerals (phyllosilicate minerals), minerals which impart plasticity and harden when fired and/or dried, and variable amounts of water trapped in the mineral structure by polar attraction. Organic materials which do not impart plasticity may also be a part of _____ deposits.
   a. 1509 Istanbul earthquake
   b. 1703 Genroku earthquake
   c. 1700 Cascadia earthquake
   d. Clay

64. _____ are performed by geotechnical engineers or engineering geologists to obtain information on the physical properties of soil and rock around a site to design earthworks and foundations for proposed structures and for repair of distress to earthworks and structures caused by subsurface conditions. A geotechnical investigation will include surface exploration and subsurface exploration of a site. Sometimes, geophysical methods are used to obtain data about sites.
   a. Geotechnical investigations
   b. Water table
   c. Geogrid
   d. Crosshole sonic logging

65. _____ is the application of scientific methods and engineering principles to the acquisition, interpretation, and use of knowledge of materials of the Earth's crust and earth materials for the solution of engineering problems. It is the applied science of predicting the behavior of the Earth and its various materials towards making the Earth more habitable to human activities.

_____ embraces the fields of soil mechanics and rock mechanics, and many of the engineering aspects of geology, geophysics, hydrology, and related sciences.

   a. Geopetal
   b. Lisasion
   c. Gibraltar Arc
   d. Geotechnics

66. _____ is water located beneath the ground surface in soil pore spaces and in the fractures of lithologic formations. A unit of rock or an unconsolidated deposit is called an aquifer when it can yield a usable quantity of water. The depth at which soil pore spaces or fractures and voids in rock become completely saturated with water is called the water table.

a. Groundwater
b. 1509 Istanbul earthquake
c. Depression focused recharge
d. 1700 Cascadia earthquake

67. _____ is a method of testing deep foundations to obtain information about their capacity and integrity, and in some cases, to monitor their installation. It is codified by D4945-00 - Standard Test Method for High-Strain Dynamic Testing of Piles.

_____ encompasses dynamic pile monitoring, applicable only to driven piles, and dynamic load testing, which is applicable to any type of deep foundation.

a. Wave equation analysis
b. Geosynthetics
c. Tieback
d. High strain dynamic testing

68. _____ is a safe and efficient form of excavation. However it is totally unsuitable for archaeological excavation. Using a powerful vacuum and high pressure water, precise holes, trenches and tunnels can be cut to the required size and proportion.
a. Wave equation analysis
b. Tieback
c. Hydro excavation
d. Shaft construction

69. _____ is a broad term used to describe the phenomenon that occurs when water invades a confined space in a structural support and upon freezing causes structural fracture as the ice expands.

The phenomenon has been blamed for the recent failure of a ski gondola in the Canadian ski resort of Whistler, B.C.

Rock slope failures can occur due to the presence of water; _____ occurs when water between joint or fissure surfaces freezes and expands.

a. AASHTO Soil Classification System
b. Ice jacking
c. AL 333
d. AL 129-1

70. _____ is a very soft phyllosilicate mineral that typically forms in microscopic crystals, forming a clay. _____, a member of the smectite family, is a 2:1 clay, meaning that it has 2 tetrahedral sheets sandwiching a central octahedral sheet.
a. 1700 Cascadia earthquake
b. Montmorillonite
c. 1703 Genroku earthquake
d. 1509 Istanbul earthquake

71. A _____ is a field test used in geotechnical engineering. The test is performed on a compacted base to establish it's percentage of compaction. With the use of a 3/4' diameter rod a hole is created in the compacted base by hammering the rod into the base to produce a hole that the densometer's probe can be inserted into.
a. Dynamic load testing
b. Geotechnical investigations
c. Soil nailing
d. Nuclear Densometer Test

72. The _____ is a method of analyzing the ability of deep foundations to resist loads applied in the lateral direction. This method uses the finite element method and p-y graphs to find a solution. P-y graphs are graphs which relate the force applied to soil to the lateral deflection of the soil.

a. 1509 Istanbul earthquake
c. 1700 Cascadia earthquake
b. Soil gradation
d. P-y method

73. The _____ of an earth (rock) material is a measure of its ability to be excavated with conventional excavation equipment. A material may be classified as rippable, marginally rippable or non-rippable. The _____ of a material is often evaluated by an engineering geologist and/or geophysicist utilizing the seismic refraction equipment
    a. 1700 Cascadia earthquake
    c. Rippability
    b. Soil gradation
    d. 1509 Istanbul earthquake

74. _____ -- also known as rip rap, rubble, shot rock or rock armour -- is rock or other material used to armor shorelines, streambeds, bridge abutments, pilings and other shoreline structures against scour, water or ice erosion.

    It is made from a variety of rock types, commonly granite, limestone or occasionally concrete rubble from building and paving demolition. It is used to protect coastlines and structures from erosion by the sea, rivers, or streams.

    a. Silt fence
    c. Geologic preliminary investigation
    b. Sediment trap
    d. Riprap

75. A _____ is a long anchor bolt, for stabilizing rock excavations, which may be tunnels or rock cuts. It transfers load from the unstable exterior, to the confined (and much stronger) interior of the rock mass.

    They were first used in mining starting in the 1890s, with systematic use documented at the St Joseph Lead Mine in the US in the 1920s.

    a. Dynamic load testing
    c. Nuclear Densometer Test
    b. Wave equation analysis
    d. Rock bolt

76. The _____, a construction approach popularized by architect Frank Lloyd Wright, is a type of foundation that uses loose stone or rubble to minimize the use of concrete and improve drainage. It is considered more environmentally friendly than other types of foundation because cement manufacturing requires the use of enormous amounts of energy and contributes significantly to global warming. However, some soil environments are not suitable for this kind of foundation; particularly expansive or poor load-bearing (< 1 ton/sf) soils.
    a. Soil nailing
    c. High strain dynamic testing
    b. Geomembranes
    d. Rubble trench foundation

77. A _____ is a temporary pond built on a construction site to capture eroded or disturbed soil that is washed off during rain storms, and protect the water quality of a nearby stream, river, lake, or bay. The sediment-laden soil settles in the pond before the runoff is discharged. Sediment basins are typically used on construction sites of 5 acres (20,000 m^2) or more, where there is sufficient room.
    a. Silt fence
    c. Sediment basin
    b. Mitigation of seismic motion
    d. Riprap

78. A _____ is a practice or device designed to keep eroded soil on a construction site, so that it does not wash off and cause water pollution to a nearby stream, river, lake, or bay. Sediment controls are usually employed together with erosion controls, which are designed to prevent or minimize erosion and thus reduce the need for sediment controls.

- Check dam
- Diversion dike
- Fiber rolls
- Sand bag barrier
- Sediment basin
- Sediment trap
- Silt fence
- Storm drain inlet protection
- Straw bale barrier
- Turbidity curtain

Chemical treatment of sediment, commonly called an active treatment system, is a relatively new form of _____ for the construction industry. It is designed to reduce turbidity in nearby water bodies and involves collection of sediment-laden stormwater in a basin or tank, and adding a chemical flocculant.

a. Mitigation of seismic motion
c. Riprap
b. Sediment control
d. Geologic preliminary investigation

79. A _____ is a temporary device installed on a construction site to capture eroded or disturbed soil that is washed off during rain storms, and protect the water quality of a nearby stream, river, lake, or bay. The trap is basically an embankment built along a waterway or low-lying area on the site. They are typically installed at the perimeter of a site and above storm drain inlets, to keep sediment from entering the drainage system.

a. Silt fence
c. Sediment basin
b. Sediment control
d. Sediment trap

80. _____ concerns the building of vertical openings such as Raises and Shafts. Shafts are vertical openings used for supplying equipment, personnel, and support systems to the horizontal tunnel where the pipeline is installed. They can be temporary or permanent, Which need large size excavations.

a. Rock bolt
c. Geotechnical investigations
b. Shaft construction
d. Dynamic load testing

81. _____ is soil or rock derived granular material of a grain size between sand and clay. _____ may occur as a soil or as suspended sediment in a surface water body. It may also exist as soil deposited at the bottom of a water body.

a. 1700 Cascadia earthquake
c. 1703 Genroku earthquake
b. 1509 Istanbul earthquake
d. Silt

82. A _____ is a temporary sediment control device used on construction sites to protect water quality in nearby streams, rivers, lakes and bays. A typical fence consists of a piece of synthetic filter fabric (also called a geotextile) stretched between a series of wooden or metal stakes. The stakes are installed on the downhill side of the fence, and the bottom edge of the fabric is trenched in the soil and backfilled on the uphill side.

a. Mitigation of seismic motion
b. Geologic preliminary investigation
c. Silt fence
d. Sediment trap

83. A _____ is a reinforced-concrete diaphragm wall used to build tunnels, to open cuts, and to lay foundations in areas of soft earth close to open water or with a high ground water table.

Slurry walls are typically constructed by starting with a set of guide walls, typically 1 metre (3.3 ft) deep and 0.5 metre (1.6 ft) thick, constructed on the ground surface. A special clamshell-shaped digger or a hydromill trench cutter is used to excavate the slurry trench guided by the guide walls.

a. Rubble trench foundation
b. Dynamic load testing
c. Geosynthetics
d. Slurry wall

84. _____ occurs when weight of livestock or heavy machinery compresses soil, causing it to lose pore space. Affected soils become less able to absorb rainfall, thus increasing runoff and erosion. Plants have difficulty in compacted soil because the mineral grains are pressed together, leaving little space for air and water, which are essential for root growth.
a. 1509 Istanbul earthquake
b. Soil compaction
c. 1703 Genroku earthquake
d. 1700 Cascadia earthquake

85. _____ refers to the process by which a sediment progressively loses its porosity due to the effects of loading. This forms part of the process of lithification. When a layer of sediment is originally deposited, it contains an open framework of particles with the pore space being usually filled with water.
a. Diamond Head
b. Geothermal
c. Compaction
d. Combe

86. _____ describes the sizes of individual particles in soil. A sieve analysis and a hydrometer analysis are used to determine _____.

The gradation of a soil can be assessed by the values of the coefficient of uniformity and of the coefficient of gradation of the analysed sample (the latter is also known as the coefficient of curvature.)

a. 1509 Istanbul earthquake
b. Rippability
c. 1700 Cascadia earthquake
d. Soil gradation

87. A _____ is a practice or procedure used to assess the particle size distribution of a granular material.

The size distribution is often of critical importance to the way the material performs in use. A _____ can be performed on any type of non-organic or organic granular materials including sands, crushed rock, clays, granite, feldspars, coal, soil, a wide range of manufactured powders, grain and seeds, down to a minimum size depending on the exact method.

a. 1703 Genroku earthquake
b. Sieve analysis
c. 1509 Istanbul earthquake
d. 1700 Cascadia earthquake

88. _____ is a technique in which soil slopes, excavations or retaining walls are reinforced by the insertion of relatively slender elements - normally steel reinforcing bars. The bars are usually installed into a pre-drilled hole and then grouted into place or drilled and grouted simultaneously. They are usually installed untensioned at a slight downward inclination.
   a. Wave equation analysis
   b. Tieback
   c. Rubble trench foundation
   d. Soil nailing

89. A _____ is a horizontal wire or rod, or a helical anchor used to reinforce retaining walls for stability. With one end of the _____ secured to the wall, the other end is anchored to a stable structure, such as a concrete deadman which has been driven into the ground or anchored into earth with sufficient resistance. The _____-deadman structure resists forces that would otherwise cause the wall to lean, as for example, when a seawall is pushed seaward by water trapped on the landward side after a heavy rain.
   a. Tieback
   b. Wave equation analysis
   c. Hydro excavation
   d. Crosshole sonic logging

90. A _____ is an instrument designed to measure very small changes from the horizontal level, either on the ground or in structures. A similar term, in less common usage, is the inclinometer. They are used extensively for monitoring volcanos, the response of dams to filling, the small movements of potential landslides, the orientation and volume of hydraulic fractures, and the response of structures to various influences such as loading and foundation settlement.
   a. 1700 Cascadia earthquake
   b. Tiltmeter
   c. 1703 Genroku earthquake
   d. 1509 Istanbul earthquake

91. The _____ is the level at which the ground water pressure is equal to atmospheric pressure. It may be conveniently visualized as the 'surface' of the ground water in a given vicinity. It usually coincides with the phreatic surface, but can be many feet above it.
   a. Crosshole sonic logging
   b. Shaft construction
   c. Rock bolt
   d. Water table

92. _____ is a numerical method of analysis for the behavior of driven foundation piles. It predicts the pile capacity versus blow count relationship (bearing graph) and pile driving stress. The model mathematically represents the pile driving hammer and all its accessories (ram, cap, and cap block), as well as the pile, as a series of lumped masses and springs in a one-dimensional analysis.
   a. Geosynthetics
   b. Geogrid
   c. Rubble trench foundation
   d. Wave equation analysis

93. A _____ is a type of geothermal power plant that allows cooler geothermal reservoirs to be used than with dry steam and flash steam plants. They are used when the temperature of the water is less than 175 °C (350 °F.) With binary cycle geothermal power plants, pumps are used to pump hot water from a geothermal well, through a heat exchanger, and the cooled water is returned to the underground reservoir.
   a. Geothermal desalination
   b. Binary cycle power plant
   c. Hot Dry Rock Geothermal Energy
   d. Geothermal power

94. In geology, _____ refers to heat sources within the planet. _____ is technically an adjective (e.g., _____ energy) but in U.S. English the word has attained frequent use as a noun.

The planet's internal heat was originally generated during its accretion, due to gravitational binding energy, and since then additional heat has continued to be generated by decay heat from the radioactive decay of elements.

a. Combe
c. Dali

b. Diamond Head
d. Geothermal

95. A _____ system is a central heating and/or air conditioning system that actively pumps heat to or from the shallow ground. It uses the earth as either a source of heat in the winter, or as a coolant in the summer. This design takes advantage of moderate temperatures in the shallow ground to boost efficiency and reduce operational costs.
a. Geothermal power
c. Geothermal heat pump

b. Hot Dry Rock Geothermal Energy
d. Geothermal gradient

96. _____ is a type of geothermal power production that uses the high temperatures that can be found in rocks a few kilometers below ground. Electricity is generated by pumping high pressure water down a borehole into the hot rock. The water travels through fractures in the rock, capturing the heat of the rock until it is forced out of a second borehole as very hot water, which is converted into electricity using either a steam turbine or a binary power plant system.
a. Geothermal gradient
c. Geothermal heat pump

b. Hot Dry Rock Geothermal Energy
d. Geothermal desalination

1. _____ is a proven process under development for the production of fresh water using heat energy. Claimed benefits of this method of desalination are that it requires less maintenance than reverse osmosis membranes and that the primary energy input is from geothermal heat, which is a low-environmental-impact source of energy.

Around 1995, entrepreneur Douglas Firestone from Nevada came up with an idea to use geothermal water directly as a source for desalination.

   a. Hot Dry Rock Geothermal Energy
   b. Geothermal power
   c. Geothermal heat pump
   d. Geothermal desalination

2. In geology, _____ refers to heat sources within the planet. _____ is technically an adjective (e.g., _____ energy) but in U.S. English the word has attained frequent use as a noun.

The planet's internal heat was originally generated during its accretion, due to gravitational binding energy, and since then additional heat has continued to be generated by decay heat from the radioactive decay of elements.

   a. Geothermal
   b. Combe
   c. Diamond Head
   d. Dali

3. The _____ is the rate of increase in temperature per unit depth in the Earth. It varies with location and is typically measured by determining the bottom open-hole temperature after borehole drilling. To achieve accuracy the drilling fluid needs time to reach the ambient temperature.

   a. Hot Dry Rock Geothermal Energy
   b. Geothermal gradient
   c. Geothermal power
   d. Geothermal desalination

4. A _____ system is a central heating and/or air conditioning system that actively pumps heat to or from the shallow ground. It uses the earth as either a source of heat in the winter, or as a coolant in the summer. This design takes advantage of moderate temperatures in the shallow ground to boost efficiency and reduce operational costs.

   a. Geothermal power
   b. Geothermal gradient
   c. Hot Dry Rock Geothermal Energy
   d. Geothermal heat pump

5. _____ is power extracted from heat stored in the earth. This geothermal energy originates from the original formation of the planet, from radioactive decay of minerals, and from solar energy absorbed at the surface. It has been used for space heating and bathing since ancient roman times, but is now better known for generating electricity.

   a. Geothermal desalination
   b. Geothermal gradient
   c. Geothermal power
   d. Geothermal heat pump

6. _____ is the process by which the freezing of water-saturated soil causes the deformation and upward thrust of the ground surface. This process can damage plant roots through breaking or desiccation, cause cracks in pavement, and damage the foundations of buildings, even below the frost line. Moist, fine-grained soil at certain temperatures is most susceptible to _____.

   a. 1700 Cascadia earthquake
   b. 1703 Genroku earthquake
   c. 1509 Istanbul earthquake
   d. Frost heaving

Chapter 3. Test Preparation Part 3

7. The _____, also known as frost depth or freezing depth, is most commonly the depth that the groundwater in soil is expected to freeze. The frost depth depends on the climatic conditions of an area, the heat transfer properties of the soil and adjacent materials, and on nearby heat sources. For example, snow cover and asphalt insulate the ground and homes can heat the ground
   a. 1509 Istanbul earthquake
   b. 1703 Genroku earthquake
   c. Frost line
   d. 1700 Cascadia earthquake

8. An _____ is the result of a sudden release of energy in the Earth's crust that creates seismic waves. They are recorded with a seismometer or the related and mostly obsolete Richter magnitude, with a magnitude 3 or lower _____ being mostly imperceptible and magnitude 7 causing serious damage over large areas.
   a. AL 333
   b. AL 129-1
   c. AASHTO Soil Classification System
   d. Earthquake

9. An _____ is a rapid flow of snow down a slope, from either natural triggers or human activity. Typically occurring in mountainous terrain, an _____ can mix air and water with the descending snow. Powerful avalanches have the capability to entrain ice, rocks, trees, and other material on the slope; however avalanches are always initiated in snow, are primarily composed of flowing snow, and are distinct from mudslides, rock slides, rock avalanches, and serac collapses from an icefall.
   a. AL 129-1
   b. AASHTO Soil Classification System
   c. Avalanche
   d. AL 333

10. A _____ is a crevasse that forms where the moving glacier ice separates from the stagnant ice above. It is often a serious obstacle for mountaineers, who sometimes abbreviate '_____' to "schrund".

In a corrie or cirque, the _____ is positioned at the rear, parallel to the back wall of the corrie.

   a. Bergschrund
   b. Pastonian Stage
   c. Cordilleran Ice Sheet
   d. Snowball Earth

11. A _____ is a huge crack formed by two glaciers colliding. Accelerations in glacier speed cause extension and can initiate a _____. Crevasses often have vertical or near-vertical walls, which can then melt and create seracs, arches, etc.; these walls sometimes expose layers that represent the glacier's stratigraphy.
   a. Geohazard
   b. Solifluction
   c. Sturzstrom
   d. Crevasse

12. A _____ known as a frost quake may be caused by a sudden cracking action in frozen soil or rock saturated with water or ice. As water seeps down into the rock, it freezes and expands, putting stress on surrounding rock. This builds up until it is relieved explosively in a _____.
   a. Sturzstrom
   b. Cryoseism
   c. Geohazard
   d. Debris flow

13. A _____ is a fast moving mass of unconsolidated, saturated debris that looks like flowing concrete. They differentiate from a mudflow by terms of the viscosity of the flow. Flows can carry clasts ranging in size from clay particles to boulders, and also often contains a large amount of woody debris.

a. Sturzstrom
c. Rockfall
b. Geohazard
d. Debris flow

14. _____ is loose sand whose bulk density is reduced by blowing air through it and which yields easily to weight or pressure. It acts similarly to regular quicksand, but it does not contain any water and does not operate on the same principle. _____ is an example of a granular material.
   a. Fech fech
   b. Salt glacier
   c. Sediment
   d. Dry quicksand

15. _____ is a colloid hydrogel consisting of fine granular matter (such as sand or silt), clay, and salt water. In the name, as in that of quicksilver (mercury), 'quick' does not mean 'fast,' but 'living' (cf. the expression the quick and the dead.)
   a. Bovey Beds
   b. Salt glacier
   c. Quick clay
   d. Quicksand

16. An _____ is a downslope viscous flow of fine grained materials that have been saturated with water, and moves under the pull of gravity. They are an intermediate type of mass wasting that is between downhill creep and mudflow. The types of materials that are susceptible to earthflows are clay, fine sand and silt, and fine-grained pyroclastic material.
   a. AL 129-1
   b. AL 333
   c. AASHTO Soil Classification System
   d. Earthflow

17. A _____ can be defined as a geological state that represents or has the potential to develop further into a situation leading to damage or uncontrolled risk . This definition implies that geohazards are widespread phenomena that are related to geological and environmental conditions and involve long-term and/or short-term geological processes. Geohazards can thus be relatively small features, but they can also attain huge dimensions (e.g. submarine or surface landslide) and affect local and regional socio-economy (e.g. tsunamis) to a large extent.
   a. Rockfall
   b. Geohazard
   c. Predator trap
   d. Debris flow

18. A _____ is a type of mudflow or landslide composed of pyroclastic material and water that flows down from a volcano, typically along a river valley. The term '_____' originated in the Javanese language of Indonesia.
   a. 1509 Istanbul earthquake
   b. 1703 Genroku earthquake
   c. 1700 Cascadia earthquake
   d. Lahar

19. _____ were originally defined by Coffin and Eldholm (1992) as areas of Earth's surface that contain very large volumes of magmatic rocks (typically basalt but including rhyolites) erupted over extremely short geological time intervals of a few million years or less. These provinces are not associated with normal plate tectonic magmatism, i. e. mid-ocean ridges and island arcs.
   a. Large igneous provinces
   b. Rock cycle
   c. Metamorphic zone
   d. Serpentinite

20. A _____, also referred to as a lake overturn, is a rare type of natural disaster in which carbon dioxide (CO_2) suddenly erupts from deep lake water, suffocating wildlife, livestock and humans. Such an eruption may also cause tsunamis in the lake as the rising CO_2 displaces water. Scientists believe landslides, volcanic activity, or explosions can trigger such an eruption.

Chapter 3. Test Preparation Part 3   41

a. 1509 Istanbul earthquake
c. 1703 Genroku earthquake
b. Limnic eruption
d. 1700 Cascadia earthquake

21. _____ is the geomorphic process by which soil, regolith, and rock move downslope under the force of gravity. Types of _____ include creep, slides, flows, topples, and falls, each with its own characteristic features, and taking place over timescales from seconds to years. _____ occurs on both terrestrial and submarine slopes, and has been observed on Earth, Mars, and Venus.
  a. 1703 Genroku earthquake
  c. 1700 Cascadia earthquake
  b. 1509 Istanbul earthquake
  d. Mass wasting

22. A _____ is the geological name given to pockets of oxygen-poor air which can be lethal to any human or animal life inside. The term comes from Swahili and means 'evil wind.' They are created when an odorless and invisible gas such as carbon dioxide accumulates in pockets low to the ground. CO_2 is heavier than air (oxygen and nitrogen) which causes it to stay close to the ground, and is also undetectable by human olfactory or most visual conditions.
  a. Seismic refraction
  c. 1509 Istanbul earthquake
  b. Strainmeter
  d. Mazuku

23. _____ is an informal term to indicate a tsunami that has initial wave heights that are much larger than normal tsunami. Unlike usual tsunamis, which originate from tectonic activity and the raising or lowering of the sea floor, known megatsunamis have originated from large scale impact events such as landslides and meteor impacts.

A _____ is meant to refer to a tsunami with an initial wave amplitude measured in several tens, hundreds or possibly thousands of metres.

  a. 1703 Genroku earthquake
  c. Megatsunami
  b. 1509 Istanbul earthquake
  d. 1700 Cascadia earthquake

24. A _____ or mudslide is the most rapid (up to 80 km/h, or 50 mph) and fluid type of downhill mass wasting. It is a rapid movement of a large mass of mud formed from loose earth and water. Similar terms are mudslide (not very liquid), mud stream, debris flow (e.g. in high mountains), j>ökulhlaup, and lahar
  a. 1700 Cascadia earthquake
  c. 1703 Genroku earthquake
  b. 1509 Istanbul earthquake
  d. Mudflow

25. A _____ is a natural hazard such as a tar pit. Predators become attracted to struggling animals that have become entrapped in viscous or glutinous material, such as a heavy sedimentary deposit or tar and, in the process, become entrapped themselves. More predators, scavengers, insects and birds become attracted to this mounting accumulation of carrion, until a wide variety of animals are caught and ultimately killed by the hazard.
  a. Predator trap
  c. Sturzstrom
  b. Geohazard
  d. Solifluction

26. _____ refers to quantities of rock falling freely from a cliff face. A _____ is a fragment of rock (a block) detached by sliding, toppling, or falling, that falls along a vertical or sub-vertical cliff, proceeds down slope by bouncing and flying along ballistic trajectories or by rolling on talus or debris slopes,'e; (Varnes, 1978.) Alternatively, a '_____ is the natural downward motion of a detached block or series of blocks with a small volume involving free falling, bouncing, rolling, and sliding'.

a. Cryoseism
b. Predator trap
c. Sturzstrom
d. Rockfall

27. In geology, _____ is a type of mass wasting where waterlogged sediment slowly moves downslope over impermeable material. It can occur in any climate where the ground is saturated by water, though it is most often found in periglacial environments where the ground is permanently frozen, under which conditions the process is often called gelifluction. During warm seasonal periods the surface layer melts and slides over the frozen underlayer, slowly moving downslope due to frost heave that occurs normal to the slope.
a. Rockfall
b. Solifluction
c. Predator trap
d. Sturzstrom

28. A _____ is a rare, unique type of landslide consisting of soil and rock which is characterized by having a great horizontal movement when compared to its initial vertical drop - as much as 20 or 30 times the vertical distance. Sturzstroms are similar to glaciers, mudslides, and lava flows. Sturzstroms flow across land fairly easily, and their mobility increases when volume increases.
a. Debris flow
b. Geohazard
c. Cryoseism
d. Sturzstrom

29. A _____ or super volcanic eruption is a volcanic eruption which is substantially larger than any volcano in historic times (generally accepted to be greater than 1,000 cubic kilometres.) They occur when magma in the Earth rises into the crust from a hotspot but is unable to break through the crust. Pressure builds in a large and growing magma pool until the crust is unable to contain the pressure.
a. 1509 Istanbul earthquake
b. Supervolcano
c. 1700 Cascadia earthquake
d. Pit crater

30. A _____ is an opening in a planet's surface or crust, which allows hot, molten rock, ash, and gases to escape from below the surface. Volcanic activity involving the extrusion of rock tends to form mountains or features like mountains over a period of time.
a. 1509 Istanbul earthquake
b. Volcano
c. 1700 Cascadia earthquake
d. 1703 Genroku earthquake

31. _____ is the use of the principles of geology to reconstruct and understand the history of the Earth . It focuses on geologic processes that change the Earth's surface and subsurface; and the use of stratigraphy, structural geology and paleontology to tell the sequence of these events. It also focuses on the evolution of plants and animals during different time periods in the geological timescale.
a. 1509 Istanbul earthquake
b. Historical geology
c. Logarithmic Spiral Beach
d. Rockall

32. _____ is the historical geological state of a particular area including such things as reconstructions of previous configurations of the Earth's continents, the history and evolution of the Earth's surface geological configuration, the formation and development of continents, and so on.

There are several related fields of research that are involved in _____, including Plate tectonics, in which case is used to study the history and movements of the earths continents.

a. Chatham Rise
c. Paleogeology

b. Paleoseismology
d. Geosyncline

33. _____ describes geological events that account for the stratigraphy, petrology and structure seen in rocks or earth materials.
   a. Patagonian Ice Sheet
   c. First appearance datum

   b. Paleoseismology
   d. Geological history

34. The _____ was a cratonic sequence that extended from the end of the Mississippian through the Permian periods. It is the unconformity between this sequence and the preceding Kaskaskia that divides the Carboniferous into the Mississippian and Pennsylvanian periods in North America.

Like the Kaskaskia sequence, Absaroka sedimentary deposits were dominated by detrital or siliclastic rocks.

   a. AL 129-1
   c. AASHTO Soil Classification System

   b. AL 333
   d. Absaroka sequence

35. In the Mesozoic Era, _____ was a land area which is now an eastern part of the USA, separated from Laramidia by the Western Interior Seaway, which shrank and became the Pierre Seaway and finally dried up. Laramidia was roughly what is now the western cordillera area of the USA and Canada.

From the Turonian period of the Late Cretaceous to the very beginning of the Paleocene, _____ was separated from the rest of North America.

   a. AL 333
   c. AASHTO Soil Classification System

   b. AL 129-1
   d. Appalachia

36. The _____ Era is one of three geologic eras of the Phanerozoic eon. The division of time into eras dates back to Giovanni Arduino, in the 18th century, although his original name for the era now called the '_____' was 'Secondary' (making the modern era the 'Tertiary'.)

The _____ was a time of tectonic, climatic and evolutionary activity. The continents gradually shifted from a state of connectedness into their present configuration; the drifting provided for speciation and other important evolutionary developments.

   a. Mesozoic
   c. 1509 Istanbul earthquake

   b. 1700 Cascadia earthquake
   d. 1703 Genroku earthquake

37. An _____ contains aragonite and high-magnesium calcite as the primary inorganic carbonate precipitates. Therefore, the chemical conditions of the seawater must be notably high in magnesium content for a _____ to form. This is in contrast to a calcite sea in which low-magnesium calcite is the primary inorganic marine calcium carbonate precipitate.
   a. AL 333
   c. AASHTO Soil Classification System

   b. Aragonite sea
   d. AL 129-1

38. The _____, is a geologic eon before the Proterozoic and Paleoproterozoic, before 2.5 Ga (billion years ago, or 2,500 Ma.) Instead of being based on stratigraphy, this date is defined chronometrically. The lower boundary (starting point) has not been officially recognized by the International Commission on Stratigraphy, but it is usually set to 3.8 Ga, at the end of the Hadean eon.
   a. AL 333
   b. AL 129-1
   c. AASHTO Soil Classification System
   d. Archean

39. The _____ establishes a geologic timescale for prehistoric Asian fauna beginning 58.7 Mya during the Paleogene and continuing through to the Middle Pleistocene (0.33 Ma.) These periods are referred to as ages, stages, or intervals and were established using geographic place names where fossil materials where obtained.

The basic unit of measure is the first/last boundary statement.

   a. Asian land mammal ages
   b. AL 333
   c. AASHTO Soil Classification System
   d. AL 129-1

40. The _____ occupies more than half of the continent of Australia. It occupies the portion of Australia west of a line running north-south roughly from the eastern shore of Arnhem Land on the Bay or Gulf of Carpentaria to the Eyre Peninsula in the state of South Australia, and skirting to the west of the Simpson Desert in the interior. The plateau has an average elevation of between 305 and 460 m. The shield is fractured into a number of distinct blocks, including the Pilbara craton in the North and the Yilgarn craton in the Southwest. Some of these blocks have been raised to form uplands; others have been depressed, forming lowlands and basins.
   a. AL 129-1
   b. AASHTO Soil Classification System
   c. AL 333
   d. Australian Shield

41. The _____ is an inconstant limestone deposited in a warm shallow sea near the eastern margin of the Iapetus Ocean. It occurs in England in the Ludlow series of Silurian rocks, between the Upper and Lower Ludlow Shales. It derives its name from Aymestry, Herefordshire, where it may be seen on both sides of the river Lugg.
   a. AASHTO Soil Classification System
   b. Aymestry Limestone
   c. AL 333
   d. AL 129-1

42. The _____ was an ancient tectonic plate that existed from the Cambrian period to the Carboniferous period. The _____ collided against Siberia, to form the Ural Mountains about 500 million years ago. The _____, however, fused onto the Eurasian Plate when the _____ collided against Siberia when the Ural Mountains were completely formed.
   a. Fault trace
   b. Farallon Plate
   c. Sonoma orogeny
   d. Baltic Plate

43. The Bering land bridge was a land bridge roughly 1,000 miles (1,600 km) north to south at its greatest extent, which joined present-day Alaska and eastern Siberia at various times during the Pleistocene ice ages. It was not glaciated because snowfall was extremely light due to the southwesterly winds from the Pacific Ocean having lost their moisture over the fully glaciated Alaska Range. The grassland steppe including the land bridge and stretching for several hundred miles into the continents on either side has been called _____.
   a. Tethyan Trench
   b. Beringia
   c. Tyrrell Sea
   d. Patagonian Ice Sheet

Chapter 3. Test Preparation Part 3   45

44. A _____ is one in which low-magnesium calcite is the primary inorganic marine calcium carbonate precipitate. An aragonite sea is the alternate seawater chemistry in which aragonite and high-magnesium calcite are the primary inorganic carbonate precipitates. The Early Paleozoic and the Middle to Late Mesozoic oceans were predominantly calcite seas, whereas the Middle Paleozoic through the Early Mesozoic and the Cenozoic (including today) are characterized by aragonite seas (Wilkinson et al., 1985; Wilkinson and Given, 1986; Morse and Mackenzie, 1990; Lowenstein et al., 2001; Palmer and Wilson, 2004.)

  a. Calcite sea
  b. 1509 Istanbul earthquake
  c. 1703 Genroku earthquake
  d. 1700 Cascadia earthquake

45. In chemistry, a _____ is a salt or ester of carbonic acid.

To test for the presence of the _____ anion in a salt, the addition of dilute mineral acid (e.g. hydrochloric acid) will yield carbon dioxide gas.

_____-containing salts are industrially and mineralogically ubiquitous.

  a. 1703 Genroku earthquake
  b. 1700 Cascadia earthquake
  c. 1509 Istanbul earthquake
  d. Carbonate

46. _____ are surfaces of synsedimentarily cemented carbonate layers that have been exposed on the seafloor (Wilson and Palmer, 1992.) A hardground is essentially, then, a lithified seafloor. Ancient hardgrounds are found in limestone sequences and distinguished from later-lithified sediments by evidence of exposure to normal marine waters.

  a. 1703 Genroku earthquake
  b. 1700 Cascadia earthquake
  c. 1509 Istanbul earthquake
  d. Carbonate hardgrounds

47. The _____ age is the first or earliest or oldest Geochronological 'geologic age' of the Late Cretaceous Epoch. Like all geological time units the _____ age is associated with a Chronostratigraphic stratum or 'geologic stage' of the same name, the '_____ stage' Each belong to the Cretaceous period and Cretaceous system as well.

  a. Geologic record
  b. Global Standard Stratigraphic Age
  c. Chronozone
  d. Cenomanian

48. The _____ Era, is the most recent of the three classic geological eras and covers the period from 65.5 million years ago to the present. It is marked by the Cretaceous-Tertiary extinction event at the end of the Cretaceous that saw the demise of the last non-avian dinosaurs and the end of the Mesozoic Era. The _____ era is ongoing.

  a. 1700 Cascadia earthquake
  b. 1509 Istanbul earthquake
  c. 1703 Genroku earthquake
  d. Cenozoic

49. The _____ is an area of ocean floor to the east of New Zealand, forming part of the Zealandia continent. It stretches for some 1000 kilometres from near the South Island in the west, to the Chatham Islands in the east.

Geologically and tectonically, the _____ can be thought of as an extension of the eastern South Island. It was largely dry land at the end of the Cretaceous (65.5 million years ago) and formed a large peninsula extending from New Zealand to the Chatham Islands at that time. This was characterized by a volcanic landscape. Fossils found on the Chatham Islands characterize the flora and fauna of the _____ in the late Mesozoic.

a. Cornbrash
b. Storegga Slides
c. Cratonic sequence
d. Chatham Rise

50. A _____ or chron is a slice of time that begins at a given identifiable event and ends at another. In the fossil record such tracer events are usually keyed to disappearance (extinction) of a widely distributed and rapidly changing species or the appearance of such a species in the geological record. They are used especially in the various disciplines related to Geology, notably in stratigraphy where relative dating is employed.
   a. Geologic record
   b. Law of superposition
   c. Chronozone
   d. Relative dating

51. The _____ is the northwest section of the Canadian Shield and stretches from southern Saskatchewan and Alberta to northern Nunavut. It has a very complex geological history punctuated by at least seven distinct regional tectonometamorphic intervals, including many discrete accretionary magmatic events. The Western Churchill province is the part of the _____ that is exposed north and west of the Hudson Bay.
   a. Churchill craton
   b. Sebakwe proto-craton
   c. Craton
   d. Wyoming craton

52. A _____ is an old and stable part of the continental crust that has survived the merging and splitting of continents and supercontinents for at least 500 million years. Some are over two billion years old. They are generally found in the interiors of continents and are characteristically composed of ancient crystalline basement crust of lightweight felsic igneous rock such as granite.
   a. Sebakwe proto-craton
   b. Kalahari craton
   c. Superior craton
   d. Craton

53. The _____ is an ancient tectonic plate that comprises parts of present-day Anatolia, Iran, Afghanistan, Tibet, Indochina and Malaya regions. The _____ was formerly part of the ancient supercontinent of Pangaea. Pangaea was shaped like a vast 'C', facing east, and inside of the 'C' was the Paleo-Tethys Ocean.
   a. Nazca Plate
   b. Cimmerian Plate
   c. Solomon Sea Plate
   d. Kermadec Plate

54. The _____ was a major ice sheet that covered, during glacial periods of the Quaternary, a large area of North America. This included the following areas:

   - Western Montana
   - The Idaho Panhandle
   - Northern Washington state down to about Seattle and Spokane, Washington
   - All of British Columbia
   - The southwestern third or so of Yukon territory
   - All of the Alaska Panhandle
   - South Central Alaska
   - The Alaska Peninsula
   - Almost all of the continental shelf north of the Strait of Juan de Fuca

The ice sheet covered up to two and a half million square kilometres at the Last Glacial Maximum and probably more than that in some previous periods, when it may have extended into the northeast extremity of Oregon and the Salmon River Mountains in Idaho. It is probable, though, that its northern margin also migrated south due to the influence of starvation caused by very low levels of precipitation.

At its eastern end the _____ merged with the Laurentide ice sheet at the Continental Divide, forming an area of ice that contained one and a half times as much water as the Antarctic ice sheet does today.

a. Quaternary glaciation
b. Cordilleran Ice Sheet
c. Pre-Pastonian Stage
d. Pastonian Stage

55. In geology, _____ was the name applied to the uppermost member of the Bathonian stage of the Jurassic formation in England. It is an old English agricultural name applied in Wiltshire to a variety of loose rubble or brash which, in that part of the country, forms a good soil for growing corn. The name was adopted by William Smith for a thin band of shelly limestone which, in the south of England, breaks up in the manner indicated.
a. Chatham Rise
b. Cratonic sequence
c. First appearance datum
d. Cornbrash

56. A _____ refers to a very large-scale lithostratigraphic sequence that covers a complete marine transgressive-regressive cycle across a craton. They are also known as 'megasequences', 'stratigraphic sequences', or simply 'sequences.'

They were first proposed by Lawrence Sloss in 1963; each one represents a time when epeiric seas deposited sediments across the craton, while the upper and lower edges of the sequence are bounded by craton-wide unconformities eroded when the seas receded.

These sequences may in part represent eustatic or global change in sea level; however, when the proper names are used they usually refer to the North American continent.

a. Cratonic sequence
b. First appearance datum
c. Tethyan Trench
d. Geosyncline

57. The _____ , usually abbreviated K for its German translation Kreide, is a geologic period and system from circa >145.5 >± 4 to >65.5 >± 0.3 million years ago . In the geologic timescale, the _____ follows on the Jurassic period and is followed by the Paleogene period. It is the youngest period of the Mesozoic era, and at 80 million years long, the longest period of the Phanerozoic eon. The end of the _____ defines the boundary between the Mesozoic and Cenozoic eras.
a. Coniacian
b. Santonian
c. Cretaceous
d. Hauterivian

58. _____ is the study of astronomically forced climate cycles within sedimentary successions. Astronomical cycles are variations of the Earth's orbit around the sun due to the gravitational interaction with other masses within the solar system. Due to this cyclicity solar irradiation differs through time on different hemispheres and seasonality is affected.
a. Sequence stratigraphy
b. Polystrate
c. Cyclostratigraphy
d. Bedrock

59. _____ is the concept of geologic time first recognized in the 11th century by the Persian geologist and polymath, Avicenna , and the Chinese naturalist and polymath Shen Kuo (1031-1095.) In the Western world, the modern scientific concept was developed in the 1700s by Scottish geologist James Hutton.

Science in succeeding centuries has established the age of the Earth as between four and five billion years, with an exceedingly long history of change and development.

  a. 1703 Genroku earthquake
  b. 1700 Cascadia earthquake
  c. Deep time
  d. 1509 Istanbul earthquake

60. _____ is a name given by geologists to the former landmass in the southern North Sea that connected the island of Great Britain to mainland Europe during the last ice age. Geological surveys have suggested that _____ was a large area of dry land that stretched from Britain's east coast across to the present coast of the Netherlands and the western coasts of Germany and Denmark. The land was likely a rich habitat with human habitation in the Mesolithic period.

  a. Cornbrash
  b. Paleogeology
  c. Paleoseismology
  d. Doggerland

61. The _____ is the core of the Baltica proto-plate and consists of three crustal regions/segments: Fennoscandia to the northwest, Volgo-Uralia to the east, and Sarmatia to the south. Fennoscandia includes the Baltic Shield (also referred to as the Fennoscandian Shield) and has a diversified accretionary Archaean and Early Proterozoic crust, while Sarmatia has an older Archaean crust. The Volgo-Uralia region has a thick sedimentary cover, however deep drillings have revealed mostly Archaean crust.

  a. AASHTO Soil Classification System
  b. AL 333
  c. East European craton
  d. AL 129-1

62. In stratigraphy and geology, an _____ is the totality of rock strata laid down in the stratigraphic record deposited during a certain eon of the continuous geologic timescale. The _____ is not to be confused with the eon itself, which is a corresponding division of geologic time spanning a specific amount of (millions of) years, during which rocks were formed that are classified within the _____.

  a. Eonothem
  b. AL 129-1
  c. AASHTO Soil Classification System
  d. AL 333

63. An _____ is a large shallow sea that either extends far into a continent, such as the Persian Gulf, or overlies a large part of a continent.

They are usually associated with the marine transgressions of the early Cenozoic era and may be semi-cyclic--during eras of glacial recession given a period of low mountains coupled with a warming under the influence of plate tectonics. They can be warm or cold; indeed, several were present at the end of the last Ice Age, when sea levels rose more rapidly than some areas could isostatically adjust.

  a. AL 333
  b. AL 129-1
  c. Epeiric sea
  d. AASHTO Soil Classification System

64. In stratigraphy, paleontology, geology, and geobiology an _____ is the total stratigraphic record deposited during a certain corresponding span of time, an era in the geologic timescale.

It can therefore be used as a chronostratigraphic unit of time which delineates a large span of years -- less than an geological eon, but greater than its successively smaller and more refined subdivisions (geologic periods, epochs, and geologic ages.) By 3,500 Million years ago (Mya) simple life had developed on earth (the oldest known microbial fossils in Australia are dated to this figure.

a. AL 129-1
b. AASHTO Soil Classification System
c. AL 333
d. Erathem

65. An _____ is the name given to a late 19th century electric lighting apparatus designed for the examination of the strata of earth traversed by boring apparatus.

It consisted of a very powerful incandescent lamp enclosed in a metallic cylinder. One of the two semi-cylindrical sides constitutes the reflector, and the other, which is of thick glass, allows the passage of light, which illuminates the strata of earth traversed by the instrument.

a. AL 129-1
b. AL 333
c. AASHTO Soil Classification System
d. Erygmascope

66. The _____ establishes a geologic timescale for prehistoric European fauna beginning 66.5 Ma during the Paleogene and continuing through to the Middle Pleistocene (0.33 Ma.) These periods are referred to as ages, stages, or intervals and were established using geographic place names where fossil materials where obtained.

The basic unit of measure is the first/last boundary statement.

a. AL 129-1
b. AL 333
c. AASHTO Soil Classification System
d. European Land Mammal Ages

67. The _____ was an ancient oceanic plate, which began subducting under the west coast of the North American Plate-- then located in modern Utah-- as Pangaea broke apart during the Jurassic period. It is named for the Farallon Islands which are located just west of San Francisco, California.

Over time the central part of the _____ was completely subducted under the southwestern part of the North American Plate. The remains of the _____ are the Juan de Fuca, Explorer and Gorda Plates, subducting under the northern part of the North American Plate, the Cocos Plate subducting under Central America and the Nazca Plate subducting under the South American Plate.

a. Rivera Plate
b. Fault trace
c. Sonoma orogeny
d. Farallon Plate

68. The _____ was an ancient oceanic trench on the west coast of North America during the Late Cretaceous period. When the trench disappeared, it turned into the San Andreas Fault. Since then, it has spread out to the north and south.
a. 1703 Genroku earthquake
b. 1700 Cascadia earthquake
c. 1509 Istanbul earthquake
d. Farallon Trench

69. In chronostratigraphy, a _____ is a succession of rock strata laid down in an single age on the geologic timescale, which usually represents millions of years of deposition. A given _____ of rock and the corresponding age of time will by convention have the same name, and the same boundaries.
   a. Chronozone
   b. Paleomagnetism
   c. Global Standard Stratigraphic Age
   d. Stage

70. _____ is a term used by geologists and paleontologists to designate the first (oldest) appearance of a species in the geologic record. In other words, _____ represents the geologically oldest fossil of a particular species that has yet been discovered. They are frequently used to designate segments in the Geologic time scale.
   a. Storegga Slides
   b. Doggerland
   c. Geological history
   d. First appearance datum

71. The _____ covers approximately 440,000 square kilometres of central South Australia. Its Precambrian crystalline basement crustal block was cratonised ca. 1550-1450 Ma. Prior to 1550 Ma the craton comprised a number of active Proterozoic orogenic belts extending back in time to at least 2450 Ma.

The Craton can be subdivided into a number of tectonic subdomains on the basis of structure and tectonostratigraphic history.

The _____, is a distinct physiographic province of the larger West Australian Shield division. It includes the smaller Stuart Range Basin and Pimba Platform physiographic sections.

   a. Great Artesian Basin
   b. Sahara pump theory
   c. Gawler craton
   d. Canadian Shield

72. The _____ in stratigraphy, Chronostratigraphy, paleontology and other natural sciences refers to the entirety of the layers of rock strata -- depositions laid down in volcanism or by weathering detritus (clays, sands etc.) including all its fossil content and the information it yields about the history of the Earth: its past climate, geography, geology and the evolution of life on its surface. According to the Law of Superposition (first proposed in the mid-seventeenth century by the Danish naturalist Nicolas Steno) sedimentary and volcanic rocklayers are deposited on top of each other.
   a. Global Boundary Stratotype Section and Point
   b. Geologic record
   c. Law of superposition
   d. Global Standard Stratigraphic Age

73. The _____ are changes in Earth's environment as determined from geologic evidence on multi-million to billion (10^9) year time scales.

Our evidence for past temperatures comes mainly from isotopic considerations (especially $>\delta^{18}O$); the Mg/Ca ratio of foram tests, and alkenones, are also useful.

   a. Geologic temperature record
   b. Little Ice Age
   c. 1509 Istanbul earthquake
   d. Keeling Curve

74. The _____ is a chronologic schema (or idealized model) relating stratigraphy to time that is used by geologists, paleontologists and other earth scientists to describe the timing and relationships between events that have occurred during the history of the Earth. The table of geologic time spans presented here agrees with the dates and nomenclature proposed by the International Commission on Stratigraphy, and uses the standard color codes of the United States Geological Survey.

Chapter 3. Test Preparation Part 3   51

Evidence from radiometric dating indicates that the Earth is about 4.570 billion years old.

a. Geologic time scale
b. 1509 Istanbul earthquake
c. 1703 Genroku earthquake
d. 1700 Cascadia earthquake

75. _____ theory is an obsolete concept involving vertical crustal movement that has been replaced by plate tectonics to explain crustal movement and geologic features. _____ is a term still occasionally used for a subsiding linear trough that was caused by the accumulation of sedimentary rock strata deposited in a basin and subsequently compressed, deformed, and uplifted into a mountain range, with attendant volcanism and plutonism. The filling of a _____ with tons of sediment is accompanied in the late stages of deposition by folding, crumpling, and faulting of the deposits.

a. Paleogeology
b. Storegga Slides
c. Tejas sequence
d. Geosyncline

76. A _____, is an internationally agreed upon stratigraphic section which serves as the reference section for a particular boundary on the geologic time scale. The effort to define GSSPs is conducted by the International Commission on Stratigraphy, a part of the International Union of Geological Sciences. Most, but not all, GSSPs are based on paleontological changes.

a. Chronostratigraphy
b. Global Boundary Stratotype Section and Point
c. Chronozone
d. Paleomagnetism

77. In the Stratigraphy sub-discipline of Geology, a _____, is a chronological reference point and criteria in the world's rock records used to define the boundaries (a internationally sanctioned benchmark point) between different geological periods, epochs or ages on the overall geologic time scale in a chronostratigraphically useful rock layer. A world wide multidisciplinary effort has been ongoing since 1974 to define such important metrics. But such work goes slowly despite a lot of effort, as one criteria is such points and strata need be widespread and contain a identifiable sequence of layers or other unambiguous marker (identifiable or quantifiable) attributes.

a. Relative dating
b. Global Standard Stratigraphic Age
c. Geologic record
d. Paleomagnetism

78. The _____ is the geologic eon before the Archean. It started at Earth's formation about 4.6 billion years ago (4,600 Ma), and ended roughly 3.8 billion years ago, though the latter date varies according to different sources.

a. 1509 Istanbul earthquake
b. 1700 Cascadia earthquake
c. 1703 Genroku earthquake
d. Hadean

79. _____, first described by marine geologist Hartmut Heinrich, occurred during the last glacial period, or 'ice age'. During such events, armadas of icebergs broke off from glaciers and traversed the North Atlantic. The icebergs contained rock mass eroded by the glaciers, and as they melted, this matter was dropped onto the sea floor as 'ice rafted debris'.

a. Heinrich events
b. 1700 Cascadia earthquake
c. 1703 Genroku earthquake
d. 1509 Istanbul earthquake

80. An _____ is a buried erosion surface separating two rock masses or strata of different ages, indicating that sediment deposition was not continuous. In general, the older layer was exposed to erosion for an interval of time before deposition of the younger, but the term is used to describe any break in the sedimentary geologic record. The phenomenon of angular unconformities was discovered by James Hutton, who found examples at Jedburgh in 1787 and at Siccar Point in 1788.

a. AASHTO Soil Classification System
b. AL 129-1
c. AL 333
d. Unconformity

81. The _____ was an ancient oceanic tectonic plate, that lay on the west coast of North America about 195 million years ago. The _____ had a chain of volcanic islands called the Intermontane Islands. The Intermontane Islands had been accumulating as a volcanic chain somewhere out in the Pacific Ocean since Triassic time, beginning around 245 million years ago. The volcanism records yet another subduction zone. Beneath the far edge of the Intermontane microplate, another plate called the Insular Plate was sinking. This arrangement with two parallel subduction zones is unusual.
   a. Okhotsk Plate
   b. Eurasian Plate
   c. Arabian Plate
   d. Intermontane Plate

82. The _____ was an ancient oceanic trench during the Triassic time. The trench was probably 600 to 800 miles long running along the west-coast of North America. The ocean that the trench was located in was called the Slide Mountain Ocean.
   a. Intermontane Trench
   b. AL 129-1
   c. AASHTO Soil Classification System
   d. AL 333

83. _____ was the shore of the Glacial Lake Iroquois, now part of the current Lake Ontario.

The old shoreline runs west-east across Toronto, further inland. Most prominent sections above the height of the lower city include the area near St. Clair Avenue West between Bathurst and the Don River, as well as running parallel (or just south of) Davenport Road from Caledonia to Spadina Avenue.

   a. AL 129-1
   b. AL 333
   c. Iroquois Shoreline
   d. AASHTO Soil Classification System

84. The _____ was a cratonic sequence that began in the mid-Devonian, peaked early in the Mississippian, and ended by mid-Mississippian time. A major unconformity separates it from the lower Tippecanoe sequence.

The basal-that is, the lowest and oldest-units of the Kaskaskia consist of clean quartz sandstones eroded from the Appalachian orogenic belt to the east, the Ozark Dome in the center of the continent, and south from the Canadian Shield.

   a. Sauk sequence
   b. 1700 Cascadia earthquake
   c. 1509 Istanbul earthquake
   d. Kaskaskia sequence

85. The _____ is an oceanic tectonic plate under the northern Pacific Ocean south of the Near Islands segment of the Aleutian Islands. It is subducting under the North American Plate at the Aleutian Trench and is surrounded by the Pacific Plate. There is a portion of the _____ at the surface in the southern Bering Sea.
   a. Conway Reef Plate
   b. Kula Plate
   c. North Bismarck Plate
   d. Manus Plate

86. The _____ was an ancient mid-ocean ridge that existed between the Kula and Farallon plates in the Pacific Ocean during the Jurassic period. There was a small piece of this ridge off the Pacific Northwest 43 million years ago. The rest of the ridge has since been subducted beneath Alaska.

Chapter 3. Test Preparation Part 3

a. Pacific-Farallon Ridge
b. Pacific-Antarctic Ridge
c. Nazca Ridge
d. Kula-Farallon Ridge

87. _____ is a mountain pass south of modern day Downey, Idaho that is famous for being the spot at which the ancient Lake Bonneville was emptied. It is bounded by two mountain ranges; the Portneuf to the East and the Bannock to the West.

The pass was cut through a sill of resistant Paleozoic shale, limestone, and dolomite, and forms a narrow gap two miles (3 km) long.

a. Geosyncline
b. Red Rock Pass
c. Storegga Slides
d. Paleoseismology

88. A _____, in biogeography, is an isthmus or wider land connection between otherwise separate areas, which allows terrestrial animals and plants to cross over and colonise new lands. They can be created by marine regression, in which sea levels fall, exposing shallow, previously submerged sections of continental shelf; or when new land is created by plate tectonics; or occasionally when the sea floor rises due to post-glacial rebound after an ice age.

a. Land bridge
b. 1703 Genroku earthquake
c. 1509 Istanbul earthquake
d. 1700 Cascadia earthquake

89. The _____ was a massive sheet of ice that covered hundreds of thousands of square miles, including most of Canada and a large portion of the northern United States, between c. 95,000 and c. 20,000 years before the present day.

a. Laurentide ice sheet
b. 1509 Istanbul earthquake
c. 1700 Cascadia earthquake
d. 1703 Genroku earthquake

90. _____ was a separate tectonic plate in the Mesozoic. It collided with Eurasia during Cretaceous forming the present-day southern Tibet.

a. Conway Reef Plate
b. South Bismarck Plate
c. Niuafo'ou Plate
d. Lhasa Plate

91. The _____ is a geological feature which forms the south-eastern part of Yorkshire, England. The feature goes under a number of names such as 'block' or 'area' while the name of the town, Market Weighton is retained. 'Block' seems to be the most modern version but the most distinctive and widely known is 'axis'.

It takes the form of a ridge of tectonic uplift which has progressed during the period of deposition of the newer rocks from the at least the end of the Triassic (205 million years ago) onwards. Its rise has more or less kept pace with the deposition so that on the north and south sides of it, each stratum thins to nothing and in most cases, picks up again on the other side.

a. 1509 Istanbul earthquake
b. Market Weighton Axis
c. 1703 Genroku earthquake
d. 1700 Cascadia earthquake

92. The _____ is a geologic era within the Archean, spanning 3200 Mya to 2800 Mya (million years ago.) The period is defined chronometrically and is not referenced to a specific level in a rock section on Earth. Fossils from Australia show that stromatolites have lived on Earth since the _____.

a. Mesoarchean
b. Marine isotope stages
c. Siderian
d. Tonian

93. The _____ is a chiefly British geological term for the beds of red sandstone and associated rocks laid down throughout the Permian (280 million years ago) to the beginning of the Triassic (240 million years ago) that underlie the Jurassic Lias; the term distinguishes it from the Devonian Old Red Sandstone.

Its upper layers consist of mudstones, but most of the formation consists of reddish sandstones, interbedded with evaporite minerals like salt and gypsum; these indicate deposition in a hot, arid environment.

The _____ covers much of central England, where it generally forms a low-lying plain.

a. New Red Sandstone
b. 1703 Genroku earthquake
c. 1509 Istanbul earthquake
d. 1700 Cascadia earthquake

94. The _____ is an assemblage of Triassic sedimentary rocks which outcrop intermittently along the United States East Coast; the exposures extend from Massachusetts to North Carolina, with more still in Nova Scotia.

The _____ consists largely of poorly-sorted nonmarine sediments; typical rocks are conglomerate, arkose sandstone, siltstone, and shale.

a. 1509 Istanbul earthquake
b. 1700 Cascadia earthquake
c. 1703 Genroku earthquake
d. Newark Group

95. The _____ establishes a geologic timescale for prehistoric North American fauna beginning 66.5 Ma during the Paleocene and continuing through to the Middle Pleistocene (0.33 Ma.) These periods are referred to as ages, stages, or intervals and were established using geographic place names where fossil materials where obtained.

The North American Land-Mammal Age system was formalized in 1941 as a series of provincial land-mammal ages.

a. 1509 Istanbul earthquake
b. 1700 Cascadia earthquake
c. South American Mammal Ages
d. North American Mammal Ages

96. The _____ is a British rock formation of considerable importance to early paleontology. Hutton's angular unconformity at Siccar Point where 345 million year old Devonian _____ overlies 425 million year old Silurian greywacke.

The _____ describes a suite of rocks deposited in a variety of environments during the Devonian period but extending back into the late Silurian period and forward into the earliest part of the Carboniferous period.

a. AASHTO Soil Classification System
b. AL 129-1
c. AL 333
d. Old Red Sandstone

97. The _____ is a geologic period and system that began 65.5 ± 0.3 and ended 23.03 ± 0.05 million years ago and comprises the first part of the Cenozoic era. Lasting 42 million years, the _____ is most notable as being the time in which mammals evolved from relatively small, simple forms into a plethora of diverse animals in the wake of the mass extinction that ended the preceding Cretaceous Period. Some of these mammals would evolve into large forms that would dominate the land, while others would become capable of living in marine, specialized terrestrial and even airborne environments.
   a. Paleogene
   b. Hsandagolian
   c. Gashatan
   d. Mustersan

98. _____ is the study of the record of the Earth's magnetic field preserved in various magnetic minerals through time. The study of _____ has demonstrated that the Earth's magnetic field varies substantially in both orientation and intensity through time. <
   a. Geologic record
   b. Global Standard Stratigraphic Age
   c. Paleomagnetism
   d. Chronozone

99. _____ looks at geologic sediments and rocks, for signs of ancient earthquakes. It is used to supplement seismic monitoring, for the calculation of seismic hazard. _____ is usually restricted to geologic regimes that have undergone continuous sediment creation for the last few thousand years, such as swamps, lakes, river beds and shorelines.
   a. Tejas sequence
   b. First appearance datum
   c. Geological history
   d. Paleoseismology

100. In the geosciences, _____ can have two meanings. The first meaning, common in geology and paleontology, refers to a former soil preserved by burial underneath either sediments (alluvium or loess) or volcanic deposits (Volcanic ash), which in case of older deposits have lithified into rock. In Quaternary geology, sedimentology, paleoclimatology, and geology in general, it is the typical and accepted practice to use the term '_____' to designate such 'fossil' soils found buried within either sedimentary or volcanic deposits exposed in all continents as illustrated by Rettallack (2001), Kraus (1999), and innumerable other published papers and books.
   a. 1509 Istanbul earthquake
   b. 1700 Cascadia earthquake
   c. Paleosol
   d. 1703 Genroku earthquake

101. The _____ is the earliest of three geologic eras of the Phanerozoic eon. The _____ spanned from roughly 542 to 251 million years ago (ICS, 2004), and is subdivided into six geologic periods; from oldest to youngest they are: the Cambrian, Ordovician, Silurian, Devonian, Carboniferous, and Permian.

The _____ covers the time from the first appearance of abundant, soft-shelled fossils to the time when the continents were beginning to be dominated by large, relatively sophisticated reptiles and modern plants. The lower (oldest) boundary was classically set at the first appearance of creatures known as trilobites and archeocyathids.

   a. 1700 Cascadia earthquake
   b. 1509 Istanbul earthquake
   c. 1703 Genroku earthquake
   d. Paleozoic

102. The _____ was a large elongated and narrow ice sheet that covered all of Chile south of approximately present-day Puerto Montt during the Llanquihue glaciation. Some maps have the _____ connected to the icecaps of the Altiplano by continuous glaciers all the way through the Andes.

The ice sheet extended beyond the crest of the Andes into Argentina, but because of the dryness of the climate it did not reach beyond present-day lakes such as the Yagagtoo, Musters, and Colhue Huapi.

   a. Cornbrash
   b. First appearance datum
   c. Paleoseismology
   d. Patagonian Ice Sheet

103. The _____ Eon is the current eon in the geologic timescale, and the one during which abundant animal life has existed. It covers roughly 545 million years and goes back to the time when diverse hard-shelled animals first appeared.
   a. 1700 Cascadia earthquake
   b. Phanerozoic
   c. 1703 Genroku earthquake
   d. 1509 Istanbul earthquake

104. The _____, along with the Kaapvaal craton (the Kaapvaal province of South Africa) are the only remaining areas of pristine Archaean 3.6-2.7 Ga crust on Earth. Similarities of their rock records, especially the similarities in the overlying Late Archean sequences of both these cratons, suggest that they were once part of the Vaalbara supercontinent, and then believed to have belonged to Ur continent.

The _____ comprises a mid-Archaean granite-greenstone terrane and an overlying late-Archaean volcano-sedimentary sequence called the Hamersley Basin.

   a. 1700 Cascadia earthquake
   b. Pilbara craton
   c. 1509 Istanbul earthquake
   d. 1703 Genroku earthquake

105. The _____ is an informal name for the supereon comprising the eons of the geologic timescale that came before the current Phanerozoic eon. It spans from the formation of Earth around 4500 Mya (million years ago) to the evolution of abundant macroscopic hard-shelled animals, which marked the beginning of the Cambrian, the first period of the first era of the Phanerozoic eon, some 542 Mya. It is named after the Roman name for Wales - Cambria - where rocks from this age were first studied.
   a. 1703 Genroku earthquake
   b. 1509 Istanbul earthquake
   c. 1700 Cascadia earthquake
   d. Precambrian

106. _____ or River Warren was a prehistoric river that drained Lake Agassiz in central North America between 11,700 and 9,400 years ago. The enormous outflow from this lake carved a mighty valley now occupied by the much-smaller Minnesota River and the Upper Mississippi River.

Lake Agassiz was formed from the meltwaters of the Laurentide Ice Sheet during the Wisconsonian glaciation of the last ice age.

   a. Glacial River Warren
   b. 1703 Genroku earthquake
   c. 1509 Istanbul earthquake
   d. 1700 Cascadia earthquake

107. The _____ was a massive waterfall on the glacial River Warren initially located in present-day Saint Paul, Minnesota, United States. The waterfall was an impressive 2700 feet (823 m) across and 175 feet (53 m) tall, over 10 times as wide as Niagara Falls

Chapter 3. Test Preparation Part 3 57

The area now occupied by the Twin Cities generally consisted of a 155 foot (47 m) thick layer of St. Peter Sandstone, under a 16 foot (5 m) thick layer of shale, under a 35 foot (11 m) thick layer of Platteville limestone. These layers were the result of an Ordovician Period sea which covered east-central Minnesota 500 million years ago.

a. 1509 Istanbul earthquake
b. 1703 Genroku earthquake
c. 1700 Cascadia earthquake
d. River Warren Falls

108. The _____ explains how flora and fauna left Africa to penetrate the Middle East and beyond to Europe and Asia. African pluvial periods are associated with a 'wet Sahara' phase during which larger lakes and more rivers exist.
a. Canadian Shield
b. Musgrave Block
c. Gawler craton
d. Sahara pump theory

109. The _____ paleontological site is located in the city of Santa Maria, Rio Grande do Sul, in Brazil. It belongs to the Caturrita Formation and the Santa Maria Formation. It is located in the neighborhood of Castelinho.The early sauropodomorph dinosaur Saturnalia was discovered at this site, along with rhynchosaurs and many other fossil specimens.

The first terrestrial reptile fossil discovered in South America came from this site in 1902.

a. Gunflint Chert
b. Hamilton Quarry
c. Lakota Formation
d. Sanga da Alemoa

110. The _____ was the earliest of the six cratonic sequences that have occurred during the Phanerozoic (followed by the Tippecanoe, Kaskaskia, Absaroka, Zu>ñi, and Tejas.) It dates from the late Proterozoic through the early Ordovician, though the marine transgression did not begin in earnest until the middle Cambrian.

At its peak, most of North America was covered by the shallow Sauk Sea, save for parts of the Canadian Shield and the islands of the Transcontinental Arch.

a. Sauk sequence
b. 1509 Istanbul earthquake
c. Tippecanoe sequence
d. 1700 Cascadia earthquake

111. A _____ is a late Archean supercraton thought to be parental to the Slave craton. The shape and size of this supercraton are currently unknown.
a. Planar deformation features
b. Cap carbonates
c. Tidal scour
d. Sclavia craton

112. _____ is a relatively new branch of geology that attempts to link subdivide sedimentary deposits into unconformity bound units on a variety of scales and explain these stratal units in terms of control by relative sea-level changes and variations in sediment supply. The essence of the method is mapping of strata based on identification of surfaces which are assumed to represent time lines (e.g. subaerial unconformities, maximum flooding surfaces), and therefore placing stratigraphy in chronostratigraphic framework. _____ is sometimes a useful alternative to a lithostratigraphic approach, which emphasizes similarity of aspect of rocks rather than time significance, but suffers from issues of testibility and the non-uniqueness of many of the predicted stratal geometries.

a. Biozones
b. Cyclostratigraphy
c. Bedrock
d. Sequence stratigraphy

113. _____ is a two mile wide topographic terrace with an average height of 20 feet deposited by the Ohio River. It was formed many years ago when the Mississippi River flowed west of Sikeston. This Southeast Missouri ridge runs from area of Haywood City south through Sikeston towards the historic Mississippi River town of New Madrid, Missouri.
a. 1700 Cascadia earthquake
b. 1509 Istanbul earthquake
c. 1703 Genroku earthquake
d. Sikeston Ridge

Chapter 4. Test Preparation Part 4

1. The _____ is a Canadian geological formation located in the Northwest Territories. This craton is approximately 300,000 square kilometres (120,000 sq mi) in size and forms part of the Canadian Shield. It is dominated by ca. 2.73-2.63 Ga greenstones and turbidite sequences and ca. 2.72-2.58 Ga plutonic rock, with large parts of the craton underlain by older gneiss and granitoid units.

   a. 1700 Cascadia earthquake
   b. 1509 Istanbul earthquake
   c. 1703 Genroku earthquake
   d. Slave craton

2. A _____ is an old and stable part of the continental crust that has survived the merging and splitting of continents and supercontinents for at least 500 million years. Some are over two billion years old. They are generally found in the interiors of continents and are characteristically composed of ancient crystalline basement crust of lightweight felsic igneous rock such as granite.

   a. Kalahari craton
   b. Sebakwe proto-craton
   c. Superior craton
   d. Craton

3. _____ refers to hypotheses regarding paleoclimatic global-scale glaciation, claiming that the Earth's surface was nearly or entirely frozen at some points in its past. The occurrence of _____ remains controversial. Proponents claim it best explains sedimentary deposits generally regarded as of glacial origin at tropical latitudes and other enigmatic features of the geological record.

   a. Bergschrund
   b. Cordilleran Ice Sheet
   c. Snowball Earth
   d. Pre-Pastonian Stage

4. The _____ establishes a geologic timescale for prehistoric South American fauna beginning 64.5 Ma during the Paleogene and continuing through to the Middle Pleistocene (0.33 Ma.) These periods are referred to as ages, stages, or intervals and were established using geographic place names where fossil materials where obtained.

   The basic unit of measure is the first/last boundary statement.

   a. North American Mammal Ages
   b. 1509 Istanbul earthquake
   c. 1700 Cascadia earthquake
   d. South American Mammal Ages

5. _____ is a biogeographical region of Southeastern Asia that comprises the Maritime Southeast Asia islands of Sumatra, Java, Borneo, and surrounding smaller islands. The eastern boundary of _____ is the Wallace Line, identified by Alfred Russel Wallace, which marks the eastern boundary of the Asia's land mammal fauna, and is the boundary of the Indomalaya and Australasia ecozones. The islands east of the Wallace line are known as Wallacea, and are considered part of Australasia.

   a. 1700 Cascadia earthquake
   b. 1509 Istanbul earthquake
   c. 1703 Genroku earthquake
   d. Sundaland

6. In geology, a _____ is a landmass comprising more than one continental core, or craton. The assembly of cratons and accreted terranes that form Eurasia qualifies as a _____ today.

   Most commonly, paleogeographers employ the term _____ to refer to a single landmass consisting of all the modern continents.

   a. Supercontinent
   b. 1703 Genroku earthquake
   c. 1509 Istanbul earthquake
   d. 1700 Cascadia earthquake

7. The _____ forms the core of both the North American continent and the Canadian Shield. It extends from Quebec in the east to eastern Manitoba in the west. The western margin extends from northern Minnesota through eastern Manitoba to northwestern Ontario.

The formation of the _____ is best explained within the context of 2.72-2.68 Ga accretion of small continental plates and trapped oceanic terranes in a tectonic regime resembling that of the rapidly changing southwestern Pacific Ocean. The craton is made up of a collage of small continental fragments of Mesoarchean age and Neoarchean oceanic plates and tracts of oceanic crust that consists of the following domains: Northern Superior, North Caribou, Winnipeg River, Marmion, Minnesota River Valley, Opatica, and Goudalie.

  a. Craton
  b. Kalahari craton
  c. Sebakwe proto-craton
  d. Superior craton

8. The _____ was the last major marine transgression across the North American craton. Following the late Cretaceous regression that ended the Zuñi sequence, the oceans advanced again early in the Cenozoic, peaking during the Paleocene and Eocene epochs. There were no dramatic epeiric seas in North America; indeed, the Atlantic coast advanced only as far as the Mississippi Embayment.
  a. Red Rock Pass
  b. Cornbrash
  c. Storegga Slides
  d. Tejas sequence

9. The _____ was an ancient oceanic trench that existed in the northern part of the Tethys Ocean during the middle Mesozoic to early Cenozoic eras.

The _____ formed when the Cimmerian Plate was subducting under eastern Laurasia, around 200 million years ago, in the Early Jurassic. The _____ extended at its greatest during Late Cretaceous to Paleocene, from what is now Greece to the Western Pacific Ocean.

  a. Geosyncline
  b. Tethyan Trench
  c. Geological history
  d. Red Rock Pass

10. The _____ is a chronologic schema (or idealized model) relating stratigraphy to time that is used by geologists, paleontologists and other earth scientists to describe the timing and relationships between events that have occurred during the history of the Earth. The table of geologic time spans presented here agrees with the dates and nomenclature proposed by the International Commission on Stratigraphy, and uses the standard color codes of the United States Geological Survey.

Evidence from radiometric dating indicates that the Earth is about 4.570 billion years old.

  a. 1700 Cascadia earthquake
  b. 1509 Istanbul earthquake
  c. 1703 Genroku earthquake
  d. Geologic time scale

11. The _____ divides the history of Earth's Moon into five generally recognized periods: the Copernican, Eratosthenian, Imbrian (Late and Early epochs), Nectarian, and Pre-Nectarian. The boundaries of this time scale are related to large impact events that have modified the lunar surface, changes in crater morphology that occur through time, and the size-frequency distribution of craters superposed on geological units. The absolute ages for these periods have been constrained by radiometric dating of samples obtained from the lunar surface.

a. 1703 Genroku earthquake
b. 1700 Cascadia earthquake
c. 1509 Istanbul earthquake
d. Lunar Geological Timescale

12. The _____ was the cratonic sequence--that is, the marine transgression--that followed the Sauk sequence; it extended from roughly the middle Ordovician to the early Devonian.

After the regression of the Sauk Sea early in the Ordovician, the exposed craton for a time underwent vigorous erosion, due to being located in a tropical climate; indeed, at this point in the Phanerozoic the North American continent roughly straddled the equator.

The Tippecanoe transgression ended this period of erosion, beginning with the deposition of clean sandstones across the craton, followed by abundant carbonate deposition.

a. Tippecanoe sequence
b. 1700 Cascadia earthquake
c. Sauk sequence
d. 1509 Istanbul earthquake

13. The _____, was the major mountain building event that formed the Precambrian Canadian Shield, the North American craton, and the forging of the initial North American continent. It is the largest Paleoproterozoic orogenic belt in the world. It consists of a network of belts that were formed by Proterozoic crustal accretion and the collision of pre-existing Archean continents.

a. Kaikoura Orogeny
b. Laramide orogeny
c. Pan-African orogeny
d. Trans-Hudson orogeny

14. _____ refers to natural mountain building, and may be studied as a tectonic structural event, (b) as a geographical event, and (c) a chronological event. Orogenic events (a) cause distinctive structural phenomena and related tectonic activity, (b) affect certain regions of rocks and crust, and (c) happen within a specific period of time.

a. Alleghenian orogeny
b. Alpine orogeny
c. Orogeny
d. AASHTO Soil Classification System

15. The _____ is another name for prehistoric Hudson Bay, namely as it existed during the retreat of the Laurentide Ice Sheet.

Roughly 8,000 years BP, the Laurentide Ice Sheet thinned and split into two lobes, one centered over Quebec-Labrador, the other over Keewatin. This drained Glacial Lake Ojibway, a massive proglacial lake south of the ice sheet, leading to the formation of the early _____.

a. Tethyan Trench
b. Paleoseismology
c. Paleogeology
d. Tyrrell Sea

16. An _____ is a buried erosion surface separating two rock masses or strata of different ages, indicating that sediment deposition was not continuous. In general, the older layer was exposed to erosion for an interval of time before deposition of the younger, but the term is used to describe any break in the sedimentary geologic record. The phenomenon of angular unconformities was discovered by James Hutton, who found examples at Jedburgh in 1787 and at Siccar Point in 1788.

a. AL 333
b. Unconformity
c. AASHTO Soil Classification System
d. AL 129-1

17. The _____ is located in the west-central United States and west-central Canada -- more specifically, in Montana, Wyoming, southern Alberta, southern Saskatchewan, and parts of northern Utah. Also called the Wyoming province, it is the initial core of the continental crust of North America.

The _____ was sutured together with the Superior and Hearne-Rae cratons in the mountain-building episode that created the Trans-Hudson Suture Zone to form the core of North America (Laurentia.).

a. Craton
b. Superior craton
c. Kalahari craton
d. Wyoming craton

18. The _____ is a large craton which constitutes the bulk of the Western Australian land mass. It is bounded by a mixture of sedimentary basins and Proterozoic fold and thrust belts. Zircon grains in the Jack Hills, Narryer Terrane have been dated at ~4.27 Ga, with one detrital zircon dated as old as 4.4 Ga.

The _____ appears to have been assembled between ~2.94 and 2.63 Ga by the accretion of a multitude of formerly present blocks or terranes of existing continental crust, most of which formed between 3.2 Ga and 2.8 Ga.

a. Sahara pump theory
b. Gawler craton
c. Canadian Shield
d. Yilgarn Craton

19. _____, is the process of coastal sediments returning to the visible portion of a beach or foreshore following a submersion event. A sustainable beach or foreshore often goes through a cycle of submersion during rough weather then _____ during calmer periods. If a coastline is not in a healthy sustainable condition, then erosion can be more serious and _____ does not fully restore the original volume of the visible beach or foreshore leading to permanent beach or foreshore loss.

a. Accretion
b. AASHTO Soil Classification System
c. AL 129-1
d. AL 333

20. _____ pertain to the activity of the winds and more specifically, to the winds' ability to shape the surface of the Earth and other planets. Winds may erode, transport, and deposit materials, and are effective agents in regions with sparse vegetation and a large supply of unconsolidated sediments. Although water is much more powerful than wind, _____ are important in arid environments such as deserts.

a. AL 333
b. Aeolian processes
c. AASHTO Soil Classification System
d. AL 129-1

21. _____ is a form of coastal or river erosion, when the bed load is eroded by itself. Rocks are hit together as they travel downstream, suspended in the river, and are broken up into smaller rocks. This process also makes them rounder and smoother.

a. AL 129-1
b. AASHTO Soil Classification System
c. AL 333
d. Attrition

Chapter 4. Test Preparation Part 4

22. _____ describes the erosion of hard ocean substrates - and less often terrestrial substrates - by living organisms by a number of mechanisms. Marine _____ can be caused by mollusks, polychaete worms, phoronids, sponges, crustaceans, echinoids, and fish; it can occur on coastlines, on coral reefs, and on ships; its mechanisms include biotic boring, drilling, rasping, and scraping. On dry land, _____ is typically performed by pioneer plants or plant-like organisms such as lichen, and mostly chemical (e.g. by acidic secretions on limestone) or mechanical (e.g. by roots growing into cracks) in nature.

 a. 1703 Genroku earthquake
 b. 1509 Istanbul earthquake
 c. 1700 Cascadia earthquake
 d. Bioerosion

23. A _____ is a substance produced by life processes. It may be either constituents, or secretions, of plants or animals.

Examples

- Coal and oil are possible examples of constituents which may have undergone changes over geologic time periods.
- Chalk and limestone are examples of secretions (marine animal shells) which are of geologic age.
- Cotton and wood are biogenic constituents of contemporary origin.
- Pearls, silk and ambergris are examples of secretions of contemporary origin.

 a. Wave pounding
 b. Hydraulic action
 c. Spheroidal weathering
 d. Biogenic substance

24. _____ are sandy depressions in a sand dune ecosystem (psammosere) caused by the removal of sediments by wind.

_____ occur in partially vegetated dunefields or sandhills. A blowout forms when a patch of protective vegetation is lost, allowing strong winds to 'blow out' sand and form a depression.

 a. 1509 Istanbul earthquake
 b. 1700 Cascadia earthquake
 c. 1703 Genroku earthquake
 d. Blowouts

25. _____ is the removal of sediment such as sand and rocks from around bridge abutments or piers. Scour, caused by swiftly moving water, can scoop out scour holes, compromising the integrity of the bridge.

_____ is one of the three main causes of bridge failure.

 a. 1703 Genroku earthquake
 b. 1509 Istanbul earthquake
 c. Bridge scour
 d. 1700 Cascadia earthquake

26. _____ is a weathering phenomenon of rock surface induration. It is observed commonly in: felsic alkaline rocks, such as nepheline syenite, phonolite and trachyte; pyroclastic rocks, as pyroclastic flow deposit, fine air-fall deposits and vent-filling pyroclastic deposits; sedimentary rocks, as sandstone and mudstone.

a. Patterned ground
b. Case hardening
c. Gibraltar Arc
d. Geomechanics

27. _____ refers to the process by which a sediment progressively loses its porosity due to the effects of loading. This forms part of the process of lithification. When a layer of sediment is originally deposited, it contains an open framework of particles with the pore space being usually filled with water.
   a. Compaction
   b. Combe
   c. Geothermal
   d. Diamond Head

28. _____ is the (natural or artificial) process of formation of solid crystals precipitating from a solution, melt or more rarely deposited directly from a gas. _____ is also a chemical solid-liquid separation technique, in which mass transfer of a solute from the liquid solution to a pure solid crystalline phase occurs.

The _____ process consists of two major events, nucleation and crystal growth.

   a. Crystallization
   b. 1509 Istanbul earthquake
   c. 1703 Genroku earthquake
   d. 1700 Cascadia earthquake

29. _____ are geographical features found on coastlines and created by long shore drift. Made out of sand and shingle, and later stabilised by vegetation, _____ are triangular-shaped accretions and extend seawards.

_____ develop mainly as a result of long shore drift that occurs in two directions, merging two spits into a triangular protrusion into the sea by converging the material onto one location.

   a. Longshore drift
   b. 1509 Istanbul earthquake
   c. 1700 Cascadia earthquake
   d. Cuspate forelands

30. _____ is the process by which the removal of material, through means of erosion and weathering, leads to a reduction of elevation and relief in landforms and landscapes. Exogenic processes, including the action of water, ice, and wind, predominantly involve _____. _____ can involve the removal of both solid particles and dissolved material.
   a. 1700 Cascadia earthquake
   b. Denudation
   c. 1703 Genroku earthquake
   d. 1509 Istanbul earthquake

31. _____ is the geological process by which material is added to a landform or land mass. Fluids such as wind and water, as well as sediment gravity flows, transport previously eroded sediment, which, at the loss of enough kinetic energy in the fluid, is deposited, building up layers of sediment.

_____ occurs when the forces responsible for sediment transportation are no longer sufficient to overcome the forces of particle weight and friction, which resist motion.

   a. Wave pounding
   b. Permineralization
   c. Deposition
   d. Hydraulic action

Chapter 4. Test Preparation Part 4

32. In geology and oceanography, _____ is any chemical, physical or biological change undergone by a sediment after its initial deposition and during and after its lithification, exclusive of surface alteration (weathering) and metamorphism. These changes happen at relatively low temperatures and pressures and result in changes to the rock's original mineralogy and texture. The boundary between _____ and metamorphism, which occurs under conditions of higher temperature and pressure, is gradational.
   a. Diagenesis
   b. Hydrothermal circulation
   c. Seafloor spreading
   d. Spheroidal weathering

33. A _____ is a type of intrusion in which a more mobile and ductily-deformable material is forced into brittle overlying rocks. Depending on the tectonic environment, they can range from idealized mushroom-shaped Rayleigh-Taylor instability-type structures in regions with low tectonic stress such as in the Gulf of Mexico to narrow dike (geology) dikes of material that move along tectonically-induced fractures in surrounding rock. The term was introduced by the Romanian geologist Ludovic Mrazek, who was the first to understand the principle of salt intrusion and plasticity.
   a. Rockall Basin
   b. Slyne-Erris Trough
   c. Skarn
   d. Diapir

34. _____, also called erosional _____ or downward erosion or vertical erosion is a geological process that deepens the channel of a stream or valley by removing material from the stream's bed or the valley's floor. How fast _____ occurs depends on the stream's base level, which is the lowest point to which the stream can erode. Sea level is the ultimate base level, but many streams have a higher 'temporary' base level because they empty into another body of water that is above sea level or encounter bedrock that resists erosion.
   a. Wave pounding
   b. Transgression
   c. Hydrothermal circulation
   d. Downcutting

35. _____ is the removal of solids (sediment, soil, rock and other particles) in the natural environment. It usually occurs due to transport by wind, water, or ice; by down-slope creep of soil and other material under the force of gravity; or by living organisms, such as burrowing animals, in the case of bioerosion.

_____ is distinguished from weathering, which is the process of chemical or physical breakdown of the minerals in the rocks, although the two processes may occur concurrently.

   a. AL 129-1
   b. AASHTO Soil Classification System
   c. Erosion
   d. AL 333

36. _____ or sheet joints are surface-parallel fracture systems in rock often leading to erosion of concentric slabs.
   a. Exfoliation joints
   b. AL 333
   c. AASHTO Soil Classification System
   d. AL 129-1

37. The term _____ is used in geology when one or a stack of originally flat and planar surfaces, such as sedimentary strata, are bent or curved as a result of plastic (i.e. permanent) deformation. Synsedimentary folds are those due to slumping of sedimentary material before it is lithified. Folds in rocks vary in size from microscopic crinkles to mountain-sized folds.
   a. 1509 Istanbul earthquake
   b. 1700 Cascadia earthquake
   c. 1703 Genroku earthquake
   d. Fold

38. A _____ is a series of mountainous foothills, adjacent to an orogenic belt, that form due to compression. Fold-thrust belts commonly form in the forelands adjacent to major orogens as deformation propagates outwards. They usually comprise both folds and thrust faults, commonly interrelated.
   a. Kaikoura Orogeny
   b. Pan-African orogeny
   c. Trans-Hudson orogeny
   d. Fold and thrust belt

39. In geology, _____ refers to heat sources within the planet. _____ is technically an adjective (e.g., _____ energy) but in U.S. English the word has attained frequent use as a noun.

The planet's internal heat was originally generated during its accretion, due to gravitational binding energy, and since then additional heat has continued to be generated by decay heat from the radioactive decay of elements.

   a. Dali
   b. Combe
   c. Diamond Head
   d. Geothermal

40. The _____ is the rate of increase in temperature per unit depth in the Earth. It varies with location and is typically measured by determining the bottom open-hole temperature after borehole drilling. To achieve accuracy the drilling fluid needs time to reach the ambient temperature.
   a. Geothermal power
   b. Hot Dry Rock Geothermal Energy
   c. Geothermal desalination
   d. Geothermal gradient

41. _____ is caused by gravity in contrast to the physical movement of wind and water required for other types of soil erosion. _____ involves both large scale mass wasting and smaller scale erosion. Forms of _____ include avalanche, landslide, debris flow, mudflow, and sinkhole formation.
   a. Bradyseism
   b. Rejuvenated
   c. Shutter ridge
   d. Gravitational erosion

42. _____ is a fluvial process of erosion that lengthens a stream, a valley or a gully at its head and also enlarges its drainage basin. The stream erodes away at the rock and soil at its headwaters in the opposite direction that it flows. Once a stream has begun to cut back, the erosion is sped up by the steep gradient the water is flowing down. As water erodes a path from its headwaters to its mouth at a standing body of water, it tries to cut an ever-shallower path. This leads to increased erosion at the steepest parts, which is _____.
   a. Diagenesis
   b. Headward erosion
   c. Seafloor spreading
   d. Hydrothermal circulation

43. _____ is a form of mechanical weathering caused by the force of moving water currents rushing into a crack in the rockface. The water compresses the air in the crack, pushing it right to the back. As the wave retreats, the highly pressurised air is suddenly released with explosive force, capable of chipping away the rockface over time.
   a. Diagenesis
   b. Hydraulic action
   c. Deposition
   d. Permineralization

44. _____ in its most general sense is the circulation of hot water. _____ occurs most often in the vicinity of sources of heat within the Earth's crust. This generally occurs near volcanic activity, but can occur in the deep crust related to the intrusion of granite, or as the result of orogeny or metamorphism.

Chapter 4. Test Preparation Part 4   67

a. Wave pounding
b. Permineralization
c. Seafloor spreading
d. Hydrothermal circulation

45. _____ is an umbrella term for the various processes by which magmas undergo bulk chemical change during the partial melting process, cooling, emplacement of eruption.

When a rock melts it melts to form a liquid, the liquid is known as a primary melt. Primary melts have not undergone any differentiation and represent the starting composition of a magma.

a. AL 129-1
b. Igneous differentiation
c. Ultra-high-temperature metamorphism
d. AASHTO Soil Classification System

46. The _____ was a crucial event early in the history of Earth with respect to the future of life on our planet. When the mass and temperature of the newly forming planet reached a critical level, the denser iron, held in the outer layers, sank towards the centre of the planet to form the core; this event is a part of planetary differentiation. The gravitational potential energy released by the sinking of the dense NiFe globules increased the temperature of the protoplanet above the melting point resulting in a global silicate magma which accelerated the process.

a. AL 129-1
b. Iron catastrophe
c. Overburden pressure
d. AASHTO Soil Classification System

47. In ecology or geoscience, the _____ is the biogeochemical cycle of iron through landforms, the atmosphere, and oceans. The _____ affects dust deposition and aerosol iron bioavailability..

a. AASHTO Soil Classification System
b. AL 129-1
c. AL 333
d. Iron cycle

48. _____, sometimes known as shore drift, is a geological process by which sediments such as sand or other materials, move along a beach shore. It uses the process of swash to push the material up the beach and backwash down the beach; until it reaches a groyne or another obstacle.

Where waves approach the coastline at an angle, when they break their swash pushes beach material up the beach at the same angle.

a. Cuspate forelands
b. 1700 Cascadia earthquake
c. Longshore drift
d. 1509 Istanbul earthquake

49. In geology, _____ is transported rock debris overlying the solid bedrock. The term is also sometimes refers to organic debris so-transported. In the largest sense, it refers to the material left behind by retreating continental glaciers.

a. Geopetal
b. Cross-bedding
c. Riegel
d. Drift

50. A _____ is a chemical reaction that takes place during the geological process of metamorphism in an amalgamate of minerals that helps determine the final stable state of the resulting metamorphic rock.

a. Metamorphic reaction
b. Type locality
c. Lake capture
d. Geostrophic current

51. _____ is the solid-state recrystallization of pre-existing rocks due to changes in physical and chemical conditions, primarily heat, pressure, and the introduction of chemically active fluids. Both mineralogical, chemical and crystallographic changes can occur during this process.

Three types of _____ exist: dynamic, contact and regional.

  a. Leaverite
  b. Pumice raft
  c. Paralithic
  d. Metamorphism

52. _____ is the chemical alteration of a rock by hydrothermal and other fluids.

_____ can occur via the action of hydrothermal fluids from an igneous or metamorphic source.

In the igneous environment, _____ creates skarns, greisen, and may affect hornfels in the contact metamorphic aureole adjacent to an intrusive rock mass.

  a. Dalradian
  b. Porphyroblast
  c. Greenschist
  d. Metasomatism

53. A _____ is an underwater mountain range, typically having a valley known as a rift running along its spine, formed by plate tectonics. This type of oceanic ridge is characteristic of what is known as an oceanic spreading center, which is responsible for seafloor spreading. The uplifted sea floor results from convection currents which rise in the mantle as magma at a linear weakness in the oceanic crust, and emerge as lava, creating new crust upon cooling.

  a. Diagenesis
  b. Hydraulic action
  c. Mid-ocean ridge
  d. Spheroidal weathering

54. _____ is the overthrusting of continental crust by oceanic crust or mantle rocks at a destructive plate boundary. It can occur during an orogeny.

_____ occurs where a fragment of continental crust is caught with resulting overthrusting of oceanic mafic and ultramafic rocks from the mantle onto the continental crust.

  a. East Pacific Rise
  b. Elastic rebound theory
  c. Azores-Gibraltar Transform Fault
  d. Obduction

55. The various theories of _____ explain how the various types of mineral deposits form within the Earth's crust. _____ theories are very dependent on the mineral or commodity.

_____ theories generally involve three components: source, transport or conduit, and trap.

  a. AASHTO Soil Classification System
  b. AL 129-1
  c. AL 333
  d. Ore genesis

56. _____ is a process of fossilization in which mineral deposits form internal casts of organism. Carried by water, these minerals fill the spaces within organic tissue. Because of the nature of the casts, _____ is particularly useful in studies of the internal structures of organisms, usually of plants.

a. Deposition b. Permineralization
c. Hydrothermal circulation d. Saltation

57. _____ are defined as juvenile forming eruptions as a result of interaction between water and magma. They are different from magmatic and phreatic eruptions. The products of _____ contain juvenile clasts, unlike phreatic eruptions and are the result of interaction between magma and water unlike magmatic eruptions.
   a. 1700 Cascadia earthquake b. 1509 Istanbul earthquake
   c. 1703 Genroku earthquake d. Phreatomagmatic eruptions

58. In geology, solid-state _____ is a metamorphic process that occurs under situations of intense temperature and pressure where grains, atoms or molecules of a rock or mineral are packed closer together, creating a new crystal structure. The basic composition remains the same. This process can be illustrated by observing how snow recrystallizes to ice without melting.
   a. 1703 Genroku earthquake b. 1700 Cascadia earthquake
   c. Recrystallization d. 1509 Istanbul earthquake

59. The _____ is a fundamental concept in geology that describes the dynamic transitions through geologic time among the three main rock types: sedimentary, metamorphic, and igneous. Each type of rock is altered or destroyed when it is forced out of its equilibrium conditions. An igneous rock such as basalt may break down and dissolve when exposed to the atmosphere, or melt as it is subducted under a continent.
   a. Metamorphic rock b. Migmatite
   c. Large igneous provinces d. Rock cycle

60. _____ is a transliteration of the Arabic word for a salt flat. They are supratidal, forming along arid coastlines and are characterized by evaporite-carbonate deposits with some siliciclastics. They form subareal, prograding and shoaling-upward sequences that have an average thickness of a meter or less.
   a. 1509 Istanbul earthquake b. Sabkha
   c. 1703 Genroku earthquake d. 1700 Cascadia earthquake

61. _____ is concerned with the geometries and processes associated with the presence of significant thicknesses of rock salt within a sequence of rocks. This is due both to the low density of salt, which does not increase with burial, and its low strength.

Structures may form during continued sedimentary loading, without any external tectonic influence, due to gravitational instability.

   a. Teilzone b. Zechstein
   c. Subfossil d. Salt tectonics

62. In geology, _____ is a specific type of particle transport by fluids such as wind, or the denser fluid water. It occurs when loose material is removed from a bed and carried by the fluid, before being transported back to the surface. Examples include pebble transport by rivers, sand drift over desert surfaces, soil blowing over fields, or even snow drift over smooth surfaces such as those in the Arctic or Canadian Prairies.
   a. Stoping b. Hydrothermal circulation
   c. Diagenesis d. Saltation

63. _____ occurs at mid-ocean ridges, where new oceanic crust is formed through volcanic activity and then gradually moves away from the ridge. _____ helps explain continental drift in the theory of plate tectonics.
   a. Spheroidal weathering
   b. Stoping
   c. Mid-ocean ridge
   d. Seafloor spreading

64. _____ is any particulate matter that can be transported by fluid flow, and which eventually is deposited.

They are most often transported by water (fluvial processes) transported by wind (aeolian processes) and glaciers. Beach sands and river channel deposits are examples of fluvial transport and deposition, though _____ also often settles out of slow-moving or standing water in lakes and oceans.

   a. Brickearth
   b. Bovey Beds
   c. Salt glacier
   d. Sediment

65. The phrase _____ is used to describe the movement of solid particles (sediment) and the processes that govern their motion. _____ is typically due to a combination of the force of gravity acting on the sediment, and/or the movement of the fluid in which the sediment is entrained. This is typically studied in natural systems, where the particles are clastic rocks (sand, gravel, boulders, etc.), mud, or clay; the fluid is air, water, or ice; and the force of gravity is due to the sloping surface on which the particles are resting.
   a. 1509 Istanbul earthquake
   b. 1703 Genroku earthquake
   c. 1700 Cascadia earthquake
   d. Sediment transport

66. Study of geological _____ is related to the study of structural geology, rock microstructure or rock texture and fault mechanics.

_____ is the response of a rock to deformation usually by compressive stress and forms particular textures. _____ can be homogeneous or non-homogeneous, and may be pure _____ or simple _____.

   a. Crenulation
   b. Sag pond
   c. Petermann Orogeny
   d. Shear

67. The _____ has been defined as a Late Permian to Early Triassic tectonic event that deformed Upper Paleozoic oceanic facies rocks and emplaced them over the Upper Paleozoic margin of northern Nevada.
   a. Cocos Plate
   b. Fault trace
   c. Farallon Plate
   d. Sonoma orogeny

68. _____ is a type of chemical weathering that creates rounded boulders and helps to create domed monoliths. This should not be confused with stream abrasion, a physical process which also creates rounded rocks on a much smaller scale. A good example of _____ can be found in the Alabama Hills area of eastern California.
   a. Transgression
   b. Spheroidal weathering
   c. Mid-ocean ridge
   d. Headward erosion

69. In Hydrology, _____ is the flow of water down the trunk or stem of a plant. In tropical rainforests, where this kind of flow can be substantial, erosion gulleys can form at the base of the trunk. However in more temperate climates _____ levels are low and have little erosional power.

a. Flownet
b. Hydraulic conductivity
c. Stemflow
d. Specific storage

70. _____ is a process accommodating the ascent of magmatic bodies from their sources in the mantle (geology) or lower crust to the surface. The process involves the mechanical disintegration of the surrounding country/host rock, typically through fracturing due to pressure increases associated with thermal expansion of the host rock in proximity of the interface with the melt. Once fractures are formed, melt and/or volatiles will typically invade, widening the fracture and promoting the foundering of host rock blocks (i.e. stoped blocks.)
   a. Seafloor spreading
   b. Spheroidal weathering
   c. Headward erosion
   d. Stoping

71. In geology, _____ is the process that takes place at convergent boundaries by which one tectonic plate moves under another tectonic plate, sinking into the Earth's mantle, as the plates converge. A _____ zone is an area on Earth where two tectonic plates move towards one another and _____ occurs. Rates of _____ are typically measured in centimeters per year, with the average rate of convergence being approximately 2 to 8 centimeters per year (about the rate a fingernail grows.)
   a. Juan de Fuca Ridge
   b. Panthalassa
   c. Subduction
   d. Copperbelt Province

72. _____ is the sustainable cyclic portion of coastal erosion where coastal sediments move from the visible portion of a beach to the submerged nearshore region, and later return to the original visible portion of the beach. The recovery portion of the sustainable cycle of sediment behaviour is (accretion.)

The sediment that is submerged during rough weather forms landforms including storm bars.

   a. Dali
   b. Geothermal
   c. Compaction
   d. Submersion

73. The term _____ refers to the part of the large-scale ocean circulation that is driven by global density gradients created by surface heat and freshwater fluxes. The adjective thermohaline derives from thermo- referring to temperature and -haline referring to salt content, factors which together determine the density of sea water. Wind-driven surface currents (such as the Gulf Stream) head polewards from the equatorial Atlantic Ocean, cooling all the while and eventually sinking at high latitudes (forming North Atlantic Deep Water.)
   a. 1700 Cascadia earthquake
   b. 1703 Genroku earthquake
   c. Thermohaline circulation
   d. 1509 Istanbul earthquake

74. _____ is an erosion process which is carried out by the tidal movement of water. Examples of this hydrological process can be found in many areas of the world. Two locations in the United States where _____ is the predominant shaping force is the San Francisco Bay and the Elkhorn Slough.
   a. Palynomorph
   b. Fort Union Formation
   c. Marine clay
   d. Tidal scour

75. A _____ landslide is a distinctive landslide type which may occur when a stronger material such as sandstone or limestone overlies a weaker material such as shale and an eroding agent undercuts the weaker lower layer. The type was first recognized by Parry Reiche in 1937, and takes its name from Toreva, Arizona. Toreva blocks exhibit a characteristic backward rotation toward the parent cliff.

a. Toreva block
b. Gravitational erosion
c. Rejuvenated
d. Bradyseism

76. A marine _____ is a geologic event during which sea level rises relative to the land and the shoreline moves toward higher ground, resulting in flooding. They can be caused either by the land sinking or the ocean basins filling with water (or decreasing in capacity.) Transgresssions and regressions may be caused by tectonic events such as orogenies, severe climate change such as ice ages or isostatic adjustments following removal of ice or sediment load.
   a. Mid-ocean ridge
   b. Wave pounding
   c. Transgression
   d. Deposition

77. The field of _____ encompasses the analysis of static and dynamic stability of slopes of earth and rock-fill dams, slopes of other types of embankments, excavated slopes, and natural slopes in soil and soft rock.

Earthen slopes can develop a cut-spherical weakness zone. The probability of this happening can be calculated in advance using a simple 2-D circular analysis package.

   a. Reynolds' dilatancy
   b. Lateral earth pressure
   c. Groundwater-related subsidence
   d. Slope stability

78. A _____ is an opening in a planet's surface or crust, which allows hot, molten rock, ash, and gases to escape from below the surface. Volcanic activity involving the extrusion of rock tends to form mountains or features like mountains over a period of time.
   a. 1700 Cascadia earthquake
   b. 1703 Genroku earthquake
   c. 1509 Istanbul earthquake
   d. Volcano

79. _____ is the rock that constitutes the wall of an area undergoing geologic activity. Examples are the rock along the neck of a volcano, on the edge of a pluton that is being emplaced, along a fault plane, enclosing a mineral deposit, or where a vein or dike is being emplaced.

In volcanoes, _____ can often become broken off of the wall and incoporated into the erupted volcanic rock.

   a. 1509 Istanbul earthquake
   b. Wall rock
   c. 1703 Genroku earthquake
   d. 1700 Cascadia earthquake

80. _____ is the 'sledge hammer' effect of tonnes of water crashing against cliffs. It shakes and weakens the rocks leaving them open to attack from hydraulic action and abrasion. Eroded material gets carried away by the waves.
   a. Wave pounding
   b. Diagenesis
   c. Transgression
   d. Deposition

81. The _____ is a volcanic hotspot in central British Columbia, Canada. It is situated on the Interior Plateau, a large region that lies between the Cariboo and Monashee Mountains to the east, and the Hazelton Mountains, Coast Mountains and Cascade Range to the west. As a geologic hotspot, it is a place that has experienced active volcanism over a long period of time.

a. AASHTO Soil Classification System
b. AL 129-1
c. AL 333
d. Anahim hotspot

82. The _____ is a volcanic hotspot located at the Azores in the northern Atlantic Ocean. It has interactions with the Mid-Atlantic Ridge which lies just west of the hotspot.
   a. AL 333
   b. AASHTO Soil Classification System
   c. Azores hotspot
   d. AL 129-1

83. _____ is a lower Cretaceous locality in Siberia, on the left bank of the Vitim River. The Zaza Formation sediments exposed at _____ are represented mostly by sandstones, siltstones, marls and bituminous shales. The total thickness if the section is about 80 m.
   a. Thrace Basin
   b. Juan Fernandez hotspot
   c. Neocomian
   d. Baissa

84. The _____ is a volcanic hotspot located in the Southern Ocean. The hotspot created the Balleny Islands, which forms a chain that extends for about 160 km in a northwest-southeast direction.
   a. 1700 Cascadia earthquake
   b. 1703 Genroku earthquake
   c. 1509 Istanbul earthquake
   d. Balleny hotspot

85. The _____ is a geological formation in Burkhant, Mongolia, that dates to the late Cretaceous period. The exact age is uncertain, with two competing hypotheses; based on comparisons with other formations, the Bayan Shireh fauna seems to correspond best with the Turonian through early Campanian stages of the Late Cretaceous, about 93 to 80 million years ago. However, examination of the magnetostratigraphy of the formation seems to confirm that the entire Bayan Shireh lies within the Cretaceous Long Normal, which lasted only until the end of the Santonian stage, giving a possible Cenomanian through Santonian age, or between 98 and 83 million years ago.
   a. Bayan Shireh Formation
   b. 1700 Cascadia earthquake
   c. 1703 Genroku earthquake
   d. 1509 Istanbul earthquake

86. The _____ is the supposed 'hotspot' (or mantle plume) proposed to explain the Bermuda Rise (a cluster of extinct volcanoes in the Atlantic Ocean, including the island of Bermuda), and also invoked by Cox and Van Arsdale to explain the origin of the Mississippi Embayment and by Nunn to explain the Sabine Uplift (southwest of the Mississippi Embayment.)

A hotspot origin for the Bermuda Rise has never been strongly supported, and has been largely shut out by a detailed and tightly argued paper by Vogt and Jung.

Evidence cited against a hotspot origin include: 1) Lack of a chain of age-progressive seamounts, such as with the Hawaiian-Emperor or Great Meteor seamount chains.

   a. Canary hotspot
   b. Bermuda hotspot
   c. New England hotspot
   d. 1509 Istanbul earthquake

87. The _____ is a volcanic hotspot, located 180 kilometers west of the Queen Charlotte Islands in the Pacific Ocean.

Almost all magma created by the hotspot has the composition of basalt, and so the volcanoes are constructed almost entirely of this igneous rock. The eruptions from the _____ are effusive eruptions because basaltic magma is relatively fluid compared with magmas typically involved in more explosive eruptions, such as the andesitic magmas that produce some of the spectacular and dangerous eruptions around the margins of the Pacific Ocean.

   a. 1509 Istanbul earthquake
   c. 1700 Cascadia earthquake
   b. 1703 Genroku earthquake
   d. Bowie hotspot

88. The _____ -- also called the Laurentian Plateau, or Bouclier Canadien -- is a massive geological shield covered by a thin layer of soil that forms the nucleus of the North American or Laurentia craton. It has a deep, common, joined bedrock region in eastern and central Canada and stretches North from the Great Lakes to the Arctic Ocean, covering over half of Canada; it also extends south into the northern reaches of the United States. Population is scarce, and industrial development is minimal, although the region has a large hydroelectric power potential.
   a. Sahara pump theory
   c. Yilgarn Craton
   b. Great Artesian Basin
   d. Canadian Shield

89. The _____ is a volcanic hotspot believed to be located at the Canary Islands off the north-western coast of Africa, although alternative theories to explain the volcanism there exist. The _____ is believed to be underlain by a mantle plume that is relatively deep. It is believed to have first appeared about 60 million years ago.
   a. 1509 Istanbul earthquake
   c. Jan Mayen hotspot
   b. New England hotspot
   d. Canary hotspot

90. The _____ is a volcanic hotspot located off the Oregon/Washington coast of the United States. The hotspot is at the Juan de Fuca Ridge, and has made the Cobb-Eickelberg Seamount chain. The Axial Seamount is the hotspot's most recent eruptive center, which last erupted in 1998.
   a. Galapagos hotspot
   c. Marquesas hotspot
   b. Pitcairn hotspot
   d. Cobb hotspot

91. A _____ refers to a very large-scale lithostratigraphic sequence that covers a complete marine transgressive-regressive cycle across a craton. They are also known as 'megasequences', 'stratigraphic sequences', or simply 'sequences.'

They were first proposed by Lawrence Sloss in 1963; each one represents a time when epeiric seas deposited sediments across the craton, while the upper and lower edges of the sequence are bounded by craton-wide unconformities eroded when the seas receded.

These sequences may in part represent eustatic or global change in sea level; however, when the proper names are used they usually refer to the North American continent.

   a. Cratonic sequence
   c. Tethyan Trench
   b. Geosyncline
   d. First appearance datum

Chapter 4. Test Preparation Part 4

92. The _____ is a volcanic hotspot that takes advantage of weak spots in the Indo-Australian Plate to feed magma to the volcanoes of Eastern Australia. It does not produce a single chain of volcanoes like the Hawaiian Islands. Tweed Volcano in New South Wales is a large shield volcano that was formed by the hotspot about 23 million years ago and has one of the biggest erosion calderas in the world.
   a. AL 129-1
   b. AASHTO Soil Classification System
   c. AL 333
   d. East Australia hotspot

93. The _____ is a volcanic hotspot located in the southeastern Pacific Ocean. The hotspot created the Sala y Gómez Ridge which includes Easter Island and the Pukao Seamount which is at the ridge's young western edge.
   a. AL 129-1
   b. AASHTO Soil Classification System
   c. AL 333
   d. Easter hotspot

94. The _____ is a volcanic hotspot which is responsible for the volcanic activity which forms the volcanoes in Western Germany of northwestern Europe. It is thought to have formed the Eifel volcanic field.
   a. AL 333
   b. Eifel hotspot
   c. AASHTO Soil Classification System
   d. AL 129-1

95. The _____ is a hotspot which is partly responsible for the high volcanic activity which has formed the island of Iceland.

Iceland is one of the most active volcanic regions in the world, with eruptions occurring on average roughly every five years. About a third of the basaltic lavas erupted in recorded history have been produced by Icelandic eruptions.

   a. AASHTO Soil Classification System
   b. AL 333
   c. AL 129-1
   d. Iceland hotspot

96. The _____ is a volcanic hotspot responsible for the volcanic activity that has formed the island of Jan Mayen in the northern Atlantic Ocean.
   a. Jan Mayen hotspot
   b. 1509 Istanbul earthquake
   c. New England hotspot
   d. Canary hotspot

97. The geological unit called _____ is composed of Eocene and Oligocene deposits, laid above karstic limestone formations of the Campagnien, in the North of the Aquitaine Basin. The kaolin clays of Charentes belong to this mainly continental, tertiary formation often referred as e;siderolithice;, of which the principal outcrop is situated in the South of the Charente Maritime department, 35 miles going North-East from Bordeaux city. The quarries are scattered along a 20 mile long, 7 mile wide, North - South band.
   a. 1703 Genroku earthquake
   b. 1700 Cascadia earthquake
   c. Charentes Basin
   d. 1509 Istanbul earthquake

98. The _____ is a volcanic hotspot at the Kerguelen Plateau in the Southern Indian Ocean. The _____ has produced basaltic lava for about 130 million years and has also produced the Kerguelen Islands, Heard Island and the McDonald Islands.
   a. Neocomian
   b. Mediterranean Ridge
   c. Tristan hotspot
   d. Kerguelen hotspot

99. The _____ is a volcanic hotspot responsible for the volcanic activity that has formed the Louisville seamount chain in the southern Pacific Ocean.

The _____ is believed to lie close to the Pacific-Antarctic Ridge, although its exact location is, however, uncertain.

The _____ has produced the Louisville seamount chain, which is one of the longest seamount chains on Earth, stretching some 4,300 km (2,672 mi) from the Pacific-Antarctic Ridge where it subducts under the Indo-Australian Plate as part of the Pacific Plate.

   a. Galapagos hotspot
   c. Marquesas hotspot
   b. Louisville hotspot
   d. Pitcairn hotspot

100. The _____ was a hotspot that existed about 1,267 million years ago across Canada from the Northwest Territories and Nunavut. It is responsible for the Mackenzie dike swarm, which is the largest dike swarm on Earth. During its formation, eruption of plateau lavas near the Coppermine River, built an extensive volcanic plateau about 1,200 million years ago with an area of about 170,000 km² (65,000 sq mi) representing a volume of lavas of at least 500,000 km³ (120,000 mi³.)
   a. 1509 Istanbul earthquake
   c. Mackenzie hotspot
   b. 1703 Genroku earthquake
   d. 1700 Cascadia earthquake

101. The _____ is a volcanic hotspot in the central Pacific Ocean. It is responsible for the Marquesas Islands, a group of 12 volcanic islands and are one of the five archipelagos of French Polynesia.
   a. Galapagos hotspot
   c. Louisville hotspot
   b. Pitcairn hotspot
   d. Marquesas hotspot

102. The _____ is a wide ridge in the bed of the Mediterranean Sea, running along a rough quarter circle from Calabria, south of Crete, to the southwest corner of Turkey, and from there eastwards south of Turkey, including Cyprus. According to tectonic theory, it is caused by the African Plate subducting under the Eurasian and Anatolian plates. As the African Plate moves slowly north-northeastward, it is plowing up the sediment layers of the Mediterranean, lifting them from the seabed, and in one area already, above sea level, causing the island of Cyprus.
   a. Thrace Basin
   c. Tristan hotspot
   b. Mediterranean Ridge
   d. Messinian evaporite

103. _____ is the last age of the Miocene epoch. It spans the time between 7.246 ± 0.005 Ma and 5.332 ± 0.005 Ma (million years ago.) It is named after the _____ evaporite deposit, which was named after Messina in Sicily.
   a. Messinian
   c. 1703 Genroku earthquake
   b. 1509 Istanbul earthquake
   d. 1700 Cascadia earthquake

104. The _____ deposit is a geological deposit of evaporites which was found on Sicily and named after the city of Messina. It was later found to underlie much of the bed of the Mediterranean. It was formed during the Messinian salinity crisis, which see for more information.
   a. Thrace Basin
   c. Messinian evaporite
   b. Kerguelen hotspot
   d. Neocomian

105. The _____, also referred to as the Messinian Event, is a period when the Mediterranean Sea evaporated partly or completely dry during the Messinian period of the Miocene epoch, 5.96 million years ago.

In the first observation of the result of the episode, Professor Charles Mayer-Eymar (1826-1907) of Zurich studied some fossils between gypsum-bearing, brackish and freshwater layers and identified them as having been deposited just before the end of the Miocene Epoch. In a publication of 1867 he named the period the Messinian, for the region of Messina, Sicily; since then salt-bearing and gypsum-bearing layers in many Mediterranean countries have been dated to that period.

   a. Thrace Basin   b. Neocomian
   c. Juan Fernandez hotspot   d. Messinian salinity crisis

106. In geology, _____ was a name given to the lowest stage of the Cretaceous system. It was introduced by Jules Thurmann in 1835 on account of the development of these rocks at Neuchâtel (Neocomum), Switzerland. It has been employed in more than one sense.
   a. Neocomian   b. Messinian evaporite
   c. Kerguelen hotspot   d. Juan Fernandez hotspot

107. The _____, also referred to as the Great Meteor hotspot, is a long-lived volcanic hotspot in the Atlantic Ocean. The hotspot's most recent eruptive center is the Great Meteor Seamount and probably created a short line of mid to late-Tertiary age seamounts on the African Plate but appears to be currently inactive.

The _____ track is used to estimate the movement of the North American Plate away from the African Plate from early Cretaceous period to the present.

   a. 1509 Istanbul earthquake   b. Canary hotspot
   c. Jan Mayen hotspot   d. New England hotspot

108. _____ is a term used to describe the distinct, and often symmetrical geometric shapes formed by ground material in periglacial regions. Typically found in remote regions of the Arctic, Antarctica, and the Australian outback, but also found anywhere that freezing and thawing of soil alternate, the geometric shapes and patterns associated with _____ are often mistaken as artistic human creations. The nature of _____ puzzled scientists for ages.
   a. Lithotope   b. Seismic inversion
   c. Fabric   d. Patterned ground

109.

The _____ is a distinct geologic fault in Southern Europe, running S-shaped about 1000 km from the Tyrrhenian Sea through the whole Southern Alps as far as Hungary. It forms the division between the Adriatic plate and the European plate. The term Insubric line is sometimes used to address the whole _____, but it is more commonly used to mean just a western part of it.

   a. Valais Ocean   b. Lepontin dome
   c. Penninic thrustfront   d. Periadriatic Seam

110. The _____ is a volcanic hotspot which is responsible for the volcanic activity which forms the volcanoes in New Mexico, United States.

The _____ is believed to have been the origin of the Raton-Clayton volcanic field which is an extensive volcanic field with no observed activity in modern times.

a. 1700 Cascadia earthquake
b. 1703 Genroku earthquake
c. 1509 Istanbul earthquake
d. Raton hotspot

111. The _____, a prominent circular feature in the Sahara desert of Mauritania near Ouadane, has attracted attention since the earliest space missions because it forms a conspicuous bull's-eye in the otherwise rather featureless expanse of the desert. Described by some as looking like an outsized ammonite in the desert, the structure, which has a diameter of almost 50 kilometres (30 miles), has become a landmark for space shuttle crews. Initially interpreted as a meteorite impact structure because of its high degree of circularity, it is now thought to be a symmetrical uplift (circular anticline or dome) that has been laid bare by erosion.

a. 1509 Istanbul earthquake
b. 1703 Genroku earthquake
c. 1700 Cascadia earthquake
d. Richat Structure

112. The _____ is a volcanic hotspot located in the southern Atlantic Ocean. It is responsible for the island of St. Helena and the St. Helena Seamount chain. It is one the oldest known hotspots on Earth, which began to produce basaltic lava about 145 million years ago.

a. Messinian evaporite
b. Messinian salinity crisis
c. Mediterranean Ridge
d. Saint Helena hotspot

113. The European side of Turkey is called the _____. It is the largest and thickest Tertiary sedimentary basin in Turkey. The basin is triangular shaped, trends WNW-ESE and was formed by extension in late Middle Eocene to latest Oligocene times.

a. Juan Fernandez hotspot
b. Tristan hotspot
c. Thrace Basin
d. Neocomian

114. The _____ is a volcanic hotspot which is responsible for the volcanic activity which forms the volcanoes in the southern Atlantic Ocean. It is thought to have formed the island of Tristan da Cunha and the Walvis Ridge on the African Plate.

a. Tristan hotspot
b. Thrace Basin
c. Mediterranean Ridge
d. Juan Fernandez hotspot

115. A _____ is a section of large diameter pipe fitted to the top of the blowout preventers that the flow line attaches to via a side outlet, to allow the drilling fluid to flow back over the shale shakers to the mud tanks.

a. Bell nipple
b. Swivel
c. Crown block
d. Mud pump

116. A _____ is the generalised term for any narrow shaft drilled in the ground, either vertically or horizontally. A _____ may be constructed for many different purposes including the extraction of water or other liquid (such as petroleum) or gases (such as natural gas), as part of a geotechnical investigation or environmental site assessment, for mineral exploration, or as a pilot hole for installing piers or underground utilities. Boreholes used as water wells are described in more depth in that article.

a. 1700 Cascadia earthquake
b. 1509 Istanbul earthquake
c. 1703 Genroku earthquake
d. Borehole

117. In machining, _____ is the process of enlarging a hole that has already been drilled (or cast), by means of a single-point cutting tool (or of a _____ head containing several such tools), for example as in _____ a cannon barrel. _____ is used to achieve greater accuracy of the diameter of a hole, and can be used to cut a tapered hole.

The term _____ is also sometimes used for drilling a hole, especially with respect to tunnels and wells in the earth.

a. 1703 Genroku earthquake
b. Boring
c. 1509 Istanbul earthquake
d. 1700 Cascadia earthquake

118. _____ is large diameter pipe that is assembled and inserted into a recently drilled section of a borehole and typically cemented into place.

_____ that is cemented in place aids the drilling process in several ways:

- Prevent contamination of fresh water well zones.
- Prevent unstable upper formations from caving-in and sticking the drill string or forming large caverns.
- Provides a strong upper foundation to use high-density drilling fluid to continue drilling deeper.
- Isolates different zones (that may have different pressures or fluids - known as zonal isolation) in the drilled formations from one another.
- Seals off high pressure zones from the surface, avoiding potential for a blowout
- Prevents fluid loss into or contamination of production zones.
- Provides a smooth internal bore for installing production equipment

A slightly different metal string, called production tubing, is often used without cement in the smallest _____ of a well completion to contain production fluids and convey them to the surface from an underground reservoir.

In the planning stages of a well a drilling engineer, usually with input from geologists and others, will pick strategic depths at which the hole will need to be cased in order for drilling to reach the desired total depth. This decision is often based on subsurface data such as formation pressures, strengths, and makeup, and is balanced against the cost objectives and desired drilling strategy.

a. 1509 Istanbul earthquake
b. Casing
c. 1703 Genroku earthquake
d. 1700 Cascadia earthquake

119. A _____ is a large metal flange welded or screwed on to the top of the conductor pipe (also known as drive-pipe) or the casing and is used to bolt the surface equipment to, such as the blowout preventers (for well drilling) or the Christmas tree (for well production.)

The _____, when installed, is typically tested to very strict pressure and leak-off parameters to insure viability under blowout conditions, before any surface equipment is installed.

a. Mud tank
c. Differential sticking
b. Casing head
d. Possum belly

120. _____ is a long section of connected oilfield pipe that is lowered into a wellbore and cemented. The pipe joints are typically about 40 ft [12 m] in length, male threaded on each end and connected with short lengths of double-female threaded pipe called couplings.

Casing is run to protect or isolate formations adjacent to the wellbore.

a. Rock core
c. Directional drilling
b. Flow line
d. Casing string

Chapter 5. Test Preparation Part 5

1. _____ is a very large diameter pipe that is set into the ground to prevent the loose surface soil from caving into the hole as the upper portion of the borehole is being drilled.

_____ is tyically set, on petroleum wells, before any drilling operations are performed. It is usually set with special pile-driving or spudder rigs, though the drilling rig is sometimes used to save time and money.

   a. Mud tank
   b. Casing head
   c. Differential sticking
   d. Conductor pipe

2. A _____ unit is installed on an offshore jackup rig to apply upward tension on the conductor. The _____ is installed into the conductor deck and is usually removable in order to protect the unit during transit.

The drilling conductor is the first and outer tubular which runs from the drilling rig into the seabed.

   a. Core drill
   b. Down-The-Hole Drill
   c. Conductor tensioner
   d. Flow line

3. A _____ is a drill specifically designed to remove a cylinder of material, much like a hole saw. The material left inside the drill bit is referred to as the core.

Core drills are used for many applications, either where the core needs to be preserved (the drilling apparatus used in obtaining a core sample is often referred to as a corer), or where drilling can be done more rapidly since much less material needs to be removed than with a standard bit.

   a. Flow line
   b. Mud motor
   c. Core drill
   d. Deep well drilling

4. A _____ is the stationary section of a block and tackle that contains a set of pulleys or sheaves through which the drill line (wire rope) is threaded or reeved and is opposite and above the traveling block.

The combination of the traveling block, _____ and wire rope drill line gives the ability to lift weights in the hundreds of thousands of pounds. On larger drilling rigs, when raising and lowering the derrick, line tensions over a million pounds are not unusual.

   a. Possum belly
   b. Drill pipe
   c. Drill bit
   d. Crown block

5. _____ involves drilling (a well) to a desired 'deep' depth of 10,000 ft or more.

_____ is sometimes more importantly characterized by the requirement of having the drill bit finally positioned within a specified radius of its surface starting location. This sometimes requires maneuvering the direction (azimuth) of the drill bit by various techniques (kicking) so as to arrive at the desired location at both the desired depth and within a specified radius of the starting point.

a. Core drill
b. Down-The-Hole Drill
c. Flow line
d. Deep well drilling

6. Desanders and desilters are drilling rig equipment with a set of hydrocyclones that separates sand and silt from the drilling fluid. _____ is installed after shakers and degasser but before desilter. _____ removes those abrasive solids from the drilling mud which cannot be removed by shakers.
   a. Casing head
   b. Crown block
   c. Desander
   d. Mud pump

7. A _____, more generally known in the oil industry as simply a 'survey', is the measurement of a borehole's departure from the vertical, measured in degrees (>°.)

   - When a well plan dictates the drilling of a straight borehole, surveys are periodically taken to ensure that it will hit its target and also to ensure that it does not trespass underneath different property lines. These surveys can be taken fairly simply with a mechanical drift recorder more commonly known as a Totco or Totco barrel This device is run inside the drill string attached to a wire on a wireline unit, down to the bottom of the drill pipe where the device (which is simply an inverted pendulum with a timer that punches a pin-hole onto a round paper tab delineated with concentric circles indicating increments of degrees) measures the angle of the hole and then is pulled back out to visually inspect to determine the angle. There are versions of this device that actually take a picture on film and are often used in situations where the azimuth (direction) needs to be determined also.

   - When a well plan dictates a directional or horizontal borehole, more sophisticated tools are normally used. One such tool is the MWD (measurement while drilling) tool that uses electronic accelerometers and gyroscopes, to continually take surveys while drilling (as the name suggests) and also measures the azimuth (direction.) This tool is attached to the drill string itself and requires extra support personnel to use and interpret the data, and its costs are much more substantial.

   a. 1509 Istanbul earthquake
   b. Deviation survey
   c. 1700 Cascadia earthquake
   d. 1703 Genroku earthquake

8. _____ is a problem that occurs when drilling a well with a greater well bore pressure than formation pressure, as is usually the case. The drill pipe is pressed against the wellbore wall so that part of its circumference will see only reservoir pressure, while the rest will continue to be pushed by wellbore pressure. As a result the pipe becomes stuck to the wall, and can require millions of pounds of force to remove, which may prove impossible.
   a. Differential sticking
   b. Drill bit
   c. Conductor pipe
   d. Crown block

9. _____, commonly called horizontal directional drilling or HDD, is a steerable trenchless method of installing underground pipes, conduits and cables in a shallow arc along a prescribed bore path by using a surface launched drilling rig, with minimal impact on the surrounding area. _____ is used when trenching or excavating is not practical. _____ minimizes environmental disruption.
   a. 1700 Cascadia earthquake
   b. 1703 Genroku earthquake
   c. 1509 Istanbul earthquake
   d. Directional boring

Chapter 5. Test Preparation Part 5

10. In machining, _____ is the process of enlarging a hole that has already been drilled (or cast), by means of a single-point cutting tool (or of a _____ head containing several such tools), for example as in _____ a cannon barrel. _____ is used to achieve greater accuracy of the diameter of a hole, and can be used to cut a tapered hole.

The term _____ is also sometimes used for drilling a hole, especially with respect to tunnels and wells in the earth.

- a. 1700 Cascadia earthquake
- b. 1703 Genroku earthquake
- c. 1509 Istanbul earthquake
- d. Boring

11. _____ is the practice of drilling non-vertical wells. It can be broken down into three main groups: Oilfield _____, Utility Installation _____ (or H.D.D., Horizontal _____, Directional boring) and in-seam _____ (Coal-Bed methane.)

Many prerequisites enabled this suite of technologies to become productive.

- a. Rotary steerable system
- b. Rock core
- c. Deep well drilling
- d. Directional drilling

12. A _____, as it is known in the oil industry, is an oil well with a borehole that deviates from a vertically straight line. This is normally an intentional decision and done purposefully, to hit several target sands, for instance.
- a. Drill line
- b. Conductor pipe
- c. Traveling block
- d. Directional well

13. A _____ is either a pneumatic or hydraulic powered rock or ground drill placed on the bottom of a drill string.

DTH is short for down-the-hole. Since the DTH method was originally developed to drill large-diameter holes downwards in surface-drilling applications, its name originated from the fact that the percussion mechanism followed the bit down into the hole.

- a. Deep well drilling
- b. Mud motor
- c. Flow line
- d. Down-The-Hole Drill

14. A _____, is a device attached to the end of the drill string that breaks apart, cuts or crushes the rock formations when drilling a wellbore (water, gas or oil.)

The _____ is hollow and has jets to allow for the expulsion of the drilling fluid at high velocity and high pressure to help clean the bit and help to break apart the rock (for softer formations.)

- a. Free point
- b. Flow show
- c. Mud pump
- d. Drill bit

15. In a drilling rig, the _____ is a multi-thread, twisted wire rope that is threaded or reeved through the traveling block and crown block to facilitate the lowering and lifting of the drill string into and out of the wellbore.

On larger diameter lines, tension strengths over a million pounds are possible.

To Make a connection is to add another segment of drill pipe onto the top the drill string.

    a. Casing head
    b. Conductor pipe
    c. Flow show
    d. Drill line

16. _____ is hollow, thick-walled, steel tubing that is used on drilling rigs to facilitate the drilling of a wellbore and comes is a variety of sizes, strengths and weights but are typically 30 to 33 feet in length. They are hollow to allow drilling fluid to be pumped through them, down the hole and back up the annulus. Because it is designed to support its own weight for combined lengths that often exceed 1 mile down into the crust of the Earth, the case hardened steel tubes are expensive, and owner's spend considerable efforts to re-use them after finishing a well, replacing the drill stems with thinner walled tubular casing, tapping the natural resources of oil reservoirs.

    a. Flow show
    b. Drill pipe
    c. Drill bit
    d. Desander

17. In geotechnical engineering, _____ is a fluid used to drill boreholes into the earth. Often used while drilling oil and natural gas wells and on exploration drilling rigs, drilling fluids are also used for much simpler boreholes, such as water wells. The three main categories of drilling fluids are Water based muds (which can be dispersed and non dispersed), non aqueous muds, usually called oil based mud, and gaseous _____, in which a wide range of gases can be used.

    a. Geosteering
    b. Drilling fluid
    c. Core drill
    d. Conductor tensioner

18. _____ is a process that occurs in a well being drilled with higher wellbore pressure than formation pressure. The liquid component of the drilling fluid (known as the mud filtrate) continues to 'invade' the porous and permeable formation until the solids present in the mud, commonly bentonite, clog enough pores to form a mud cake capable of preventing further invasion.

If invasion is severe enough, and reservoir pressures are unable to force the fluid and associated particles out entirely when the well starts producing, the amount of oil and gas a well can produce can be permanently reduced.

    a. 1700 Cascadia earthquake
    b. 1509 Istanbul earthquake
    c. 1703 Genroku earthquake
    d. Drilling fluid invasion

19. _____ is a system for increasing the diameter of the casing or liner of an oil well by up to 20% after it has been run down-hole.

Two challenges facing the Oil ' Gas industry are accessing new reservoirs that currently cannot be reached economically and maintaining profitable production from producing older fields. _____ is considered one of the most revolutionary technologies which will benefit the oil and gas industry within the last 10 years.

    a. AL 129-1
    b. AASHTO Soil Classification System
    c. Underbalanced drilling
    d. Expandable tubular technology

Chapter 5. Test Preparation Part 5

20. _____ describes an extreme form of Directional drilling that achieves horizontal well departures beyond the conventional, or achieves particularly challenging geometries of a well in terms of horizontal versus vertical offsets from the surface location. The aim of _____ are either to reach a larger area from one surface drilling location, or to keep a well for a longer distance in a reservoir in order to maximise its productivity and drainage capability. The challenges in _____ are in cleaning of the hole and managing of the significant torsion in the drill string as well as any buckling of drill string or casing that is caused by the well geometry and length.

   a. Underbalanced drilling
   b. AASHTO Soil Classification System
   c. AL 129-1
   d. Extended Reach Drilling

21. The _____ is a type of drilling equipment whereby there is no contact with the drilling surface.

Therefore in theory, the drill never wears down.

The tool expels an ultra hot hydrogen flame (~4000 °C) which causes small inconsistencies in the rock to fracture and fly away and thus 'drill' surface.

   a. 1700 Cascadia earthquake
   b. 1509 Istanbul earthquake
   c. Kelly hose
   d. Flame jet drill

22. A _____, used on a drilling rig, is a large diameter pipe (typically a section of casing) that is connected to the bell nipple (under the drill floor) and extends to the possum belly (on the mud tanks) and acts as a return line, (for the drilling fluid as it comes out of the hole), to the mud tanks.

The _____ will typically have equipment attached to it, such as a flow show which shows whether drilling fluid is flowing down the _____ or not and any changes in that flow. High-pressure jets are typically attached along its length to dislodge any obstructions (such as drill cuttings collecting in one spot) that may occur.

   a. Mud motor
   b. Down-The-Hole Drill
   c. Flow line
   d. Rock core

23. A _____ is a device on a drilling rig that is attached to the flow line and has a paddle that swings out as the flow of drilling fluid passes by it. The angle of the paddle increases as the volume of drilling fluid increases and pushes it out further and vice versa.

The purpose of the _____ is to allow the driller (and other rig personnel) to monitor the flow of drilling fluid as it comes out of the hole.

   a. Desander
   b. Crown block
   c. Free point
   d. Flow show

24. _____ is a common method known in the oil field practice which involves deploying a wireline to estimate the depth at which the drill string can get stuck during drilling.

   a. Casing head
   b. Traveling block
   c. Directional well
   d. Free point

25. In the process of drilling a borehole, _____ is the act of adjusting the borehole position (inclination and azimuth angles) on the fly to reach one or more geological targets. These changes are based on geological information gathered while drilling.

From 2D and 3D models of underground substructures, deviated wells (2D and 3D) are planned in advance to achieve specific goals: exploration, fluids production, fluids injection or technical.

   a. Down-The-Hole Drill
   b. Geosteering
   c. Flow line
   d. Mousehole

26. A _____ is a flexible, steel reinforced, high pressure hose that connects the standpipe to the kelly and allows free vertical movement of the kelly while facilitating the flow of drilling fluid through the system and down the drill string.
   a. Kelly hose
   b. 1509 Istanbul earthquake
   c. 1700 Cascadia earthquake
   d. Shale shakers

27. The _____ viscometer is a simple device for measuring viscosity from the time it takes a known volume of liquid to flow from the base of a cone through a short tube. It is particularly used by mud engineers to check the quality of drilling mud. A modern plastic _____

It consists of a cone 6 inches (152 mm) across and 12 inches in height (305 mm) to the apex of which is fixed a tube 2 inches (50.8 mm) long and 3/16 inch (4.76 mm) internal diameter. A mesh is fixed near the top across half the cone.

   a. 1509 Istanbul earthquake
   b. 1700 Cascadia earthquake
   c. 1703 Genroku earthquake
   d. Marsh funnel

28. The _____ is the storage area on a drilling rig where the next joint of drilling pipe is held until needed. This hole is in the floor of the rig, bored into the earth for a short ways, and usually lined with a metal casing known as a scabbard. .
   a. Conductor tensioner
   b. Deep well drilling
   c. Rotary steerable system
   d. Mousehole

29. A _____ works on an oil well drilling rig, and is responsible for the drilling fluid, also known as drilling mud which lubricates the drill bit and clears cuttings from the borehole.

Mud is a vital part of drilling operations. It provides hydrostatic pressure on the borehole wall to prevent uncontrolled production of reservoir fluids, lubricates and cools the drill bit, carries the drill cuttings up to the surface and forms a 'filter-cake' on the borehole wall to prevent drilling fluid invasion.

   a. 1700 Cascadia earthquake
   b. 1703 Genroku earthquake
   c. 1509 Istanbul earthquake
   d. Mud engineer

30. _____ is a type of borehole logging performed by the mud logger, that provides well owners with information about the lithology and fluid content of the borehole. Although most commonly used in petroleum exploration, it is also used when drilling water wells and in mineral exploration, where drilling mud is the circulating medium used to lift cuttings out of the hole. In hydrocarbon exploration, hydrocarbon surface gas detectors record the level of natural gas brought up in the mud.

a. 1703 Genroku earthquake
b. Mud logging
c. 1509 Istanbul earthquake
d. 1700 Cascadia earthquake

31. _____ refers to a Progressive Cavity Positive Displacement Pump placed in the Drill String to provide additional power to the bit while drilling. The PCPD Pump uses Drilling Fluid (commonly referred to as Drilling Mud, or just Mud) to create eccentric motion in the power section of the motor which is transferred as concentric power to the drill bit. The _____ uses different rotor and stator configurations to provide optimum performance for the desired drilling operation, typically increasing the number of lobes and length of power assembly for greater horsepower.

a. Flow line
b. Mud motor
c. Geosteering
d. Core drill

32. A _____ is a reciprocating plunger device designed to circulate drilling fluid down the drill string and back up the annulus.

They come in a variety of sizes and configuations but for the typical petroleum drilling rig, the triplex (three plunger) _____ is the pump of choice.

a. Flow show
b. Desander
c. Crown block
d. Mud pump

33. A _____ is an open-top container, typically made of steel, used as a reserve store for the active circulation of the drilling fluid on a drilling rig. They are often called mud pits, which comes from the fact that they used to be nothing more than pits dug out of the earth.

The tanks are open-top and will have walkways on top of them to allow traversing and visual observation of the drilling fluid and to monitor the level of fluid in the tanks.

a. Wellbore
b. Mud tank
c. Drill pipe
d. Drill line

34. A _____, on a drilling rig, is a metal container at the head of the shale shaker that receives the flow of drilling fluid and is directly connected to and at the end of the flow line.

The purpose of the _____ is to slow the flow of the drilling fluid (after it has gained momentum from coming down through the flow line) so that it does not shoot off of the shale shakers.

a. Mud pump
b. Swivel
c. Mud tank
d. Possum belly

35. A _____ is a special type of drill core and is a long tube looking run of rock obtained from the subsurface by drilling using a drilling rig. Usually using a method called mud rotary and cutting with a 2 inch bit and can be a few feet in length to hundreds of feet in length.

a. Mousehole
b. Rock core
c. Core drill
d. Drilling fluid

36. A _____ is a new form of drilling technology used in directional drilling. It employs the use of specialized downhole equipment to replace conventional directional tools such as mud motors. They are generally programmed by the MWD engineer or directional driller who transmits commands using surface equipment (typically using either pressure fluctuations in the mud column or variations in the drill string rotation) which the tool understands and gradually steers into the desired direction. In other words, a tool designed to drill directionally with continuous rotation from the surface, eliminating the need to slide a steerable motor.
 a. Deep well drilling
 b. Flow line
 c. Rock core
 d. Rotary steerable system

37. _____ are devices that remove drill cuttings from the drilling fluid while circulating and drilling. There are many different designs and research into the best design is constantly ongoing since solids control is vital in keeping down costs associated with the drilling fluid.
 a. 1509 Istanbul earthquake
 b. Kelly hose
 c. 1700 Cascadia earthquake
 d. Shale shakers

38. The _____, is a mud volcano in the subdistrict of Porong, Sidoarjo in East Java, Indonesia that has been ongoing since May 2006. Approximately 2,500 m³ (88,000 cubic feet) of mud are expelled per day, which is equivalent to the contents of a dozen Olympic-size swimming pools. It appears that the flow will continue indefinitely.
 a. Sidoarjo mud flow
 b. 1509 Istanbul earthquake
 c. 1703 Genroku earthquake
 d. 1700 Cascadia earthquake

39. _____ is a term often used in the oilfield to describe the process of injecting cement slurry into a zone, generally for pressure-isolation purposes. The term probably originated from the concept that enough water is 'squeezed' out of the slurry to render it unflowable, so the portion that has actually entered the zone will stay in place when the squeeze pressure is removed. After surface indications (e.g., pressure reaching a predetermined maximum) that a squeeze has been attained, any still-pumpable cement slurry remaining in the drill pipe or tubing ideally can be reverse circulated out before it sets.
 a. Squeeze job
 b. 1703 Genroku earthquake
 c. 1509 Istanbul earthquake
 d. 1700 Cascadia earthquake

40. A _____ is a mechanical device used on a drilling rig that hangs directly under the traveling block and directly above the kelly, that provides the ability for the kelly (and subsequently the drill string) to rotate while allowing the traveling block to remain in a stationary rotational position (yet allow vertical movement up and down the derrick) while simultaneously allowing the introduction of drilling fluid into the drill string.
 a. Desander
 b. Mud tank
 c. Possum belly
 d. Swivel

41. A _____ is the free moving section of a block and tackle that contains a set of pulleys or sheaves through which the drill line (wire rope) is threaded or reeved and is opposite (and under) the crown block (the stationary section.)

The combination of the _____, crown block and wire rope drill line gives the ability to lift weights in the hundreds of thousands of pounds. On larger drilling rigs, when raising and lowering the derrick, line tensions over a million pounds are not unusual.

 a. Directional well
 b. Casing head
 c. Free point
 d. Traveling block

42. _____ is a procedure used to drill oil and gas wells where the pressure in the wellbore is kept lower than the fluid pressure in the formation being drilled. As the well is being drilled, formation fluid flows into the wellbore and up to the surface. This is the opposite of the usual situation, where the wellbore is kept at a pressure above the formation to prevent formation fluid entering the well.

a. AL 129-1
b. AASHTO Soil Classification System
c. Underbalanced drilling
d. Extended Reach Drilling

43. A _____ is any hole drilled for the purpose of exploration for or extraction of natural resources such as water, gas or oil where a well may be produced and a resource is extracted for a protracted period of time.

It is often used interchangeably with drill hole or borehole though typically a 'borehole' is referred to in ore mining exploratory drilling or pilot holes for installing piers or underground utilities or any other of a number of single use hole drilling.

a. Wellbore
b. Swivel
c. Traveling block
d. Directional well

44. _____ or electrical resistivity imaging (ERI) is a geophysical technique for imaging sub-surfaces structures from electrical measurements made at the surface, or by electrodes in one or more boreholes. It is closely related to the medical imaging technique electrical impedance tomography (EIT), and mathematically is the same inverse problem. In contrast to medical EIT however _____ is essentially a direct current method.

a. AL 333
b. AL 129-1
c. AASHTO Soil Classification System
d. Electrical resistivity tomography

45. An _____ is a configuration of electrodes used for measuring either an electric current or voltage. Some electrode arrays can operate in a bidirectional fashion, in that they can also be used to provide a stimulating pattern of electric current or voltage.

Common arrays include:

- Schlumberger (Wenner)
- Wenner alpha
- Wenner beta
- Wenner gamma
- Pole-pole
- Dipole-dipole
- Pole-dipole
- Equatorial dipole-dipole

a. Electrode array
b. AL 333
c. AASHTO Soil Classification System
d. AL 129-1

46. _____ is geophysical technique that investigates the subsurface. There are many different kinds of imaging techniques, all which are based on applied physics.

Types of _____ include

- Electrical resistivity tomography
- Ground-penetrating radar
- Induced polarization
- Seismic tomography and Reflection seismology

a. 1703 Genroku earthquake
b. 1700 Cascadia earthquake
c. 1509 Istanbul earthquake
d. Geophysical imaging

47. _____ in archaeology most often refers to ground-based physical sensing techniques used for archaeological imaging or mapping. Remote sensing and marine surveys are also used in archaeology, but are generally considered separate disciplines. Other terms, such as 'geophysical prospection' and 'archaeological geophysics' are generally synonymous.

a. 1700 Cascadia earthquake
b. Geophysical survey
c. 1509 Istanbul earthquake
d. 1703 Genroku earthquake

48. _____ is a geophysical method that uses radar pulses to image the subsurface. This non-destructive method uses electromagnetic radiation in the microwave band (UHF/VHF frequencies) of the radio spectrum, and detects the reflected signals from subsurface structures. GPR can be used in a variety of media, including rock, soil, ice, fresh water, pavements and structures.

a. 1703 Genroku earthquake
b. 1700 Cascadia earthquake
c. 1509 Istanbul earthquake
d. Ground-penetrating radar

49. _____ is a geophysical imaging technique used to identify subsurface materials, such as ore. The method is similar to electrical resistivity tomography, in that an electric current is induced into the subsurface through two electrodes, and voltage is monitored through two other electrodes.

Time domain _____ methods measure the voltage decay or chargeability over a specified time interval after the induced voltage is removed.

a. AL 129-1
b. AASHTO Soil Classification System
c. AL 333
d. Induced polarization

50. _____ is a low frequency, pulse-limited radar sounder and altimeter used on the ESA Mars Express mission. It features ground-penetrating radar capabilities, which uses synthetic aperture techniques and a secondary receiving antenna to isolate subsurface reflections.

a. MARSIS
b. 1703 Genroku earthquake
c. 1509 Istanbul earthquake
d. 1700 Cascadia earthquake

51. _____ is one of a number of methods used in archaeological geophysics. Magnetic surveys record spatial variation in the earth's magnetic field. In archaeology, magnetic surveys are used to detect and map archaeological artifacts and features.

a. Magnetic survey
c. 1700 Cascadia earthquake
b. 1703 Genroku earthquake
d. 1509 Istanbul earthquake

52. The _____ of rock mass classification was developed in Norway in 1974 by Nick Barton, Lien, R., and Lunde, J at NGI (Norwegian Geotechnical Institute.) The system was developed on the basis of an analysis of 212 tunnel case histories from Scandinavia. It is a quantitative classification system and is an engineering system facilitating the design of tunnel supports.
   a. Rock Mass Rating
   c. 1700 Cascadia earthquake
   b. Q-system
   d. 1509 Istanbul earthquake

53. The _____ system is a geomechanical classification system for rocks, developed by Z. T. Bieniawski between 1972 and 1973.

The following six parameters are used to classify a rock mass using the _____ system

1. Uniaxial compressive strength of rock material
2. Rock Quality Designation (RQD)
3. Spacing of discontinuities
4. Condition of discontinuities
5. Groundwater conditions
6. Orientation of discontinuities

Each of the six parameters is assigned a value corresponding to the characteristics of the rock. These values are derived from field surveys. The sum of the six parameters is the '_____ value', which lies between 0 and 100.

a. Rock Structure Rating
c. 1509 Istanbul earthquake
b. 1700 Cascadia earthquake
d. Rock Mass Rating

54. _____ is a quantitative method for describing quality of a rock mass and then appropriate ground support.

The _____ concept introduced a rating system for a rock masses. It was the sum of weighted values in this classification system.

a. 1700 Cascadia earthquake
c. Rock Mass Rating
b. Rock Structure Rating
d. 1509 Istanbul earthquake

55. _____ is the name given to a series of fourteen softish grey and brown clays, with layers of sand, of Upper Eocene age, which are found in the Hampshire Tertiary basin, where they are particularly well exposed in the cliffs of Barton, Hordwell, and in the Isle of Wight. The area was covered with an inland sea, and the temperature was higher than at the present day.

Above the highly fossiliferous Barton Clay, which is said to contain about 600 species, there is a sandy series with few fossils; these are the Headon Hill or Barton Sands.

a. Quicksand
b. Fech fech
c. Dry quicksand
d. Barton Beds

56. _____ consists of thick deposits of soft, unconsolidated silty clay, which is saturated with water; these soil layers are situated at the bottom of certain estuaries, which are normally in temperate regions that have experienced cyclical glacial cycles. Example locations are Cape Cod Bay, Chongming Dongtan Reserve in Shanghai, China, Banc d'Arguinpreserve in Mauritania, The Bristol Channel in the United Kingdom, Mandø Island in the Wadden Sea in Denmark, Florida Bay, San Francisco Bay, Bay of Fundy, Casco Bay and Morro Bay. _____ manifests low shear strength, high compressibility and low permeability, making it hazardous to build upon in seismically active regions like the San Francisco Bay Area.
   a. 1703 Genroku earthquake
   b. 1700 Cascadia earthquake
   c. Bay mud
   d. 1509 Istanbul earthquake

57. _____ is sand that is black in colour. One type of _____ is a heavy, glossy, partly magnetic mixture of usually fine sands, found as part of a placer deposit. Another type of _____, found on beaches near a volcano, consists of tiny fragments of lava.
   a. Slyne-Erris Trough
   b. Rockall Basin
   c. Black sand
   d. Skarn

58. _____ is a naturally occurring granular material composed of finely divided rock and mineral particles.

As the term is used by geologists, _____ particles range in diameter from 0.0625 (or $>^1\!/_{16}$ mm, or 62.5 micrometers) to 2 millimeters. An individual particle in this range size is termed a _____ grain.

   a. 1700 Cascadia earthquake
   b. 1703 Genroku earthquake
   c. 1509 Istanbul earthquake
   d. Sand

59. _____, in geology, is a deposit of clay, often full of boulders, which is formed in and beneath glaciers and ice-sheets wherever they are found, but is in a special sense the typical deposit of the Glacial Period in northern Europe and North America.
   a. Boulder clay
   b. Brickearth
   c. Dry quicksand
   d. Sediment

60. _____ is a naturally occurring material composed primarily of fine-grained minerals, which show plasticity through a variable range of water content, and which can be hardened when dried and/or fired. _____ deposits are mostly composed of _____ minerals (phyllosilicate minerals), minerals which impart plasticity and harden when fired and/or dried, and variable amounts of water trapped in the mineral structure by polar attraction. Organic materials which do not impart plasticity may also be a part of _____ deposits.
   a. 1703 Genroku earthquake
   b. 1700 Cascadia earthquake
   c. 1509 Istanbul earthquake
   d. Clay

61. The _____ or Bovey Formation is a deposit of sands, clays and lignite, probably over 1000 ft. thick, that lies in a sedimentary basin termed the Bovey Basin which extends from Bovey Tracey to Newton Abbot in South Devon, England. The Bovey Basin lies along the line of the Sticklepath fault and owes its existence to subsidence along this fault.
   a. Fech fech
   b. Dry quicksand
   c. Salt glacier
   d. Bovey Beds

Chapter 5. Test Preparation Part 5

62. _____ is originally a wind-blown loess dust deposited under extremely cold, dry conditions that can be used for making house bricks. The _____ is normally represeneted on 1:50,000 solid and drift edition geological maps. In the Thames Valley area, where the _____ overlies certain River Terrace Gravels, this has been reclassified on more recent maps as the 'Langley Silt Complex'.
   a. Brickearth
   b. Dry quicksand
   c. Quick clay
   d. Salt glacier

63. In geology, _____ was the name given by W. Whitaker in 1861 to a peculiar deposit of stiff red, brown or yellow clay containing unworn whole flints as well as angular shattered fragments, also with a variable admixture of rounded flint, quartz, quartzite and other pebbles. It occurs in sheets or patches of various sizes over a large area in the south of England, from Hertfordshire on the north to Sussex on the south, and from Kent on the east to Devon on the west. It almost always lies on the surface of the Upper Chalk, but in Dorset it passes on to the Middle and Lower Chalk, and in Devon it is found on the Chert-Beds of the Selbornian group (A. J. Jukes-Browne, The _____, its Origin and Distribution, Q.J.G.S., vol.
   a. Clay-with-Flints
   b. 1700 Cascadia earthquake
   c. 1703 Genroku earthquake
   d. 1509 Istanbul earthquake

64. A _____ is a desert surface that is covered with closely packed, interlocking angular or rounded rock fragments of pebble and cobble size.

Several theories have been proposed for their formation. The more common theory is that they form by the gradual removal of the sand, dust and other fine grained material by the wind and intermittent rain leaving only the larger fragments behind.

   a. 1509 Istanbul earthquake
   b. 1703 Genroku earthquake
   c. 1700 Cascadia earthquake
   d. Desert pavement

65. _____ is loose sand whose bulk density is reduced by blowing air through it and which yields easily to weight or pressure. It acts similarly to regular quicksand, but it does not contain any water and does not operate on the same principle. _____ is an example of a granular material.
   a. Salt glacier
   b. Fech fech
   c. Sediment
   d. Dry quicksand

66. _____ is a colloid hydrogel consisting of fine granular matter (such as sand or silt), clay, and salt water. In the name, as in that of quicksilver (mercury), 'quick' does not mean 'fast,' but 'living' (cf. the expression the quick and the dead.)
   a. Quicksand
   b. Salt glacier
   c. Bovey Beds
   d. Quick clay

67. _____ is a clay that is prone to large volume changes that are directly related to changes in water content. Mitigation of the effects of _____ on structures built in areas with expansive clays is a major challenge in geotechnical engineering. Cities built on top of clay compact the clay beneath as groundwater is drawn down and water is wringed out of the clay.
   a. AL 333
   b. AL 129-1
   c. AASHTO Soil Classification System
   d. Expansive clay

68. _____ is a very fine powder caused by the erosion of clay-limestone terrain, pulverulent soil under a thin crust common in deserts. It is not determinable from the surface and can therefore pose a significant transportation hazard acting as a surprise 'trap' as the ground collapses beneath a vehicle miring it in a quicksand-like substance.

_____ is common in the Qattara Depression, making that portion of the Sahara Desert deemed impassable to most vehicles.

   a. Bovey Beds   b. Quicksand
   c. Salt glacier   d. Fech fech

69. The _____ is the largest submarine accumulation of sediment on Earth. Material is carried from the mouth of the Ganges Delta in Bangladesh through a series of underwater canyons, some of which are more than 1,500 miles (2,414km) in length. The material is then carried along the floor of the Bay of Bengal up to 30 degrees latitude from where it began.
   a. Ganges Fan   b. 1700 Cascadia earthquake
   c. 1509 Istanbul earthquake   d. 1703 Genroku earthquake

70. Sediments deposited into lakes that have come from glaciers are called _____. These lakes include ice margin lakes or other types formed from glacial erosion or deposition. Sediments in the bedload and suspended load are carried into lakes and deposited.
   a. 1700 Cascadia earthquake   b. 1509 Istanbul earthquake
   c. Bull Lake glaciation   d. Glaciolacustrine deposits

71. _____ is a homogeneous, typically nonstratified, porous, friable, slightly coherent, often calcareous, fine-grained, silty, pale yellow or buff, windblown (aeolian) sediment. It generally occurs as a widespread blanket deposit that covers areas of hundreds of square kilometers and tens of meters thick. _____ often stands in either steep or vertical faces.
   a. 1700 Cascadia earthquake   b. 1703 Genroku earthquake
   c. Loess   d. 1509 Istanbul earthquake

72. _____ is a type of clay found in coastal regions around the world. In the northern, deglaciated regions, it can sometimes be quick clay, which is notorious for being involved in landslides.

Clay particles can self-assemble into various configurations, each with totally different properties.

   a. Marine clay   b. Teilzone
   c. Basin and Range   d. Salt tectonics

73. A _____ is any glacially formed accumulation of unconsolidated glacial debris (soil and rock) which can occur in currently glaciated and formerly glaciated regions, such as those areas acted upon by a past ice age. This debris may have been plucked off the valley floor as a glacier advanced or it may have fallen off the valley walls as a result of frost wedging. Moraines may be composed of silt like glacial flour to large boulders.
   a. 1509 Istanbul earthquake   b. 1700 Cascadia earthquake
   c. 1703 Genroku earthquake   d. Moraine

Chapter 5. Test Preparation Part 5

74. _____ is an accumulation of partially decayed vegetation matter. _____ forms in wetlands or peatlands, variously called bogs, moors, muskegs, pocosins, mires, and _____ swamp forests. By volume there are about 4 trillion mÂ³ of _____ in the world covering a total of around 2% of global land mass (about 3 million km^2), containing about 8 billion terajoules of energy.
   a. 1703 Genroku earthquake
   b. 1509 Istanbul earthquake
   c. Peat
   d. 1700 Cascadia earthquake

75. _____ is a unique form of highly sensitive marine clay, with the tendency to change from a relatively stiff condition to a liquid mass when it is disturbed.

Undisturbed _____ resembles a water-saturated gel. When a mass of _____ undergoes sufficient stress, however, it instantly turns into a flowing ooze, a process known as liquefaction.

   a. Boulder clay
   b. Brickearth
   c. Quicksand
   d. Quick clay

76. A _____ is a flow of salt (typically halite) that is created when a rising diapir in a salt dome breaches the surface, much like toothpaste from a tube. Gravity causes the salt to flow like glaciers into adjacent valleys. Most of the flow occurs during the winter, when the salt is wet, as the strength of salt is critically dependent on its water content.
   a. Sediment
   b. Bovey Beds
   c. Brickearth
   d. Salt glacier

77. _____ is any particulate matter that can be transported by fluid flow, and which eventually is deposited.

They are most often transported by water (fluvial processes) transported by wind (aeolian processes) and glaciers. Beach sands and river channel deposits are examples of fluvial transport and deposition, though _____ also often settles out of slow-moving or standing water in lakes and oceans.

   a. Salt glacier
   b. Bovey Beds
   c. Sediment
   d. Brickearth

78. _____ is soil or rock derived granular material of a grain size between sand and clay. _____ may occur as a soil or as suspended sediment in a surface water body. It may also exist as soil deposited at the bottom of a water body.
   a. 1509 Istanbul earthquake
   b. Silt
   c. 1700 Cascadia earthquake
   d. 1703 Genroku earthquake

79. _____ refer to geological deposits typically of Quaternary age. These recent unconsolidated sediments may include stream channel and floodplain deposits, beach sands, talus gravels and glacial drift and moraine. All pre-quaternary deposits are referred to as bedrock.
   a. Superficial deposits
   b. Concretion
   c. Jasperoid
   d. Conglomerate

80. _____ is unsorted glacial sediment. Glacial drift is a general term for the coarsely graded and extremely heterogeneous sediments of glacial origin. Glacial _____ is that part of glacial drift which was deposited directly by the glacier.

a. 1703 Genroku earthquake
b. 1700 Cascadia earthquake
c. 1509 Istanbul earthquake
d. Till

81. _____ is the scientific study of earthquakes and the propagation of elastic waves through the Earth. The field also includes studies of earthquake effects, such as tsunamis as well as diverse seismic sources such as volcanic, tectonic, oceanic, atmospheric, and artificial processes . A related field that uses geology to infer information regarding past earthquakes is paleoseismology.
a. 1509 Istanbul earthquake
b. 1700 Cascadia earthquake
c. Seismology
d. 1703 Genroku earthquake

82. Scale-invariance is also the main rule for faults and earthquakes. However, an apparent exception confuses this picture: the _____, which is a repeating, large earthquake that appears more frequently than local seismic monitoring would suggest . Characteristic earthquakes are usually defined from paleoseismology observations .
a. Seismotectonics
b. Microtremor
c. Morley-Vine-Matthews hypothesis
d. Characteristic earthquake

83. An _____ is the result of a sudden release of energy in the Earth's crust that creates seismic waves. They are recorded with a seismometer or the related and mostly obsolete Richter magnitude, with a magnitude 3 or lower _____ being mostly imperceptible and magnitude 7 causing serious damage over large areas.
a. AASHTO Soil Classification System
b. AL 129-1
c. AL 333
d. Earthquake

84. _____ are events where a local area experiences sequences of many earthquakes striking in a relatively short period of time. The length of time used to define the swarm itself varies, but the United States Geological Survey points out that an event may be on the order of days, weeks, or months. They are differentiated from earthquakes succeeded by a series of aftershocks by the observation that no single earthquake in the sequence is obviously the main shock.
a. AL 333
b. Earthquake swarms
c. AASHTO Soil Classification System
d. AL 129-1

85. _____ is used in the mining industry to probe the contents of ore deposits. By withdrawing a small diameter core of rock from the orebody, geologists can perform examinations like Assay and determining the lithology of the rock.

Early diamond drilling opened up many new areas for mineral mining, and was related to a boom in mineral exploration in remote locations.

a. AL 333
b. AL 129-1
c. AASHTO Soil Classification System
d. Exploration diamond drilling

86. The _____ of an earthquake describes the inelastic deformation in the source region that generates the seismic waves. In the case of a fault-related event it refers to the orientation of the fault plane that slipped and the slip vector and is also known as a fault-plane solution. Focal mechanisms are derived from a solution of the moment tensor for the earthquake, which itself is estimated by an analysis of observed seismic waveforms.
a. 1509 Istanbul earthquake
b. Seismotectonics
c. Morley-Vine-Matthews hypothesis
d. Focal mechanism

Chapter 5. Test Preparation Part 5

87. A _____ is defined as a faint earth tremor caused by natural phenomena, such as winds and ocean waves. Thus a _____ is a small and long-continuing oscillation of the ground. The term is most commonly used to refer to the dominant background seismic noise signal on Earth, which arises from wave action in the oceans.
   a. Microtremor
   b. Seismotectonics
   c. Normal Move Out
   d. Microseism

88. _____ is a low amplitude (in the order of micrometres) ambient vibration of the ground caused by man-made or atmospheric disturbances. Observation of microtremors can give useful information on dynamic properties of the site such as predominant period and amplitude. _____ observations are easy to perform, inexpensive and can be applied to places with low seismicity as well, hence, _____ measurements can be used conveniently for seismic microzonation .
   a. Seismotectonics
   b. Supershear earthquake
   c. Normal Move Out
   d. Microtremor

89. The _____, also known as the Vine-Matthews-Morley hypothesis was the first key scientific test of the seafloor spreading theory of continental drift.

Geophysicists Frederick John Vine and Lawrence W. Morley independently realized that if the seafloor spreading theory was correct, then the rocks surrounding the mid-oceanic ridges should show symmetric patterns of magnetization reversals, a record of the earth's geomagnetic reversals, captured in the cooling volcanic rocks. Morley's letters to Nature and Journal of Geophysical Research were both rejected, so Vine and his adviser Drummond Hoyle Matthews were first to publish in 1963.

   a. Supershear earthquake
   b. Microtremor
   c. Morley-Vine-Matthews hypothesis
   d. Normal Move Out

90. _____ is a term used in seismics and geophysics to describe the effect of the separation between receiver and source on the arrival time of a reflection that does not dip, abbreviated _____. Filters and correcting algorithims must be used to properly image the subsurface.

In a land-based seismic survey blasts of dynamite or vibroseis units are used to create waves that will reflect off different layers of rock and are collected by equally spaced geophones or receivers placed along the surface.

   a. Normal Move Out
   b. Seismotectonics
   c. Supershear earthquake
   d. Microtremor

91. _____ is the process of transforming seismic reflection data into a quantitative rock property description of a reservoir. _____ may be pre-or post-stack, deterministic, stochastic or geostatistical, and typically includes other reservoir measurements such as well logs and cores.

Seismic surveys are routinely performed to gather information about the geology of an oil or gas field.

   a. Seismic to simulation
   b. Fahlband
   c. Lithotope
   d. Seismic inversion

92. A _____ is used to measure and compare the severity of earthquakes.

Two fundamentally different but equally important types of scales are commonly used by seismologists to describe earthquakes. The original force or energy of an earthquake is measured on a magnitude scale, while the intensity of shaking occurring at any given point on the Earth's surface is measured on an intensity scale.

a. Seismic scale
b. Surface wave magnitude
c. Moment magnitude scale
d. China Seismic Intensity Scale

93. _____ is the process and associated techniques used to develop highly accurate static and dynamic 3D models of hydrocarbon reservoirs for use in predicting future production, placing additional wells, and evaluating alternative reservoir management scenarios. The process is successful if the model accurately reflects the original well logs, seismic data and production history.

Reservoir models are constructed to gain a better understanding of the subsurface that leads to informed well placement, reserves estimation and production planning.

a. Forebulge
b. Geological survey
c. Platform
d. Seismic to simulation

94. _____ is the study of the relationship between earthquakes, tectonics and individual faults. It seeks to understand which faults are responsible for seismic activity in an area by analysing a combination of regional tectonics, recent instrumentally recorded events, accounts of historical earthquakes and geomorphological evidence. This information can then be used to quantify the seismic hazard of an area.

a. Normal Move Out
b. Microtremor
c. Supershear earthquake
d. Seismotectonics

95. A _____ is an earthquake in which the propagation of the rupture along the fault surface occurs at speeds in excess of the seismic shear wave velocity. This causes a form of sonic boom to occur.

During seismic events along a fault surface the displacement initiates at the focus and then propagates outwards.

a. Morley-Vine-Matthews hypothesis
b. Microtremor
c. Normal Move Out
d. Supershear earthquake

96. _____ is a discipline that applies principles of engineering mechanics, e.g. kinematics, dynamics, fluid mechanics, and mechanics of material, to predict the mechanical behavior of soils. Together with Rock mechanics, it is the basis for solving many engineering problems in civil engineering (geotechnical engineering), geophysical engineering and engineering geology. Some of the basic theories of _____ are the basic description and classification of soil, effective stress, shear strength, consolidation, lateral earth pressure, bearing capacity, slope stability, and permeability.

a. Vibro replacement stone columns
b. Shear strength
c. Reynolds' dilatancy
d. Soil mechanics

97. The _____ is an engineering property of granular materials. The _____ is the maximum angle of a stable slope determined by friction, cohesion and the shapes of the particles.

When bulk granular materials are poured onto a horizontal surface, a conical pile will form. The internal angle between the surface of the pile and the horizontal surface is known as the _____ and is related to the density, surface area, and coefficient of friction of the material.

   a. AL 333
   b. AL 129-1
   c. AASHTO Soil Classification System
   d. Angle of repose

98. In geotechnical engineering, _____ is the capacity of soil to support the loads applied to the ground. The _____ of soil is the maximum average contact pressure between the foundation and the soil which should not produce shear failure in the soil. Ultimate _____ is the theoretical maximum pressure which can be supported without failure; while allowable _____ is the ultimate _____ divided by a factor of safety.
   a. Vibro replacement stone columns
   b. Lateral earth pressure
   c. Critical state soil mechanics
   d. Bearing capacity

99. _____ use capacitance to measure the dielectric permittivity of a surrounding medium. One application for such a device is measuring the water content of soil, where the volume of water in the total volume of soil most heavily influences the dielectric permittivity of the soil because the dielectric of water (80) is much greater than the other constituents of the soil (mineral soil: 4, organic matter: 4, air: 1.) When the amount of water changes in the soil, a probe will measure a change in capacitance due to the change in dielectric permittivity that can be directly correlated with a change in water content.
   a. Hydraulic conductivity
   b. Specific storage
   c. Capacitance sensors
   d. Stemflow

100. _____ is the component of shear strength of a rock or soil that is independent of interparticle friction.

In soils, true _____ is caused by one of three things:

   1. Electrostatic forces in stiff overconsolidated clays (which may be lost through weathering)
   2. Cementing by Fe_2O_3, $CaCO_3$, NaCl, etc
   3. Root _____

There can also be apparent _____. This is caused by:

   1. Negative capillary pressure (which is lost upon wetting)
   2. Pore pressure response during undrained loading (which is lost through time)

   a. Compaction
   b. Combe
   c. Diamond Head
   d. Cohesion

101. _____ is a process by which soils decrease in volume. It occurs when stress is applied to a soil that causes the soil particles to pack together more tightly, therefore reducing its bulk volume. When this occurs in a soil that is saturated with water, water will be squeezed out of the soil.

a. Groundwater-related subsidence
b. Pore water pressure
c. Vibro replacement stone columns
d. Consolidation

102. _____ is the area of Soil Mechanics that encompasses the conceptual models that represent the mechanical behavior of saturated remolded soils based on the Critical State concept. The Critical State concept is an idealization of the observed behavior of saturated remoulded clays in triaxial compression tests, and it is assumed to apply to undisturbed soils. It states that soils and other granular materials, if continuously distorted (sheared) until they flow as a frictional fluid, will come into a well-defined critical state.

a. Pore water pressure
b. Critical state soil mechanics
c. Slope stability
d. Reynolds' dilatancy

103. In fluid dynamics, the _____ is a phenomenological equation, which relates the head loss -- or pressure loss -- due to friction along a given length of pipe to the average velocity of the fluid flow. The equation is named after Henry Darcy and Julius Weisbach.

The _____ contains a dimensionless friction factor, known as the Darcy friction factor.

Head loss can be calculated with

$$h_f = f \cdot \frac{L}{D} \cdot \frac{V^2}{2g}$$

where

- h_f is the head loss due to friction;
- L is the length of the pipe;
- D is the hydraulic diameter of the pipe (for a pipe of circular section, this equals the internal diameter of the pipe);
- V is the average velocity of the fluid flow, equal to the volumetric flow rate per unit cross-sectional wetted area;
- g is the local acceleration due to gravity;
- f is a dimensionless coefficient called the Darcy friction factor. It can be found from a Moody diagram.

a. 1703 Genroku earthquake
b. Darcy-Weisbach equation
c. 1509 Istanbul earthquake
d. 1700 Cascadia earthquake

104. The _____ is a pressure-dependent model for determining whether a material has failed or undergone plastic yielding. The criterion was introduced to deal with the plastic deformation of soils. It and its many variants have been applied to rock, concrete, polymers, foams, and other pressure-dependent materials.

a. 1700 Cascadia earthquake
b. 1703 Genroku earthquake
c. 1509 Istanbul earthquake
d. Drucker-Prager yield criterion

105. Karl von Terzaghi first proposed the relationship for _____ in 1936. For him, the term effective meant the calculated stress that was effective in moving soil, or causing displacements. It represents the average stress carried by the soil skeleton.
   a. AL 333
   b. Effective stress
   c. AASHTO Soil Classification System
   d. AL 129-1

106. A _____ is a graphical representation of two-dimensional steady-state groundwater flow through aquifers. Construction of a _____ is often used for solving groundwater flow problems where the geometry makes analytical solutions impractical. The method is often used in civil engineering, hydrogeology or soil mechanics as a first check for problems of flow under hydraulic structures like dams or sheet pile walls.
   a. Stemflow
   b. Hydraulic conductivity
   c. Flownet
   d. Specific storage

1. _____ sensor is an instrument developed for measuring soil moisture content. The instrument has an oscillating circuit, the sensing part of the sensor is embedded in the soil, and the operating frequency will depend on the value of soil's dielectric constant.

There are two types of sensors:

- Capacitance probe, or fringe capacitance sensor. Capacitance probes use capacitance to measure the dielectric permittivity of the soil. The volume of water in the total volume of soil most heavily influences the dielectric permittivity of the soil because the dielectric of water is much greater than the other constituents of the soil (mineral soil: 4, organic matter: 4, air: 1.) Thus, when the amount of water changes in the soil, the probe will measure a change in capacitance (from the change in dielectric permittivity) that can be directly correlated with a change in water content. Circuitry inside some commercial probes change the capacitance measurement into a proportional millivolt output. Other configuration are like the neutron probe where an access tube made of PVC is installed in the soil. The probe consists of sensing head at fixed depth. The sensing head consists of an oscillator circuit, the frequency is determined by an annular electrode, fringe-effect capacitor, and the dielectric constant of the soil.

- Electrical impedance sensor, which consists of soil probes and using electrical impedance measurement. The most common configuration is based on the standing wave principle (Gaskin ' Miller, 1996.)

a. 1700 Cascadia earthquake
b. 1509 Istanbul earthquake
c. 1703 Genroku earthquake
d. Frequency domain

2. _____ is the subsidence (or the sinking) of land resulting from groundwater extraction, and a major problem in the developing world as major metropolises swell without adequate regulation and enforcement, as well as a being a common problem in the developed world. One estimate has 80% of serious land subsidence problems associated with the excessive extraction of groundwater , making it a growing problem throughout the world.
a. Pore water pressure
b. Lateral earth pressure
c. Groundwater-related subsidence
d. Vibro replacement stone columns

3. In geology, engineering, and surveying, _____ is the motion of a surface (usually, the Earth's surface) as it shifts downward relative to a datum such as sea-level. The opposite of _____ is uplift, which results in an increase in elevation. There are several types of _____.
a. Subsidence
b. 1700 Cascadia earthquake
c. 1703 Genroku earthquake
d. 1509 Istanbul earthquake

4. _____, symbolically represented as K, is a property of vascular plants, soil or rock, that describes the ease with which water can move through pore spaces or fractures. It depends on the intrinsic permeability of the material and on the degree of saturation. Saturated _____, K_{sat}, describes water movement through saturated media.
a. Flownet
b. Specific storage
c. Stemflow
d. Hydraulic conductivity

5. A _____ is a type of mudflow or landslide composed of pyroclastic material and water that flows down from a volcano, typically along a river valley. The term '_____' originated in the Javanese language of Indonesia.
a. 1700 Cascadia earthquake
b. 1509 Istanbul earthquake
c. 1703 Genroku earthquake
d. Lahar

6. _____ is the pressure that soil exerts in the horizontal plane. The common applications of _____ theory are for the design of ground engineering structures such as retaining walls, basements, tunnels, and to determine the friction on the sides of deep foundations.

To describe the pressure a soil will exert, a _____ coefficient, K, is used. K is the ratio of lateral (horizontal) pressure to vertical pressure (K = σ_h'/σ_v'). Thus horizontal earth pressure is assumed to be directly proportional to the vertical pressure at any given point in the soil profile.

   a. Reynolds' dilatancy   b. Vibro replacement stone columns
   c. Shear strength   d. Lateral earth pressure

7. _____, lithostatic pressure, and vertical stress are terms that denote the pressure or stress imposed on a layer of soil or rock by the weight of overlying material.

The _____ at a depth z is given by

,

where >ρ(z) is the density of the overlying rock at depth z and g is the acceleration due to gravity. p_0 is the datum pressure, like the pressure at the surface.

   a. AL 129-1   b. AASHTO Soil Classification System
   c. Iron catastrophe   d. Overburden pressure

8. _____ in the earth sciences (commonly symbolized as κ a rock or k) is a measure of the ability of a material (typically unconsolidated material) to transmit fluids. It is of great importance in determining the flow characteristics of hydrocarbons in oil and gas reservoirs, and of groundwater in aquifers. It is typically measured in the lab by application of Darcy's law under steady state conditions or, more generally, by application of various solutions to the diffusion equation for unsteady flow conditions.
   a. Permeability   b. Saltwater intrusion
   c. 1700 Cascadia earthquake   d. 1509 Istanbul earthquake

9. _____ refers to the pressure of groundwater held within a soil or rock, in gaps between particles (pores.) For example, in a high permeability soil, the pressure would be close to hydrostatic in no flow conditions. It is also referred to as tensiometer pressure.
   a. Soil mechanics   b. Critical state soil mechanics
   c. Pore water pressure   d. Shear strength

10. _____ is a measure of the void spaces in a material, and is measured as a fraction, between 0-1, or as a percentage between 0-100%. The term is used in multiple fields including ceramics, metallurgy, materials, manufacturing, earth sciences and construction.

Used in geology, hydrogeology, soil science, and building science, the _____ of a porous medium (such as rock or sediment) describes the fraction of void space in the material, where the void may contain, for example, air or water.

   a. 1700 Cascadia earthquake
   b. 1509 Istanbul earthquake
   c. Saltwater intrusion
   d. Porosity

11. _____ is a unique form of highly sensitive marine clay, with the tendency to change from a relatively stiff condition to a liquid mass when it is disturbed.

Undisturbed _____ resembles a water-saturated gel. When a mass of _____ undergoes sufficient stress, however, it instantly turns into a flowing ooze, a process known as liquefaction.

   a. Quick clay
   b. Quicksand
   c. Brickearth
   d. Boulder clay

12. _____ is a naturally occurring material composed primarily of fine-grained minerals, which show plasticity through a variable range of water content, and which can be hardened when dried and/or fired. _____ deposits are mostly composed of _____ minerals (phyllosilicate minerals), minerals which impart plasticity and harden when fired and/or dried, and variable amounts of water trapped in the mineral structure by polar attraction. Organic materials which do not impart plasticity may also be a part of _____ deposits.

   a. 1509 Istanbul earthquake
   b. 1700 Cascadia earthquake
   c. Clay
   d. 1703 Genroku earthquake

13. _____ is a colloid hydrogel consisting of fine granular matter (such as sand or silt), clay, and salt water. In the name, as in that of quicksilver (mercury), 'quick' does not mean 'fast,' but 'living' (cf. the expression the quick and the dead.)

   a. Quick clay
   b. Bovey Beds
   c. Quicksand
   d. Salt glacier

14. Study of geological _____ is related to the study of structural geology, rock microstructure or rock texture and fault mechanics.

_____ is the response of a rock to deformation usually by compressive stress and forms particular textures. _____ can be homogeneous or non-homogeneous, and may be pure _____ or simple _____.

   a. Petermann Orogeny
   b. Crenulation
   c. Sag pond
   d. Shear

15. _____ in reference to soil is a term used to describe the maximum strength of soil at which point significant plastic deformation or yielding occurs due to an applied shear stress. There is no definitive '_____' of a soil as it depends on a number of factors affecting the soil at any given time and on the frame of reference, in particular the rate at which the shearing occurs.

Two theories are commonly used to estimate the _____ of a soil depending on the rate of shearing as a frame of reference.

a. Critical state soil mechanics
c. Shear strength
b. Soil mechanics
d. Consolidation

16. The field of _____ encompasses the analysis of static and dynamic stability of slopes of earth and rock-fill dams, slopes of other types of embankments, excavated slopes, and natural slopes in soil and soft rock.

Earthen slopes can develop a cut-spherical weakness zone. The probability of this happening can be calculated in advance using a simple 2-D circular analysis package.

a. Lateral earth pressure
c. Groundwater-related subsidence
b. Reynolds' dilatancy
d. Slope stability

17. _____ describes the behavior of soils that, when loaded, suddenly go from a solid state to a liquefied state, or having the consistency of a heavy liquid. Liquefaction is more likely to occur in loose to moderate saturated granular soils with poor drainage, such as silty sands or sands and gravels capped or containing seams of impermeable sediments . During loading, usually cyclic undrained loading, e.g. earthquake loading, loose sands tend to decrease in volume, which produces an increase in their porewater pressures and consequently a decrease in shear strength, i.e. reduction in effective stress.

a. 1700 Cascadia earthquake
c. 1703 Genroku earthquake
b. 1509 Istanbul earthquake
d. Soil liquefaction

18. _____, storativity (S), specific yield (S_y) and specific capacity are material physical properties that characterize the capacity of an aquifer to release groundwater from storage in response to a decline in hydraulic head. For that reason they are sometimes referred to as 'storage properties'. In the field of hydrogeology, these properties are often determined using some combination of field hydraulic tests (e.g., aquifer tests) and laboratory tests on aquifer material samples.

a. Flownet
c. Stemflow
b. Hydraulic conductivity
d. Specific storage

19. _____ is the property of some non-Newtonian pseudoplastic fluids to show a time-dependent change in viscosity; the longer the fluid undergoes shear stress, the lower is its viscosity. A thixotropic fluid is a fluid which takes a finite time to attain equilibrium viscosity when introduced to a step change in shear rate. However, this is not a universal definition; the term is sometimes applied to pseudoplastic fluids without a viscosity/time component.

a. 1509 Istanbul earthquake
c. Thixotropy
b. 1703 Genroku earthquake
d. 1700 Cascadia earthquake

20. _____, in materials science, is defined as the volume of voids in a mixture divided by the volume of solids. This figure is relevant in composites, in mining (particular with regard to the properties of tailings), and in soil science. In geotechnics the _____ is represented by the symbol e.

a. 1700 Cascadia earthquake
c. 1703 Genroku earthquake
b. 1509 Istanbul earthquake
d. Void ratio

21. The _____ are a basic measure of the nature of a fine-grained soil. Depending on the water content of the soil, it may appear in four states: solid, semi-solid, plastic and liquid. In each state the consistency and behavior of a soil is different and thus so are its engineering properties.

a. AL 333 　　　　　　　　　　　　　　　b. AL 129-1
c. AASHTO Soil Classification System 　　d. Atterberg limits

22. The _____ is an in situ testing method used to determine the geotechnical engineering properties of soils and delineating soil stratigraphy. It was initially developed in the 1950s at the Dutch Laboratory for Soil Mechanics in Delft to investigate soft soils. Based on this history it has also been called the 'Dutch cone test'.
   a. Proctor compaction test 　　　　　　　b. Cone penetration test
   c. 1509 Istanbul earthquake 　　　　　　d. 1700 Cascadia earthquake

23. The _____ and the related modified _____ are tests to determine the maximum practically-achievable density of soils and aggregates, and are frequently used in geotechnical engineering.

The test consists of compacting the soil or aggregate to be tested into a standard mould using a standardized compactive energy at several different levels of moisture content. The maximum dry density and optimum moisture content is determined from the results of the test.

   a. 1700 Cascadia earthquake 　　　　　b. Proctor compaction test
   c. R-value 　　　　　　　　　　　　　　d. 1509 Istanbul earthquake

24. _____ refers to the process by which a sediment progressively loses its porosity due to the effects of loading. This forms part of the process of lithification. When a layer of sediment is originally deposited, it contains an open framework of particles with the pore space being usually filled with water.
   a. Compaction 　　　　　　　　　　　　b. Diamond Head
   c. Geothermal 　　　　　　　　　　　　d. Combe

25. The _____ test, California Test 301, measures the response of a compacted sample of soil or aggregate to a vertically applied pressure under specific conditions. This test is used by Caltrans for pavement design, replacing the California bearing ratio test. Many other agencies have adopted the California pavement design method, and specify _____ testing for subgrade soils and road aggregates.
   a. R-value 　　　　　　　　　　　　　　b. 1509 Istanbul earthquake
   c. 1700 Cascadia earthquake 　　　　　d. Proctor compaction test

26. A _____ is a practice or procedure used to assess the particle size distribution of a granular material.

The size distribution is often of critical importance to the way the material performs in use. A _____ can be performed on any type of non-organic or organic granular materials including sands, crushed rock, clays, granite, feldspars, coal, soil, a wide range of manufactured powders, grain and seeds, down to a minimum size depending on the exact method.

   a. 1509 Istanbul earthquake 　　　　　b. Sieve analysis
   c. 1700 Cascadia earthquake 　　　　　d. 1703 Genroku earthquake

27. In geology, _____ refers to heat sources within the planet. _____ is technically an adjective (e.g., _____ energy) but in U.S. English the word has attained frequent use as a noun .

The planet's internal heat was originally generated during its accretion, due to gravitational binding energy, and since then additional heat has continued to be generated by decay heat from the radioactive decay of elements.

   a. Geothermal
   b. Combe
   c. Dali
   d. Diamond Head

28. A _____ system is a central heating and/or air conditioning system that actively pumps heat to or from the shallow ground. It uses the earth as either a source of heat in the winter, or as a coolant in the summer. This design takes advantage of moderate temperatures in the shallow ground to boost efficiency and reduce operational costs.
   a. Geothermal power
   b. Geothermal gradient
   c. Hot Dry Rock Geothermal Energy
   d. Geothermal heat pump

29. An _____ is the result of a sudden release of energy in the Earth's crust that creates seismic waves. They are recorded with a seismometer or the related and mostly obsolete Richter magnitude, with a magnitude 3 or lower _____ being mostly imperceptible and magnitude 7 causing serious damage over large areas.
   a. AASHTO Soil Classification System
   b. AL 129-1
   c. Earthquake
   d. AL 333

30. _____ is an informal term to indicate a tsunami that has initial wave heights that are much larger than normal tsunami. Unlike usual tsunamis, which originate from tectonic activity and the raising or lowering of the sea floor, known megatsunamis have originated from large scale impact events such as landslides and meteor impacts.

A _____ is meant to refer to a tsunami with an initial wave amplitude measured in several tens, hundreds or possibly thousands of metres.

   a. 1509 Istanbul earthquake
   b. Megatsunami
   c. 1700 Cascadia earthquake
   d. 1703 Genroku earthquake

31. The _____ was a tsunami devastating the coasts of the Maliakos and Euboic Gulf, Greece, in the summer of 426 BC. The event led the Greek historian Thucydides to inquire into the origin of the natural phenomena, coming to the conclusion that the tsunami must have been caused by an earthquake. Thucydides thus became the first in the history of natural science to correlate quake and wave in terms of cause and effect.
   a. 426 BC Maliakos Gulf tsunami
   b. 1509 Istanbul earthquake
   c. 1703 Genroku earthquake
   d. 1700 Cascadia earthquake

32. The _____, also called the Laurentian Slope earthquake and the South Shore Disaster, was a magnitude 7.2 earthquake that occurred on November 18, 1929 in the Atlantic Ocean off the south coast of Newfoundland.

The earthquake was centered on the edge of the Grand Banks of Newfoundland, about 400 kilometres (250 mi) south of the island. It was felt as far away as New York and Montreal.

   a. 1700 Cascadia earthquake
   b. 1929 Grand Banks earthquake
   c. 1703 Genroku earthquake
   d. 1509 Istanbul earthquake

33. The _____ is an Archean stratovolcano, located 480 kilometres (298 miles) northwest of Yellowknife, Northwest Territories, Canada. The volcano constitutes the Back Group of the Yellowknife Supergroup and is somewhat anomalous in the Slave craton because it has undergone only a low degree of deformation and is subhorizontal. The southern half of the complex is exposed at the crest of a small dome.

- a. 1509 Istanbul earthquake
- b. 1700 Cascadia earthquake
- c. 1703 Genroku earthquake
- d. Back River volcanic complex

34. _____ is an extinct volcano in the Virunga Mountains of the Great Rift Valley. It straddles the border of Rwanda and the Democratic Republic of the Congo, but the summit is located in Rwanda. It is located approximately 35 km northeast of the town of Goma and adjacent Lake Kivu

_____, like all of the peaks in the Virunga Mountain Range, is a volcano created by rift action on the forming divergent boundary which is slowly bisecting the African plate

- a. 1509 Istanbul earthquake
- b. 1700 Cascadia earthquake
- c. 1703 Genroku earthquake
- d. Mount Bisoke

35. _____ is an extinct volcano in the Cascade Volcanic Arc in Washington, United States. Glacially eroded remnants of this volcano rise above the Deming Glacier, part of the glacier system of Mount Baker.

The volcano was last active between 500,000 and 300,000 years ago..Mount Baker, a much younger volcano, sits on top of lava erupted from _____ Volcano.

- a. 1509 Istanbul earthquake
- b. 1700 Cascadia earthquake
- c. Black Buttes
- d. 1703 Genroku earthquake

36. _____ is a remarkably abrupt pinnacle of volcanic rock located in Garibaldi Provincial Park of British Columbia, Canada. At 2,319 m (7,608 ft) above sea level, the upper spire is visible from a great distance in all directions. It is particularly noticeable from the Sea-to-Sky Highway just south of Whistler, British Columbia.

_____ is considered to be the remnant of an extinct andesitic stratovolcano which formed between about 1.3 and 1.1 million years ago. Following glacial dissection, renewed volcanism produced the lava dome and flow forming its summit about 170,000 years ago. According to Natural Resources Canada, _____ was 'perhaps the conduit for lava within a cinder-rich volcano. The loose cinder has eroded, leaving only the hard lava core.' The exposed lava rock of the core is loose and friable.

- a. Broken Top
- b. Mount Overlord
- c. 1509 Istanbul earthquake
- d. Black Tusk

37. In machining, _____ is the process of enlarging a hole that has already been drilled (or cast), by means of a single-point cutting tool (or of a _____ head containing several such tools), for example as in _____ a cannon barrel. _____ is used to achieve greater accuracy of the diameter of a hole, and can be used to cut a tapered hole.

The term _____ is also sometimes used for drilling a hole, especially with respect to tunnels and wells in the earth.

Chapter 6. Test Preparation Part 6

a. 1700 Cascadia earthquake
c. 1509 Istanbul earthquake

b. 1703 Genroku earthquake
d. Boring

38. The _____ is an extinct Plio-Pleistocene volcanic zone with at least 32 cinder cones and small shield volcanoes lying within a radius of 13 miles (21 km) of Kelly Butte, which is approximately 4 miles (6 km) east of downtown Portland, Oregon, in the United States. The zone became active at least 2.7 million years ago, and has been extinct for about 300,000 years.

The Portland metropolitan area, including suburbs, is one of the few places in the continental United States to have extinct volcanoes within a city's limits; Bend, Oregon is another.

a. 1509 Istanbul earthquake
c. 1703 Genroku earthquake

b. Boring Lava Field
d. 1700 Cascadia earthquake

39. _____ is a mountain located near Kelowna on the west shore of Okanagan Lake, British Columbia, Canada. It is the remnants of a former stratovolcano created nearly 60 million years ago. Between four and six different glacial periods over the past 50 million years have eroded the volcano to produce _____.

_____ is composed primarily of rhyolite and andesite, which gives the mountain its yellow, tan and pinkish colours on the north and south flanks. The more prominent black and dark gray east and north-east face is dacite.

a. 1703 Genroku earthquake
c. 1509 Istanbul earthquake

b. 1700 Cascadia earthquake
d. Mount Boucherie

40. _____ is an extinct stratovolcano in Oregon state which has been highly eroded by glaciation. It is located south of the Three Sisters group of volcanoes in the Cascade Range of central Oregon and within the Three Sisters Wilderness. _____ is about 20 miles (32 km) west of Bend, Oregon in Deschutes County.

Pleistocene eruptions originally created a broad shield of basaltic andesite. Intermittently, more silicic magma was erupted, ranging from andesite to dacite to rhyodacite. Intrusive dikes and pyroclastic flow deposits can also be found in the layers of _____'s flanks. Ice Age glaciers have carved into the volcano on three sides, exposing its internal structure.

a. Mount Overlord
c. 1509 Istanbul earthquake

b. Nevado Sajama
d. Broken Top

41. The _____ is located in present-day southwest Idaho. The volcano erupted during the Miocene, between ten and twelve million years ago, spreading a thick blanket of ash in the Bruneau-Jarbidge event and forming a caldera. Animals were suffocated and burned in pyroclastic flows within a hundred miles of the event, and died of slow suffocation and starvation much farther away, notably at Ashfall Fossil Beds, located 1000 miles downwind in northeastern Nebraska, where a foot of ash was deposited.

a. 1700 Cascadia earthquake
c. Bruneau-Jarbidge caldera

b. 1703 Genroku earthquake
d. 1509 Istanbul earthquake

42. A _____ is a cauldron-like volcanic feature usually formed by the collapse of land following a volcanic eruption such as the one at Yellowstone National Park. They are sometimes confused with volcanic craters.
   a. Caldera
   b. 1703 Genroku earthquake
   c. 1509 Istanbul earthquake
   d. 1700 Cascadia earthquake

43. _____ is a hill overlooking Ballarat in Victoria, Australia. Formed from an extinct volcano, it rises to 719 metres (2451 ft) above sea level. The mountain was originally named Mt. Bonan Yowing. It and nearby Mount Warrenheip are the only two forested volcanic cones in Victoria.
   a. 1700 Cascadia earthquake
   b. 1509 Istanbul earthquake
   c. 1703 Genroku earthquake
   d. Mount Buninyong

44. _____, located in Northeastern New Mexico, was designated a U.S. National Monument on August 9, 1916. It is an example of an extinct cinder cone volcano that is part of the Raton-Clayton Volcanic Field.

_____ is a well-preserved, relatively young (58,000 to 62,000 years old), symmetrical cinder cone. It rises steeply from the surrounding grassland plains to an elevation of 8,182 feet above sea level. The irregular rim of the crater is about a mile in circumference and the crater about 400 feet deep.

   a. 1703 Genroku earthquake
   b. 1509 Istanbul earthquake
   c. Capulin Volcano National Monument
   d. 1700 Cascadia earthquake

45. A _____ is an opening in a planet's surface or crust, which allows hot, molten rock, ash, and gases to escape from below the surface. Volcanic activity involving the extrusion of rock tends to form mountains or features like mountains over a period of time.
   a. 1700 Cascadia earthquake
   b. 1509 Istanbul earthquake
   c. Volcano
   d. 1703 Genroku earthquake

46. _____ is a stratovolcano in southwestern British Columbia, Canada, located 22 km (14 mi) of Tulameen and 29 km (18 mi) north of Snass Mountain. It is the highest point in the Bedded Range.

_____ is a major preserved feature in the Miocene age Pemberton Volcanic Belt that was erupting about 21 to 22 million years ago.

   a. 1700 Cascadia earthquake
   b. Coquihalla Mountain
   c. 1703 Genroku earthquake
   d. 1509 Istanbul earthquake

47. The Corner Rise Seamounts are a chain of extinct submarine volcanoes in the northern Atlantic Ocean east of the New England Seamount chain.

Seamounts within the _____ chain include:

- Bean Seamount
- Caloosahatchee Seamount
- Corner Seamount
- Goode Peak
- Kukenthal Peak
- MacGregor Seamount
- Milne-Edwards Peak
- Rockaway Seamount
- Verrill Peak
- Yakutat Seamount

a. 1703 Genroku earthquake
c. 1509 Istanbul earthquake

b. Corner Rise Seamount
d. 1700 Cascadia earthquake

48. _____ is the name of a volcanic tuff cone on the Hawaiian island of Oahu. _____ is part of the complex of cones, vents, and their associated eruption flows that are collectively known to geologists as the Honolulu Volcanic Series, eruptions from the Ko'olau Volcano that took place long after the volcano formed and had gone dormant.

a. Compaction
c. Combe

b. Diamond Head
d. Submersion

49. _____ is an extinct volcano in the Hegau region of Baden-W>ürttemberg in southern Germany. About 20 miles from Lake Constance, it lies in the German city of Singen

_____ began forming, along with the chain of volcanoes in the Hegau region, about 7-8 million years ago, when a layer of volcanic ash and stone was laid down. The magma consists of Phonolite. In the following millions of years, the core was opened 260 metres beneath the surface by the glaciers from the ice age. This formed the core that is now exposed, after the ensuing millions of years of erosion.

a. La Garita Caldera
c. 1509 Istanbul earthquake

b. 1700 Cascadia earthquake
d. Hohentwiel

50. The _____ is a name given to an extinct shield volcano in British Columbia, Canada. It is not a mountain range in the normal sense, because it was formed as a single volcano that has been eroded for the past 5 million years. It lies on the Chilcotin Plateau, located some 350 kilometers (217 mi) north-northwest of Vancouver and 30 km north of Anahim Lake.

The _____ began erupting about 5 million years ago and has grown steadily since then. Like all of the Anahim volcanoes, the _____ has its origins in the Anahim hotspot--a plume of magma rising from the Earth's mantle in central British Columbia. The hotspot remains in a fixed position, while the North American Plate drifts over it at a rate of 2 to 3.3 centimetres per year. The upwelling of the hot magma creates volcanoes, and each individual volcano erupts for a few million years before the movement of the plate carries it away from the rising magma.

a. AL 333
b. AL 129-1
c. AASHTO Soil Classification System
d. Ilgachuz Range

51. _____ is an extinct volcano located 2900 feet (884 meters) beneath the city of Jackson, Mississippi, under the Mississippi Coliseum. It is the only volcano located directly below a major population center or capital city in the United States. The volcano was discovered in 1819.
   a. 1509 Istanbul earthquake
   b. 1703 Genroku earthquake
   c. Jackson Volcano
   d. 1700 Cascadia earthquake

52. _____ is the oldest of five volcanoes that make up the island of HawaiÊ»i. It is believed to have breached sea level more than 500,000 years ago and to have last erupted 120,000 years ago. Toward the end of its shield-building stage 250,000 to 300,000 years ago, a landslide destroyed the northeast flank of the volcano, reducing its height by over 1,000 m (3,281 ft) and traveling 130 km (81 mi) across the sea floor.
   a. 1703 Genroku earthquake
   b. Kohala
   c. 1509 Istanbul earthquake
   d. 1700 Cascadia earthquake

53. _____ is a large volcanic caldera located in the San Juan volcanic field in the San Juan Mountains in southwestern Colorado, United States, to the west of the town of La Garita, Colorado. The eruption that created the _____ was, perhaps, the largest known explosive eruption in all of Earth's history.

The _____ is one of a number of calderas that formed during a massive ignimbrite flare-up in Colorado, Utah and Nevada from 40-25 million years ago, and was the site of truly enormous eruptions about 28-26 million years ago, during the Oligocene Epoch.

   a. 1700 Cascadia earthquake
   b. 1509 Istanbul earthquake
   c. Sierra Grande
   d. La Garita Caldera

54. The _____ is a mountain range and a lava-field province in New South Wales, Australia.

The _____ starts from the volcanic plateau known as the Barrington Tops and runs for about 100 km westwards, forming the northern boundary of the Hunter Valley district. Parts of the _____ form the watershed between the coastal and inland drainage of New South Wales and thus form a component of the Great Dividing Range.

   a. 1700 Cascadia earthquake
   b. 1509 Istanbul earthquake
   c. 1703 Genroku earthquake
   d. Liverpool Range

55. _____ is a very large mountain which is an extinct stratovolcano, situated at the northwest limit of Deception Plateau, 50 miles inland from the Ross Sea and just east of the head of Aviator Glacier in Victoria Land. Its assymetrial cone is on the edge of a plateau above Aviator Glacier. While most of the cone is ice-covered, _____ does have a 1.2 mile (.8 kilometer) diameter caldera.
   a. Broken Top
   b. Nevado Sajama
   c. 1509 Istanbul earthquake
   d. Mount Overlord

Chapter 6. Test Preparation Part 6   113

56. The _____ is a massive 3,069 m (10,069 ft) shield volcano on R>éunion, one of the volcanic islands in the Mascarene Archipelago in the southwestern Indian Ocean. It is considered to be the highest point in the Indian Ocean. The _____ was formed by the R>éunion hotspot and emerged from the sea about two million years ago.
   a. 1703 Genroku earthquake
   b. Piton des Neiges
   c. 1509 Istanbul earthquake
   d. 1700 Cascadia earthquake

57. The _____ is a large and wide eroded Late Devonian caldera complex, located in the northern Appalachian Mountains of southwestern New Brunswick, Canada. It is one of few noticeable pre-Cenozoic calderas, and its formation is associated to a period of crustal thinning that followed the Acadian orogeny in the northern Appalachian Mountains. It sits relatively near to the coastline.
   a. Mount Pleasant Caldera
   b. 1703 Genroku earthquake
   c. 1509 Istanbul earthquake
   d. 1700 Cascadia earthquake

58. _____ is an extinct volcanic tuff cone located in Honolulu, Hawaii. It is the location of the National Memorial Cemetery of the Pacific.

The crater was formed some 75,000 to 100,000 years ago during the Honolulu period of secondary volcanic activity. A crater resulted from the ejection of hot lava through cracks in the old coral reefs which, at the time, extended to the foot of the Koolau Mountain Range.

   a. 1700 Cascadia earthquake
   b. 1509 Istanbul earthquake
   c. 1703 Genroku earthquake
   d. Punchbowl Crater

59. _____ is a 324 m (1,063 ft) tall extinct volcano that forms the southwestern headland of Easter Island, a Chilean island in the Pacific Ocean; it was formed of basaltic lava flows in the Pleistocene with its youngest rocks dated at between 150,000 and 210,000 years ago. Rapa Nui, with _____ and the volcanoes Terevaka ' Poike. To the South are the ruins at Orongo, as well as the islets Motu Nui, Moto Kau Kau ' Motu Iti.
   a. Thirtynine Mile volcanic field
   b. 1509 Istanbul earthquake
   c. 1700 Cascadia earthquake
   d. Rano Kau

60. _____ is an extinct volcanic field located in the state of New Mexico, United States. Capulin Volcano National Monument is located in the volcanic field. It is thought to have formed by the Raton hotspot.
   a. 1703 Genroku earthquake
   b. 1509 Istanbul earthquake
   c. 1700 Cascadia earthquake
   d. Raton-Clayton volcanic field

61. _____ is an extinct stratovolcano and the highest peak in Bolivia. The mountain is located in Sajama National Park in the southwest area of the country some 16-24 km (10-15 mi) from the border with Chile. The peak is an isolated cone, but is geologically complex, with lava domes of andesitic and rhyodactic composition overlain by an andesitic stratovolcano. The date of the most recent eruption is uncertain, although Holocene activity is assigned to the volcano by many. Some of the highest growing trees in the world are found on the volcano, where Polylepis tarapacana have been found growing up to 5200m.
   a. Mount Overlord
   b. Nevado Sajama
   c. Broken Top
   d. 1509 Istanbul earthquake

62. _____ is the highest volcano in Antarctica, a member of the Volcanic Seven Summits. It is a massive, mainly snow-covered shield volcano which is the highest and most imposing of the five extinct volcanic mountains that comprise the Executive Committee Range of Marie Byrd Land. The feature is marked by a spectacular 5 km wide caldera on the southern side and stands NE of Mount Waesche in the southern part of the range.

- a. 1509 Istanbul earthquake
- b. 1700 Cascadia earthquake
- c. 1703 Genroku earthquake
- d. Mount Sidley

63. _____ is a range of volcanic mountains in Lincoln and Otero counties of south-central New Mexico. The range is about 40 miles from north to south and 20 miles wide, and is dominated by _____ Peak, whose highest point is at 12,005 feet The peak is located 10 miles west-northwest of Ruidoso and 30 miles north-northeast of Alamogordo.

_____ is a massive complex of volcanic rocks including pyroclastic materials, lava flows, and intrusions. An ancient and heavily eroded volcanic pile, it is the largest mid-Tertiary volcanic complex east of the Rio Grande with an estimated volume of erupted products of 185 cubic miles (770 km^3).

- a. 1703 Genroku earthquake
- b. 1509 Istanbul earthquake
- c. Sierra Blanca
- d. 1700 Cascadia earthquake

Chapter 7. Test Preparation Part 7

1. _____ is an extinct shield volcano in northeastern New Mexico that rises 2,200 feet above the surrounding plain. It is part of the inactive Raton-Clayton volcanic field.

U.S. Highway 64 and U.S. Highway 87 run along the north and east of the volcano with the town of Des Moines just to the northeast.

a. 1700 Cascadia earthquake
b. La Garita Caldera
c. 1509 Istanbul earthquake
d. Sierra Grande

2. _____ is an extinct volcano in the southwestern Cascade Mountains in the U.S. state of Washington Washington. In September 1902 _____ was the center of the Yacolt Burn, the largest fire in Washington history, which took 38 lives and burned over 238,000 acres (963 km^2) The smoke was so thick that street lights glowed at noon in Seattle 160 miles (260 km) away.

With the loss of vegetative ground cover, a series of rockslides occurred on the slopes of _____ and neighboring uplands that were also affected by the fire.

a. 1700 Cascadia earthquake
b. 1509 Istanbul earthquake
c. Silver Star Mountain
d. 1703 Genroku earthquake

3. A _____ is a cauldron-like volcanic feature usually formed by the collapse of land following a volcanic eruption such as the one at Yellowstone National Park. They are sometimes confused with volcanic craters.
a. 1700 Cascadia earthquake
b. 1509 Istanbul earthquake
c. 1703 Genroku earthquake
d. Caldera

4. _____ is a large extinct caldera complex in Kenora District of Northwestern Ontario, Canada. It is one the world's best preserved mineralized Neoarchean caldera complexes, containing well-preserved mafic-intermediate pillow lavas, pillow breccias, hyaloclastite and peperites, submarine lava domes and dome-associated breccia deposits. The complex is some 2.7 billion years old with a minimum strike length of 30 km (19 mi).
a. 1703 Genroku earthquake
b. 1509 Istanbul earthquake
c. 1700 Cascadia earthquake
d. Sturgeon Lake Caldera

5. The _____ are a small circular complex of eroded volcanic lava domes which rise above the flat plains of the Central Valley of California in the United States. The highest peak, South Butte, reaches about 2,130 feet above sea level. The Buttes are located just outside of Yuba City, California in the Sacramento Valley, the northern part of the Central Valley.

The _____ were formed over 1.5 million years ago by a now-extinct volcano. Some geological references suggested that it represents the southernmost of the Cascade Volcanoes, but there are significant differences in age and form compared to the other volcanoes in that range. The questions about their origin and connection to other regional volcanic activity are the subject of ongoing research.

a. 1509 Istanbul earthquake
b. 1703 Genroku earthquake
c. 1700 Cascadia earthquake
d. Sutter Buttes

6. The _____ is an extinct volcanic field located in Park and Teller counties, Colorado, northwest of Cripple Creek and southeast of South Park. The area was the site of significant volcanism in the Tertiary Period about 35 million years ago. Ashfall and lahars (mudflows) from the volcanoes created the conditions for fossilization at what is now Florissant Fossil Beds National Monument.
   a. 1700 Cascadia earthquake
   b. Rano Kau
   c. 1509 Istanbul earthquake
   d. Thirtynine Mile volcanic field

7. _____ is a Pleistocene volcano in the Cascade Range of Oregon. It is a deeply glaciated shield volcano and consists mainly of basaltic andesite lava.
   a. Three Fingered Jack
   b. 1509 Istanbul earthquake
   c. 1703 Genroku earthquake
   d. 1700 Cascadia earthquake

8. The _____ are a group of low mountains in central Germany, located in the middle of the state of Hesse. They are the product of ancient volcanic activity and are separated from the Rh>ön Mountains by the Fulda River and its valley. Bismarck tower on the Taufstein

Arising approximately 19 million years ago, the Vogelsberg, Germany's only shield volcano, is also Central Europe's largest basalt formation, consisting of a multitude of layers which, having flowed over each other, fall downward from their peak in ring-shaped terraces to the base.

   a. 1703 Genroku earthquake
   b. 1700 Cascadia earthquake
   c. 1509 Istanbul earthquake
   d. Vogelsberg Mountains

9. The _____ was the extension of the River Rhine and other rivers into what is now the English Channel during periods of low sea level during the ice ages. .
   a. Channel River
   b. 1703 Genroku earthquake
   c. 1509 Istanbul earthquake
   d. 1700 Cascadia earthquake

10. The name _____, derived from the ancient Greek _____, was given by geologists to a river which flowed where the Baltic Sea is now (Overeem, et al., 2002.) The fluvial system was better known as the 'Baltic River System' (Bijlsma, 1981; Gibbard, 1988.)

The _____ began about 40 million years ago in the Eocene. About 12 million years ago in the Miocene the _____ reached the North Sea area, where it began to build an immense delta with its sediment. The _____ disappeared in the early Middle Pleistocene.

   a. Eridanos
   b. AASHTO Soil Classification System
   c. AL 333
   d. AL 129-1

11. _____ or River Warren was a prehistoric river that drained Lake Agassiz in central North America between 11,700 and 9,400 years ago. The enormous outflow from this lake carved a mighty valley now occupied by the much-smaller Minnesota River and the Upper Mississippi River.

Lake Agassiz was formed from the meltwaters of the Laurentide Ice Sheet during the Wisconsinan glaciation of the last ice age.

Chapter 7. Test Preparation Part 7

    a. 1700 Cascadia earthquake
    c. 1509 Istanbul earthquake
    b. 1703 Genroku earthquake
    d. Glacial River Warren

12. The _____ is the term used for the pre-glacial river that began the creation of the valley in Silurian age shales and limestones now occupied by Lake Ontario. The valley was greatly deepened by glacial action during the Ice age.

The original flow is thought to have been westward beginning from the Laurentian shield in the present area of the St. Lawrence River to eventually join the Mississippi River drainage system.

    a. AASHTO Soil Classification System
    c. AL 129-1
    b. AL 333
    d. Ontarian River

13. The _____ is a chronologic schema (or idealized model) relating stratigraphy to time that is used by geologists, paleontologists and other earth scientists to describe the timing and relationships between events that have occurred during the history of the Earth. The table of geologic time spans presented here agrees with the dates and nomenclature proposed by the International Commission on Stratigraphy, and uses the standard color codes of the United States Geological Survey.

Evidence from radiometric dating indicates that the Earth is about 4.570 billion years old.

    a. 1703 Genroku earthquake
    c. 1509 Istanbul earthquake
    b. 1700 Cascadia earthquake
    d. Geologic time scale

14. The _____ is a subdivision of the Middle Jurassic epoch of the geologic timescale that extends from about 175.6 Ma to about 171.6 Ma . It was preceded by the Toarcian era and succeeded by the Bajocian.
    a. AL 129-1
    c. Aalenian
    b. AASHTO Soil Classification System
    d. AL 333

15. _____ is a stage of the Cretaceous period.

_____ is a term proposed in 1842 by A. d'Orbigny for that stage of the Cretaceous system which comes above the Aptian and below (before) the Cenomanian (Pal. France. Cret. ii.). Approximate time range is 112.0 ± 1.0 Ma to 99.6 ± 0.9 Ma (million years ago).

    a. AASHTO Soil Classification System
    c. Aptian
    b. AL 129-1
    d. Albian

16. In the geologic timescale, the _____ is the lower age of the Middle Triassic epoch and lasted from 245 million years ago until 237 million years ago, approximately. The _____ age succeeds the Olenekian age of the Lower Triassic epoch and precedes the Ladinian age of the Middle Triassic epoch.

The earliest potential dinosaur fossil to date is a partial pubis from _____-age rocks of the Moenkopi Formation, Arizona.

    a. Olenekian
    c. Anisian
    b. AASHTO Soil Classification System
    d. Induan

17. _____ stage is a faunal stage of the Early Cretaceous epoch in the geologic timescale, that extends from 125.0 >± 1.0 Ma to 112.0 >± 1.0 Ma (million years ago), approximately. The _____ stage succeeds the Barremian stage and precedes the Albian stage, all in the same epoch.

- Pictetia
- Eogaudryceras
- Georgioceras
- Lithancylus
- Salfeldiella
- Zuercherella

- Eotetragonites
- Pseudosaynella
- Roloboceras
- Helicancylus
- Procheloniceras
- Prodeshayesites
- Shastoceras
- Ammonitoceras
- Australiceras
- Cheloniceras
- Cicatrites
- Colombiceras
- Dufrenoya
- Melchiorites
- Parahoplites

Tropaeum imperator

- Hypacanthoplites
- Sinzovia
- Trochleiceras
- Mathoceratites
- Metahamites
- Neosilesites
- Protanisoceras
- Ammonoceratites
- Beudanticeras
- Gyaloceras
- Hulenites
- Knemiceras
- Uhligella
- Acanthohoplites
- Acanthoplites
- Argonauticeras
- Burckhardites
- Cloioceras
- Diadochoceras
- Diodochoceras
- Eodouvilleiceras
- Epancyloceras
- Epicheloniceras

- Gargasiceras
- Jauberticeras
- Kazanskyella
- Mathoceras
- Megatyloceras
- Miyakoceras
- Nodosohoplites
- Nolaniceras
- Protacanthoplites
- Somalites
- Theganoceras
- Tropaeum
- Gabbioceras
- Tetragonites
- Desmoceras
- Hamites

- Vectibelus
- Conoteuthis

- Tetrabelus
- Peratobelus
- Parahibolites

- Heminautilus
- Carinonautilus

- Zhuralevia

- Euphylloceras

- Adygeya
- Naefia

- Boluochia zhengi
- Chaoyangia beishanensis
- Confuciusornis sanctus
- Cuspirostrisornis houi
- Jeholornis prima
- Jixiangornis orientalis
- Largirostrornis sexdentoris
- Longchengornis sanyanensis
- Longipteryx chaoyangensis
- Sapeornis chaoyangensis
- Sinornis santensis/Cathayornis yandica
- Songlingornis linghensis
- Yanornis martini
- Yixianornis grabaui

- Sarcosuchus

- Hybodus
- Jinanichthys longicephalus
- Lycoptera davidi
- Lycoptera muroii
- Peipiaosteus pani

- Protosephurus liui
- Sinamia zdanskyi

- Anhanguera
- Araripedactylus dehmi
- Araripesaurus castilhoi
- Arthurdactylus conandoylei
- Boreopterus cuiae
- Brasileodactylus araripensis
- Cearadactylus atrox
- Chaoyangopterus zhangi
- Dsungaripterus weii
- Dsungaripterus brancai
- Eoazhdarcho liaoxiensis
- Eopteranodon lii
- Gegepterus changi
- Haopterus gracilis
- Hongshanopterus lacustris
- Huaxiapterus benxiensis
- Huaxiapterus corollatus
- Huaxiapterus jii
- Istiodactylus latidens
- Istiodactylus sinensis
- Jidapterus edentus
- Liaoningopterus gui
- Liaoxipterus brachyognathus
- Lonchodectes
- Longchengpterus zhaoi
- Ludodactylus sibbicki
- Nemicolopterus crypticus
- Nurhachius ignaciobritoi
- Ornithocheirus simus
- Ornithocheirus mesembrinus
- Pricesaurus megalodon
- Santanadactylus
- Sinopterus dongi
- Sinopterus gui
- Tapejara navigans
- Tapejara wellnhoferi
- Thalassodromeus sethi
- Tropeognathus mesembrinus
- Tropeognathus robustus
- Tupandactylus imperator

Antlers Formation, Cedar Mountain Formation, Cloverly Formation, Elrhaz Formation, Jiufotang Formation, Little Atherfield, Mazong Shan, Potomac Formation, Santana Formation, Twin Mountains Formation, Xinminbao Group, Yixian Formation

a. AASHTO Soil Classification System
c. Early Cretaceous

b. AL 129-1
d. Aptian

18. _____ is the first age of the Miocene Epoch. It spans the time between 23.03 ± 0.05 Ma and 20.43 ± 0.05 Ma (million years ago.) The _____ Stage succeeds the Chattian age of the Oligocene Epoch and precedes the Burdigalian Stage.

a. AL 129-1
c. Early Miocene

b. AASHTO Soil Classification System
d. Aquitanian

19. The _____, is a geologic eon before the Proterozoic and Paleoproterozoic, before 2.5 Ga (billion years ago, or 2,500 Ma.) Instead of being based on stratigraphy, this date is defined chronometrically. The lower boundary (starting point) has not been officially recognized by the International Commission on Stratigraphy, but it is usually set to 3.8 Ga, at the end of the Hadean eon.

a. AL 333
c. AASHTO Soil Classification System

b. Archean
d. AL 129-1

20. The _____ establishes a geologic timescale for prehistoric Asian fauna beginning 58.7 Mya during the Paleogene and continuing through to the Middle Pleistocene (0.33 Ma.) These periods are referred to as ages, stages, or intervals and were established using geographic place names where fossil materials where obtained.

The basic unit of measure is the first/last boundary statement.

a. AL 129-1
c. AL 333

b. AASHTO Soil Classification System
d. Asian land mammal ages

21. _____ Age, _____ Age, _____ Era, _____ Period and _____ Eon were terms used before 1950 to describe the age of rocks formed before the appearance of life in the geologic sequence. The word '_____' is derived from the Greek a- meaning without and zoön meaning animal , it was first used to mean without life.

_____ was used as early as 1846 by a geologist named Adams, and gradually replaced the earlier term Primitive. Due to the controversy over evolution, '_____' was replaced, by 1900, in most usages by the term 'Archaean' or 'Archaeozic'.

a. AL 129-1
c. AL 333

b. AASHTO Soil Classification System
d. Azoic

22. In the geologic timescale, the _____ is an age of the Middle Jurassic epoch of the Jurassic period of the Mesozoic era of the Phanerozoic eon. It lasted from approximately 171.6 Ma to around 167.7 Ma (million years ago.) The _____ age succeeds the Aalenian age and precedes the Bathonian age, all in the same epoch.

a. La Voulte-sur-Rhone
   b. Bathonian
   c. Toarcian
   d. Bajocian

23. The _____ faunal stage was a period of geological time between 130.0 ± 1.5 mya (million years ago) and 125.0 ± 1.0 mya.) It is considered to be of the Early Cretaceous epoch, in which it constituted the earliest part of the obsolete Gallic (according to some classifications the Urgonian) epoch. It is preceded by the Hauterivian and followed by the Aptian stage.
   a. Valanginian
   b. Berriasian
   c. Hauterivian
   d. Barremian

24. The _____ (also known as the Auversian) is a stage of the middle Eocene Epoch. It spans the time between 40.4 ± 0.2 Ma and 37.2 ± 0.2 Ma
   a. Ypresian
   b. Bartonian
   c. 1509 Istanbul earthquake
   d. Lutetian

25. _____ refers to 9 informal subdivisions of the lunar Pre-Nectarian geologic period.

The motivation for creating the _____ subdivisions was to place 30 pre-Nectarian impact basins into 9 relative age groups. The relative age of the first basin in each group is based on crater densities and superposition relationships, whereas the other basins are included based on weaker grounds.

   a. Stenian
   b. Siderian
   c. Calymmian
   d. Basin Groups

26. In the geologic timescale the _____ epoch is a stage during the Middle Jurassic, of the Mesozoic era of the Phanerozoic eon. It lasted from approximately 167.7 Ma to around 164.7 Ma (million years ago.) The _____ age succeeds the Bajocian age and precedes the Callovian age.
   a. La Voulte-sur-Rhone
   b. Toarcian
   c. Hettangian
   d. Bathonian

27. In the geologic timescale, _____ is a stage of the Early Cretaceous epoch, and the first of the entire Cretaceous period. It spanned between 145.5 >± 4.0 Ma and 140.2 >± 3.0 Ma (million years ago.) The _____ stage succeeds the Tithonian stage of the Late Jurassic epoch and precedes the Valanginian stage of the Early Cretaceous epoch.
   a. Santonian
   b. Campanian
   c. Hauterivian
   d. Berriasian

28. The _____ is the first geologic period in the Mesoproterozoic Era and lasted from 1600 Ma to 1400 Ma (million years ago.) Instead of being based on stratigraphy, these dates are defined chronometrically.

The period is characterised by expansion of existing platform covers, or by new platforms on recently cratonized basements.

   a. Marine Isotopic Stage 11
   b. Cryptic era
   c. Mesoarchean
   d. Calymmian

29. The _____ age is the first or earliest or oldest Geochronological 'geologic age' of the Late Cretaceous Epoch. Like all geological time units the _____ age is associated with a Chronostratigraphic stratum or 'geologic stage' of the same name, the '_____ stage' Each belong to the Cretaceous period and Cretaceous system as well.
   a. Geologic record
   b. Global Standard Stratigraphic Age
   c. Chronozone
   d. Cenomanian

30. The _____ Era, is the most recent of the three classic geological eras and covers the period from 65.5 million years ago to the present. It is marked by the Cretaceous-Tertiary extinction event at the end of the Cretaceous that saw the demise of the last non-avian dinosaurs and the end of the Mesozoic Era. The _____ era is ongoing.
   a. 1700 Cascadia earthquake
   b. 1509 Istanbul earthquake
   c. 1703 Genroku earthquake
   d. Cenozoic

31. _____ is the branch of stratigraphy that studies the age of rock strata in relation to time.

The ultimate aim of _____ is to arrange the sequence of deposition and the time of deposition of all rocks within a geological region, and eventually, the entire geologic record of the Earth.

The standard stratigraphic nomenclature is a chronostratigraphic system based on palaeontological intervals of time defined by recognised fossil assemblages (biostratigraphy.)

   a. Global Standard Stratigraphic Age
   b. Geologic record
   c. Paleomagnetism
   d. Chronostratigraphy

32. A _____ or chron is a slice of time that begins at a given identifiable event and ends at another. In the fossil record such tracer events are usually keyed to disappearance (extinction) of a widely distributed and rapidly changing species or the appearance of such a species in the geological record. They are used especially in the various disciplines related to Geology, notably in stratigraphy where relative dating is employed.
   a. Relative dating
   b. Chronozone
   c. Geologic record
   d. Law of superposition

33. The _____ is an informal term that refers to the earliest geologic evolution of the Earth and Moon. It is the oldest era of the (informal) Hadean eon, and it is commonly accepted to have begun close to 4567.17 million (about 4.6 billion) years ago when the Earth and Moon formed. No samples exist to date the transition between the _____ and the following Basin Groups era for the Moon, though sometimes it is stated that this era ended 4150 million years ago for one or both of these bodies.
   a. Mesoarchean
   b. Permo-Carboniferous
   c. Marine isotope stages
   d. Cryptic era

34. In the geologic record the _____ erathem and the _____ era in the geologic timescale correspond to one another in the dual system of classification of rock strata laid down beginning 4000 Ma to 3600 Ma (million years ago.)

It was formerly officially unnamed and usually referred to as the first part of the Early Archean (now an obsolescent name) together with the later Paleoarchean era. It is the first part of the Archaean Eon, preceded by the 'informal' Hadean eon, during which the Earth was considered to be essentially molten.

a. AASHTO Soil Classification System
b. AL 129-1
c. AL 333
d. Eoarchean

35. The '_____' is a term usually defined as Earth's first billion years, or gigayear. On the geologic time scale, the '_____' comprises all of the Hadean eon (itself unofficially defined), as well as the Eoarchean and part of the Paleoarchean eras of the Archean eon.

This period of Earth's history, being its earliest, involved the planet's condensation from a solar nebula and accretion from meteorites, as well as the formation of the earliest atmosphere and hydrosphere.

a. AL 129-1
b. AASHTO Soil Classification System
c. Early Earth
d. AL 333

36. The _____ is the second geologic period in the Mesoproterozoic era and lasted from 1400 Ma ago to 1200 Ma (million years ago.) Instead of being based on stratigraphy, these dates are defined chronometrically.

Evidence of a eukaryotic red algae, Bangiomorpha pubescens, has been identified from ca. 1200 Ma old rocks in the Hunting Formation (Somerset Island, Canada).

a. AL 333
b. AASHTO Soil Classification System
c. Ectasian
d. AL 129-1

37. The _____ Period is the last geological period of the Neoproterozoic Era and of the Proterozoic Eon, immediately preceding the Cambrian Period, the first period of the Paleozoic Era and of the Phanerozoic Eon. Its status as an official geological period was ratified in 2004 by the International Union of Geological Sciences (IUGS), making it the first new geological period declared in 120 years. The type section is in the Flinders Ranges in South Australia.

a. AASHTO Soil Classification System
b. AL 333
c. AL 129-1
d. Ediacaran

38. In stratigraphy and geology, an _____ is the totality of rock strata laid down in the stratigraphic record deposited during a certain eon of the continuous geologic timescale. The _____ is not to be confused with the eon itself, which is a corresponding division of geologic time spanning a specific amount of (millions of) years, during which rocks were formed that are classified within the _____.

a. AL 129-1
b. AASHTO Soil Classification System
c. AL 333
d. Eonothem

39. In stratigraphy, paleontology, geology, and geobiology an _____ is the total stratigraphic record deposited during a certain corresponding span of time, an era in the geologic timescale.

It can therefore be used as a chronostratigraphic unit of time which delineates a large span of years -- less than an geological eon, but greater than its successively smaller and more refined subdivisions (geologic periods, epochs, and geologic ages.) By 3,500 Million years ago (Mya) simple life had developed on earth (the oldest known microbial fossils in Australia are dated to this figure.

Chapter 7. Test Preparation Part 7

a. AASHTO Soil Classification System
c. AL 129-1
b. AL 333
d. Erathem

40. The _____ establishes a geologic timescale for prehistoric European fauna beginning 66.5 Ma during the Paleogene and continuing through to the Middle Pleistocene (0.33 Ma.) These periods are referred to as ages, stages, or intervals and were established using geographic place names where fossil materials where obtained.

The basic unit of measure is the first/last boundary statement.

a. AL 129-1
c. AASHTO Soil Classification System
b. AL 333
d. European Land Mammal Ages

41. The _____ in stratigraphy, Chronostratigraphy, paleontology and other natural sciences refers to the entirety of the layers of rock strata -- depositions laid down in volcanism or by weathering detritus (clays, sands etc.) including all its fossil content and the information it yields about the history of the Earth: its past climate, geography, geology and the evolution of life on its surface. According to the Law of Superposition (first proposed in the mid-seventeenth century by the Danish naturalist Nicolas Steno) sedimentary and volcanic rocklayers are deposited on top of each other.
  a. Global Boundary Stratotype Section and Point
  c. Law of superposition
  b. Global Standard Stratigraphic Age
  d. Geologic record

42. The term _____ refers to large geologic time intervals. Geologists traditionally subdivide Earth history into a hierarchy of named intervals: eons, eras, periods, etc. (e.g. Jurassic Period of the Mesozoic Era.)
  a. Cryptic era
  c. Neoarchean
  b. Geon
  d. Permo-Carboniferous

43. A _____, is an internationally agreed upon stratigraphic section which serves as the reference section for a particular boundary on the geologic time scale. The effort to define GSSPs is conducted by the International Commission on Stratigraphy, a part of the International Union of Geological Sciences. Most, but not all, GSSPs are based on paleontological changes.
  a. Paleomagnetism
  c. Chronostratigraphy
  b. Chronozone
  d. Global Boundary Stratotype Section and Point

44. In the Stratigraphy sub-discipline of Geology, a _____, is a chronological reference point and criteria in the world's rock records used to define the boundaries (a internationally sanctioned benchmark point) between different geological periods, epochs or ages on the overall geologic time scale in a chronostratigraphically useful rock layer. A world wide multidisciplinary effort has been ongoing since 1974 to define such important metrics. But such work goes slowly despite a lot of effort, as one criteria is such points and strata need be widespread and contain a identifiable sequence of layers or other unambiguous marker (identifiable or quantifiable) attributes.
  a. Global Standard Stratigraphic Age
  c. Geologic record
  b. Relative dating
  d. Paleomagnetism

45. The _____ is the geologic eon before the Archean. It started at Earth's formation about 4.6 billion years ago (4,600 Ma), and ended roughly 3.8 billion years ago, though the latter date varies according to different sources.
  a. 1703 Genroku earthquake
  c. 1509 Istanbul earthquake
  b. 1700 Cascadia earthquake
  d. Hadean

46. The _____ is the first stage of the Early Triassic epoch. It spans the time between 251 ± 0.4 Ma and 249.7 ± 0.7 Ma This stage follows the mass extinction event of the late Permian period.
   a. AASHTO Soil Classification System
   b. Olenekian
   c. Early Triassic
   d. Induan

47.

Interglacial periods that occurred during Pleistocene times have been recently put under investigation, in order to better understand our present and future climates. In fact, paleoclimatic interpretations often depends on observations drawn from the study of modern/historical processes. In order to better estimate the 'e;natural range'e; of climatically important mechanisms, it seems crucial to attempt detailed comparisons of the present interglacial (i.e., the Holocene) with previous warm periods of the Quaternary, such as _____

   a. Permo-Carboniferous
   b. Siderian
   c. Marine isotope stages
   d. Marine Isotopic Stage 11

48. In chronostratigraphy, a _____ is a succession of rock strata laid down in an single age on the geologic timescale, which usually represents millions of years of deposition. A given _____ of rock and the corresponding age of time will by convention have the same name, and the same boundaries.
   a. Global Standard Stratigraphic Age
   b. Chronozone
   c. Paleomagnetism
   d. Stage

49. The _____ is a geologic era within the Archean, spanning 3200 Mya to 2800 Mya (million years ago.) The period is defined chronometrically and is not referenced to a specific level in a rock section on Earth. Fossils from Australia show that stromatolites have lived on Earth since the _____.
   a. Siderian
   b. Mesoarchean
   c. Tonian
   d. Marine isotope stages

50. The _____ Era is a geologic era that occurred between 1600 Ma and 1000 Ma (million years ago.)

The major events of this era are the formation of the Rodinia supercontinent, the breakup of the Columbia supercontinent, and the evolution of sexual reproduction.

   a. 1700 Cascadia earthquake
   b. 1509 Istanbul earthquake
   c. 1703 Genroku earthquake
   d. Mesoproterozoic

51. The _____ is a geologic era within the Archaean. It spans the period of time from 2,800 to 2,500 million years ago-- the period being defined chronometrically and not referenced to a specific level in a rock section on Earth. Oxygenic photosynthesis first evolved in this era and was accountable for the oxygen catastrophe which was to happen later in the paleoproterozoic from a poisonous buildup of oxygen in the atmosphere, produced by these oxygen producing photoautotrophs, which evolved earlier in the _____.
   a. Cryptic era
   b. Geon
   c. Neoarchean
   d. Stenian

Chapter 7. Test Preparation Part 7

52. The _____ establishes a geologic timescale for prehistoric North American fauna beginning 66.5 Ma during the Paleocene and continuing through to the Middle Pleistocene (0.33 Ma.) These periods are referred to as ages, stages, or intervals and were established using geographic place names where fossil materials where obtained.

The North American Land-Mammal Age system was formalized in 1941 as a series of provincial land-mammal ages.

   a. 1700 Cascadia earthquake
   b. South American Mammal Ages
   c. 1509 Istanbul earthquake
   d. North American Mammal Ages

53. The _____ is the third geologic period in the Paleoproterozoic Era and lasted from 2050 Ma to 1800 Ma (million years ago.) Instead of being based on stratigraphy, these dates are defined chronometrically.

Latter half of the period was an episode of intensive orogeny on virtually all continents.

   a. AL 129-1
   b. Orosirian
   c. AL 333
   d. AASHTO Soil Classification System

54. The _____ is a geologic era within the Archaean. It spans the period of time 3600 Ma to 3200 Ma (million years ago)--the period being defined chronometrically and not referenced to a specific level in a rock section on Earth. The oldest ascertained life form (Well-preserved bacteria older than 3.46 billion years found in Western Australia) is from this era.
   a. Geon
   b. Marine Isotopic Stage 11
   c. Neoarchean
   d. Paleoarchean

55. The _____ is a geologic period and system that began 65.5 ± 0.3 and ended 23.03 ± 0.05 million years ago and comprises the first part of the Cenozoic era. Lasting 42 million years, the _____ is most notable as being the time in which mammals evolved from relatively small, simple forms into a plethora of diverse animals in the wake of the mass extinction that ended the preceding Cretaceous Period. Some of these mammals would evolve into large forms that would dominate the land, while others would become capable of living in marine, specialized terrestrial and even airborne environments.
   a. Gashatan
   b. Mustersan
   c. Hsandagolian
   d. Paleogene

56. The _____ is the first of the three sub-divisions of the Proterozoic occurring between >1,600 to 2,500 million years ago. This is when the continents first stabilized. This is also when Cyanobacteria evolved, a type of bacteria which uses the biochemical process of photosynthesis to produce energy and oxygen.

During this era the earliest surviving mountain belt appears, in the Wopmay Fault Zone of Canada (West of Hudson Bay, 2100-1800 million years ago).

   a. Paleoproterozoic
   b. 1703 Genroku earthquake
   c. 1700 Cascadia earthquake
   d. 1509 Istanbul earthquake

57. The _____ refers to the time period including the latter parts of the Carboniferous and early part of the Permian period. _____ rocks are in places not differentiated because of the presence of transitional fossils, and also where no conspicuous stratigraphic break is present.

_____ time, about 300 million years ago, was a period of great glaciation. The widespread distribution of _____ glacial sediments in South America, Africa, Madagascar, Arabia, India, Antarctica and Australia was one of the major pieces of evidence for the theory of continental drift, and led ultimately to the concept of a supercontinent, Pangea.

- a. Marine Isotopic Stage 11
- b. Neoarchean
- c. Permo-Carboniferous
- d. Siderian

58. The _____ Eon is the current eon in the geologic timescale, and the one during which abundant animal life has existed. It covers roughly 545 million years and goes back to the time when diverse hard-shelled animals first appeared.
- a. 1700 Cascadia earthquake
- b. 1509 Istanbul earthquake
- c. 1703 Genroku earthquake
- d. Phanerozoic

59. The _____ is the second geologic period in the Paleoproterozoic Era and lasted from 2300 Ma to 2050 Ma (million years ago.) Instead of being based on stratigraphy, these dates are defined chronometrically.

The Bushveld Complex and other similar intrusions formed during this period.

- a. Neoarchean
- b. Permo-Carboniferous
- c. Rhyacian
- d. Marine isotope stages

60. The _____ stage is an age of the geologic timescale from >1,400 to 800 million years ago. The name _____ was used in a number of older geologic timescales but is in the most recent timescales of the ICS replaced by the Stenian, Ectasian and Tonian periods of the Neo- and Mesoproterozoic eras.
- a. Geon
- b. Riphean
- c. Mesoarchean
- d. Cryptic era

61. The Sicilian European Stage is a European faunal stage in the period of geological time between 0.781 +/- 0.005 Ma and 0.26 Ma (million years ago.) It is considered to be in the middle of the Pleistocene epoch.

The _____ starts with the Brunhes-Matuyama magnetic reversal at the end of the Calabrian.

- a. Tyrrhenian
- b. Pleistocene
- c. Sicilian Stage
- d. Late Pleistocene

62. The _____ is the first geologic period in the Paleoproterozoic Era and lasted from 2500 Ma to 2300 Ma (million years ago.) Instead of being based on stratigraphy, these dates are defined chronometrically.

Abundance of banded iron formations (BIFs) peaked early this period.

- a. Riphean
- b. Siderian
- c. Neoarchean
- d. Calymmian

Chapter 7. Test Preparation Part 7

63. The _____ establishes a geologic timescale for prehistoric South American fauna beginning 64.5 Ma during the Paleogene and continuing through to the Middle Pleistocene (0.33 Ma.) These periods are referred to as ages, stages, or intervals and were established using geographic place names where fossil materials where obtained.

The basic unit of measure is the first/last boundary statement.

a. South American Mammal Ages
b. North American Mammal Ages
c. 1509 Istanbul earthquake
d. 1700 Cascadia earthquake

64. The _____ is the final geologic period in the Paleoproterozoic Era and lasted from 1800 Ma to 1600 Ma (million years ago.) Instead of being based on stratigraphy, these dates are defined chronometrically.

During this period the first complex single-celled life appeared.

a. Pliensbachian
b. Statherian
c. Thermochronology
d. Serravallian

65. The _____ is the final geologic period in the Mesoproterozoic Era and lasted from 1200 Ma to 1000 Ma (million years ago.) Instead of being based on stratigraphy, these dates are defined chronometrically.

Name derives from narrow polymetamorphic belts formed over this period.

a. Rhyacian
b. Stenian
c. Tonian
d. Geon

66. _____ was an ancient continent which formed approximately 2.5 billion years ago in the Neoarchean era. It consisted of the Canadian and Siberian shields, and is now roughly situated in the Arctic around the current North Pole. _____ joined with the continents Atlantica and Nena about one billion years ago to form the supercontinent, Rodinia.

a. Arctica
b. Atlantica
c. Ur
d. Asiamerica

67. _____ was a large island formed from the Laurasian landmass and separated by shallow continental seas from Eurasia to the West and eastern North America to the East. This region incorporated what are now China, Mongolia, western USA and western Canada. Fossil evidence tells us that it was home to many dinosaurs and archaic mammals.

a. Asiamerica
b. Atlantica
c. Euramerica
d. Ur

68. _____ was an ancient continent theorised to have formed about two billion years ago. About 200 million years later, it became part of the major supercontinent Columbia. 300 million years later, Columbia broke up; _____ became part of the minor supercontinent Nena, along with Baltica, Arctica, and the East Antarctic craton.

a. Ur
b. Atlantica
c. Asiamerica
d. Euramerica

69. _____ was an ancient microcontinent or terrane whose history formed much of the older rocks of Western Europe, Atlantic Canada, and parts of the coastal United States.

The early development of _____ is believed to have been in volcanic arcs near a subduction zone on the margin of Gondwana. Some material may have accreted from volcanic island arcs which formed further out in the ocean and later collided with Gondwana as a result of plate tectonic movements.

   a. AL 333
   b. AL 129-1
   c. AASHTO Soil Classification System
   d. Avalonia

70. _____ is a name applied by geologists to a late-Proterozoic, early-Palaeozoic continent that now includes the East European craton of northwestern Eurasia. _____ was created as an entity not earlier than 1.8 billion years ago. Before this time, the three segments/continents that now comprise the East European craton were in different places on the globe. _____ existed on a tectonic plate called the Baltic Plate.
   a. Cimmeria
   b. Baltica
   c. Congo craton
   d. Laurentia

71. _____ was an ancient microcontinent or terrane whose history affected many of the older rocks of central Chile and western Argentina. It was once separated by oceanic crust from the Cuyania terrane to which it accreted at ~420-390 Ma when Cuyania was already amalgamated with Gondwana.
   a. 1509 Istanbul earthquake
   b. 1703 Genroku earthquake
   c. Chilenia
   d. 1700 Cascadia earthquake

72. _____ was an ancient microcontinent that existed about 200 million years ago. It rifted north from Gondwana during the Late Carboniferous and collided against eastern Laurasia (the Siberian continent) during the Late Triassic together with the Chinese continents. The collision created new mountain ranges between Siberia and _____.
   a. Congo craton
   b. North China craton
   c. Laurentia
   d. Cimmeria

73. The _____, covered by the Palaeozoic-to-recent Congo basin, is an ancient Precambrian craton that with four others (the Kaapvaal, Zimbabwe, Tanzania, and West African cratons) makes up the modern continent of Africa. These cratons were formed between about 3.6 and 2.0 billion years ago and have been tectonically stable since that time. All of these cratons are bounded by younger fold belts formed between 2.0 billion and 300 million years ago.
   a. North China craton
   b. Laurentia
   c. Cimmeria
   d. Congo craton

74. A _____ is an old and stable part of the continental crust that has survived the merging and splitting of continents and supercontinents for at least 500 million years. Some are over two billion years old. They are generally found in the interiors of continents and are characteristically composed of ancient crystalline basement crust of lightweight felsic igneous rock such as granite.
   a. Craton
   b. Superior craton
   c. Sebakwe proto-craton
   d. Kalahari craton

75. _____ or Precordillera terrane was an ancient microcontinent or terrane whose history affected many of the older rocks of Cuyo in Argentina. It was separated by oceanic crust from the Chilenia terrane which accreted into it at ~420-390 Ma when _____ was already amalgamated with Gondwana.

a. 1700 Cascadia earthquake
b. Cuyania
c. 1703 Genroku earthquake
d. 1509 Istanbul earthquake

76. _____ was a minor supercontinent created in the Devonian as the result of a collision between the Laurentian, Baltica and Avalonia cratons (Caledonian orogeny).

_____ became a part of the major supercontinent Pangaea in the Permian. In the Jurassic, when Pangaea rifted into two continents, Gondwana and Laurasia, _____ was a part of Laurasia.

a. Asiamerica
b. Ur
c. Atlantica
d. Euramerica

77. _____ , originally Gondwanaland is the name given to a southern precursor-supercontinent and then as a remnant separated from Laurasia 180->200 million years ago during the breakup of the Pangaea supercontinent that existed about 500 to 200 Ma ago into two large segments. While the corresponding northern hemisphere continent Laurasia moved further north, the nearly equal in area _____ included most of the landmasses in today's southern hemisphere, including Antarctica, South America, Africa, Madagascar, Australia-New Guinea, and New Zealand, as well as Arabia and the Indian subcontinent, which have now moved into the Northern Hemisphere.

a. Gondwana
b. 1509 Istanbul earthquake
c. 1703 Genroku earthquake
d. 1700 Cascadia earthquake

78. The _____ occupies a large portion of South Africa and consists of the Kaapvaal, the Zimbabwe craton, the Limpopo belt, and the Namaqua Belt. It has formed a stable unit for the past 2.3 billion years (2.3 Ga.) As such, it contains some of the oldest known rocks and microfossils in the world.

a. Wyoming craton
b. Superior craton
c. Craton
d. Kalahari craton

79. _____ is a small continental region in the interior of Asia. It consists of that area north and east of the Aral Sea, south of the Siberian craton and west of the Altai Mountains and Lake Balkhash. Politically, it comprises most of Kazakhstan and has a total area of around 1.3 million km^2.

It is believed that present-day _____ is chiefly a collage of early Paleozoic volcanic island arcs and some small continental terranes. These were joined together during the Ordovician to form what was at the time an isolated continent of its own.

a. 1700 Cascadia earthquake
b. 1703 Genroku earthquake
c. 1509 Istanbul earthquake
d. Kazakhstania

80. The _____ is an underwater volcanic large igneous province in the Indian Ocean. It lies about 3,000 km to the southwest of Australia and is nearly three times the size of Japan. The plateau extends for more than 2,200 km in a northwest-southeast direction and lies in deep water.

The plateau was produced by the Kerguelen hotspot, starting with or following the breakup of Gondwanaland about 130 million years ago. There is a small portion of the plateau that breaks sea level, forming the Kerguelen Islands, Heard Island and the McDonald Islands. Intermittent volcanism continues on Heard and McDonald islands.

a. Kerguelen Plateau
b. Circum-Superior Belt
c. North Atlantic Igneous Province
d. High Arctic Large Igneous Province

81. _____, like all craton land, was created as continents moved about the surface of the Earth, bumping into other continents and drifting away.

Many times in its past, _____ has been a separate continent as it is now in the form of North America. During other times in its past, _____ has been part of a supercontinent.

a. Cimmeria
b. South China
c. North China craton
d. Laurentia

82. The _____ is one of the smaller continental cratons of the Earth. It covers a total area of around 1.7 million square kilometres (655,500 square miles) in the northeast of China , most of Korea and the southern part of Mongolia, and has a shape quite akin to a funnel, with a long east-west axis in the western part and two shorter perpendicular axes in the eastern half.

The _____ is composed of several major blocks that have been heavily tilted and folded over time as a result of collisions with other continental land masses.

a. Congo craton
b. Cimmeria
c. Laurentia
d. North China craton

83. _____ was the supercontinent that is theorized to have existed during the Paleozoic and Mesozoic eras about 250 million years ago, before the component continents were separated into their current configuration.

The name was first used by the German originator of the continental drift theory, Alfred Wegener, in the 1920 edition of his book The Origin of Continents and Oceans , in which a postulated supercontinent _____ played a key role.

The single enormous ocean which surrounded Pangaea is known as Panthalassa.

a. 1509 Istanbul earthquake
b. 1700 Cascadia earthquake
c. 1703 Genroku earthquake
d. Pangea

84. _____ continent or as Yangtze craton, was an ancient continent that contained today's South and Southeast China, Indochina, and parts of Southeast Asia _____ had been part of many past supercontinents, including Rodinia, Pannotia, Gondwana, Pangaea, Laurasia and Eurasia.

a. North China craton
b. Cimmeria
c. Congo craton
d. South China

85. _____ is the Earth's theorized first supercontinent. According to radiometric data of the encompassing cratons that constituted _____, it is believed to have existed 3.3 billion years ago (3.3 Ga) and possibly as far back as 3.6 Ga. Evidence includes geochronological and palaeomagnetic studies between the two Archaean cratons (protocontinents) called the Kaapvaal craton (the Kaapvaal province of South Africa) and the Pilbara craton (the Pilbara region of Western Australia.)

Chapter 7. Test Preparation Part 7

a. 1509 Istanbul earthquake
c. 1703 Genroku earthquake
b. 1700 Cascadia earthquake
d. Vaalbara

86. The _____ was a Mesozoic-era seaway that lay along the northern border of Laurasia.
a. Boreal Sea
b. Pannonian Sea
c. Pan-African Ocean
d. Superocean

87. The _____ was an ancient ocean that existed between North America and the Insular Islands during the Paleozoic time. Like the earlier Slide Mountain Ocean the _____ had a subduction zone on the ocean floor called the Insular Trench. The closure of the _____ occurred about 115 million years ago, during the mid Cretaceous period.
a. Bridge River Ocean
b. 1703 Genroku earthquake
c. 1509 Istanbul earthquake
d. 1700 Cascadia earthquake

88. The _____, also called the Panamanic Seaway or Inter-American Seaway was an ancient body of water that once separated North America from South America. It formed in the Mesozoic (200-154 mya) during the separation of the Pangaean supercontinent, and closed when the Panamanian isthmus was formed by volcanic activity in the late Pliocene (2.76-2.54 mya.)

The closure of the _____ had tremendous effects on oceanic circulation and the biogeography of the adjacent seas, isolating many species and triggering speciation and diversification of tropical and sub-tropical marine fauna.

a. Superocean
b. Proto-Tethys Ocean
c. Sundance Sea
d. Central American Seaway

89. The _____ was a temporary inlet of the Atlantic Ocean, created by the retreating glaciers during the close of the last ice age. The Sea once included lands in what are now the Canadian provinces of Quebec and Ontario, as well as parts of the American states of New York and Vermont.

The mass of ice from the continental ice sheets had depressed the rock beneath it over millennia, causing it to rebound once the ice melted.

a. 1703 Genroku earthquake
b. Champlain Sea
c. 1509 Istanbul earthquake
d. 1700 Cascadia earthquake

90. The _____ was an ocean that existed in the Neoproterozoic and Paleozoic eras of the geologic timescale (between 600 and 400 million years ago.) The _____ was situated in the southern hemisphere, between the paleocontinents of Laurentia, Baltica and Avalonia. The ocean disappeared with the Caledonian, Taconic and Acadian orogenies, when these three continents joined to form one big landmass called Laurussia.
a. AASHTO Soil Classification System
b. AL 129-1
c. AL 333
d. Iapetus Ocean

91. _____ was an ancient, small ocean that existed near the end of the Precambrian time to the Silurian. It was between Baltica and the Siberian continent, with the bordering oceans of Panthalassa to the north, Proto-Tethys to the northeast, and Paleo-Tethys to the south and east. The ocean formed when a minor supercontinent of Proto-Laurasia (shortly after the break-up of Pannotia, about 600 mya) rifted and created three separated continents - Laurentia, Baltica, and Siberia, the ocean was between Siberia and Baltica.
   a. Khanty Ocean
   b. Paratethys
   c. Central American Seaway
   d. Pannonian Sea

92. _____ was an hypothesized paleo-ocean which may have been a global ocean that surrounded the supercontinent Rodinia in the Neoproterozoic Era, about 1 billion to 750 million years ago. The _____ may be essentially identical to, or the precursor of, the hypothesized Pan-African Ocean which followed the rifting of Rodinia. The Panthalassa (proto-Pacific Ocean) developed in the Neoproterozoic Era at the expense by subduction of the global _____.
   a. Juan de Fuca Ridge
   b. Mirovia
   c. Motagua Fault
   d. Subduction

93. The _____ was an ancient Paleozoic ocean. It was located between the paleocontinent Gondwana and the so called Hunic terranes. These are divided into the European Hunic (today the crust under parts of Central Europe (called 'Armorica') and Iberia) and Asiatic Hunic (today the crust of China and parts of eastern Central Asia.)
   a. Slide Mountain Ocean
   b. Paleo-Tethys Ocean
   c. Sundance Sea
   d. Paratethys

94. The _____ is a hypothesized paleo-ocean whose closure created the supercontinent of Pannotia. The ocean may have existed before the break-up of a supercontinent of Rodinia. The ocean closed before the beginning of the Phanerozoic Eon, when the Panthalassa ocean expanded, and was eventually replaced by it.
   a. Pan-African Ocean
   b. Sundance Sea
   c. Superocean
   d. Piemont-Liguria Ocean

95. The _____ was a shallow ancient sea located in the area today known as the Pannonian Plain in Central Europe. The _____ existed during the Pliocene, when three to four kilometres of marine sediments were deposited in the Pannonian Basin.

The _____ was part of the Paratethys Sea that got separated during the later part of the Miocene Epoch (around 10 million years ago).

   a. Rheic Ocean
   b. Pannonian Sea
   c. Superocean
   d. Paleo-Tethys Ocean

96. _____ was the vast global ocean that surrounded the supercontinent Pangaea, during the late Paleozoic and the early Mesozoic eras. It included the Pacific Ocean to the west and north and the Tethys Ocean to the southeast. It became the Pacific Ocean, following the closing of the Tethys basin and the breakup of Pangaea, which created the Atlantic, Arctic, and Indian Ocean basins.
   a. Subduction
   b. Thrust fault
   c. Mirovia
   d. Panthalassa

Chapter 7. Test Preparation Part 7

97. The _____ ocean, _____ sea or just _____ was a large shallow sea that stretched from the region north of the Alps over Central Europe to the Aral sea in western Asia. The sea was formed during the Oligocene epoch (after 34 million years ago) when it was separated from the Tethys Ocean to the south by the formation of the Alps, Carpathians, Dinarides, Taurus and Elburz mountains. During its long existence the _____ was at times reconnected with the Tethys or its successors, the Mediterranean Sea or Indian Ocean.
   a. Central American Seaway
   b. Pan-African Ocean
   c. Paratethys
   d. Slide Mountain Ocean

98. The Piemont-Liguria basin or the _____ was a former piece of oceanic crust that is seen as part of the Tethys Ocean. Together with some other oceanic basins that existed between the continents Europe and Africa the _____ is called the Western or Alpine Tethys Ocean.

The _____ was formed in the Jurassic period, when the paleocontinents Laurasia (to the north, with Europe) and Gondwana (to the south, with Africa) started to move away from each other.

   a. Paleo-Tethys Ocean
   b. Piemont-Liguria Ocean
   c. Sundance Sea
   d. Superocean

99. The _____ was an ancient ocean that existed from the latest Ediacaran to the Carboniferous (550-330 Ma.) It was an ocean predecessor of the later Paleo-Tethys Ocean. The ocean formed when Pannotia disintegrated, Proto-Laurasia (Laurentia, Baltica, and Siberia) rifted away from a supercontinent that will become Gondwana.
   a. Proto-Tethys Ocean
   b. Khanty Ocean
   c. Paratethys
   d. Central American Seaway

100. The _____ was a Paleozoic ocean between the large continent Gondwana to the south and the microcontinents Avalonia and others to the north. It formed during the Cambrian and was destroyed during the Hercynian (European name) and Alleghenian (North American name) orogenies during the Carboniferous.
   a. Sundance Sea
   b. Rheic Ocean
   c. Paratethys
   d. Superocean

101. The _____ was an ancient ocean that existed between the Intermontane Islands and North America sometime during the Triassic time beginning around 245 million years ago. The name comes from the Slide Mountain Terrane, a region made of rocks from the floor of the ancient ocean. There was a subduction zone on the Slide Mountain Oceans floor called the Intermontane Trench where the Intermontane Plate was being subducted under North America.
   a. Piemont-Liguria Ocean
   b. Superocean
   c. Rheic Ocean
   d. Slide Mountain Ocean

102. The _____ was an epeiric sea which existed in North America during the mid to late Jurassic Period of the Mesozoic Era. It was an arm of what is now the Arctic Ocean, and extended through what is now western Canada into the central western United States. The sea receded when highlands to the west began to rise.

The _____ did not occur at a single time; geological evidence suggests that the Sea was actually a series of five successive marine transgressions--each separated by an erosional hiatus--which advanced and receded from the middle Jurassic onward.

a. Piemont-Liguria Ocean
b. Superocean
c. Pan-African Ocean
d. Sundance Sea

103. A _____ is an ocean which surrounds a supercontinent. It is less commonly defined as any ocean larger than the current Pacific Ocean. Named global superoceans include Mirovia, which surrounded the supercontinent Rodinia, and Panthalassa, which surrounded the supercontinent Pangaea.
   a. Superocean
   b. Khanty Ocean
   c. Pannonian Sea
   d. Sundance Sea

104. The _____ was an ocean that existed between the continents of Gondwana and Laurasia during the Mesozoic era before the opening of the Indian Ocean.

About 250 million years ago, during the Triassic, a new ocean began forming in the southern end of the Paleo-_____. A rift formed along the northern continental shelf of Southern Pangaea (Gondwana.) Over the next 60 million years, that piece of shelf, known as Cimmeria, traveled north, pushing the floor of the Paleo-_____ under the eastern end of Northern Pangaea (Laurasia). The _____ formed between Cimmeria and Gondwana, directly over where the Paleo-Tethys used to be.

   a. 1509 Istanbul earthquake
   b. 1700 Cascadia earthquake
   c. Tethys Ocean
   d. 1703 Genroku earthquake

105. The _____ or Turgai Strait was a large shallow body of salt water of the Mesozoic and Cenozoic Eras. It extended north of the present-day Caspian Sea to the 'paleo-Arctic' region, and was in existence from Middle Jurassic to Oligocene times, from approximately 160 to 29 million years ago.

The _____ was not absolutely continuous throughout this entire era, though it was a persistent and predominating feature in its region; it 'fragmented southern Europe and southwestern Asia into many large islands, and separated Europe from Asia.'

The division of the Eurasian landmass by the _____ had the effect of isolating animal populations.

   a. Carpolite
   b. Xanioascus
   c. Fasciculus
   d. Turgai Sea

106. _____ was a small, ancient ocean that was situated between Siberia and Baltica. The ocean formed in the Late Ordovician epoch, when large islands from Siberia collided with Baltica, which was now part of a minor supercontinent of Euramerica. The islands also caused _____'s precursor, Khanty Ocean to close.
   a. AL 129-1
   b. AASHTO Soil Classification System
   c. AL 333
   d. Ural Ocean

107. The _____ is a disappeared piece of oceanic crust which was situated between the continent Europe and the microcontinent Iberia or so called Briançonnais microcontinent. The _____ is together with other small disappeared oceanic basins often called the Alpine or Western Tethys Ocean.
   a. Greywacke zone
   b. Lepontin dome
   c. Periadriatic Seam
   d. Valais Ocean

108. The _____ was an ancient tectonic plate that fused onto the Antarctic Plate.

The plate was in existence during the Late Cretaceous and early Tertiary periods adjacent to eastern Marie Byrd Land.

a. 1509 Istanbul earthquake
b. 1703 Genroku earthquake
c. 1700 Cascadia earthquake
d. Bellingshausen Plate

1. The _____ was a fragment of the older, Phoenix Plate. The _____ was subducting under West Antarctica. The subduction of the _____ stopped before 83 Ma, and became fused onto the Antarctic Peninsula.
   a. Charcot Plate
   b. 1700 Cascadia earthquake
   c. 1509 Istanbul earthquake
   d. 1703 Genroku earthquake

2. The _____ was an ancient oceanic plate that began subducting under the west-coast of North America around the early Cretaceous time. The _____ had a chain of active volcanic islands that were called the Insular Islands. These volcanic Islands however collided then fused onto the west-coast of North America when the _____ jammed then shut down ending the subduction zone.
   a. AL 129-1
   b. AASHTO Soil Classification System
   c. AL 333
   d. Insular Plate

3. The _____ was an ancient tectonic plate, which began subducting beneath the eastern Eurasian Plate during 130 - 100 Ma. The rapid plate motion of the _____ caused the northward drift of north-west Japan and the outer zone of south-west Japan. Sanbagawa metamorphic rocks were formed in the eastern margin of the drifting land mass, while Abukuma metamorphic rocks were formed in its western margin.
   a. Izanagi Plate
   b. AASHTO Soil Classification System
   c. AL 333
   d. AL 129-1

4. _____ is the study of climate change taken on the scale of the entire history of Earth. It uses records from ice sheets, tree rings, sediment, and rocks to determine the past state of the climate system on Earth.
   a. 1703 Genroku earthquake
   b. 1700 Cascadia earthquake
   c. 1509 Istanbul earthquake
   d. Paleoclimatology

5. The _____ was one of the most severe climatic events of the Holocene period in terms of impact on cultural upheaval. Starting in >≈2200 BC, it probably lasted the entire 22nd century BC. It is very likely to have caused the collapse of the Old Kingdom in Egypt as well as the Akkadian Empire in Mesopotamia.
   a. 1700 Cascadia earthquake
   b. 1509 Istanbul earthquake
   c. 1703 Genroku earthquake
   d. 4.2 kiloyear BP aridification event

6. The _____ was one of the most intense aridification events during the Holocene. It ended the Neolithic Subpluvial and probably initiated the desiccation of the Sahara desert. Thus, it also triggered worldwide migration to river valleys, e.g. from central North Africa to the Nile valley, what eventually led to the emergence of first complex, highly organised, state-level societies in the 4th millennium BC.
   a. 5.9 kiloyear event
   b. 1703 Genroku earthquake
   c. 1509 Istanbul earthquake
   d. 1700 Cascadia earthquake

7. The _____ is the term that climatologists have adopted for a sudden decrease in global temperatures that occurred approximately 8,200 years before the present, or c. 6200 BCE, and which lasted for the next two to four centuries. Milder than the Younger Dryas cold spell that preceded it, but more severe than the Little Ice Age that would follow, the 8.2 kiloyear cooling was a significant exception to general trends of the Holocene climatic optimum.
   a. Mousterian Pluvial
   b. Neolithic Subpluvial
   c. Stadial
   d. 8.2 kiloyear event

8. The _____ was an extended wet and rainy period in the climate history of North Africa. It began c. 120,000 years before the present (ybp), lasted approximately 30,000 years, and ended c. 90,000 ybp. The _____ spanned the end of the Lower Paleolithic and the start of the Middle Paleolithic eras -- an interval that is also sometimes identified as the Achulean (250-90 kybp).
   a. AL 129-1
   b. AL 333
   c. AASHTO Soil Classification System
   d. Abbassia Pluvial

9. In geology and climatology, a _____ was an extended period of abundant rainfall lasting many thousands of years. The term is especially applied to such periods during the Pleistocene Epoch. A minor, short _____ may be termed a 'subpluvial'.
   a. 1509 Istanbul earthquake
   b. 1700 Cascadia earthquake
   c. 1703 Genroku earthquake
   d. Pluvial

10. The _____ was an important episode of cooling in the climate history of the Earth, during the deglaciation at the close of the last ice age. It illustrates the complexity of the climate changes at the transition from the Pleistocene to the Holocene Epoch.
    a. Impact winter
    b. AASHTO Soil Classification System
    c. Antarctic Cold Reversal
    d. AL 129-1

11. The _____ is an alternative, less dramatic name for the Oxygen Catastrophe reflecting the idea that although oxygen would be toxic to some anaerobic organisms, there is little or no evidence to suggest that the extinction of these organisms was as dramatic as was originally supposed.
    a. AASHTO Soil Classification System
    b. AL 333
    c. AL 129-1
    d. Atmospheric oxygenation event

12. The _____ is the name for an early Pleistocene stage used in the British Isles. It precedes the Cromerian Stage and follows the Pastonian Stage. This stage consists of alternating glacial and interglacial phases instead of being a continuous glacial epoch. It is equivalent to the European Bavellan, Waalian, and Eburonian stages combined and Marine Isotope stages 22 to (60?). The _____ and Marine Isotope Stage 22 ended about 866,000 years ago.
    a. Pastonian Stage
    b. Snowball Earth
    c. Beestonian stage
    d. Pre-Pastonian Stage

13. In chronostratigraphy, a _____ is a succession of rock strata laid down in an single age on the geologic timescale, which usually represents millions of years of deposition. A given _____ of rock and the corresponding age of time will by convention have the same name, and the same boundaries.
    a. Chronozone
    b. Stage
    c. Global Standard Stratigraphic Age
    d. Paleomagnetism

14. _____ are North Atlantic climate fluctuations occurring every >≈1,470 years throughout the Holocene. Eight such events have been identified. _____ may be the interglacial relatives of the glacial Dansgaard-Oeschger events.

The theory of 1,500-year climate cycles in the Holocene was postulated by Gerard C. Bond of the Lamont-Doherty Earth Observatory at Columbia University, mainly based on petrologic tracers of drift ice in the North Atlantic.

a. Keeling Curve
b. 1509 Istanbul earthquake
c. Little Ice Age
d. Bond events

15. _____ were plants that may have formed a belt of vegetation around the Northern Hemisphere during the Eocene epoch. These included forests composed of large, fast-growing trees (such as Dawn Redwood) as far north as 80°N.
a. 1703 Genroku earthquake
b. Boreotropical flora
c. 1509 Istanbul earthquake
d. 1700 Cascadia earthquake

16. The _____ is the name for an early Pleistocene stage used in the British Isles. It precedes the Pre-Pastonian Stage (Baventian Stage). The exact timing of the beginning and end of the _____ is currently unknown. It is only known that it is equivalent to the Tiglian C1-4b Stage of Europe and early Pre-Illinoian Stage of North America.
a. Glaciolacustrine deposits
b. 1700 Cascadia earthquake
c. 1509 Istanbul earthquake
d. Bramertonian Stage

17. The _____ is a glacial period that began roughly 200,000 years ago and ended 130,000 years ago when several large sheets of ice moved down the Buffalo River valley from the north and from the Teton Range in the west. The name _____ itself is derived from the well-preserved moraines found in the vicinity of Bull Lake near the Wind River Mountains.

The glacial till from this period is most apparent around Jenny Lake.

a. 1700 Cascadia earthquake
b. 1509 Istanbul earthquake
c. Bull Lake glaciation
d. Glaciolacustrine deposits

18. The _____ occurred approximately 488 million years ago. It was the first major extinction event in the Phanerozoic eon and it eliminated many brachiopods and conodonts, and severely reduced the number of trilobite species. The _____ ended the Cambrian period, and led into the Ordovician period in the Paleozoic era.
a. Middle Miocene disruption
b. 1509 Istanbul earthquake
c. Toarcian turnover
d. Cambrian-Ordovician extinction event

19. The _____ is the naturally occurring reversible chemical reaction with summary equation $CaSiO_3+CO_2<=>CaCO_3+SiO_2$.

Equilibrium of the carbonate-silicate reaction is generally shifted in the favor of carbonate formation under near surface temperature and pressure conditions, but shifts to silicate formation at temperatures above 300 °C. Therefore, at the Earth's surface silicates are converted to carbonate sediments, but these sediments are converted back to silicates during the subduction process.

a. 1509 Istanbul earthquake
b. Carbonate-silicate geochemical cycle
c. 1703 Genroku earthquake
d. 1700 Cascadia earthquake

20. The _____ was a temporary inlet of the Atlantic Ocean, created by the retreating glaciers during the close of the last ice age. The Sea once included lands in what are now the Canadian provinces of Quebec and Ontario, as well as parts of the American states of New York and Vermont.

Chapter 8. Test Preparation Part 8

The mass of ice from the continental ice sheets had depressed the rock beneath it over millennia, causing it to rebound once the ice melted.

a. Champlain Sea
b. 1509 Istanbul earthquake
c. 1703 Genroku earthquake
d. 1700 Cascadia earthquake

21. The _____, which occurred approximately 65.5 million years ago (Ma), was a large-scale mass extinction of animal and plant species in a geologically short period of time. Widely known as the K-T extinction event, it is associated with a geological signature known as the K-T boundary, usually a thin band of sedimentation found in various parts of the world. K is the traditional abbreviation for the Cretaceous Period derived from the German name Kreidezeit, and T is the abbreviation for the Tertiary Period.

a. 1700 Cascadia earthquake
b. 1509 Istanbul earthquake
c. 1703 Genroku earthquake
d. Cretaceous-Tertiary extinction event

22. The _____ is the name for a middle Pleistocene stage used in the in the British Isles that is known as the Cromerian Complex in Europe. It precedes the Anglian Stage and follows the Beestonian Stage in the British Iles. The Cromerian Complex in Europe is subdivided into 3 glacial periods and 4 interglacial periods. Similarly, the _____ of the British Isles is known to consist of multiple glacial and interglacial periods. Both the _____ and Complex are equivalent to Marine Isotope stages 13 to 21.

a. 1703 Genroku earthquake
b. 1509 Istanbul earthquake
c. 1700 Cascadia earthquake
d. Cromerian Stage

23. _____ is the study of astronomically forced climate cycles within sedimentary successions. Astronomical cycles are variations of the Earth's orbit around the sun due to the gravitational interaction with other masses within the solar system. Due to this cyclicity solar irradiation differs through time on different hemispheres and seasonality is affected.

a. Cyclostratigraphy
b. Sequence stratigraphy
c. Bedrock
d. Polystrate

24. The _____ was a period of low solar activity lasting from about 1790 to 1830. Like the Maunder Minimum and Spörer Minimum, the _____ coincided with a period of lower-than-average global temperatures. The Oberlach Station in Germany, for example, experienced a 2.0° C decline over 20 years.

a. 1700 Cascadia earthquake
b. 1509 Istanbul earthquake
c. 1703 Genroku earthquake
d. Dalton Minimum

25. _____, once called the _____ Interglacial period, is temporally equivalent to the Sangamonian Stage (sensu stricto) in North America, the Ipswichian Stage in the UK, and the Riss-W>ürm interglacial in the Alps. This stage is second-to-latest interglacial period of the Ice Age. It began about 130,000 years ago. Changes in orbital parameters from today (greater obliquity and eccentricity, and perihelion), known as the Milankovitch cycle, probably led to greater seasonal temperature variations in the Northern Hemisphere, although global annual means temperatures were probably similar to those of the Holocene.

a. AL 333
b. Eemian
c. AL 129-1
d. AASHTO Soil Classification System

26. The _____ were the most severe and protracted short-term episodes of cooling in the Northern Hemisphere in the last 2,000 years. The event is thought to have been caused by an extensive atmospheric dust veil, most likely resulting from a large volcanic eruption in the tropics though the exact location remains unknown. Its effects were widespread, causing unseasonal weather, crop failures and famines worldwide.
   a. AL 129-1
   b. AASHTO Soil Classification System
   c. AL 333
   d. Extreme weather events of 535-536

27. The _____ or problem describes the apparent contradiction between observations of liquid water early in the Earth's history and the astrophysical expectation that the Sun's output would be only 70% as intense during that epoch as it is during the modern epoch. The issue was raised by astronomers Carl Sagan and George Mullen in 1972.

According to the Standard Solar Model, stars similar to the Sun should gradually brighten over their life time.

   a. 1509 Istanbul earthquake
   b. 1700 Cascadia earthquake
   c. Faint young Sun paradox
   d. 1703 Genroku earthquake

28. The _____ are changes in Earth's environment as determined from geologic evidence on multi-million to billion (10^9) year time scales.

Our evidence for past temperatures comes mainly from isotopic considerations (especially $>\delta^{18}O$); the Mg/Ca ratio of foram tests, and alkenones, are also useful.

   a. Keeling Curve
   b. Little Ice Age
   c. 1509 Istanbul earthquake
   d. Geologic temperature record

29. _____, first described by marine geologist Hartmut Heinrich, occurred during the last glacial period, or 'ice age'. During such events, armadas of icebergs broke off from glaciers and traversed the North Atlantic. The icebergs contained rock mass eroded by the glaciers, and as they melted, this matter was dropped onto the sea floor as 'ice rafted debris'.
   a. 1700 Cascadia earthquake
   b. 1703 Genroku earthquake
   c. 1509 Istanbul earthquake
   d. Heinrich events

30. _____ was a glacial lake that formed approximately 15,000 years ago in the late Pleistocene epoch. After the Laurentide ice sheet retreated, glacial ice melt accumulated at the terminal moraine and blocked up the Connecticut River, creating the long, narrow lake. The lake existed for approximately 3,000 years after which a combination of erosion and continuing geological changes likely caused it to drain.
   a. 1700 Cascadia earthquake
   b. 1509 Istanbul earthquake
   c. 1703 Genroku earthquake
   d. Lake Hitchcock

31. The _____ is a dispute over the reconstructed estimates of Northern Hemisphere mean temperature changes over the past millennium, especially the particular reconstruction of Michael E. Mann, Raymond S. Bradley and Malcolm K. Hughes, frequently referred to as the MBH98 reconstruction.

A quasi-global instrumental temperature record exists from approximately 1850; but to construct a millennial-scale record proxies for temperature are required; issues arise over the faithfulness with which these proxies reflect actual temperature change, their geographical coverage, and the statistical methods used to combine them.

a. 1509 Istanbul earthquake
b. 1700 Cascadia earthquake
c. 1703 Genroku earthquake
d. Hockey stick controversy

32. The _____ was a warm period during roughly the interval 9,000 to 5,000 years B.P.. This event has also been known by many other names, including: Hypsithermal, Altithermal, Climatic Optimum, Holocene Optimum, Holocene Thermal Maximum, and Holocene Megathermal.

This warm period was followed by a gradual decline until about 2,000 years ago.

a. Middle Bronze Age Cold Epoch
b. Maunder Minimum
c. Medieval Warm Period
d. Holocene Climate Optimum

33. _____ had a profound effect on landscapes in many areas that were covered by ice at the Last Glacial Maximum. The many valleys of the Cairngorms, a mountainous region in the Eastern Scottish Highlands are littered with deposits from this period. Changes in sea level during the Holocene.

- Terminal moraine
- Altered river courses

The modern Ohio River was formed when the river was temporarily dammed just southwest of Louisville, Kentucky, creating a large lake until the dam burst. The Ohio River largely supplanted the former Teays River drainage system, which was disrupted by the glaciers.

a. 1509 Istanbul earthquake
b. 1700 Cascadia earthquake
c. 1703 Genroku earthquake
d. Holocene glacial retreat

34. The _____ is the name given to a cooling event in South America between 11,400 and 10,200 ^{14}C years BP. This cooling began about 550 years before the Younger Dryas cooling in the Northern Hemisphere, and both periods ended at about the same time.
a. Tyrrhenian
b. Pleistocene
c. Sicilian Stage
d. Huelmo/Mascardi Cold Reversal

35. The general term '_____' or, more precisely, 'glacial age' denotes a geological period of long-term reduction in the temperature of the Earth's surface and atmosphere, resulting in an expansion of continental ice sheets, polar ice sheets and alpine glaciers. Within a long-term _____, individual pulses of extra cold climate are termed 'glaciations'. Glaciologically, _____ implies the presence of extensive ice sheets in the northern and southern hemispheres; by this definition we are still in an _____
a. AL 333
b. AASHTO Soil Classification System
c. Ice age
d. AL 129-1

36. The _____ is the name used by Quaternary geologists in North America to designate the period of geologic time during which the middle Pleistocene sediments comprising the Illinoian Glacial Lobe were deposited. It precedes the Sangamonian Stage and follows the Pre-_____ in North America. The _____ is defined as the period of geologic time during which the glacial tills and outwash, which comprise the bulk of the Glasford Formation accumulated to create the Illinoian Glacial Lobe.

a. AL 333
b. AL 129-1
c. AASHTO Soil Classification System
d. Illinoian Stage

37. The _____ was a period of unusually cold climate in the North Atlantic region, lasting from about 900 BC to about 300 BC, with an especially cold wave in 450 BC during the expansion of ancient Greece. It was followed by the Roman Age Optimum (200 BC - 300 AD.)
   a. AL 129-1
   b. AL 333
   c. AASHTO Soil Classification System
   d. Iron Age Cold Epoch

38. The _____ was part of an early conceptual climatic and chronological framework composed of four glacial and interglacial stages used by early geomorphologists and Quaternary geologists to subdivide glacial and nonglacial deposits within north-central United States. From youngest to oldest, they were the Wisconsin (glacial), Sangamonian (interglacial), Illinoian (glacial), Yarmouthian (Yarmouth)(interglacial), Kansan (glacial), Aftonian (interglacial), and Nebraskan (glacial) stages. As developed between 1894 and 1909, the Kansan Stage was based on a model that assumed that the Pleistocene deposits contained only two glacial tills and one volcanic ash bed within Nebraska and Kansas.
   a. 1700 Cascadia earthquake
   b. 1509 Istanbul earthquake
   c. 1703 Genroku earthquake
   d. Kansan glaciation

39. The _____ is a graph showing the variation in concentration of atmospheric carbon dioxide since 1958. It is based on continuous measurements taken at the Mauna Loa Observatory in Hawaii under the supervision of Charles David Keeling. Keeling's measurements showed the first significant evidence of rapidly increasing carbon dioxide levels in the atmosphere.
   a. 1509 Istanbul earthquake
   b. Geologic temperature record
   c. Little Ice Age
   d. Keeling Curve

40. The _____ is a geological signature, usually a thin band, dated to (65.5 ± 0.3) Ma (million years ago). The boundary marks the end of the Mesozoic era and the beginning of the Cenozoic era, and is associated with the Cretaceous-Tertiary extinction event, a mass extinction.
   a. Shiva crater
   b. 1509 Istanbul earthquake
   c. 1700 Cascadia earthquake
   d. K-T boundary

41. The _____ refers to the time of maximum extent of the ice sheets during the last glaciation (the Würm or Wisconsin glaciation), approximately 20,000 years ago. This extreme persisted for several thousand years.

At this time, ice sheets covered the whole of Iceland and all but the southern extremity of the British Isles.

   a. 1703 Genroku earthquake
   b. 1700 Cascadia earthquake
   c. 1509 Istanbul earthquake
   d. Last Glacial Maximum

42. The _____ was the most recent glacial period within the current ice age, occurring in the Pleistocene epoch. It began about 110,000 years ago and ended about 9,600 - 9,700 BC. During this period there were several changes between glacier advance and retreat. The maximum extent of glaciation was approximately 18,000 years ago. While the general pattern of global cooling and glacier advance was similar, local differences in the development of glacier advance and retreat make it difficult to compare the details from continent to continent.

a. 1509 Istanbul earthquake
b. 1700 Cascadia earthquake
c. 1703 Genroku earthquake
d. Last glacial period

43. The _____ was a period of cooling occurring after a warmer North Atlantic era known as the Medieval Warm Period. While not a true ice age, the term was introduced into scientific literature by Fran>çois E. Matthes in 1939. Climatologists and historians working with local records no longer expect to agree on either the start or end dates of this period, which varied according to local conditions.
 a. Little Ice Age
 b. Keeling Curve
 c. 1509 Istanbul earthquake
 d. Geologic temperature record

44.

Interglacial periods that occurred during Pleistocene times have been recently put under investigation, in order to better understand our present and future climates. In fact, paleoclimatic interpretations often depends on observations drawn from the study of modern/historical processes. In order to better estimate the 'e;natural range'e; of climatically important mechanisms, it seems crucial to attempt detailed comparisons of the present interglacial (i.e., the Holocene) with previous warm periods of the Quaternary, such as _____

 a. Marine Isotopic Stage 11
 b. Marine isotope stages
 c. Siderian
 d. Permo-Carboniferous

45. The _____ is the name given to the period roughly from 1645 to 1715, when sunspots became exceedingly rare, as noted by solar observers of the time. It is named after the solar astronomer Edward W. Maunder (1851-1928) who studied changes of sunspots latitudes in different times and also during second part of 17th Century. Edward Maunder published two papers in 1890 and 1894 and he cited earlier papers written by Gustav Sp>örer.
 a. Paleocene-Eocene Thermal Maximum
 b. Medieval Warm Period
 c. Middle Bronze Age Cold Epoch
 d. Maunder Minimum

46. The _____ or Medieval Climate Optimum was a time of warm climate in the North Atlantic region, lasting from about the tenth century to about the fourteenth century. It was followed by the a cooler period in the North Atlantic termed as the Little Ice Age. The _____ is often invoked in discussions of global warming.
 a. Middle Bronze Age Cold Epoch
 b. Maunder Minimum
 c. Paleocene-Eocene Thermal Maximum
 d. Medieval Warm Period

47. The _____ was a period of unusually cold climate in the North Atlantic region, lasting from about 1800 BC to about 1500 BC. It was followed by the Bronze Age Optimum.

During that epoch, a series of severe volcanic eruptions occurred, including Mount Vesuvius (Avellino eruption, >≈1660 BC), Mount Aniakchak (>≈1645 BC), and Thera (Minoan eruption, >≈1620 BC.)

 a. Maunder Minimum
 b. Paleocene-Eocene Thermal Maximum
 c. Medieval Warm Period
 d. Middle Bronze Age Cold Epoch

48. _____ are the collective effect of changes in the Earth's movements upon its climate axial tilt, and precession of the Earth's orbit determined climatic patterns on Earth, resulting in 100,000-year ice age cycles of the Quaternary glaciation over the last few million years. The Earth's axis completes one full cycle of precession approximately every 26,000 years. At the same time, the elliptical orbit rotates, more slowly, leading to a 21,000-year cycle between the seasons and the orbit.
- a. Milankovitch Theory
- b. Global Boundary Stratotype Section and Point
- c. Global Standard Stratigraphic Age
- d. Paleomagnetism

49. The _____ was an extended wet and rainy period in the climate history of North Africa. It occurred during the Upper Paleolithic era, beginning around 50,000 years before the present (ybp), lasting 20,000 years, and ending around 30,000 ybp.

During the _____, the now-desiccated regions of northern Africa were well-watered, bearing lakes, swamps, and river systems that no longer exist.

- a. Mousterian Pluvial
- b. Stadial
- c. Neolithic Subpluvial
- d. Piora Oscillation

50. The _____ describes the documented cooling trend in the Earth's climate during the Holocene, following the retreat of the Wisconsin glaciation, the most recent glacial period. _____ has followed the hypsithermal or Holocene Climatic Optimum, the warmest point in the Earth's climate during the current interglacial stage. The _____ has no well-marked universal beginning: local conditions and ecological inertia affected the onset of detectably cooler (and wetter) conditions.
- a. 1700 Cascadia earthquake
- b. 1703 Genroku earthquake
- c. 1509 Istanbul earthquake
- d. Neoglaciation

51. The _____ -- sometimes called the Holocene Wet Phase -- was an extended period (from about 7,000 BC to about 3,000 BC) of wet and rainy conditions in the climate history of northern Africa. It was both preceded and followed by much drier periods.

The _____ was the most recent of a number of periods of 'Wet Sahara' or 'Green Sahara' during which the region was much moister and supported a richer biota and human population than the present-day desert.

- a. Mousterian Pluvial
- b. Stadial
- c. Piora Oscillation
- d. Neolithic Subpluvial

52. The _____ transgression was a period of unusually warm climate during the Holocene Epoch. It began in the 5000 BCE to 4900 BCE era, and lasted to about 4100 BCE (different climate indices at different locations over the globe yield slightly varying chronologies.) The _____ was a period of generally clement and balmy weather conditions that favored plant growth; in the dendrochronology of the bristlecone pine, which extends back from the modern era to 6700 BCE, the single best year for the growth of the pine was 4850 BCE, early in the _____ era.
- a. AL 129-1
- b. AASHTO Soil Classification System
- c. Impact winter
- d. Older Peron

53. The _____ was a massive environmental change believed to have happened during the Siderian period at the beginning of the Paleoproterozoic era of the Precambrian, about 2.4 billion years ago. It is also called the Oxygen Crisis, Oxygen Revolution, or The Great Oxidation.

When evolving lifeforms developed oxyphotosynthesis about 3.5 billion years ago, molecular oxygen was initially produced in limited quantities. With time, this oxygen accumulated and eventually caused an ecological crisis to the biodiversity of the time, as oxygen was toxic to the microscopic anaerobic organisms dominant then.

a. AL 333
b. AL 129-1
c. AASHTO Soil Classification System
d. Oxygen Catastrophe

54. The Paleocene/Eocene boundary, 55.8 million years ago, was marked by the most rapid and significant climatic disturbance of the Cenozoic Era. A sudden global warming event, leading to the _____, and formerly known as the 'Initial Eocene' or 'Late Paleocene Thermal Maximum', (IETM/LPaleocene-Eocene Thermal Maximum)), is associated with changes in oceanic and atmospheric circulation, the extinction of numerous deep-sea benthic foraminifera, and a major turnover in mammalian life on land which is coincident with the emergence of many of today's major mammalian orders.

The event saw global temperatures rise by around 6 °C over 20,000 years, with a corresponding rise in sea level as the whole of the oceans warmed.

a. Paleocene-Eocene Thermal Maximum
b. Medieval Warm Period
c. Middle Bronze Age Cold Epoch
d. Maunder Minimum

55. The Pastonian interglacial, now called the _____, is the name for an early Pleistocene stage used in the British Isles. It precedes the Beestonian Stage and follows the Pre-_____. This stage started 1.816 Ma (million years ago) at the beginning of Marine Oxygen Isotope Stage 64.

a. Pre-Pastonian Stage
b. Snowball Earth
c. Bergschrund
d. Pastonian Stage

56. The _____, informally known as the Great Dying, was an extinction event that occurred 251.4 million years ago, forming the boundary between the Permian and Triassic geologic periods. It was the Earth's most severe extinction event, with up to 96 percent of all marine species and 70 percent of terrestrial vertebrate species becoming extinct; it is the only known mass extinction of insects. 57% of all families and 83% of all genera were killed off.

a. 1509 Istanbul earthquake
b. Middle Miocene disruption
c. Toarcian turnover
d. Permian-Triassic extinction event

57. The _____ was an abrupt cold and wet period in the climate history of the Holocene Epoch; it is generally dated to the period of c. 3200 to 2900 BCE. Some researchers associate the _____ with the end of the Atlantic climate regime, and the start of the Sub-Boreal, in the Blytt-Sernander sequence of Holocene climates.

a. Mousterian Pluvial
b. Stadial
c. Neolithic Subpluvial
d. Piora Oscillation

58. The _____ or Baventian Stage, is the name for an early Pleistocene stage used in the British Isles. It precedes the Pastonian Stage and follows the Bramertonian Stage. This stage ended 1.806 Ma (million years ago) at the end of Marine Isotope Stage 65. It is not currently known when this stage started.

a. Quaternary glaciation
b. Wolstonian Stage
c. Cordilleran Ice Sheet
d. Pre-Pastonian Stage

59. The _____ Period is the geologic time period after the Neogene Period, spanning 1.805 +/- 0.005 million years ago to the present. The _____ includes two geologic epochs: the Pleistocene and the Holocene Epoch.

There is an ongoing debate of the status of _____ -- a recent proposal from International Commission on Stratigraphy (ICS) was to make _____ a subperiod under Neogene, but that was retracted after criticism from International Union for _____ Research (INQUA), so instead ICS and INQUA agreed to erect _____ as an Era, above Neogene, and to place the base for _____ at 2.588 >± 3.005, the base for Gelasian Stage.

a. Quaternary
b. Gawler craton
c. Canadian Shield
d. Musgrave Block

60. _____, also known as the Pleistocene glaciation, the current ice age or simply the ice age, refers to the period of the last few million years in which permanent ice sheets were established in Antarctica and perhaps Greenland, and fluctuating ice sheets have occurred elsewhere The major effects of the ice age were erosion and deposition of material over large parts of the continents, modification of river systems, creation of millions of lakes, changes in sea level, development of pluvial lakes far from the ice margins, isostatic adjustment of the crust, and abnormal winds. It affected oceans, flooding, and biological communities.

a. Pre-Pastonian Stage
b. Snowball Earth
c. Pastonian Stage
d. Quaternary glaciation

61. The _____ explains how flora and fauna left Africa to penetrate the Middle East and beyond to Europe and Asia. African pluvial periods are associated with a 'wet Sahara' phase during which larger lakes and more rivers exist.

a. Canadian Shield
b. Musgrave Block
c. Gawler craton
d. Sahara pump theory

62. The _____ is the name used by Quaternary geologists to designate the last interglacial period in North America. The _____ precedes the Wisconsinan Stage and follows the Illinoian Stage in North America.

The _____, originally the Sangamon interglacial stage, is defined on the basis of the Sangamon Soil, a paleosol, which is developed in contemporaneous colluvium and older glacial tills and loesses and overlain by Wisconsinan loesses or tills.

a. 1703 Genroku earthquake
b. 1700 Cascadia earthquake
c. 1509 Istanbul earthquake
d. Sangamonian Stage

63. _____ refers to hypotheses regarding paleoclimatic global-scale glaciation, claiming that the Earth's surface was nearly or entirely frozen at some points in its past. The occurrence of _____ remains controversial. Proponents claim it best explains sedimentary deposits generally regarded as of glacial origin at tropical latitudes and other enigmatic features of the geological record.

a. Pre-Pastonian Stage
b. Cordilleran Ice Sheet
c. Snowball Earth
d. Bergschrund

64. A _____ is a period of colder temperatures during the warm period separating the glacial periods of an ice age, of insufficient duration or intensity to be considered a glaciation, or glacial period. Notable stadials include the Older and Younger Dryas events and the Little Ice Age.

An interstadial is a warmer period during a glaciation of insufficient duration or intensity to be considered an interglacial.

a. Neolithic Subpluvial
b. Mousterian Pluvial
c. Piora Oscillation
d. Stadial

65. The _____ is the name for a middle Pleistocene stage that precedes the Ipswichian Stage (Eemian Stage in Europe) and follows the Hoxnian Stage in the British Isles. The _____ apparently includes three periods of glaciation. The _____ is temporally analogous to the Warthe Stage and Saalian Stage in northern Europe and the Riss glaciation in the Alps.

a. Pastonian Stage
b. Bergschrund
c. Wolstonian Stage
d. Quaternary glaciation

66. The _____ was 1816, in which severe summer climate abnormalities destroyed crops in Northern Europe, the American Northeast and eastern Canada. Historian John D. Post has called this 'the last great subsistence crisis in the Western world'. It appears to have been caused by a volcanic winter.

a. 1700 Cascadia earthquake
b. 1703 Genroku earthquake
c. 1509 Istanbul earthquake
d. Year Without a Summer

67. In biostratigraphy, an _____, abundance zone, or peak zone is the area of a teilzone where a particular fossil taxon reaches a higher level of abundance.

a. Acme zone
b. AL 129-1
c. AASHTO Soil Classification System
d. AL 333

68. An _____ is a small organic fossil, present from approximately >2,500 million years ago to the present. Their diversity reflects major ecological events such as the appearance of predation and the Cambrian explosion.

In general, any small, non-acid soluble (i.e. non-carbonate, non-siliceous) organic structure that can not otherwise be accounted for is classified as an _____.

a. AL 333
b. AL 129-1
c. AASHTO Soil Classification System
d. Acritarch

69. _____ are the organisms which live on, in also known as the benthic zone. They live in or near marine sedimentary environments, from tidal pools along the foreshore, out to the continental shelf, and then down to the abyssal depths.

Many organisms adapted to deep-water pressure cannot survive in the upper parts of the water column.

a. 1509 Istanbul earthquake
b. 1700 Cascadia earthquake
c. 1703 Genroku earthquake
d. Benthos

70. A _____ is the length of time represented by a biostratigraphic zone. They are named after characteristic fossil organisms or taxa that characterise that interval in time.

a. Biochron
b. Conodont Alteration Index
c. Bromalites
d. Stegocephalia

71. _____ are skeletal fragments of marine or land organisms that are found in sedimentary rocks laid down in a marine environment--especially limestone varieties, some of which take on distinct textures and coloration from their predominate _____--that geologists, archaeologists and paleontologists use to date a rock strata to a particular geological era.

_____ used for such relative dating purposes can be whole fossils or broken fragments of organisms. Their preponderance can give a rough guide to life diversity in the historic biosphere, but absolute counts much depend on water conditions such as the depth of the deposition, local currents, as well as wave strength in large body of water such as lake.

a. Bioclasts
b. Turgai Sea
c. Carpolite
d. Choia

72. Biostratigraphic units or _____ are intervals of geological strata that are defined on the basis of their characteristic fossil taxa.

A biostratigraphic unit may be defined on the basis of a single taxon or combinations of taxa, on relative abundances of taxa, or variations in features related to the distribution of fossils. The same strata may be zoned differently depending on the diagnostic criteria or fossil group chosen, so there may be several, sometimes overlapping, biostratigraphic units in the same interval.

a. Bedrock
b. Sequence stratigraphy
c. Biozones
d. Polystrate

73. _____ are the fossilised remains of material sourced from the digestive system of organisms. As such, they can be broadly considered to be trace fossils. The most well-known types of _____ are fossilised faeces or coprolites.

a. Principle of faunal succession
b. Proximodorsal process
c. Bromalites
d. Labyrinthodont

74. Characteristic of the Neoproterozoic and Cambrian epochs, the heterogeneous group called _____ are calcareous colonial microfossils, which include many morphologically dissimilar organisms, whose effect in massive aggregations, in association with shelly metazoans, was to lay down the earliest recognizable reef systems: compare Archaeocyathids. The earliest recognizable patch reefs date to the Tommotian. Individual _____ laid down calcium carbonate in tubules, threads, chambered structures and other forms.

a. Stegocephalia
b. Calcimicrobes
c. Cambrian explosion
d. Bromalites

75. The _____ or Cambrian radiation was the seemingly rapid appearance of most major groups of complex animals around 530 million years ago, as evidenced by the fossil record. This was accompanied by a major diversification of other organisms, including animals, phytoplankton, and calcimicrobes. Before about 580 million years ago, most organisms were simple, composed of individual cells occasionally organized into colonies.

a. Conodont Alteration Index
b. Romer's Gap
c. Labyrinthodont
d. Cambrian explosion

76. The _____ or Agronomic revolution, evidenced in trace fossils, is the diversification of animal burrowing during the early Cambrian period.

   a. Cambrian substrate revolution
   b. 1700 Cascadia earthquake
   c. 1509 Istanbul earthquake
   d. 1703 Genroku earthquake

77. A _____ is an organism outline of a fossil. It is a type of fossil found in any rock when organic material is compressed, leaving a thick carbon film.

When an organism is buried under many layers of sediment, pressure and heat may build up, leaving this thin film of carbon residue on rock surfaces.

   a. Derived fossil
   b. Carbonaceous film
   c. Compression fossil
   d. Copalite

78. The _____, also called the Panamanic Seaway or Inter-American Seaway was an ancient body of water that once separated North America from South America. It formed in the Mesozoic (200-154 mya) during the separation of the Pangaean supercontinent, and closed when the Panamanian isthmus was formed by volcanic activity in the late Pliocene (2.76-2.54 mya.)

The closure of the _____ had tremendous effects on oceanic circulation and the biogeography of the adjacent seas, isolating many species and triggering speciation and diversification of tropical and sub-tropical marine fauna.

   a. Sundance Sea
   b. Proto-Tethys Ocean
   c. Superocean
   d. Central American Seaway

79. In paleontology, a _____ is a fossil which was reconstructed with elements coming from more than a single species (or genus) of animal. A now classic example of _____ is Protoavis.

   - Brontosaurus
   - Lametasaurus
   - Palaeosaurus
   - Protoavis
   - Ultrasauros

   a. Trackway
   b. Chimera
   c. Calcimicrobes
   d. Principle of faunal succession

80. A _____ is a species which changes physically, morphologically, genetically, and/or behaviorally over time on an evolutionary scale such that the originating species and the species it becomes could not be classified as the same species had they existed at the same point in time. Throughout this change, there is only one species in the lineage living at any point in time, as opposed to cases where one species branches off into many through divergent evolution. As opposed to paleospecies, '_____' is the general term for the elements of a sequential succession of species evolving into another, anywhere in time, for any length of time, with or without having extant descendants.

   a. 1509 Istanbul earthquake
   b. 1703 Genroku earthquake
   c. Chronospecies
   d. 1700 Cascadia earthquake

81. _____ is the branch of stratigraphy that studies the age of rock strata in relation to time.

The ultimate aim of _____ is to arrange the sequence of deposition and the time of deposition of all rocks within a geological region, and eventually, the entire geologic record of the Earth.

The standard stratigraphic nomenclature is a chronostratigraphic system based on palaeontological intervals of time defined by recognised fossil assemblages (biostratigraphy.)

   a. Chronostratigraphy
   b. Geologic record
   c. Global Standard Stratigraphic Age
   d. Paleomagnetism

82. In geology the term _____ refers to the system of forces that tend to decrease the volume of or shorten rocks. Compressive strength refers to the maximum compressive stress that can be applied to a material before failure occurs. In tectonics, plates are always subjected to compressive stress.

   a. Geodiversity
   b. Leaverite
   c. Seismic to simulation
   d. Compression

83. A _____ is a fossil preserved in sedimentary rock that has undergone physical compression. While it is uncommon to find animals preserved as good compression fossils, it is very common to find plants preserved this way. The reason for this is that physical compression of the rock often leads to distortion of the fossil.

   a. Derived fossil
   b. Fossil wood
   c. Compression fossil
   d. Copalite

84. _____ are the preserved remains or traces of animals, plants, and other organisms from the remote past. The totality of _____, both discovered and undiscovered, and their placement in fossiliferous rock formations and sedimentary layers (strata) is known as the fossil record. The study of _____ across geological time, how they were formed, and the evolutionary relationships between taxa (phylogeny) are some of the most important functions of the science of paleontology.

   a. 1509 Istanbul earthquake
   b. 1700 Cascadia earthquake
   c. Fossils
   d. 1703 Genroku earthquake

85. _____ is a paleontological and archaeological site located in Do>ña Ana County, New Mexico. It was excavated in the late 1920s under the direction of Chester Stock. Unfortunately, Stock never published the fossil fauna from the excavations. Instead, R. P. Conkling, who had drawn scientific attention to the site, published very preliminary lists of mammals identified by Stock and birds identified by Howard. Several authors have done research on portions the recovered fossil fauna. Excavated before modern dating techniques were developed, little is known about the chronology except some apparently is Holocene and much is Pleistocene in age.

a. 1509 Istanbul earthquake
b. 1700 Cascadia earthquake
c. 1703 Genroku earthquake
d. Conkling Cavern

86. The _____ is used to estimate the maximum temperature reached by a sedimentary rock using thermal alteration of conodont fossils. Conodonts in fossiliferous carbonates are prepared by dissolving the matrix with acid, since the conodonts are composed of apatite and thus do not dissolve. The fossils are then compared to the index under a microscope.
   a. Palynofacies
   b. Dubiofossil
   c. Principle of faunal succession
   d. Conodont Alteration Index

87. The _____ is an anatomical feature of the pectoral skeleton in archosaurs, including maniraptoran dinosaurs. It is sometimes called the biceps tubercle. It is also sometimes called the coracoid tuber or biceps tuber.
   a. Conodont Alteration Index
   b. Principle of faunal succession
   c. Proximodorsal process
   d. Coracoid tubercle

88. The phrase _____ refers to the fact that some clades (groups) of organisms which survive mass extinctions either become extinct a few million years after the mass extinction or fail to recover in numbers and diversity.
   a. Signor-Lipps effect
   b. Local extinction
   c. Habitat fragmentation
   d. Dead Clade Walking

89. The term _____ is a portmanteau word used in geology and paleontology for a problematic structure that looks like a fossil, but whose biologic origin is uncertain. It has been mainly used for remains found in rocks dating from the early history of the Earth , but is also applicable in other settings such as problematic microbe-like forms in meteorites.
   a. Calcimicrobes
   b. Labyrinthodont
   c. Paleopathology
   d. Dubiofossil

90. The _____ are ancient life-forms of the Ediacaran Period, which represent the earliest known complex multicellular organisms. They appeared soon after the Earth thawed from the Cryogenian period's extensive glaciers, and largely disappeared soon before the rapid appearance of biodiversity known as the Cambrian explosion, which saw the first appearance in the fossil record of the basic patterns and body-plans that would go on to form the basis of modern animals. Little of the diversity of the _____ would be incorporated in this new scheme, with a distinct Cambrian biota arising and usurping the organisms that dominated the Ediacaran fossil record.
   a. AL 333
   b. AL 129-1
   c. AASHTO Soil Classification System
   d. Ediacara biota

91. An _____ is a chipped flint nodule. They were once thought to have been artefacts, the earliest stone tools, but are now believed to be naturally produced by geological processes such as glaciation.

The first eoliths were collected in Kent by Benjamin Harrison, an amateur naturalist and archaeologist, in 1885 (though the name '_____' wasn't coined until 1892, by J. Allen Browne.)

   a. Eolith
   b. AL 129-1
   c. AL 333
   d. AASHTO Soil Classification System

92. _____ is the archaeological or paleontological term for a group of associated animal fossils found together in a given stratum.

The principle of faunal succession is used in biostratigraphy to determine each biostratigraphic unit, or biozone. The biostratigraphic unit being a section of geological strata that is defined on the basis of its characteristic fossil taxa or _____.

    a. Faunal assemblage
    b. 1703 Genroku earthquake
    c. 1700 Cascadia earthquake
    d. 1509 Istanbul earthquake

93. In paleontology, a _____ is the occurrence of abundant fern spores in the fossil record, usually immediately (in a geological sense) after an extinction event. The spikes are believed to represent a large, temporary increase in the number of ferns relative to other terrestrial plants after the extinction or thinning of the latter, probably because fern dispersal is more rapid over large geographic areas, since single-celled fern spores are more easily distributed by the wind than are seeds. Fern spikes are most associated with the Cretaceous-Tertiary extinction event, although they have been found at other events such as at the Triassic-Jurassic boundary.

    a. Fern spike
    b. 1509 Istanbul earthquake
    c. 1700 Cascadia earthquake
    d. Petrifaction

94. _____ is a term used by geologists and paleontologists to designate the first (oldest) appearance of a species in the geologic record. In other words, _____ represents the geologically oldest fossil of a particular species that has yet been discovered. They are frequently used to designate segments in the Geologic time scale.

    a. Doggerland
    b. Geological history
    c. First appearance datum
    d. Storegga Slides

95. The _____ in stratigraphy, Chronostratigraphy, paleontology and other natural sciences refers to the entirety of the layers of rock strata -- depositions laid down in volcanism or by weathering detritus (clays, sands etc.) including all its fossil content and the information it yields about the history of the Earth: its past climate, geography, geology and the evolution of life on its surface. According to the Law of Superposition (first proposed in the mid-seventeenth century by the Danish naturalist Nicolas Steno) sedimentary and volcanic rocklayers are deposited on top of each other.

    a. Global Boundary Stratotype Section and Point
    b. Geologic record
    c. Law of superposition
    d. Global Standard Stratigraphic Age

96. An _____ is a fossilised footprint. This is a type of trace fossil. Over the years, many have been found, giving important clues about the behaviour (and foot structure and stride) of the animals that made them.

    a. Ichnite
    b. AL 129-1
    c. AASHTO Soil Classification System
    d. Ichnofabric index

97. The _____ is a method used to quantify the degree of bioturbation in a sedimentary rock. It involved grading the amount of trace fossil activity on a scale of 1-5; a value of 1 indicates that bioturbation is entirely absent, whereas the highest grade would involve a bedding plane containing over 60% trace fossil cover. This index can be applied in either a vertical or horizontal aspect.

    a. AASHTO Soil Classification System
    b. AL 129-1
    c. Ichnofabric index
    d. Oldhamia

98. An _____ is any disarticulated remains of a fish found in the fossil record, most often a scale, denticle or tooth.

a. Ichthyolith
c. AASHTO Soil Classification System
b. AL 129-1
d. AL 333

99. _____ are fossils used to define and identify geologic periods They work on the premise that, although different sediments may look different depending on the conditions under which they were laid down, they may include the remains of the same species of fossil. If the species concerned were short-lived, then it is certain that the sediments in question were deposited within that narrow time period.
   a. Allotrioceras
   b. Index fossils
   c. Indian bead
   d. Invertebrate paleontology

100. _____, a form of Phyletic dwarfism, is the process and condition of the reduction in size of large animals - almost always mammals - when their gene pool is limited to a very small environment, primarily islands. The intentional breeding of _____ is called dwarfing.

This effect has made itself manifest many times throughout natural history, including dinosaurs, like Europasaurus, and modern animals such as elephants and human beings.

   a. AASHTO Soil Classification System
   b. AL 129-1
   c. AL 333
   d. Insular dwarfism

101. An _____ is an animal lacking a vertebral column. The group includes 98% of all animal species -- all animals except those in the Chordate subphylum Vertebrata (fish, reptiles, amphibians, birds, and mammals.)

Carolus Linnaeus' Systema Naturae divided these animals into only two groups, the Insecta and the now-obsolete vermes (worms.)

   a. AL 333
   b. Invertebrate
   c. AASHTO Soil Classification System
   d. AL 129-1

102. The _____ includes all the living organisms - the ecosystem - of northeastern China between 133 to 120 million years ago. This is the Lower Cretaceous ecosystem which left fossils in the Yixian Formation and Jiufotang Formation. It is also believed to have left fossils in the Sinuiju series of North Korea.The ecosystem in the Lower Cretaceous was dominated by wetlands and numerous lakes (not rivers, deltas, or marine habitats.)
   a. 1700 Cascadia earthquake
   b. Jehol Biota
   c. 1703 Genroku earthquake
   d. 1509 Istanbul earthquake

103. _____ refers to a type of limestone quarried in the Florida Keys, in particular from Windley Key fossil quarry, which is now a State Park of Florida. The limestone is Pleistocene in age, and the rock primarily consists of scleractinian coral, such as Elkhorn coral and Brain coral.
   a. Porcellanite
   b. Keystone
   c. Concretion
   d. Superficial deposits

104. The _____ is an Early Devonian (Emsian) facies that includes a Lagerstätte in the Northern Eifel hills, at Willwerath near Prüm, Rhineland-Palatinate, Germany. In it Jaekelopterus rhenaniae, a giant eurypterid was discovered. The _____ was first described in 1919 by Rudolf Richter.

a. Klerf Formation
b. 1509 Istanbul earthquake
c. 1703 Genroku earthquake
d. 1700 Cascadia earthquake

Chapter 9. Test Preparation Part 9

1. _____ in Bulgaria was used as a hunters' shelter as early as the Lower Paleolithic (1,6 million BP) marks an older route of early humans' from Africa to Europe via the Balkans, prior to the currently suggested route across Gibraltar, and probably keeps the earliest evidence of human symbolic behaviour ever found. Here have been found the earliest European Gravette flint assemblages.

   a. 1509 Istanbul earthquake
   b. Kozarnika cave
   c. 1703 Genroku earthquake
   d. 1700 Cascadia earthquake

2. _____ is a geological process occurring when areas of submerged seafloor are exposed above the sea level. The opposite event, marine transgression, occurs when flooding from the sea covers previously exposed land.

   Evidence of _____ and transgression occurs throughout the fossil record, and these fluctuations are thought to have caused (or contributed to) several mass extinctions, among them the Permian-Triassic extinction event (250 million years ago) and Cretaceous-Tertiary extinction event (65 Ma.)

   a. Marine regression
   b. 1509 Istanbul earthquake
   c. 1703 Genroku earthquake
   d. 1700 Cascadia earthquake

3. A _____ is a multi-layered sheet of micro-organisms, mainly bacteria and archaea. They grow at interfaces between different types of material, mostly on submerged or moist surfaces but a few survive in deserts. They colonize environments ranging in altitude from 10 km above sea level to more than 20 km below the surface of the oceans and as much as 30 km below the surfaces of rocks and sediments, and in temperature from from -40>°C to +120>°C.

   a. 1509 Istanbul earthquake
   b. 1703 Genroku earthquake
   c. Microbial mat
   d. 1700 Cascadia earthquake

4. The _____ is a sub-epoch of the Miocene Epoch made up of two stages: the Langhian and Serravallian stages. The _____ is followed by the Early Miocene.

   The sub-epoch lasted from 15.97 >± 0.05 mya to 11.608 >± 0.005 Mya (million years ago.)

   a. Middle Miocene
   b. Thermochronology
   c. Statherian
   d. Langhian

5. The term _____, alternatively the Middle Miocene extinction or Middle Miocene extinction peak, refers to a wave of extinctions of terrestrial and aquatic life forms that occurred around the middle of the Miocene Epoch, c. 14.8 to 14.5 million years ago, during the Langhian stage of the Miocene.

   Researchers dispute the full extent of the extinctions in the middle Miocene; the most extreme estimates assert that 30% of the mammalian genera of the early Miocene epoch went extinct in the disruption -- though other scientists rate the event much less severe.

   a. Middle Miocene disruption
   b. 1509 Istanbul earthquake
   c. Toarcian turnover
   d. Permian-Triassic extinction event

6. A _____ is a term used in anthropology, archaeology, and paleontology for a method of intelligent guesswork. A people who are well studied are used as a substitute for a more ancient and poorly known culture that may have lived in a similar way. The behaviors and beliefs of the known culture then serve as a model for what is not known about the ancient culture.

a. 1700 Cascadia earthquake
b. Model culture
c. 1703 Genroku earthquake
d. 1509 Istanbul earthquake

7. _____ is an ichnogenus describing burrows produced by organisms mining underneath microbial mats. It was common from the Ediacaran into the Cambrian, when it was forced into progressively deeper waters to avoid the increasing predation.
a. Ichnofabric index
b. AL 129-1
c. AASHTO Soil Classification System
d. Oldhamia

8. _____ is a growing and comparatively new discipline which combines the methods and findings of the natural science biology with the methods and findings of the earth science paleontology. It is occasionally referred to as 'geobiology.'

Paleobiological research uses biological field research of current biota and of fossils millions of years old to answer questions about the molecular evolution and the evolutionary history of life. In this scientific quest, macrofossils, microfossils and trace fossils are typically analyzed.

a. 1509 Istanbul earthquake
b. Petrifaction
c. 1700 Cascadia earthquake
d. Paleobiology

9. _____ is the study of parasites from the past, and their interactions with hosts and vectors; it is a subfield of Paleontology, the study of living organisms from the past. Some authors define this term more narrowly, as '_____ is the study of parasites in archaeological material.' (p. 103) K.J. Reinhard suggests that the term 'archaeoparasitology' be applied to '...

a. 1509 Istanbul earthquake
b. 1700 Cascadia earthquake
c. 1703 Genroku earthquake
d. Paleoparasitology

10. _____ is the study of ancient diseases. It is useful in understanding the past history of diseases, and uses this understanding to predict its course in the future.

A paleopathologist is one who studies old and diseased things, specifically, diseases of human and animal as inferred from recent or fossilized skeletal remains.

a. Palynofacies
b. Paleopedological record
c. Paleopathology
d. Romer's Gap

11. The _____ is, essentially, the fossil record of soils. The _____ consists chiefly of paleosols buried by flood sediments, or preserved at geological unconformities, especially plateau escarpments or sides of river valleys. Other fossil soils occur in areas where volcanic activity has covered the ancient soils.
a. Palynofacies
b. Proximodorsal process
c. Labyrinthodont
d. Paleopedological record

12. _____ studies examine the preservation of particulate organic matter and palynomorphs to provide information on the depositional environment of sediments and depositional palaeoenvironments of sedimentary rocks. The term _____ was introduced by the French geologist Combaz in 1964. _____ studies are often linked to investigations of the palynology and organic geochemistry of sedimentary rocks.

a. Palynofacies
b. Conodont Alteration Index
c. Cambrian explosion
d. Labyrinthodont

13. A _____ or upright fossil describes a fossil of a single organism (such as a tree trunk) that runs through more than one geological stratum. Entire 'fossil forests' have been discovered. They are found worldwide and are common in the Eastern United States, Eastern Canada, England, France, Germany, and Australia, especially in areas where coal seams are present.
   a. Polystrate
   b. Cyclostratigraphy
   c. Sequence stratigraphy
   d. Bedrock

14. _____ are the preserved remains or traces of animals, plants, and other organisms from the remote past. The totality of _____, both discovered and undiscovered, and their placement in fossiliferous rock formations and sedimentary layers (strata) is known as the fossil record. The study of _____ across geological time, how they were formed, and the evolutionary relationships between taxa (phylogeny) are some of the most important functions of the science of paleontology.
   a. 1700 Cascadia earthquake
   b. 1703 Genroku earthquake
   c. Fossils
   d. 1509 Istanbul earthquake

15. _____ are various groups of fishes that lived before recorded history; a few, such as the coelacanth still exist today and are considered living fossils. Their study is paleoichthyology.

The first fish and the first vertebrates, were the ostracoderms, which appeared in the Cambrian Period, about 510 million years ago, and became extinct at the end of the Devonian, about 350 million years ago.

   a. Prehistoric fish
   b. 1700 Cascadia earthquake
   c. 1703 Genroku earthquake
   d. 1509 Istanbul earthquake

16. _____ are various groups of insects that lived before recorded history. Insects inhabited Earth since before the time of the dinosaurs. Many modern insects had already evolved to very similar forms even before the dawning of the dinosaur and lived alongside them and beyond up to the present day.
   a. Trackway
   b. Calcimicrobes
   c. Prehistoric insects
   d. Coracoid tubercle

17. The _____ is based on the observation that sedimentary rock strata contain fossilised flora and fauna, and that these fossils succeed each other vertically in a specific, reliable order that can be identified over wide horizontal distances. A fossilized Neanderthal bone will never be found in the same stratum as a fossilised Megalosaurus, for example, because the two species lived during different geological periods, separated by many millions of years. This allows for strata to be identified and dated by the fossils found within.
   a. Palynofacies
   b. Principle of faunal succession
   c. Trackway
   d. Labyrinthodont

18. The _____ is a feature of the skeleton of archosaurs. It may be a pair of tabs or blade - shaped flanges on the pelvis, and serves as an anchor point for the attachment of leg muscles. This process is of particular importance in the anatomy and comparative morphology of Mesozoic birds and advanced maniraptoran dinosaurs.

a. Prehistoric insects
b. Proximodorsal process
c. Coracoid tubercle
d. Labyrinthodont

19. _____ of a species occurs where there are no more living members of that species, but members of a daughter species or subspecies remain alive. As all species must have an ancestor of a previous species, much of evolution is believed to occur through _____. However, it is difficult to prove that any particular fossil species is pseudoextinct unless genetic information has been preserved.
   a. Functional extinction
   b. Local extinction
   c. Field of Bullets
   d. Pseudoextinction

20. _____ are inorganic objects, markings, or impressions that might be mistaken for fossils. _____ may be misleading, as some types of mineral deposits can mimic lifeforms by forming what appear to be highly detailed or organized structures. One common example is when manganese oxides crystallize with a characteristic treelike or dendritic pattern along a rock fracture.
   a. Pseudofossils
   b. 1509 Istanbul earthquake
   c. 1703 Genroku earthquake
   d. 1700 Cascadia earthquake

21. A _____ is the jaw of a polychaete annelid, a common type of fossil-producing segmented worm useful in invertebrate paleontology. Scolecodonts are common and diverse microfossils, which range from the Cambrian period (around half a billion years ago at the start of the Paleozoic era) to the present. However, scolecodonts are reported most commonly from Ordovician, Silurian and Devonian marine deposits of the Paleozoic era.
   a. 1703 Genroku earthquake
   b. 1700 Cascadia earthquake
   c. 1509 Istanbul earthquake
   d. Scolecodont

22. The _____ is a paleontological principle proposed by Philip W. Signor and Jere H. Lipps which states that, since the fossil record of organisms is never complete, neither the first nor the last organism in a given taxon will be recorded as a fossil.

The most spectacular example is the coelacanth, which was thought to have become extinct in the very late Cretaceous - until a live specimen was caught in 1938.

But the _____ is more important for the difficulties it raises in paleontology:

- It makes it very difficult to be confident about the timing and speed of mass extinctions, and this makes it difficult to test theories about the causes of mass extinctions. For example the extinction of the dinosaurs was long thought to be a gradual process, but evidence collected since the late 1980s suggests it was abrupt, which is consistent with the idea that an asteroid impact caused it.
- The uncertainty about when a taxon first appeared makes it difficult to be confident about the ancestry of specific genera. For example if the earliest known fossil of genus X is much earlier than the earliest known fossil of genus Y and genus Y has all the features of genus X plus a few of its own, it is natural to suppose that X is an ancestor of Y. But this hypothesis could be called into question at any time by the finding of a fossil of Y that is earlier than any known fossil of X - unless an even older fossil of genus X is found, and so on.

Chapter 9. Test Preparation Part 9   159

   a. Field of Bullets
   c. Pseudoextinction
   b. Local extinction
   d. Signor-Lipps effect

23. The _____ are mineralized fossils, many only a few millimetres long, with a nearly continuous record from the latest stages of the Ediacaran to the end of the Early Cambrian period. They are very diverse, and there is no formal definition of '_____' or 'small shelly fossils'. Almost all are from earlier rocks than more familiar fossils such as trilobites.
   a. 1509 Istanbul earthquake
   c. 1703 Genroku earthquake
   b. 1700 Cascadia earthquake
   d. Small shelly fauna

24. _____ is an old term for early (generally large) amphibians, comprising all pre-Jurassic and some later extinct large amphibians of more or less salamander-like build. The term was coined in 1868 by American palaentologist Edward Drinker Cope and comes from Greek stego cephalia - 'roofed head', and refer to the copious amounts of dermal armour some of the larger forms evidently had. Originally, the term was used as a systematic unit at the rank of order.
   a. Conodont Alteration Index
   c. Prehistoric insects
   b. Cambrian explosion
   d. Stegocephalia

25. _____ are a class of animals that includes mammals and everything closer to mammals than to other living amniotes. In classical systematics, the non-mammalian members are described as mammal-like reptiles, and are sometimes referred to as 'proto-mammals' or 'stem-mammals'. _____ are one of the two major groups of amniote, the other being the sauropsids
   a. Cambrian explosion
   c. Dubiofossil
   b. Calcimicrobes
   d. Synapsids

26. An _____ is an animal lacking a vertebral column. The group includes 98% of all animal species -- all animals except those in the Chordate subphylum Vertebrata (fish, reptiles, amphibians, birds, and mammals.)

Carolus Linnaeus' Systema Naturae divided these animals into only two groups, the Insecta and the now-obsolete vermes (worms.)

   a. AASHTO Soil Classification System
   c. AL 129-1
   b. AL 333
   d. Invertebrate

27. In biostratigraphy, a local-range zone, topozone or _____ is the stratigraphic range of the rock unit between the first and last appearance datum of a particular taxon in a local area. It is a subset of the global biozone for that taxon. For the _____ data to be meaningful, the local area must be identified.
   a. Zechstein
   c. Primordial water
   b. Tidal scour
   d. Teilzone

28. The _____ Eon is the current eon in the geologic timescale, and the one during which abundant animal life has existed. It covers roughly 545 million years and goes back to the time when diverse hard-shelled animals first appeared.
   a. Phanerozoic
   c. 1509 Istanbul earthquake
   b. 1703 Genroku earthquake
   d. 1700 Cascadia earthquake

29. A _____ is an ancient route of travel for people and/or animals. In biology, a _____ can be a set of impressions in the soft earth, usually a set of footprints, left by an animal. A fossil _____ is the fossilized imprint of a _____.

a. Trackway
b. Dubiofossil
c. Principle of faunal succession
d. Cambrian explosion

30. The _____ or Turgai Strait was a large shallow body of salt water of the Mesozoic and Cenozoic Eras. It extended north of the present-day Caspian Sea to the 'paleo-Arctic' region, and was in existence from Middle Jurassic to Oligocene times, from approximately 160 to 29 million years ago.

The _____ was not absolutely continuous throughout this entire era, though it was a persistent and predominating feature in its region; it 'fragmented southern Europe and southwestern Asia into many large islands, and separated Europe from Asia.'

The division of the Eurasian landmass by the _____ had the effect of isolating animal populations.

a. Carpolite
b. Fasciculus
c. Xanioascus
d. Turgai Sea

31. In some natural sciences, _____ is the typical or representative location and is typically the first example of a newly discovered or described object. Often it is namesake for the term.

It is most commonly used in geology for formations, structures, rock types, minerals and fossils.

a. Sea-level curve
b. Type locality
c. Pneumatolysis
d. Patterned ground

32. An _____ is the collision of a large meteorite, asteroid, comet, or other celestial object with the Earth or another planet. Impact events have been a plot and background element in science fiction since knowledge of real impacts became established in the scientific mainstream.

a. AL 129-1
b. AASHTO Soil Classification System
c. AL 333
d. Impact event

33. The _____ occurred 367 million years ago, when one or more hypervelocity objects from space slammed into shallow marine waters at a site that is now the Devonian Guilmette Formation of the Worthington Mountains and Schell Creek Range of southeastern Nevada; the event is named for breccias of metamorphosed crushed rock deposits, found as far as the town of Alamo, Nevada (the 'Alamo Breccia'.) This catastrophic impact event resulted in what is one of the best-exposed and has become the most accurately dated impact events; it occurred within the Frasnian age of the Devonian at about 367 Ma, a moment in time that was about 3.5 Ma prior to the Frasnian/Famennian extinction events, which it is unlikely to have affected. Alamo impact breccia near Hancock Summit, Pahranagat Range, Nevada.

The actual impact site has not yet been significantly documented--even its precise diameter and its internal structural features are not yet clear enough to make speculations on the mass and trajectory genuinely useful.

a. AASHTO Soil Classification System
b. AL 129-1
c. AL 333
d. Alamo bolide impact

Chapter 9. Test Preparation Part 9

34. _____ is a form or type of tektite. It originates in an area in the eastern part of the U.S. state of Texas centered around the small town of Bedias which is about 60 miles north-north-west of Houston. They are found in about nine Texas Counties in an area of over 7000 square miles.
   a. Bediasite
   b. Marine clay
   c. Fort Union Formation
   d. Zechstein

35. _____ is an undersea crater likely to have been formed by a very large scale and relatively recent (c. 2800-3000 _____) comet or meteorite impact event. It is estimated to be about 30 km (18 mi) in diameter.

It is located to the east of Madagascar and west of Western Australia in the southern Indian ocean. Its position was determined in 2006 by the Holocene Impact Working Group using evidence of its existence from prehistoric chevron dune formations in Australia and Madagascar that allowed them to triangulate its location.

   a. 1700 Cascadia earthquake
   b. Shiva Hypothesis
   c. 1509 Istanbul earthquake
   d. Burckle Crater

36. The _____ was an explosion that occurred in the village of Cando, Spain, in the morning of January 18, 1994. There were no casualties in this incident, which has been described as being like a small Tunguska event.

Witnesses claim to have seen a fireball in the sky lasting for almost one minute. A possible explosion site was established when a local resident called the University of Santiago de Compostela to report an unknown gouge in a hillside close to the village. Up to 200 m³ of terrain was missing and trees were found displaced 100 m down the hill.

   a. 1700 Cascadia earthquake
   b. Cando event
   c. 1703 Genroku earthquake
   d. 1509 Istanbul earthquake

37. The _____ refers to the fall of the Carancas chondritic meteorite on September 15, 2007, near the village of Carancas in Peru, close to the Bolivian border and Lake Titicaca. The impact created a crater and scorched earth around its location. A local official, Marco Limache, said that boiling water started coming out of the crater, and particles of rock and cinders were found nearby as fetid, noxious gases spewed from the crater.
   a. 1700 Cascadia earthquake
   b. Carancas impact event
   c. 1509 Istanbul earthquake
   d. 1703 Genroku earthquake

38. _____ was a comet that collided with Jupiter in 1994, providing the first direct observation of an extraterrestrial collision of solar system objects. This generated a large amount of coverage in the popular media, and SL9 was closely observed by astronomers worldwide. The collision provided new information about Jupiter and highlighted its role in reducing space debris in the inner solar system.
   a. 1700 Cascadia earthquake
   b. 1509 Istanbul earthquake
   c. 1703 Genroku earthquake
   d. Comet Shoemaker-Levy 9

39. The _____, which occurred approximately 65.5 million years ago (Ma), was a large-scale mass extinction of animal and plant species in a geologically short period of time. Widely known as the K-T extinction event, it is associated with a geological signature known as the K-T boundary, usually a thin band of sedimentation found in various parts of the world. K is the traditional abbreviation for the Cretaceous Period derived from the German name Kreidezeit, and T is the abbreviation for the Tertiary Period .

a. 1700 Cascadia earthquake
b. 1703 Genroku earthquake
c. Cretaceous-Tertiary extinction event
d. 1509 Istanbul earthquake

40. The _____ was a high-energy aerial explosion over the Mediterranean Sea, around 34>°N 21>°E (between Libya and Crete, Greece) on June 6th, 2002. This explosion, similar in power to a small atomic bomb, has been related to an asteroid undetected while approaching the Earth. The object disintegrated and no part was recovered.
    a. AL 129-1
    b. Eastern Mediterranean event
    c. AASHTO Soil Classification System
    d. AL 333

41. The _____ is the currently favored scientific hypothesis for the formation of the Moon, which is thought to have formed as a result of a collision between the young Earth and a Mars-sized body that is sometimes called Theia. Evidence for this hypothesis includes moon samples which indicate the surface of the moon was once molten, the moon's apparently relatively small iron core, and evidence of similar collisions in other star systems. Questions remaining to be resolved about this hypothesis include why lunar samples do not have ratios of volatile elements, iron oxide, or siderophilic elements which would be implied by this hypothesis, as well as what evidence may suggest the earth ever had the magma ocean implied by this hypothesis.
    a. 1509 Istanbul earthquake
    b. 1700 Cascadia earthquake
    c. 1703 Genroku earthquake
    d. Giant impact hypothesis

42. In the broadest sense, the term _____ can be applied to any depression, natural or manmade, resulting from the high velocity impact of a projectile with larger body. In most common usage, the term is used for the approximately circular depression in the surface of a planet, moon or other solid body in the Solar System, formed by the hyper-velocity impact of a smaller body with the surface. This is in contrast to the pit crater which results from an internal collapse.
    a. AL 129-1
    b. AASHTO Soil Classification System
    c. AL 333
    d. Impact crater

43. _____ is the process by which impact events stir the outermost crusts of moons and other celestial objects with no atmospheres. In the particular case of the Moon, this is more often known as lunar gardening. Planetary bodies lacking an atmosphere will generally also lack any erosional processes, with the possible exception of volcanism, and as a result impact debris accumulates at the object's surface as a rough 'soil'.
    a. AL 129-1
    b. AASHTO Soil Classification System
    c. AL 333
    d. Impact gardening

44. The term _____ is closely related to the terms impact crater or meteorite impact crater, and is used in cases where erosion or burial have destroyed or masked the original topographic feature with which we normally associate the term crater. This is the fate of almost all old impact craters on Earth, unlike the ancient pristine craters preserved on the Moon and most other rocky bodies in the Solar System. _____ is synonymous with the less commonly used term astrobleme meaning 'star wound'.
    a. AASHTO Soil Classification System
    b. AL 333
    c. Impact structure
    d. AL 129-1

45. An _____ is a period of prolonged cold weather caused by the impact on the Earth of a large asteroid or comet. If such an impact occurred on land or the floor of a shallow sea, it could cause large amounts of dust or ash to be thrown into the Earth's atmosphere, blocking the Sun's light and dramatically lowering the amount of sunlight reaching the Earth's surface. _____ is one of the mechanisms proposed for extinction events, such as the asteroid impact at Chicxulub in Mexico which supposedly led to the extinction of the dinosaurs.

a. AASHTO Soil Classification System
b. Impact winter
c. AL 129-1
d. Older Peron

46. The _____ is a geological signature, usually a thin band, dated to (65.5 ± 0.3) Ma (million years ago). The boundary marks the end of the Mesozoic era and the beginning of the Cenozoic era, and is associated with the Cretaceous-Tertiary extinction event, a mass extinction.
   a. 1700 Cascadia earthquake
   b. 1509 Istanbul earthquake
   c. Shiva crater
   d. K-T boundary

47. The _____ is a period of time approximately 3.8 to 4.1 billion years ago (Ga) during which a large number of impact craters are believed to have formed on the Moon and by inference on Earth, Mercury, Venus, and Mars as well. The evidence for this event comes primarily from the dating of lunar samples, which indicates that most impact melt rocks formed in this very narrow interval of time. While many hypotheses have been put forth to explain a 'spike' in the flux of either asteroidal or cometary materials to the inner solar system, no consensus yet exists as to its cause.
   a. 1703 Genroku earthquake
   b. 1700 Cascadia earthquake
   c. 1509 Istanbul earthquake
   d. Late Heavy Bombardment

48. _____ is a meteorite impact crater located approximately 43 miles (69 km) east of Flagstaff, near Winslow in the northern Arizona desert of the United States. The site was formerly known as the Canyon Diablo Crater, and scientists generally refer to it as Barringer Crater in honor of Daniel Barringer who was first to suggest that it was produced by meteorite impact.

The crater was created about 50,000 years ago during the Pleistocene epoch when the local climate on the Colorado Plateau was much cooler and damper. At the time, the area was an open grassland dotted with woodlands inhabited by woolly mammoths, giant ground sloths, and camels.

   a. Meteor Crater
   b. Tookoonooka
   c. Vredefort crater
   d. Sudbury Basin

49. _____ is an olive-green or dull greenish vitreous substance possibly formed by a meteorite impact. It is one kind of tektite. It was named by A. Dufrnoy from Moldauthein (T>ýn nad Vltavou) in Bohemia, where it occurs.
   a. 1509 Istanbul earthquake
   b. 1703 Genroku earthquake
   c. 1700 Cascadia earthquake
   d. Moldavite

50. The _____, informally known as the Great Dying, was an extinction event that occurred 251.4 million years ago, forming the boundary between the Permian and Triassic geologic periods. It was the Earth's most severe extinction event, with up to 96 percent of all marine species and 70 percent of terrestrial vertebrate species becoming extinct; it is the only known mass extinction of insects. 57% of all families and 83% of all genera were killed off.
   a. Toarcian turnover
   b. Middle Miocene disruption
   c. 1509 Istanbul earthquake
   d. Permian-Triassic extinction event

51. The New Quebec Crater (previously known as Chubb Crater), now known as _____, is a young meteorite crater, by geological standards, located in the Ungava Peninsula of Quebec, Canada. It is 3.44 km (2.14 mi) in diameter, and is estimated to be 1.4 >± 0.1 million years old (Pleistocene.)

The crater is exposed to the surface, rising 160 m (520 ft) above the surrounding tundra and is 400 m (1,300 ft) deep.

a. Foelsche
b. Kalkkop
c. Pingualuit crater
d. Deep Bay

52. _____ are optically recognizable microscopic features in grains of silicate minerals (usually quartz or feldspar), consisting of very narrow planes of glassy material arranged in parallel sets that have distinct orientations with respect to the grain's crystal structure.

Planar deformation featuress are only produced by extreme shock compressions on the scale of meteor impacts. They are not found in volcanic environments.

a. Sclavia craton
b. Teilzone
c. Planar deformation features
d. Tidal scour

53. _____ are rare geological features that are only known to form in the bedrock beneath meteorite impact craters or underground nuclear explosions. They are evidence that the rock has been subjected to a shock with pressures in the range of 2-30 GPa.

_____ have a distinctively conical shape that radiates from the top of the cones repeating cone-on-cone in large and small scales in the same sample.

a. 1703 Genroku earthquake
b. 1509 Istanbul earthquake
c. 1700 Cascadia earthquake
d. Shatter cones

54. Named after the Hindu god of destruction, the _____ is a scientific theory that purports to explain an apparent pattern in mass extinctions caused by impact events.

The theory, created by Michael Rampino of New York University, says that gravitational disturbances caused by the Earth crossing the plane of the Milky Way galaxy are enough to disturb comets in the Oort cloud surrounding the solar system. This sends comets in towards the inner solar system, which raises the chance of an impact.

a. Suevite
b. 1509 Istanbul earthquake
c. 1700 Cascadia earthquake
d. Shiva Hypothesis

55. _____ is a form of quartz that has a microscopic structure that is different from normal quartz. Under intense pressure (but limited temperature), the crystalline structure of quartz will be deformed along planes inside the crystal. These planes, which show up as lines under a microscope, are called planar deformation features (PDFs), or shock lamellae.

a. 1703 Genroku earthquake
b. Shocked quartz
c. 1509 Istanbul earthquake
d. 1700 Cascadia earthquake

56. _____ is a rock consisting partly of melted material, typically forming a breccia containing glass and crystal or lithic fragments, formed during an impact event. It forms part of a group of rock types and structures that are known as impactites.

_____ is thought to form in and around impact craters by the sintering of molten fragments together with unmelted clasts of the country rock.

a. 1509 Istanbul earthquake
b. Shiva Hypothesis
c. 1700 Cascadia earthquake
d. Suevite

57. _____ are natural glass rocks up to a few centimeters in size, which most scientists argue were formed by the impact of large meteorites on Earth's surface. _____ are typically black or olive-green, and their shape varies from rounded to irregular.

_____ are among the 'driest' rocks, with an average water content of 0.005%.

a. 1703 Genroku earthquake
b. 1509 Istanbul earthquake
c. 1700 Cascadia earthquake
d. Tektites

58. _____ are the fragments of a larger meteorite that fell in 1879 in a remote area of Australia near the Tenham station, South Gregory, in western Queensland. Although the fall was seen by a number of people its exact date has not been established. Bright meteors were seen to be moving roughly from west to east.

Because the Tenham meterites were recovered quite soon after they fell, from a remote and dry region in which weathering and other alterations had not set in, they have been invaluable for scientific study of meteorites and their mineral contents.

a. 1509 Istanbul earthquake
b. 1703 Genroku earthquake
c. 1700 Cascadia earthquake
d. Tenham Meteorites

59. The _____ was a powerful explosion that occurred near the Podkamennaya (Lower Stony) Tunguska River in what is now Krasnoyarsk Krai of Russia, at around 7:14 a.m. on June 30, 1908 (June 17 in the Julian calendar, in use locally at the time.)

Although the cause is the subject of some debate, the explosion was most likely to have been caused by the air burst of a large meteoroid or comet fragment at an altitude of 5-10 kilometres (3-6 miles) above Earth's surface. Different studies have yielded varying estimates for the object's size, with general agreement that it was a few tens of metres across.

a. Amblypoda
b. Andrija Mohorovičić
c. Ambulocetus
d. Tunguska event

60. _____ is an informal term that may apply to two separate cases of conjectured giant impact craters hidden beneath the ice cap of Wilkes Land, East Antarctica. These are separated below under the heading Wilkes Land anomaly and Wilkes Land mascon (mass concentration), based on terms used in their principal published reference sources.

A hypothetical giant impact crater beneath the Wilkes Land ice sheet was first proposed by RA Schmidt in 1962, based on geophysical data.

a. Kebira Crater
c. Kalkkop
b. Deep Bay
d. Wilkes Land crater

61. _____ is the result of the transformation of an existing rock type, the protolith, in a process called metamorphism, which means 'change in form'. The protolith is subjected to heat and pressure (temperatures greater than 150 to 200 >°C and pressures of 1500 bars) causing profound physical and/or chemical change. The protolith may be sedimentary rock, igneous rock or another older _____.

a. Serpentinite
c. Large igneous provinces
b. Migmatite
d. Metamorphic rock

62. The _____ are groups of mineral compositions in metamorphic rocks, that are typical for a certain field in pressure-temperature space. Rocks which contain certain minerals can therefore be linked to certain tectonic settings.

The name facies was first used for specific sedimentary environments in sedimentary rocks by Swiss geologist Amanz Gressly in 1838.

a. Granoblastic
c. Hornfels
b. Metasomatism
d. Metamorphic facies

63. In geology, _____ are a body of rock with specified characteristics. Ideally, a _____ is a distinctive rock unit that forms under certain conditions of sedimentation, reflecting a particular process or environment.

The term _____ was introduced by the Swiss geologist Amanz Gressly in 1838 and was part of his significant contribution to the foundations of modern stratigraphy, [Cross and Homewood (1997)] which replaced the earlier notions of Neptunism.

a. Geothermobarometry
c. Mylonite
b. Facies
d. Quartzite

64. The _____ is a rock outcrop of Archaean tonalite gneiss in the Slave craton in Northwest Territories, Canada. The rock exposed in the outcrop formed just over four billion (4×10^9) years ago; an age based on radiometric dating of zircon crystals at 4.03 Ga, which were the oldest rocks in the world at that time. It was the oldest known rock outcrop in the world until a McGill University team reported a 4.28 billion year old outcrop on the eastern shores of Hudson Bay, 40 kilometres south of Inukjuak, Quebec, Canada.

a. AL 129-1
c. AL 333
b. AASHTO Soil Classification System
d. Acasta Gneiss

65. _____ is a common and widely distributed type of rock formed by high-grade regional metamorphic processes from pre-existing formations that were originally either igneous or sedimentary rocks. Gneissic rocks are usually medium to coarse foliated and largely recrystallized but do not carry large quantities of micas, chlorite or other platy minerals. Gneisses that are metamorphosed igneous rocks or their equivalent are termed granite gneisses, diorite gneisses, etc.

a. 1703 Genroku earthquake
c. Gneiss
b. 1509 Istanbul earthquake
d. 1700 Cascadia earthquake

66. _____ is the name given to a rock consisting mainly of hornblende amphibole, the use of the term being restricted, however, to metamorphic rocks. The modern terminology for a holocrystalline plutonic igneous rocks composed primarily of hornblende amphibole is a hornblendite, which are usually crystal cumulates. Rocks with >90% amphibole which have a feldspar groundmass may be a lamprophyre.

   a. AL 333
   b. Amphibolite
   c. AASHTO Soil Classification System
   d. AL 129-1

67. _____ is a hard, compact variety of mineral coal that has a high lustre. It has the highest carbon count and contains the fewest impurities of all coals, despite its lower calorific content.

_____ is the highest of the metamorphic rank, in which the carbon content is between 92% and 98%.

   a. AL 333
   b. AL 129-1
   c. AASHTO Soil Classification System
   d. Anthracite

68. _____ is considered a variety of the mineral zoisite. Found in Kenya and Tanzania, _____ is actually a metamorphic rock composed of intergrown green zoisite, black hornblende, and ruby. It is said to be named after the Maasai word anyoli, meaning 'green.' _____ is also referred to as ruby in zoisite or Tanganyika artstone.

   a. AL 129-1
   b. AASHTO Soil Classification System
   c. AL 333
   d. Anyolite

69. _____ is metamorphic rock which exhibits fine laminations of clay materials. Its protolith is argillite.

   a. AL 129-1
   b. Epidosite
   c. AASHTO Soil Classification System
   d. Argillaceous schist

70. _____ forms a group of medium-grade metamorphic rocks, chiefly notable for the preponderance of lamellar minerals such as micas, chlorite, talc, hornblende, graphite, and others. Quartz often occurs in drawn-out grains to such an extent that a particular form called quartz _____ is produced. By definition, _____ contains more than 50% platy and elongated minerals, often finely interleaved with quartz and feldspar.

   a. Talc carbonate
   b. Granulites
   c. Metamorphic facies
   d. Schist

71. _____ are large, lenticular eye-shaped mineral grains or mineral aggregates visible in some foliated metamorphic rocks. In cross section they have the shape of an eye.

Feldspar, quartz, and garnet are common minerals which form _____.

   a. AASHTO Soil Classification System
   b. Ultra-high-temperature metamorphism
   c. Augen
   d. AL 129-1

72. _____ is a rock that forms by the metamorphism of basalt and rocks with similar composition at high pressures and low temperatures, approximately corresponding to a depth of 15 to 30 kilometers and 200 to ~500 degrees Celsius. The blue color of the rock comes from the presence of the mineral glaucophane.

They are typically found within orogenic belts as terranes of lithology in faulted contact with greenschist or rarely eclogite facies rocks.

a. Cataclasite
c. Hornfels
b. Geothermobarometry
d. Blueschist

73. _____ is a geological term for structures formed by extension, where a rigid tabular body such as a bed of sandstone, is stretched and deformed amidst less competent surroundings. The competent bed begins to break up, forming sausage-shaped boudins.

They are typical features of sheared veins and shear zones where, due to stretching along the shear foliation and shortening perpendicular to this, rigid bodies break up.

a. Molasse basin
c. Crenulation
b. Sag pond
d. Boudinage

74. _____ is a rock composed of angular fragments of minerals or rocks in a matrix (cementing material), that may be similar or different in composition to the fragments. A _____ may have a variety of different origins, as indicated by the named types including sedimentary _____, tectonic _____, igneous _____, impact _____ and hydrothermal _____.

Sedimentary breccias are a type of clastic sedimentary rock which are composed of angular to subangular, randomly oriented clasts of other sedimentary rocks.

a. Coprolite
c. 1700 Cascadia earthquake
b. 1509 Istanbul earthquake
d. Breccia

75. _____ is a metamorphic rock that is formed by mechanical shear stress during faulting. It is either incohesive or cohesive with poor schistosity. It is usually non-foliated and consists of angular clasts in a finer-grained matrix.

a. Metasomatism
c. Jadeitite
b. Cataclasite
d. Supracrustal rocks

76. _____ is applied to any orthopyroxene-bearing granite, composed mainly of quartz, perthite or antiperthite and orthopyroxene, as an end-member of the _____ series (Classification of Igneous Rocks, 2nd ed., 2002, by R. W. Le Maitre et al.)

The _____ suite or series is a group of igneous rocks, variably metamorphosed of wide distribution and great importance in India, Ceylon, Madagascar and Africa.

The name was given by Dr T. H. Holland from the fact that the tombstone of Job Charnock, the founder of Calcutta, is made of a block of this rock.

a. Litchfieldite
c. Coldwell Complex
b. Great Dyke
d. Charnockite

77. _____ rocks are composed of fragments of pre-existing rock. The term is most commonly, but not uniquely, applied to sedimentary rocks.

_____ metamorphic rocks include breccias formed in faults, as well as some protomylonite and pseudotachylite.

a. 1703 Genroku earthquake
b. 1509 Istanbul earthquake
c. 1700 Cascadia earthquake
d. Clastic

78. _____ or _____ cleavage is a texture formed in metamorphic rocks such as phyllite, schist and some gneiss by two or more stress directions resulting in superimposed foliations.

They form when an early planar fabric is overprinted by a later planar fabric. Crenulations form by recrystallisation of mica minerals during metamorphism.

a. Michoud fault
b. Sag pond
c. Crenulation
d. Petermann Orogeny

79. _____ is a geological term that describes a series of metamorphic rocks, typically developed in the high ground which lies southeast of the Great Glen of Scotland. This was the old Celtic region of D>ál Riata (Dalriada), and in 1891 Sir A. Geikie proposed the name _____ as a convenient provisional designation for the complicated set of rocks to which it is difficult to assign a definite position in the stratigraphical sequence.

In Sir A. Geikie's words, 'they consist in large proportion of altered sedimentary strata, now found in the form of mica-schist, graphite-schist, andalusite-schist, phyllite, schistose grit, greywacke and conglomerate, quartzite, limestone and other rocks, together with epidiorites, chlorite-schists, hornblende schists and other allied varieties, which probably mark sills, lava-sheets or beds of tuff, intercalated among the sediments.

a. Metamorphic facies
b. Schist
c. Jadeitite
d. Dalradian

80. _____ is a coarse-grained mafic metamorphic rock. _____ is of special interest for at least two reasons. First, it forms at pressures greater than those typical of the crust of the Earth. Second, being unusually dense rock, _____ can play an important role in driving convection within the solid Earth.

a. AL 129-1
b. Epidosite
c. AASHTO Soil Classification System
d. Eclogite

81. _____ is a highly altered epidote and quartz bearing rock. It is the result of extreme hydrothermal fluid alteration of basalt that occurs below the black smokers within mid-oceanic ridge spreading centers. Similar altered rocks have been identified within ophiolite complexes and associated sulfide ore deposits.

a. AL 129-1
b. AASHTO Soil Classification System
c. Eclogite
d. Epidosite

82. _____ is any penetrative planar fabric present in rocks. _____ is common to rocks affected by regional metamorphic compression typical of orogenic belts. Rocks exhibiting _____ include the typical metamorphic rock sequence of slate, phyllite, schist and gneiss.

a. Greenstone belts
b. Geothermobarometry
c. Greenschist
d. Foliation

83. _____ is an informal name and in-joke in geology for any rock that has been severely brecciated and metamorphosed to a point that it is difficult or impossible to determine its origin.
   a. 1509 Istanbul earthquake
   b. 1700 Cascadia earthquake
   c. 1703 Genroku earthquake
   d. Fubarite

84. _____ is the science of measuring the previous pressure and temperature history of a metamorphic or intrusive igneous rocks. _____ is a combination of geobarometry, where a pressure of mineral formation is resolved, and geothermometry where a temperature of formation is resolved.

_____ relies upon understanding the temperature of formation of minerals within metamorphic and igneous rocks, and is particularly useful in metamorphic rocks.

   a. Cataclasite
   b. Metasomatism
   c. Geothermobarometry
   d. Hornfels

85. _____ is an anhedral phaneritic equi-granular metamorphic rock texture. _____ texture is typical of quartzite, marble and other non-foliated metamorphic rocks without porphyroblasts. Characteristics defining _____ texture include: grains visible to the unaided eye, sutured boundaries and approximately equidimensional grains.
   a. Geothermobarometry
   b. Metamorphic facies
   c. Foliation
   d. Granoblastic

86. _____ are fine to medium-grained metamorphic rocks that have experienced high temperatures of metamorphism, composed mainly of feldspars sometimes associated with quartz and anhydrous ferromagnesian minerals, with granoblastic texture and gneissose to massive structure. They are of particular interest to geologists because many _____ represent samples of the deep continental crust. Some _____ experienced decompression from deep in the Earth to shallower crustal levels at high temperature; others cooled while remaining at depth in the Earth.
   a. Metaconglomerate
   b. Geothermobarometry
   c. Cataclasite
   d. Granulites

87. _____ - also known as greenstone - is a general field petrologic term applied to metamorphic and/or altered mafic volcanic rock. The green is due to abundant green chlorite, actinolite and epidote minerals that dominate the rock. However, basalts may remain quite black if primary pyroxene does not revert to chlorite or actinolite.
   a. Hornfels
   b. Granoblastic
   c. Greenschist
   d. Mylonite

88. _____ are zones of variably metamorphosed mafic to ultramafic volcanic sequences with associated sedimentary rocks that occur within Archaean and Proterozoic cratons between granite and gneiss bodies.

The name comes from the green hue imparted by the colour of the metamorphic minerals within the mafic rocks. Chlorite, actinolite and other green amphiboles are the typical green minerals.

a. Foliation
b. Greenstone belts
c. Granoblastic
d. Metasomatism

89. _____ is the group designation for a series of contact metamorphic rocks that have been baked and indurated by the heat of intrusive igneous masses and have been rendered massive, hard, splintery, and in some cases exceedingly tough and durable. Most _____ are fine-grained, and while the original rocks may have been more or less fissile owing to the presence of bedding or cleavage planes, this structure is effaced or rendered inoperative in the _____. Though they may show banding, due to bedding, etc., they break across this as readily as along it; in fact, they tend to separate into cubical fragments rather than into thin plates.
a. Metaconglomerate
b. Slate
c. Jadeitite
d. Hornfels

90. The _____ was a significant arc accretion event in the Permian and Triassic periods affecting approximately 2,500 km of the Australian continental margin.

The _____ occurred in two main phases, a Permian accretion of previously formed passive-marginal Devonian and Carboniferous sediments in the Hunter region and mid-west region of what is now New South Wales, separated by rifting, back-arc volcanism and a later Permian to Triassic event resulting in arc accretion and metamorphism during a subduction event.

The _____ has resulted in the New England Fold Belt, a tectonic accretion of metamorphic terranes and mid-crustal granitoid intrusions, flanked by Permian to Triassic sedimentary basins which were formed distally to the now-eroded orogenic mountain belt.

a. Wianamatta shale
b. Surat Basin
c. Hawkesbury sandstone
d. Hunter-Bowen orogeny

91. _____ refers to natural mountain building, and may be studied as a tectonic structural event, (b) as a geographical event, and (c) a chronological event. Orogenic events (a) cause distinctive structural phenomena and related tectonic activity, (b) affect certain regions of rocks and crust, and (c) happen within a specific period of time.
a. Orogeny
b. AASHTO Soil Classification System
c. Alpine orogeny
d. Alleghenian orogeny

92. An _____ is used in geology to determine the degree of metamorphism a rock has experienced. Depending on the original composition of and the pressure and temperature experienced by the protolith (parent rock), chemical reactions between minerals in the solid state produce new minerals. When an _____ is found in a metamorphosed rock, it indicates the minimum pressure and temperature the protolith must have achieved in order for that mineral to form.
a. Index mineral
b. AL 129-1
c. AL 333
d. AASHTO Soil Classification System

93. _____ is a rare metamorphic rock found in blueschist grade metamorphic terrains. It is found in isolated metasomatically altered bodies within serpentinite associated with subduction zone environments. _____ consists almost entirely of jadeite pyroxene and is typically mined as a source of the ornamental rock or gemstone, jade.
a. Hornfels
b. Cataclasite
c. Jadeitite
d. Prehnite-pumpellyite facies

94. _____ is a rare, peculiar type of metasomatic alteration and occurs in two main forms; sulfidic jasperoids and hematitic jasperoids. True jasperoids are different from jaspillite, which is a form of metamorphosed chemical sedimentary rock, and from jasper which is a chemical sediment.

Sulfidic jasperoids are typical examples of silica-sulfide metasomatism of dolostones, and are found in Nevada and Iran.

a. Superficial deposits
b. Concretion
c. Porcellanite
d. Jasperoid

95. _____ is a Cornish mining term for metamorphic rock strata of sedimentary origin which were altered by heat from the intruded granites in Cornwall, England.

The deposition of the _____ strata is spread over the Devonian and Carboniferous geological periods. The sediments are not evenly spread over the county, with the Carboniferous beds being only found in the far north of Cornwall.

a. 1509 Istanbul earthquake
b. 1700 Cascadia earthquake
c. 1703 Genroku earthquake
d. Killas

96. _____ are ultramafic mantle-derived volcanic rocks. They have low SiO_2, low K_2O, low Al_2O_3, and high to extremely high MgO. They were named for their type locality along the Komati River in South Africa.

True _____ are very rare and essentially restricted to rocks of Archaean age, with few Proterozoic or Phanerozoic _____ known (although high-magnesian lamprophyres are known from the Mesozoic). This restriction in age is thought to be due to secular cooling of the mantle, which may have been up to 500 >°C hotter during the early to middle Archaean (4.5 to 2.6 Ga).

a. 1703 Genroku earthquake
b. 1700 Cascadia earthquake
c. 1509 Istanbul earthquake
d. Komatiites

97. _____ is a rare metamorphosed igneous rock. It is a variety of nepheline syenite and is composed of two near pure phases of feldspar, albite and microcline, with predominance of the first one, plus nepheline, sodalite, cancrinite and calcite. The mafic minerals, when presents, are magnetite and an iron rich biotite (lepidomelane).
a. Great Dyke
b. Charnockite
c. Coldwell Complex
d. Litchfieldite

98. _____ is the type of rock which originated from conglomerate after undergoing metamorphism. Conglomerate is easily identifiable by the pebbles or larger clasts in a matrix of sand, silt, or clay. _____ looks similar to conglomerate, besides the distorted stones.
a. Granulites
b. Slate
c. Metaconglomerate
d. Facies

99. A _____ is in geology an area where, as a result of metamorphism, the same combination of minerals occur in the bed rocks. These zones occur because most metamorphic minerals are only stable in certain intervals of temperature and pressure.

The temperature and pressure at which the mineralogical composition of a rock equilibrated can vary laterally through a metamorphic terrane.

a. Metavolcanic rock
b. Metamorphic zone
c. Large igneous provinces
d. Serpentinite

100. In geology, _____ is sediment or sedimentary rock that shows evidence of having been subjected to metamorphism. _____ is a metamorphic rock formed from sedimentary rock. These rocks are older metamophic rocks of Archaean basement complex.

a. Concretion
b. Conglomerate
c. Diatomaceous earth
d. Metasediment

101. _____ is the chemical alteration of a rock by hydrothermal and other fluids.

_____ can occur via the action of hydrothermal fluids from an igneous or metamorphic source.

In the igneous environment, _____ creates skarns, greisen, and may affect hornfels in the contact metamorphic aureole adjacent to an intrusive rock mass.

a. Greenschist
b. Dalradian
c. Porphyroblast
d. Metasomatism

102. In geology, _____ is a type of metamorphic rock. Such a rock was first produced by a volcano, either as lava or tephra. Then, the rock was buried underneath subsequent rock and was subjected to high pressures and temperatures, causing the rock to recrystallize. _____ is commonly found in greenstone belts.

a. Petrology
b. Metavolcanic rock
c. Large igneous provinces
d. Metamorphic zone

103. _____ is a rock at the frontier between igneous and metamorphic rocks. They can also be known as diatexite.

_____ forms under extreme temperature conditions during prograde metamorphism, where partial melting occurs in pre-existing rocks.

a. Metamorphic zone
b. Metamorphic rock
c. Migmatite
d. Large igneous provinces

104. _____ is a fine-grained, compact rock produced by dynamic crystallization of the constituent minerals resulting in a reduction of the grain size of the rock. It is classified as a metamorphic rock. _____ can have many different mineralogical compositions; it is a classification based on the textural appearance of the rock.

a. Metasomatism
b. Greenschist
c. Mylonite
d. Prehnite-pumpellyite facies

105. _____ is a very coarse-grained igneous rock that has a grain size of 20 mm or more; such rocks are referred to as pegmatitic.

Most _____ is composed of quartz, feldspar and mica; in essence a 'granite'. Rarer 'intermediate' and 'mafic' _____ containing amphibole, Ca-plagioclase feldspar, pyroxene and other minerals are known, found in recrystallised zones and apophyses associated with large layered intrusions.

a. 1703 Genroku earthquake
b. 1700 Cascadia earthquake
c. 1509 Istanbul earthquake
d. Pegmatite

106. The _____ was an intracontinental event that affected basement rocks of the northern Musgrave Province and Proterozoic sediments of the (now) southern Amadeus Basin between ~550-535 Ma.

Prior to the _____, which resulted in exhumation of the Musgrave Block, the Amadeus Basin was contiguous with the Officer Basin in South Australia.

The extent and effect of the _____ appears to be relatively confined, occurring most pervasively within the central northern-Musgrave Block.

a. Crenulation
b. Michoud fault
c. Sag pond
d. Petermann Orogeny

Chapter 10. Test Preparation Part 10

1. _____ is a type of foliated metamorphic rock primarily composed of quartz, sericite mica, and chlorite; the rock represents a gradation in the degree of metamorphism between slate and mica schist. Minute crystals of graphite, sericite, or chlorite impart a silky, sometimes golden sheen to the surfaces of cleavage (or schistosity.) _____ is formed from the continued metamorphism of slate.

   a. 1703 Genroku earthquake
   b. Phyllite
   c. 1509 Istanbul earthquake
   d. 1700 Cascadia earthquake

2. _____ or porcelanite, is a hard, dense rock somewhat similar in appearance to unglazed porcelain. It is often an impure variety of chert containing clay and calcareous matter.

   At Tievebulliagh, Northern Ireland _____ is a tough contact metamorphosed hornfels formed from a lateritic soil horizon within a basaltic intrusive/extrusive sequence.

   a. Superficial deposits
   b. Keystone
   c. Metasediment
   d. Porcellanite

3. A _____ is a large mineral crystal in a metamorphic rock which has grown within the finer grained groundmass. They are commonly euhedral crystals, but can also be partly to completely irregular in shape.

   The most common _____ in metapelites (metamorphosed mudstones and siltstones) are garnets and staurolites, which stand out in well foliated metapelites (such as schists) against the platy mica matrix.

   a. Granulites
   b. Jadeitite
   c. Metamorphic facies
   d. Porphyroblast

4. A _____ is a clast or mineral fragment in a metamorphic rock, surrounded by a groundmass of finer grained crystals. Porphyroclasts are fragments of the original rock before dynamic recrystallisation produced the groundmass. This means they are older than the groundmass.

   a. Hornfels
   b. Greenstone belts
   c. Porphyroclast
   d. Metasomatism

5. The _____ is a metamorphic facies typical of subseafloor alteration of the oceanic crust around mid-ocean ridge spreading centres. It is a metamorphic grade transitional between zeolite facies and greenschist facies representing a temperature range of 250 to 350 °C and a pressure range of approximately two to seven kilobars. The mineral assemblage is dependent on host composition.

   a. Metamorphic facies
   b. Geothermobarometry
   c. Facies
   d. Prehnite-pumpellyite facies

6. In geology, _____ are a body of rock with specified characteristics. Ideally, a _____ is a distinctive rock unit that forms under certain conditions of sedimentation, reflecting a particular process or environment.

   The term _____ was introduced by the Swiss geologist Amanz Gressly in 1838 and was part of his significant contribution to the foundations of modern stratigraphy, [Cross and Homewood (1997)] which replaced the earlier notions of Neptunism.

a. Quartzite
b. Mylonite
c. Geothermobarometry
d. Facies

7. _____ is a hard metamorphic rock which was originally sandstone. Sandstone is converted into _____ through heating and pressure usually related to tectonic compression within orogenic belts. Pure _____ is usually white to grey, though quartzites often occur in various shades of pink and red due to varying amounts of iron oxide .
    a. Metaconglomerate
    b. Prehnite-pumpellyite facies
    c. Metamorphic facies
    d. Quartzite

8. _____ forms a group of medium-grade metamorphic rocks, chiefly notable for the preponderance of lamellar minerals such as micas, chlorite, talc, hornblende, graphite, and others. Quartz often occurs in drawn-out grains to such an extent that a particular form called quartz _____ is produced. By definition, _____ contains more than 50% platy and elongated minerals, often finely interleaved with quartz and feldspar.
    a. Metamorphic facies
    b. Granulites
    c. Schist
    d. Talc carbonate

9. _____ is a rock composed of one or more serpentine minerals. Minerals in this group are formed by serpentinization, a hydration and metamorphic transformation of ultramafic rock from the Earth's mantle. The alteration is particularly important at the sea floor at tectonic plate boundaries.
    a. Metamorphic zone
    b. Rock cycle
    c. Serpentinite
    d. Migmatite

10. _____ or impact metamorphism describes the effects of shock-wave related deformation and heating during impact events. The formation of similar features during explosive volcanism is generally discounted due to the lack of metamorphic effects unequivocally associated with explosions and the difficulty in reaching sufficient pressures during such an event.

Planar fractures are parallel sets of multiple planar cracks or cleavages in quartz grains; they develop at the lowest pressures characteristic of shock waves (~5-8 GPa) and a common feature of quartz grains found associated with impact structures.

    a. Geothermobarometry
    b. Schist
    c. Slate
    d. Shock metamorphism

11. _____ is the solid-state recrystallization of pre-existing rocks due to changes in physical and chemical conditions, primarily heat, pressure, and the introduction of chemically active fluids. Both mineralogical, chemical and crystallographic changes can occur during this process.

Three types of _____ exist: dynamic, contact and regional.

    a. Pumice raft
    b. Leaverite
    c. Paralithic
    d. Metamorphism

12. _____ is a metamorphic rock that is usually variably colored green or red, occasionally grey, black, brown or white.

Chapter 10. Test Preparation Part 10

It usually forms by chemical metasomatism of rocks during metamorphism and in the contact zone of magmatic intrusions like granites with carbonate-rich rocks such as limestone or dolostone. Skarns in the igneous environment are associated with hornfels, marble hornfels and wider zones of calc-silicate rocks.

Skarns are in their broadest sense formed by mass and chemical transport and reactions between adjacent lithologies.

a. Rockall Basin
b. Slyne-Erris Trough
c. Diapir
d. Skarn

13. _____ is a fine-grained, foliated, homogeneous metamorphic rock derived from an original shale-type sedimentary rock composed of clay or volcanic ash through low grade regional metamorphism. The result is a foliated rock in which the foliation may not correspond to the original sedimentary layering. _____ is frequently grey in colour especially when seen en masse covering roofs.

a. Mylonite
b. Slate
c. Cataclasite
d. Geothermobarometry

14. _____ is a metamorphic rock, a talc-schist. It is largely composed of the mineral talc and is rich in magnesium. It is produced by dynamothermal metamorphism and metasomatism, which occurs at the areas where tectonic plates are subducted, changing rocks by heat and pressure, with influx of fluids, but without melting.

a. 1509 Istanbul earthquake
b. 1703 Genroku earthquake
c. 1700 Cascadia earthquake
d. Soapstone

15. _____ are rocks that were deposited on the existing basement rocks of the crust, hence the name. They may be further metamorphosed from both sedimentary and volcanic rocks.

The Isua greenstone belt contains the oldest, well preserved, supracrustals, dated at 3.8-3.7 Ga.

a. Talc carbonate
b. Slate
c. Supracrustal rocks
d. Quartzite

16. _____ is a geologic term for a suite of rock and mineral compositions found in metamorphic ultramafic rocks.

The term refers to the two most common end-member minerals found within ultramafic rocks which have undergone talc-carbonation or carbonation reactions, talc and the carbonate mineral magnesite.

_____ mineral assemblages are controlled by temperature and pressure of metamorphism and the partial pressure of carbon dioxide within metamorphic fluids, as well as by the composition of the rock.

a. Granoblastic
b. Cataclasite
c. Supracrustal rocks
d. Talc carbonate

17. In chemistry, a _____ is a salt or ester of carbonic acid.

To test for the presence of the _____ anion in a salt, the addition of dilute mineral acid (e.g. hydrochloric acid) will yield carbon dioxide gas.

_____-containing salts are industrially and mineralogically ubiquitous.

   a. Carbonate
   b. 1509 Istanbul earthquake
   c. 1703 Genroku earthquake
   d. 1700 Cascadia earthquake

18. _____ are metamorphic or tectonically deformed rocks whose fabric reflects the history of their deformation, or rocks with fabric that clearly displays coordinated geometric features that indicate continuous solid (ductile) flow during formation. Planar foliation results from a parallel orientation of platey mineral phases such as the phyllosilicates or graphite. Slender prismatic crystals such as amphibole produce a lineation in which these prisms or columnar crystals become aligned.
   a. Sag pond
   b. Michoud fault
   c. Tectonites
   d. Shear

19. _____ represents extreme crustal metamorphism with metamorphic temperatures exceeding 900 >°C. Granulite facies rocks metamorphosed at very high temperatures were identified in the early 1980s, although it took another decade for the geoscience community to recognize _____ as a common regional phenomenon.
   a. AL 129-1
   b. AASHTO Soil Classification System
   c. Ultra-high-temperature metamorphism
   d. Igneous differentiation

20. _____ are igneous and meta-igneous rocks with very low silica content (less than 45%), generally >18% MgO, high FeO, low potassium, and are composed of usually greater than 90% mafic minerals (dark colored, high magnesium and iron content.) The Earth's mantle is considered to be composed of _____.
   a. Ultramafic rocks
   b. AL 333
   c. AL 129-1
   d. AASHTO Soil Classification System

21. _____ is a calcium inosilicate mineral ($CaSiO_3$) that may contain small amounts of iron, magnesium, and manganese substituting for calcium. It is usually white. It forms when impure limestone or dolostone is subjected to high temperature and pressure sometimes in the presence of silica-bearing fluids as in skarns or contact metamorphic rocks.
   a. 1703 Genroku earthquake
   b. 1509 Istanbul earthquake
   c. 1700 Cascadia earthquake
   d. Wollastonite

22. The _____ is a tectonic plate which includes the continent of Africa, as well as oceanic crust which lies between the continent and various surrounding ocean ridges.

The westerly side is a divergent boundary with the North American Plate to the north and the South American Plate to the south forming the central and southern part of the Mid-Atlantic Ridge. The _____ is bounded on the northeast by the Arabian Plate, the southeast by the Indo-Australian Plate, the north by the Eurasian Plate and the Anatolian Plate, and on the south by the Antarctic Plate.

   a. Easter Plate
   b. Arabian Plate
   c. African Plate
   d. Eurasian Plate

23. The _____, sometimes called the Ethiopian Shield, is a geological shield located on the eastern horn of Africa and extends eastward to western Saudi Arabia and the eastern half of Madagascar.
   a. AL 333
   b. AL 129-1
   c. AASHTO Soil Classification System
   d. African Shield

24. The _____ is an extraordinary uplift of the African continent, particularly its southern half; southern Africa on average lies a full kilometer above sea level, with seemingly anomalous uplifts extending well into the south Atlantic ocean.(Nyblade and Robinson,1994),

The superswell is a relatively recent phenomenon, probably beginning between 5 and 30 million years ago.

   a. AL 333
   b. AL 129-1
   c. AASHTO Soil Classification System
   d. African superswell

25. The _____ or Appalachian orogeny is one of the geological mountain-forming events (orogeny) that formed the Appalachian Mountains and Allegheny Mountains. The term and spelling 'Alleghany Orogeny' (sic) originally proposed by H.P. Woodward (1957, 1958) is preferred usage. Approximately 350 million to 300 million years ago, in the Carboniferous period, the combined continents of Europe and Africa (Gondwana) collided with North America to form the supercontinent of Pangaea.
   a. Alpine orogeny
   b. Orogeny
   c. AASHTO Soil Classification System
   d. Alleghenian orogeny

26. _____ refers to natural mountain building, and may be studied as a tectonic structural event, (b) as a geographical event, and (c) a chronological event. Orogenic events (a) cause distinctive structural phenomena and related tectonic activity, (b) affect certain regions of rocks and crust, and (c) happen within a specific period of time.
   a. Orogeny
   b. AASHTO Soil Classification System
   c. Alleghenian orogeny
   d. Alpine orogeny

27. The _____ is one of three tectonic plates which have been moving northward over millions of years toward an inevitable collision with Eurasia. This is resulting in a mingling of plate pieces and mountain ranges extending in the west from the Pyrenees, crossing southern Europe and the Middle East, to the Himalayas and ranges of southeast Asia.

The _____ consists mostly of the Arabian peninsula; it extends northward to Turkey.

   a. Easter Plate
   b. Okhotsk Plate
   c. Eurasian Plate
   d. Arabian Plate

28. The _____ is a cratonic unit that forms part of the Congo craton of central Africa. The _____ however consists of Palaeoproterozoic granitoids and volcanics, and is overlain by a Palaeoproterozoic continental sedimentary succession, the Mporokoso Group, and does not preserve much direct evidence of Archaean protoliths.

Indirect evidence of an Archaean ancestry for the _____ is provided by detrital zircons within the Mporokoso Group, which indicate a local source area with zircons of 3.2, 3.0.

a. 1509 Istanbul earthquake
b. 1700 Cascadia earthquake
c. Bangweulu Block
d. 1703 Genroku earthquake

29. The _____, covered by the Palaeozoic-to-recent Congo basin, is an ancient Precambrian craton that with four others (the Kaapvaal, Zimbabwe, Tanzania, and West African cratons) makes up the modern continent of Africa. These cratons were formed between about 3.6 and 2.0 billion years ago and have been tectonically stable since that time. All of these cratons are bounded by younger fold belts formed between 2.0 billion and 300 million years ago.
   a. Congo craton
   b. North China craton
   c. Laurentia
   d. Cimmeria

30. A _____ is an old and stable part of the continental crust that has survived the merging and splitting of continents and supercontinents for at least 500 million years. Some are over two billion years old. They are generally found in the interiors of continents and are characteristically composed of ancient crystalline basement crust of lightweight felsic igneous rock such as granite.
   a. Superior craton
   b. Kalahari craton
   c. Sebakwe proto-craton
   d. Craton

31. _____ in Zambia covers the mineral-rich Copperbelt, and farming and bush areas to the south. It was the backbone of the Northern Rhodesian economy during British colonial rule and fuelled the hopes of the immediate post-independence period, but its economic importance was severely damaged by a crash in global copper prices in 1973 and the nationalization of the copper mines by the government of Kenneth Kaunda. The province adjoins Katanga province of the Democratic Republic of the Congo, which is similarly mineral-rich.
   a. Convergent boundary
   b. Juan de Fuca Ridge
   c. Subduction
   d. Copperbelt Province

32. _____ , originally Gondwanaland is the name given to a southern precursor-supercontinent and then as a remnant separated from Laurasia 180->200 million years ago during the breakup of the Pangaea supercontinent that existed about 500 to 200 Ma ago into two large segments. While the corresponding northern hemisphere continent Laurasia moved further north, the nearly equal in area _____ included most of the landmasses in today's southern hemisphere, including Antarctica, South America, Africa, Madagascar, Australia-New Guinea, and New Zealand, as well as Arabia and the Indian subcontinent, which have now moved into the Northern Hemisphere.
   a. 1509 Istanbul earthquake
   b. 1703 Genroku earthquake
   c. 1700 Cascadia earthquake
   d. Gondwana

33. The _____ is a linear geological feature that trends nearly north-south through the center of Zimbabwe passing just to the west of the capital, Harare. It consists of a band of short, narrow ridges and hills spanning for approximately 550 km (340 mi.) The hills become taller as the range goes north, and reach up to 1,500 feet (460 meters) above the Mvurwi Range.

Geologically the intrusion is not a dyke, but is lopolithic and Y-shaped in cross-section. It is a layered ultramafic intrusion that extends across Zimbabwe with a strike of about N10°E. The width of the intrusion varies from 3 to 12 km (7.5 mi). The _____ is unusual in that most ultramafic layered intrusions display near horizontal sill or sheet forms.

a. Litchfieldite
b. Coldwell Complex
c. Charnockite
d. Great Dyke

34. The _____ is the name given to a sedimentary succession of fluvial, lacustrine and aeolian sandstones and minor siltstones occurring on the Bangweulu Block of northern Zambia.

The succession is likely to be largely over 1.8 billion years old, and forms part of the regionally defined Muva Supergroup which occurs also in the Irumide Belt of Zambia.

a. 1703 Genroku earthquake
b. 1700 Cascadia earthquake
c. 1509 Istanbul earthquake
d. Mporokoso Group

35. The _____ was a series of major Neoproterozoic orogenic events (mountain building) which related to the formation of the supercontinents Gondwana and Pannotia about 900 million years ago.
a. Kaikoura Orogeny
b. Trans-Hudson orogeny
c. Laramide orogeny
d. Pan-African orogeny

36. The _____ is a tectonic plate that is being formed as the African Plate is splitting along the East African Rift. The part of the African Plate which lies on the other side of the rift is sometimes referred to as the Nubian Plate. As the rifting is, in geologic terms, just getting underway, these two parts of the African Plate are generally regarded as protoplates rather than as full-fledged independent plates.
a. Timor Plate
b. South American Plate
c. Niuafo'ou Plate
d. Somali Plate

37. The _____ is a geologic massif in the Swiss Alps. It contains a number of large mountain chains and parts of mountain chains.

The _____ is part of the Helvetic zone of the Alps, which consists of material originally from the European tectonic plate. The _____ has lithologies common for Paleozoic basement rocks all over Europe, deformed and metamorphosed during the Variscan orogeny.

a. Austroalpine nappes
b. AASHTO Soil Classification System
c. Aarmassif
d. AL 129-1

38. The _____ is an orogenic phase in the Tertiary that formed the mountain ranges of the Alpide belt. These mountains include the Atlas, the Pyrenees, the Alps, the Dinaric Alps, the Hellenides, the Carpathians, the Balkan, the Taurus, the Caucasus, the Alborz, the Zagros, the Hindu Kush, the Pamir, the Karakoram, and the Himalayas. Sometimes other names occur to describe the formation of separate mountain ranges: for example Carpathean orogeny for the Carpathians, Hellenic orogeny for the Hellenides or the Himalayan orogeny for the Himalayas.
a. AASHTO Soil Classification System
b. Alpine orogeny
c. Alleghenian orogeny
d. Orogeny

39. The Adriatic or _____ is a small tectonic plate carrying primarily continental crust that broke away from the African plate along a large transform fault in the Cretaceous period. The name Adriatic Plate is usually used when referring to the northern part of the plate. This part of the plate was deformed during the Alpine orogeny, when the Adriatic/_____ collided with the Eurasian plate.

a. Apulian Plate
b. AL 129-1
c. AASHTO Soil Classification System
d. AL 333

40. The _____ are a geological nappe stack in the European Alps. The Alps contain three such stacks, of which the _____ are structurally on top of the other two (meaning they were thrusted over the other two.) The name Austroalpine means Eastern Alpine, because these nappes crop out mainly in the Eastern Alps (the Alps east of the line Lake Constance - Chur - Lake Como.)
   a. Infrahelvetic complex
   b. AL 129-1
   c. AASHTO Soil Classification System
   d. Austroalpine nappes

41. The _____ or klippe is a geologic nappe and klippe that crops out in the Pennine Alps. The nappe is tectonostratigraphically on top of the Penninic nappes and by most researchers seen as Austroalpine.

The most famous outcrop of the nappe is the Matterhorn, which is made of a loose piece (klippe) of Dent Blanche material lying on top of Penninic ophiolites (Zermatt-Saas zone). Because of this it is sometimes said that the Matterhorn came from Africa

   a. Greywacke zone
   b. Dent Blanche nappe
   c. Hohe Tauern window
   d. Penninic thrustfront

42. The _____ is a major thrust fault in the Alps of eastern Switzerland. Along the thrust the Helvetic nappes were thrusted more than 100 km to the north over the external Aarmassif and Infrahelvetic complex. The thrust forms the contact between older Permo-Triassic rock layers of the Verrucano group and younger (external) Jurassic and Cretaceous limestones and Paleogene flysch and molasse.
   a. 1700 Cascadia earthquake
   b. 1703 Genroku earthquake
   c. 1509 Istanbul earthquake
   d. Glarus thrust

43. The _____ is a band of Paleozoic sedimentary rocks in the Austrian Alps. The zone is part of the Austroalpine nappes.

Mesozoic limestones crop out north of the _____, forming the Northern Calcareous Alps.

   a. Dent Blanche nappe
   b. Helvetic Zone
   c. Greywacke zone
   d. Lepontin dome

44.

The _____, Helvetic system or the Helveticum is a geologic subdivision of the Alps. The _____ crops out mainly in Switzerland, hence the name . Rocks in the _____ are sedimentary and were originally deposited at the southern margin of the European plate.

   a. Lepontin dome
   b. Helvetic Zone
   c. Helvetic nappes
   d. Hohe Tauern window

45. The _____ are a series of nappes in the Northern part of the Alps and part of the Helvetic zone. They consist of Mesozoic limestones, shales and marls that were originally deposited on the southern continental margin of the European continent. During the Alpine orogeny they were thrusted north over a d>écollement and at the same time were internally deformed by folding and thrusting.

a. Greywacke zone
b. Periadriatic Seam
c. Helvetic nappes
d. Hohe Tauern window

46. The _____ is a geological structure in the Austrian Central Eastern Alps. It is a window in the Austroalpine nappes where high-grade metamorphic rocks of the underlying Penninic nappes crop out. The structure is caused by a large dome-like antiform in the nappe stacks of the Alps.

a. Greywacke zone
b. Hohe Tauern window
c. Periadriatic Seam
d. Sesia unit

47. The _____ is a tectonic unit in the Swiss Alps. It consists of autochthonous rocks of the former southern continental margin of the European Plate.

The _____ has been overthrusted by the Helvetic nappes, that partly contain similar rocks.

a. AASHTO Soil Classification System
b. AL 129-1
c. Austroalpine nappes
d. Infrahelvetic complex

48.

The _____ is a tectonic terrane in the Italian Alps, that consists of a steeply dipping piece of the Earth's lower crust of the Apulian plate.

Geologically the _____ is considered a part of the Southern Alps. Most rocks in the zone are sedimentary, for example limestones that have been turned into marble by metamorphism. Most of the zone has been through granulite facies metamorphism and was intruded by mafic plutons.

a. Ivrea zone
b. AL 129-1
c. AASHTO Soil Classification System
d. AL 333

49. The _____ is a region of tectonic uplift in the Swiss part of the Alps. It is located in the Lepontine Alps and Glarus Alps.

The Alps north of the Periadriatic Seam are usually divided into three large nappe complexes. From bottom to top these are the Helvetic, Penninic and Austroalpine nappes. East of the dome all three are found on top of each other. The same counts for the region west of the dome, if the Sesia unit is seen as part of the Austroalpine nappes. The dome itself however only shows Penninic and Helvetic (the boundary between the two is still disputed) rocks. Apparently the uplift of the dome caused the upper Austroalpine material to be totally eroded away.

a. Lepontin dome
b. Helvetic nappes
c. Helvetic Zone
d. Penninic thrustfront

50. The _____ is a foreland basin north of the Alps, that formed during the Oligocene and Miocene epochs. The basin formed due to the flexure of the European plate under the weight of the orogenic wedge of the Alps that was forming to the south.

In geology, the name '_____' is sometimes also used in a general sense for a synorogenic (formed contemporaneously with the orogen) forelandbasin of the type north of the Alps.

a. Tectonites
b. Crenulation
c. Petermann Orogeny
d. Molasse basin

51. The _____ or the Penninicum are one of three nappe stacks and geological zones in which the Alps can be divided. In the western Alps the _____ are more obviously present than in the eastern Alps (in Austria), where they crop out as a narrow band.

Of the three nappe stacks the _____ have the highest metamorphic grade. They contain high grade metamorphic rocks of different paleogeographic origins. They were deposited as sediments on the crust that existed between the European and Apulian plates before the Alps were formed.

a. Helvetic nappes
b. Helvetic Zone
c. Dent Blanche nappe
d. Penninic nappes

52. The _____ is a major tectonic thrustfront in the French Alps. The thrustfront moves over a developing decollement horizon, and separates the high grade metamorphic rocks of the Penninic nappes from the (external) sedimentary rocks and crystalline basement of the Helvetic nappes. The last are in France often called zone Dauphin>é or Dauphinois.

a. Greywacke zone
b. Periadriatic Seam
c. Helvetic nappes
d. Penninic thrustfront

53.

The _____ is a distinct geologic fault in Southern Europe, running S-shaped about 1000 km from the Tyrrhenian Sea through the whole Southern Alps as far as Hungary. It forms the division between the Adriatic plate and the European plate. The term Insubric line is sometimes used to address the whole _____, but it is more commonly used to mean just a western part of it.

a. Valais Ocean
b. Periadriatic Seam
c. Penninic thrustfront
d. Lepontin dome

54. The Piemont-Liguria basin or the _____ was a former piece of oceanic crust that is seen as part of the Tethys Ocean. Together with some other oceanic basins that existed between the continents Europe and Africa the _____ is called the Western or Alpine Tethys Ocean.

The _____ was formed in the Jurassic period, when the paleocontinents Laurasia (to the north, with Europe) and Gondwana (to the south, with Africa) started to move away from each other.

   a. Sundance Sea
   c. Superocean
   b. Paleo-Tethys Ocean
   d. Piemont-Liguria Ocean

55. The _____ or Sesia nappe, also called the Sesia-Dent Blanche unit is a tectonic unit or terrane in the Swiss and Italian Alps. The zone crops out in the Pennine Alps and in the southeastern part of the Aosta Valley. It is widely seen as part of the Austroalpine nappes and correlated with the Dent Blanche nappe that crops out further to the northwest.

   a. Sesia unit
   c. Penninic nappes
   b. Hohe Tauern window
   d. Lepontin dome

56. The _____ are a geological subdivision of the European Alps. The _____ are the part of the Alps that are found south of the Periadriatic Seam, a major geological faultzone across the Alps. The _____ contain almost the same area as the Southern Calcareous Alps, a geographical subdivision of the Alps.

In contradiction to the Central Eastern Alps north of the Periadriatic Seam, the geology of the _____ is not characterized by nappes. Neither are high grade metamorphic rocks common in the region. The _____ are tectonically characterized by large scale thrusting and folding to the south, the dominant vergence (direction of fold asymmetry) in the region is southward.

   a. 1509 Istanbul earthquake
   c. 1703 Genroku earthquake
   b. 1700 Cascadia earthquake
   d. Southern Alps

57. The _____ is a disappeared piece of oceanic crust which was situated between the continent Europe and the microcontinent Iberia or so called Briançonnais microcontinent. The _____ is together with other small disappeared oceanic basins often called the Alpine or Western Tethys Ocean.

   a. Periadriatic Seam
   c. Greywacke zone
   b. Lepontin dome
   d. Valais Ocean

58. The _____ is a geological formation exposed in Antarctica and deposited from the Devonian to the Triassic (~400 to - million years ago 225 million years ago.) The sandstone was originally described as a formation, and upgraded to group and supergroup as time passed. It contains a sandy member known as the Beacon heights orthoquartzite.

   a. 1700 Cascadia earthquake
   c. 1703 Genroku earthquake
   b. Beacon sandstone
   d. 1509 Istanbul earthquake

59. The _____ is a prominent undersea massif, a dome-shaped region approximately 10 mi. (16 km) across and rising about 14,000 ft. (4250 m) from the sea floor, in the North Atlantic Ocean.

The massif was formed approximately 1.5-2.0 million years ago. Geologic studies of the massif have indicated that it is not composed of the black basalt typical of the ocean floor, but rather of dense green peridotite usually found in the mantle.

a. AL 333
b. AL 129-1
c. AASHTO Soil Classification System
d. Atlantis Massif

60. The _____ is a mostly oceanic tectonic plate underlying Central America and the Caribbean Sea off the north coast of South America.

Roughly 3.2 million square kilometers (1.2 million square miles) in area, the _____ borders the North American Plate, the South American Plate, the Nazca Plate and the Cocos Plate. These borders are regions of intense seismic activity, including frequent earthquakes, occasional tsunamis, and volcanic eruptions.

a. 1509 Istanbul earthquake
b. 1703 Genroku earthquake
c. 1700 Cascadia earthquake
d. Caribbean Plate

61. The _____ is a tectonic plate which includes most of the continent of Eurasia (a landmass consisting of the traditional continents of Europe and Asia), with the notable exceptions of the Indian subcontinent, the Arabian subcontinent, and the area east of the Chersky Range in East Siberia. It also includes oceanic crust extending westward to the Mid-Atlantic Ridge and northward to the Gakkel Ridge.

The easterly side is a boundary with the North American Plate to the north and a boundary with the Philippine Mobile Belt and the Philippine Sea Plate to the south, and possibly with the Okhotsk Plate and the Amurian Plate.

a. Antarctic Plate
b. Intermontane Plate
c. Arabian Plate
d. Eurasian Plate

62. The _____ is a small oceanic tectonic plate east of Iceland. The island Jan Mayen is at its northern end, and the plate stretches 500 km southwards.

It is proposed that the microplate has rifted off the North American Plate in late oligocene.

a. Jan Mayen Plate
b. Pacific Plate
c. Sunda Plate
d. Mariana Plate

63. The _____ is a tectonic plate covering most of North America, Greenland and part of Siberia. It extends eastward to the Mid-Atlantic Ridge and westward to the Chersky Range in eastern Siberia. The plate includes both continental and oceanic crust. The interior of the main continental landmass includes an extensive granitic core called a craton. Along most of the edges of this craton are fragments of crustal material called terranes, accreted to the craton by tectonic actions over the long span of geologic time. It is believed that much of North America west of the Rockies is composed of such terranes.
a. Futuna Plate
b. Niuafo'ou Plate
c. North American Plate
d. Timor Plate

64. The _____ is an oceanic tectonic plate bordering the South American Plate on the north, the South Sandwich Plate to the east, and the Antarctic Plate on the south and west.

The north and south boundaries of the plate are transform fault boundaries. At the eastern margin the Scotia has a spreading boundary between it and the small South Sandwich Plate.

a. North American Plate
b. Kermadec Plate
c. Futuna Plate
d. Scotia Plate

65. The _____ is a tectonic plate covering the continent of South America and extending eastward to the Mid-Atlantic Ridge.

The easterly side is a divergent boundary with the African Plate forming the southern part of the Mid-Atlantic Ridge. The southerly side is a complex boundary with the Antarctic Plate and the Scotia Plate.

a. South American Plate
b. South Bismarck Plate
c. Philippine Sea Plate
d. Bird's Head Plate

66. The _____ was an ancient tectonic plate that existed from the Cambrian period to the Carboniferous period. The _____ collided against Siberia, to form the Ural Mountains about 500 million years ago. The _____, however, fused onto the Eurasian Plate when the _____ collided against Siberia when the Ural Mountains were completely formed.

a. Sonoma orogeny
b. Fault trace
c. Farallon Plate
d. Baltic Plate

67. The _____ was a tectonic event or series of events in the late Neoproterozoic, about 650-550 Ma, which probably included the formation of mountains. This occurred on the margin of the Gondwana continent, involving one or more collisions of island arcs and accretion of other material at a subduction zone. The precise events, and geographical position, are uncertain, but are thought to involve the terranes of Avalonia, Armorica and Iberia.

a. 1703 Genroku earthquake
b. Cadomian Orogeny
c. 1509 Istanbul earthquake
d. 1700 Cascadia earthquake

68. _____ is made up of a sequence of sedimentary rocks of a Silurian age, dipping to the south-east. The main Silurian succession of limestones and shales comprises thirteen units spanning 200-500 m of stratigraphic thickness, being thickest in the south, and overlies a 75-125 m thick Ordovician sequence. It was deposited in a shallow, hot and salty sea, on the edge of an equatorial continent.

a. Gotland
b. 1509 Istanbul earthquake
c. 1703 Genroku earthquake
d. 1700 Cascadia earthquake

69. _____ - also known as greenstone - is a general field petrologic term applied to metamorphic and/or altered mafic volcanic rock. The green is due to abundant green chlorite, actinolite and epidote minerals that dominate the rock. However, basalts may remain quite black if primary pyroxene does not revert to chlorite or actinolite.

a. Mylonite
b. Greenschist
c. Granoblastic
d. Hornfels

70. _____ are zones of variably metamorphosed mafic to ultramafic volcanic sequences with associated sedimentary rocks that occur within Archaean and Proterozoic cratons between granite and gneiss bodies.

The name comes from the green hue imparted by the colour of the metamorphic minerals within the mafic rocks. Chlorite, actinolite and other green amphiboles are the typical green minerals.

a. Metasomatism
b. Greenstone belts
c. Granoblastic
d. Foliation

71. The _____ is a 2,800-2,600 million year old greenstone belt that spans across the Ontario-Quebec border in Canada. It is mostly made of volcanic rocks, but also includes ultramafic rocks, mafic intrusions, granitoid rocks, and early and middle Precambrian sediments.

The _____ is one of the world's largest Archean greenstone belts.

a. Abitibi greenstone belt
b. AL 129-1
c. AL 333
d. AASHTO Soil Classification System

72. The _____ is a greenstone belt located in the northern part of the Fennoscandian Shield. The region belongs to Lapland, northern Finland. The _____ is part of a much larger belt of Paleoproterozoic greenstones, a cover of metamorphosed volcanic and sedimentary rocks that cover the Archean basement, the latter which is representative of the Archaean Karelian craton.

a. 1700 Cascadia earthquake
b. 1509 Istanbul earthquake
c. 1703 Genroku earthquake
d. Central Lapland Greenstone Belt

73. The _____, also referred to as the Flin Flon-Snow Lake greenstone belt, is a Precambrian greenstone belt located in the central area of Manitoba and east-central Saskatchewan, Canada. It lies in the central portion of the Trans-Hudson orogeny and was formed by arc volcanism during the Paleoproterozoic period. The _____ is 250 km long by 75 km wide and is exposed just north of McClarty Lake.

a. Flin Flon greenstone belt
b. 1509 Istanbul earthquake
c. 1700 Cascadia earthquake
d. 1703 Genroku earthquake

74. The _____ is a 42 km long Archean greenstone belt in western Nunavut. It consists of mostly mafic volcanic rocks and contains three major gold deposits called Boston, Doris and Naartok.

a. Hope Bay greenstone belt
b. 1700 Cascadia earthquake
c. Mountain Lake cluster
d. 1509 Istanbul earthquake

75. The _____ is an Archean greenstone belt in southwestern Greenland dated at 3.8-3.7 Ga and contains the oldest known, well preserved, metavolcanic (metamorphosed mafic volcanic), metasedimentary and sedimentary rocks on Earth. It consists of five tectonic domains.

Almost all the rocks are deformed and substantially altered by metasomatism, however the transitional stages from the volcanic and sedimentary structures to schists can clearly be seen.

a. AL 333
b. AASHTO Soil Classification System
c. Isua greenstone belt
d. AL 129-1

76. The _____ is an Archean greenstone belt in western Ontario, Canada. It consists of basaltic and komatiitic volcanics ranging in age from 2,925 to 2,940 million years old and younger rhyolite-andesite volcanics ranging in age from 2,730 to 2,750 million years old.

Chapter 10. Test Preparation Part 10

a. 1703 Genroku earthquake
b. 1509 Istanbul earthquake
c. 1700 Cascadia earthquake
d. Red Lake greenstone belt

77. The _____ is a late Archean greenstone belt in northern Ontario, Canada. It is the southwestern extension of the Abitibi greenstone belt.
   a. 1509 Istanbul earthquake
   b. 1703 Genroku earthquake
   c. 1700 Cascadia earthquake
   d. Swayze greenstone belt

78. The _____ is an Archean greenstone belt in Temagami, Ontario, located 100 km (62 mi) northeast of Sudbury, Canada. It is characterized by felsic-mafic volcanic rocks and averages about 13 km (8 mi) wide and 29 km (18 mi) long with the dominant structure being a northeast trending syncline called the Tetapaga Syncline that has been modified by the emplacement of granitic rocks. The metavolcanic and metasedimentary units are composed of a different suite of volcanic rocks and clastic chemically precipitated sedimentary rocks.
   a. 1703 Genroku earthquake
   b. Temagami greenstone belt
   c. 1509 Istanbul earthquake
   d. 1700 Cascadia earthquake

79. The _____ is a tectonic plate covering the continent of Antarctica and extending outward under the surrounding oceans. The _____ has a boundary with the Nazca Plate, the South American Plate, the African Plate, the Indo-Australian Plate, the Scotia Plate and a divergent boundary with the Pacific Plate forming the Pacific-Antarctic Ridge.

The _____ is roughly 60,900,000 square kilometers.

   a. Antarctic Plate
   b. Arabian Plate
   c. Eurasian Plate
   d. Intermontane Plate

80. The _____ is a small tectonic plate or microplate located in Southeast Asia, often considered a part of the larger Eurasian Plate. The Andaman Islands, Nicobar Islands, and northwestern Sumatra are located on the plate. This island arc separates the Andaman Sea from the main Indian Ocean to the west.
   a. Burma Plate
   b. Molucca Sea Plate
   c. Sunda Plate
   d. Mariana Plate

81. The _____ is a tectonic plate that was originally a part of the ancient continent of Gondwanaland from which it split off, eventually becoming a major plate. About 50 to 55 million years ago, it fused with the adjacent Australian Plate. It is today part of the major Indo-Australian Plate, and includes the subcontinent of India and a portion of the basin under the Indian Ocean.
   a. AASHTO Soil Classification System
   b. Indian Plate
   c. AL 333
   d. AL 129-1

82. The _____ is a major tectonic plate that includes the continent of Australia and surrounding ocean, and extends northwest to include the Indian subcontinent and adjacent waters. Recent studies suggest that the _____ may be in the process of breaking up into two separate plates due primarily to stresses induced by the collision of the _____ with Eurasia along the Himalayas. The two protoplates or subplates are generally referred to as the Indian Plate and the Australian Plate.
   a. AL 129-1
   b. AASHTO Soil Classification System
   c. AL 333
   d. Indo-Australian Plate

83. _____ was a supercontinent that most recently existed as a part of the split of the Pangaean supercontinent in the late Mesozoic era. It included most of the landmasses which make up today's continents of the northern hemisphere, chiefly Laurentia (the name given to the North American craton), Baltica, Siberia, Kazakhstania, and the North China and East China cratons.
   a. 1700 Cascadia earthquake
   b. 1509 Istanbul earthquake
   c. Laurasia
   d. 1703 Genroku earthquake

84. The _____ is a volcanic hotspot located in the south-central Pacific Ocean. It is responsible for creating the Pitcairn Islands and two large seamounts called Adams and Bounty.
   a. Louisville hotspot
   b. Galapagos hotspot
   c. Marquesas hotspot
   d. Pitcairn hotspot

85. The _____ is a proposed continental tectonic plate covering Manchuria, the Korean Peninsula, Western Japan, and Primorsky Krai. It is not clear yet whether it is an independent plate or a part of the Eurasian Plate. It is bounded on the north and west by the Eurasian Plate, on the northeast by the Okhotsk Plate, and on the south by the Philippine Plate.
   a. AASHTO Soil Classification System
   b. Amurian Plate
   c. AL 129-1
   d. AL 333

86. _____ is an igneous, volcanic rock, of intermediate composition, with aphanitic to porphyritic texture. The mineral assemblage is typically dominated by plagioclase plus pyroxene and/or hornblende. Magnetite, zircon, apatite, ilmenite, biotite, and garnet are common accessory minerals.
   a. AL 333
   b. AL 129-1
   c. AASHTO Soil Classification System
   d. Andesite

87. The _____ is the most significant regional geologic distinction in the Pacific Ocean basin. It separates the mafic basaltic volcanic rocks of the Central Pacific Basin from the partially submerged continental areas of more felsic andesitic volcanic rock on its margins. The _____ parallels the subduction zones and deep oceanic trenches around the Pacific basin.
   a. AL 129-1
   b. AL 333
   c. Andesite line
   d. AASHTO Soil Classification System

88. The _____ is a small tectonic plate (microplate) located in the south Pacific north of Fiji. Clockwise from the north, it borders the Pacific Plate, Australian Plate, Conway Reef Plate, and the New Hebrides Plate. The northern and western borders are a divergent boundary while the rest of the borders are transform and convergent boundaries.
   a. Mariana Plate
   b. Bird's Head Plate
   c. Balmoral Reef Plate
   d. Nazca Plate

89. The _____ is a small tectonic plate underlying the Banda Sea in southeast Asia. This plate also carries a portion of the island of Sulawesi, the entire island of Seram, and the Banda Islands. Clockwise from the east it is bounded by the Bird's Head Plate of western New Guinea, Australian Plate, Timor Plate, Sunda Plate, and the Molucca Sea Plate.
   a. Nazca Plate
   b. Scotia Plate
   c. Banda Sea Plate
   d. New Hebrides Plate

Chapter 10. Test Preparation Part 10

90. The _____ or Blanco Fault Zone is a transform fault zone off the coast of the Pacific Northwest of the United States which runs between the Gorda Ridge to the south and the Juan de Fuca Ridge to the north. The principal feature of the Blanco zone is the Blanco Ridge, a right lateral-moving fault which also incorporates some compression, thus accounting for the uplift expressed in the ridge. The ridge is not an oceanic spreading center, despite its name, whereas the Juan de Fuca and Gorda Ridges to which it is connected are.
   a. Blanco Fracture Zone
   b. Thrust fault
   c. Subduction
   d. Gorda Ridge

91. The _____ is a small tectonic plate located north of New Guinea. It forms a subduction zone along the border with the Bird's Head Plate and the Woodlark Plate to the south. A transform boundary forms the northern border with the Pacific Plate.
   a. Conway Reef Plate
   b. Bird's Head Plate
   c. Solomon Sea Plate
   d. Caroline Plate

92. The _____ is the deepest surveyed point in the oceans, with a depth of about 11,000 metres (estimated 36,198 ft.) The exact depth is unknown. It is located in the Mariana Islands group at the southern end of the Mariana Trench.
   a. Challenger Deep
   b. Mariana Trough
   c. 1509 Istanbul earthquake
   d. 1700 Cascadia earthquake

93. The _____ is an oceanic tectonic plate beneath the Pacific Ocean off the west coast of Central America which rides upon it.

The _____ is created by sea floor spreading along the East Pacific Rise and the Cocos Ridge, specifically in a complicated area geologists call the Cocos-Nazca spreading system. From the rise the plate is pushed eastward and pushed or dragged (perhaps both) under the less dense overriding Caribbean Plate, in the process called subduction.

   a. Sonoma orogeny
   b. Rivera Plate
   c. Farallon Plate
   d. Cocos Plate

94. The _____ is a small tectonic plate (microplate) located in the south Pacific west of Fiji. It is bounded on the east and west by convergent boundaries, the western boundary is with the New Hebrides Plate while the eastern is with the Australian Plate. A short transform boundary also exists with the Balmoral Reef Plate to the north.
   a. Scotia Plate
   b. Maoke Plate
   c. New Hebrides Plate
   d. Conway Reef Plate

95. The _____ is a small (550 km x 410 km) tectonic plate or microplate in the southeastern Pacific. The plate is bounded on the west by the Pacific Plate, and the east by the Nazca Plate. The entire plate is covered by the Pacific Ocean.
   a. Arabian Plate
   b. Okhotsk Plate
   c. Intermontane Plate
   d. Easter Plate

96. The _____ is a very small tectonic plate located near the south Pacific island of Futuna. It is sandwiched between the Pacific Plate to the north and the Australian Plate to the south with the Niuafo'ou Plate to the east.
   a. Sunda Plate
   b. Bird's Head Plate
   c. Juan de Fuca Plate
   d. Futuna Plate

97. The _____ is a small tectonic plate off the west coast of South America near the Galapagos Islands. It differs from most other crustal plates in that it is rotating clockwise between three much larger crustal plates around it, the Nazca, Cocos and Pacific Plates. To its north, an even smaller microplate, the Northern _____ is likewise rotating, but counterclockwise.
   a. Kermadec Plate
   b. New Hebrides Plate
   c. Galapagos Microplate
   d. Solomon Sea Plate

98. The _____, located beneath the Pacific Ocean off the coast of northern California, is one of the northern remnants of the Farallon Plate. It is sometimes referred to (by, for example, publications from the USGS Earthquake Hazards Program) as simply the southernmost portion of the neighboring Juan de Fuca Plate, another Farallon remnant.

Unlike most tectonic plates, the _____ experiences significant deformation inside its boundaries.

   a. Gorda Plate
   b. Lhasa Plate
   c. Kermadec Plate
   d. New Hebrides Plate

99. The _____ is a small tectonic plate located at the triple junction between the Nazca Plate, Antarctic Plate and the Pacific Plate. It is moving in a clockwise direction. The Juan Fernandez Islands of Chile are not carried on this plate as may be suggested by the name.
   a. 1509 Istanbul earthquake
   b. Mariana Trough
   c. 1700 Cascadia earthquake
   d. Juan Fernandez Plate

100. The _____ is a tectonic plate arising from the Juan de Fuca Ridge, and subducting under the northerly portion of the western side of the North American Plate at the Cascadia subduction zone. It is bounded on the south by the Blanco Fracture Zone, on the north by the Nootka Fault, and along the west by the Pacific Plate. The _____ was originally part of the once-vast Farallon Plate, now largely subducted under the North American Plate, and has since fractured into three pieces.
   a. Somali Plate
   b. North Bismarck Plate
   c. Conway Reef Plate
   d. Juan de Fuca Plate

101. The _____ is a long narrow tectonic plate located west of the Kermadec Trench in the south Pacific. Also included on this plate is a portion of the North Island of New Zealand and the Kermadec Islands. It is separated from the Australian Plate by a long divergent boundary which forms a back-arc basin.
   a. Burma Plate
   b. South Bismarck Plate
   c. Juan de Fuca Plate
   d. Kermadec Plate

102. The _____ is an oceanic tectonic plate under the northern Pacific Ocean south of the Near Islands segment of the Aleutian Islands. It is subducting under the North American Plate at the Aleutian Trench and is surrounded by the Pacific Plate. There is a portion of the _____ at the surface in the southern Bering Sea.
   a. Conway Reef Plate
   b. Manus Plate
   c. North Bismarck Plate
   d. Kula Plate

103. The _____ is a tiny tectonic plate located northeast of New Guinea. It is sandwiched between the North Bismarck Plate and the South Bismarck Plate.

a. Niuafo'ou Plate
b. North American Plate
c. Timor Plate
d. Manus Plate

104. The _____ is a small tectonic plate located in western New Guinea underlying the Sudirman Range from which the highest mountain on the island- Puncak Jaya rises. To its east is a convergent boundary with the Woodlark Plate. To the south lies a transform boundary with the Australian Plate and the Bird's Head Plate lies to the west.
a. Kula Plate
b. Burma Plate
c. Maoke Plate
d. Philippine Sea Plate

105. The _____ is a small tectonic plate located west of the Mariana Trench and forms the basement of the Mariana Islands. It is separated from the Philippine Sea Plate by a long divergent boundary with numerous transform fault offsets. The boundary between the Mariana and the Pacific Plate to the east is a subduction zone with the Pacific Plate subducting beneath the Mariana.
a. New Hebrides Plate
b. Scotia Plate
c. South Bismarck Plate
d. Mariana Plate

106. The _____ is an active back-arc basin in the western Pacific Ocean (Stern et al., 2003.) It is an integral part of the Izu-Bonin-Mariana Arc system.

The _____ stretches 1300 km from north to south, about the distance from Los Angeles CA to Portland OR, Tokyo, Japan to Seoul, Korea, or London, England to Rome, Italy. The _____ has roughly the dimensions and areal extent of Japan or California. The Trough is crudely crescent-shaped, opening on the south; it is bounded to the east by the active Mariana arc, to the west by the remnant arc of the West Mariana Ridge (Karig, 1972), and to the south by the Challenger Deep, part of the Mariana Trench.

a. 1700 Cascadia earthquake
b. Juan Fernandez Plate
c. 1509 Istanbul earthquake
d. Mariana Trough

107. The _____ is a small tectonic plate that carries northern Sulawesi, the Molucca Sea and a portion of the Banda Sea in a region littered with numerous small plates. A subduction zone lies along its northern border with the Sunda Plate. A small divergent boundary exists along the Sulawesi part of the border with the Banda Sea Plate and transitions into a convergent boundary as it bisects the Banda Sea; the rest of the borders are transform boundaries.
a. Solomon Sea Plate
b. Timor Plate
c. Pacific Plate
d. Molucca Sea Plate

108. The _____ is an oceanic tectonic plate in the eastern Pacific Ocean basin off the west coast of South America.

The eastern margin is a convergent boundary subduction zone under the South American Plate and the Andes Mountains, forming the Peru-Chile Trench. The southern side is a divergent boundary with the Antarctic Plate, the Chile Rise, where seafloor spreading permits magma to rise.

a. Burma Plate
b. Bird's Head Plate
c. Lhasa Plate
d. Nazca Plate

109. The _____ is a minor tectonic plate located in the Pacific Ocean near the island nation of Vanuatu. The plate is bounded on the southwest by the Indo-Australian Plate which is subducting below it. The New Hebrides Subduction Zone is extremely active, producing over 20 earthquakes of magnitude 7 or higher in just the past 25 years.
   a. Lhasa Plate
   b. Sunda Plate
   c. Pacific Plate
   d. New Hebrides Plate

110. The _____ is a small tectonic plate located in the Bismarck Sea off the northeast coast of New Guinea. To the north it collides with the Pacific Plate and the Caroline Plate, part of the western part subducts under the Woodlark Plate of New Guinea, and it is separated from the South Bismarck Plate by a divergent boundary. Its a somewhat seismically active area.
   a. North American Plate
   b. Lhasa Plate
   c. Niuafo'ou Plate
   d. North Bismarck Plate

111. The _____ is a tectonic plate covering the Sea of Okhotsk, the Kamchatka Peninsula, and Eastern Japan. It was formerly considered a part of the North American Plate, but recent studies indicate that it is an independent plate, bounded on the north by the North American Plate. The boundary is a left-lateral moving transform fault, the Ulakhan Fault.
   a. Intermontane Plate
   b. Arabian Plate
   c. Eurasian Plate
   d. Okhotsk Plate

112. The _____ is a long narrow tectonic plate stretching from the northern end of Taiwan to the southern tip of the island of KyÅ«shÅ«. To the east lies the Ryukyu Trench and the Pacific Plate. It is separated from the Yangtze Plate (often considered part of the Eurasian Plate) by a rift that forms the Okinawa Trough which is a Back arc basin.
   a. AASHTO Soil Classification System
   b. AL 333
   c. Okinawa Plate
   d. AL 129-1

113. The _____ is an oceanic tectonic plate beneath the Pacific Ocean.

To the north the easterly side is a divergent boundary with the Explorer Plate, the Juan de Fuca Plate and the Gorda Plate forming respectively the Explorer Ridge, the Juan de Fuca Ridge and the Gorda Ridge. In the middle the easterly side is a transform boundary with the North American Plate along the San Andreas Fault and a boundary with the Cocos Plate.

   a. Lhasa Plate
   b. Somali Plate
   c. Pacific Plate
   d. Molucca Sea Plate

114. Most segments of the Philippines, including northern Luzon, are part of the _____, which is separate from the Molucca Sea Plate to the south, Sunda Plate to the southwest, the South China Sea Basin to the west and north-west, the Philippine Sea Plate to the east, and in the north ends in eastern Taiwan, the zone of active collision between the North Luzon Trough portion of the Luzon Arc and South China. The _____ has also been called the Philippine Microplate, and the Taiwan-Luzon-Mindoro Belt.
   a. 1703 Genroku earthquake
   b. 1700 Cascadia earthquake
   c. 1509 Istanbul earthquake
   d. Philippine Mobile Belt

115. The _____ is a tectonic plate beneath the Pacific Ocean to the east of the Philippines. The _____ comprises oceanic lithosphere that lies beneath the Philippine Sea, and so has been referred to in the scientific literature of the last 50 years as the _____.

Most segments of the Philippines, including northern Luzon, are part of the Philippine Mobile Belt, which is separate from the Sunda Plate to the southwest, the South China Sea Plate to the west and north-west, Taiwan to the north, and the _____ to the east.

a. Niuafo'ou Plate
b. Philippine Sea Plate
c. South American Plate
d. Burma Plate

116. In geology, a _____ or _____ line is a planar fracture in rock in which the rock on one side of the fracture has moved with respect to the rock on the other side. Large faults within the Earth's crust are the result of differential or shear motion and active _____ zones are the causal locations of most earthquakes. Earthquakes are caused by energy release during rapid slippage along a _____.

a. 1703 Genroku earthquake
b. Fault
c. 1700 Cascadia earthquake
d. 1509 Istanbul earthquake

117. The _____ is an active transform fault, located between the North American Plate and the Pacific Plate, Canada's equivalent of the San Andreas Fault. The _____ forms a triple junction on its south with the Cascadia subduction zone and the Explorer Ridge (the Queen Charlotte Triple Junction.) The fault is named for Queen Charlotte Island which lies just north of the triple junction.

a. 1509 Istanbul earthquake
b. 1703 Genroku earthquake
c. 1700 Cascadia earthquake
d. Queen Charlotte Fault

118. The _____ is a small tectonic plate (a microplate) located off the west coast of Mexico, just south of the Baja California Peninsula. It is bounded on the northwest by the East Pacific Rise, on the southwest by the Rivera Transform Fault, on the southeast by a deformation zone, and on the northeast by the Middle America Trench and another deformation zone.

The _____ is believed to have separated from the Cocos Plate located to its southeast about 5-10 million years ago.

a. Sonoma orogeny
b. Cocos Plate
c. Farallon Plate
d. Rivera Plate

119. The _____ is a minor tectonic plate to the northwest of the Solomon Islands in the south Pacific Ocean.

The tectonic regime in this part of the world is extremely complex and involves a number of minor as well as major plates.

The _____ is an oceanic crustal plate remnant which is disappearing into two subduction zones, one to its north, the other on its southwest margin.

a. Solomon Sea Plate
b. Cimmerian Plate
c. North Bismarck Plate
d. Niuafo'ou Plate

Chapter 11. Test Preparation Part 11

1. _____ is an active, broad zone of inferred left-lateral shear at the triple junction of the Australian plate, Eurasian plate, and Pacific plates, where many plate fragments exist, such as the Philippine Plate, Bird's Head Plate, Halmahera Plate and the Molucca Sea Plate. It has been implicated in numerous large earthquakes. It is one of the 2 major faults created by the Australian and Pacific plate convergence, the other being the Ramu-Markham Fault zone.
   - a. Magallanes-Fagnano Fault
   - b. Macquarie Fault Zone
   - c. Ross Lake Fault
   - d. Sorong Fault

2. The _____ is a small tectonic plate located in the southern Bismarck Sea. The eastern part of New Guinea and the island of New Britain are on this plate. Convergent boundarys line the southern border including the subduction zone responsible for the formation of New Britain and the Solomon Islands.
   - a. Bird's Head Plate
   - b. Galapagos Microplate
   - c. South Bismarck Plate
   - d. Mariana Plate

3. The _____ is a tectonic plate located in southeast Asia and commonly considered a part of the Eurasian Plate. The Sunda includes the South China Sea, the Andaman Sea, southern parts of Vietnam and Thailand along with Malaysia and the islands of Borneo, Sumatra, Java, and part of the Celebes in Indonesia, plus the south-western Philippines islands of Palawan and the Sulu Archipelago.

The Sunda is bounded by (clockwise from the east) the Philippine Sea Plate, the Bird's Head Plate (western New Guinea); the Molucca Sea, Banda Sea and Timor microplates; the Australian Plate; the Burma Plate; the Eurasian Plate; and the Yangtze Plate to the north.

   - a. Nazca Plate
   - b. Maoke Plate
   - c. Kermadec Plate
   - d. Sunda Plate

4. The _____ is a microplate in southeast Asia carrying the island of Timor and surrounding islands. The Australian Plate is subducting under the southern edge of the plate, while a small divergent boundary is located on the eastern edge. Another convergent boundary exists with the Banda Sea Plate to the north, and to the west is a transform boundary.
   - a. Burma Plate
   - b. North Bismarck Plate
   - c. Timor Plate
   - d. Nazca Plate

5. The _____ Formation is one of the world's most celebrated fossil localities, and is famous for the exceptional preservation of the fossils found within it, in which the soft parts are preserved. It is 505 million years (Middle Cambrian) in age, making it one of the earliest fossil beds to preserve the soft parts of animals. The pre-Cambrian fossil record of animals is sparse and ambiguous.
   - a. 1703 Genroku earthquake
   - b. Burgess Shale
   - c. 1509 Istanbul earthquake
   - d. 1700 Cascadia earthquake

6. The _____ are Lower Cretaceous strata located in Montana and Wyoming, in the western United States. The term now includes strata that had formerly been called the Dakota Formation in central and southern Wyoming.

In the Bighorn Basin region along the Montana - Wyoming border, the Cloverly is divided into several members.

   - a. 1509 Istanbul earthquake
   - b. Potomac Formation
   - c. 1700 Cascadia earthquake
   - d. Cloverly Formation

Chapter 11. Test Preparation Part 11

7. The _____ is an icefield located in the Canadian Rockies, astride the Continental Divide of North America. The icefield lies partly in the northwestern tip of Banff and the southern end of Jasper National Park. It is about 325 km² in area, 100 to 365 metres (328' to 1,197') in depth and receives up to seven metres (23 ft) of snowfall per year.
   a. 1700 Cascadia earthquake
   b. 1703 Genroku earthquake
   c. 1509 Istanbul earthquake
   d. Columbia Icefield

8. The _____ is a long hogback ridge at the eastern fringe of the Rocky Mountains that extends north-south from southern Wyoming through Colorado and into northern New Mexico in the United States. The ridge is prominently visible as the first line of foothills along the edge of the Great Plains. It is generally faulted along its western side, and varies in height, with gaps in numerous locations where rivers exit the mountains.
   a. 1703 Genroku earthquake
   b. 1509 Istanbul earthquake
   c. 1700 Cascadia earthquake
   d. Dakota Hogback

9. The _____ is a general term for an ill-defined early Cretaceous formation of the Rocky Mountains and Great Plains. It consists of sandy, shallow-marine deposits with intermittent mud flat sediments, and occasional stream deposits. It is an important aquifer in some areas of the Great Plains. It is made of porous sandstone more than 30 meters thick.
   a. 1509 Istanbul earthquake
   b. 1700 Cascadia earthquake
   c. Potomac Formation
   d. Dakota Sandstone

10. The _____, sometimes also called the Julesburg Basin, Denver-Julesburg Basin is a geologic structural basin centered in eastern Colorado in the United States, but extending into southeast Wyoming, western Nebraska, and western Kansas. It underlies the Denver-Aurora Metropolitan Area on the eastern side of the Rocky Mountains.

The basin consists of a large syncline of stratified Paleozoic and Mesozoic sedimentary rock layers, running north to south along the east side of the Front Range from the vicinity of Pueblo northward to Wyoming.

   a. 1700 Cascadia earthquake
   b. Raton Basin
   c. 1509 Istanbul earthquake
   d. Denver Basin

11. The _____ is a geologic unit containing sandstones, shales, and coal beds in Wyoming, Montana, and parts of adjacent states. In the Powder River Basin, it contains important economic deposits of coal, uranium, and coalbed methane.

The _____ is mostly of Paleocene age and represents a time of extensive swamps as well as fluvial and lacustrine conditions. The rocks are more sandy in southwestern Wyoming and more coal-bearing in northeast Wyoming and southeast Montana, reflecting a general change from rivers and lakes in the west to swamps in the east, but all three environments were present at various times in most locations.

   a. Planar deformation features
   b. Palynomorph
   c. Marine clay
   d. Fort Union Formation

12. The _____ is a large geologic formation in western Colorado in the United States. The largest mesa in the world, it has an area of about 500 square miles (1300 km²) and stretches for about 40 miles (65 km) east of Grand Junction between the Colorado River and the Gunnison River, its tributary to the south. The north side of the mesa is drained largely by Plateau Creek, a smaller tributary of the Colorado.

Geologically the mesa is the result of a hard volcanic basalt layer on its top. This volcanic layer, created during the birth of the modern Rocky Mountains approximately 30 million years ago, suppressed erosion compared to the surrounding sedimentary rock layers, which suffered rapid downcutting from the Colorado and the Gunnison. The top layer rests on a thick sequence of Tertiary shale and sandstone known as the Green River and Wasatch Formations.

   a. 1700 Cascadia earthquake
   b. 1703 Genroku earthquake
   c. 1509 Istanbul earthquake
   d. Grand Mesa

13. The _____ is a 3,959 square miles (10,250 km^2) endorheic drainage basin in south central Wyoming, located between the Atlantic and Pacific drainage basins. North and south of it, the water divide is defined by the Continental Divide. The water divide bifurcates to the eastern and western perimeters of the _____. The Basin is formed by a geologic anticline.
   a. Great Divide Basin
   b. 1700 Cascadia earthquake
   c. 1509 Istanbul earthquake
   d. 1703 Genroku earthquake

14. The _____ is an Eocene geologic formation that records the sedimentation in a series of intermountain lakes. The sedimentary layers were formed in a large area of interconnecting lakes a tributary of the Colorado River. The area of the formation exists as three separate basins around the Uinta Mountains of northeastern Utah: an area in northwestern Colorado east of the Uintas, a larger area in the southwest corner of Wyoming just north of the Uintas known as Lake Gosiute, and the largest area, which lies in northeastern Utah and western Colorado south of the Uintas, known as Lake Uinta.
   a. 1703 Genroku earthquake
   b. Green River Formation
   c. 1509 Istanbul earthquake
   d. 1700 Cascadia earthquake

15. A _____ is a cauldron-like volcanic feature usually formed by the collapse of land following a volcanic eruption such as the one at Yellowstone National Park. They are sometimes confused with volcanic craters.
   a. 1509 Istanbul earthquake
   b. 1700 Cascadia earthquake
   c. 1703 Genroku earthquake
   d. Caldera

16. _____ is a large volcanic caldera located in the San Juan volcanic field in the San Juan Mountains in southwestern Colorado, United States, to the west of the town of La Garita, Colorado. The eruption that created the _____ was, perhaps, the largest known explosive eruption in all of Earth's history.

The _____ is one of a number of calderas that formed during a massive ignimbrite flare-up in Colorado, Utah and Nevada from 40-25 million years ago, and was the site of truly enormous eruptions about 28-26 million years ago, during the Oligocene Epoch.

   a. 1700 Cascadia earthquake
   b. Sierra Grande
   c. La Garita Caldera
   d. 1509 Istanbul earthquake

17. The _____ is a division of Late Cretaceous rocks in the western United States. The microvertebrate fossils and dinosaurs represent important components of the latest Mesozoic vertebrate faunas. The _____ is Late Maastrichtian in age (Lancian land mammal age), and shares much fauna with the Hell Creek Formation of Montana and North Dakota, the Frenchman Formation of southwest Saskatchewan, and the lower part of the Scollard Formation of Alberta.

a. 1509 Istanbul earthquake
c. Lance Formation
b. 1700 Cascadia earthquake
d. 1703 Genroku earthquake

18. The _____ was a period of mountain building in western North America, which started in the Late Cretaceous, 70 to 80 million years ago, and ended 35 to 55 million years ago. The exact duration and ages of beginning and end of the orogeny are in dispute, as is the cause. The _____ occurred in a series of pulses, with quiescent phases intervening. The major feature that was created by this orogeny was the Rocky Mountains, but evidence of this orogeny can be found from Alaska to northern Mexico, with the easternmost extent of the mountain-building represented by the Black Hills of South Dakota.
   a. Laramide orogeny
   b. Kaikoura Orogeny
   c. Pan-African orogeny
   d. Trans-Hudson orogeny

19. _____ refers to natural mountain building, and may be studied as a tectonic structural event, (b) as a geographical event, and (c) a chronological event. Orogenic events (a) cause distinctive structural phenomena and related tectonic activity, (b) affect certain regions of rocks and crust, and (c) happen within a specific period of time.
   a. Alpine orogeny
   b. AASHTO Soil Classification System
   c. Orogeny
   d. Alleghenian orogeny

20. The _____ is a distinctive sequence of Late Jurassic sedimentary rock that is found in the western United States, which has been the most fertile source of dinosaur fossils in North America. It is composed of mudstone, sandstone, siltstone and limestone and is light grey, greenish gray, or red. Most of the fossils occur in the green siltstone beds and lower sandstones, relics of the rivers and floodplains of the Jurassic period.
   a. Morrison Formation
   b. 1703 Genroku earthquake
   c. 1509 Istanbul earthquake
   d. 1700 Cascadia earthquake

21. The _____ is a region in southeast Montana and northeast Wyoming about 120 miles (190 km) east to west and 200 miles (320 km) north to south known for its coal deposits. It is both a topographic drainage and geologic structural basin. The basin is so named because it is drained by the Powder River, although it is also drained in part by the Cheyenne River, Tongue River, Bighorn River, Little Missouri River, Platte River, and their tributaries.
   a. 1509 Istanbul earthquake
   b. 1700 Cascadia earthquake
   c. Raton Basin
   d. Powder River Basin

22. The _____ is a geologic structural basin in southern Colorado and northern New Mexico. In extent, the basin is approximately 50 miles east-west, and 90 miles north-south, in Huerfano and Las Animas Counties, Colorado, and Colfax County, New Mexico.

The sedimentary beds that form the basin are of Paleozoic, Mesozoic and Tertiary age. In the eastern part of the basin, the sedimentary section is capped by flows of basalt of Miocene age. The basin is highly asymmetrical, the beds dipping more steeply on the west side than the east.

The sedimentary rocks of the basin are extensively intruded by igneous plugs, dikes and sills of Eocene to Oligocene age. Two large granitic intrusives near the center of the basin form East Spanish Peak and West Spanish Peak.

a. 1509 Istanbul earthquake
c. Powder River Basin
b. 1700 Cascadia earthquake
d. Raton Basin

23. The _____, or the 'Trench' is sometimes called 'the valley of a thousand peaks'. It is both visually and cartographically a striking physiographic feature extending approximately 1600 km (995 mi) from Flathead Lake, Montana, to the Liard River, just south of the British Columbia-Yukon border near Watson Lake, Yukon. The general orientation of the Trench is an almost uniform 150/330 degree geographic north vector which has also become convenient for north/south aviators.

Right-lateral strike-slip fault movement on the Tintina-Northern _____ may have begun during the middle Jurassic. The fastest rates of slip probably occurred during two pulses in the middle Cretaceous and early Cenozoic, respectively, with the latter probably occurring during the Eocene. Between 750 km to > 900 km of total right-lateral movement has occurred, of which 450 km of offset has occurred since the mid-Cretaceous. The end result is that terrains to the west of the fault system have moved toward the north. In the context of plate tectonics, strike-slip movement on the Tintina-Northern _____ is also related to strike-slip movement along the San Andreas Fault.

a. Rocky Mountain Trench
c. Amblypoda
b. Andrija MohoroviÄ□iÄ‡
d. Ambulocetus

24. The _____ is a western North American sequence of Upper Jurassic age marine shales, sandy shales, and sandstones. The formation underlies the western North American Morrison Formation, the most fertile source of dinosaur fossils in the Americas, and is separated by a disconformity from the underlying Upper Triassic Chugwater Formation red beds. The _____ is known for fossils of an extinct species of marine cephalopod, Belemnites densus.

a. 1509 Istanbul earthquake
c. 1700 Cascadia earthquake
b. 1703 Genroku earthquake
d. Sundance Formation

25. The _____ was an epeiric sea which existed in North America during the mid to late Jurassic Period of the Mesozoic Era. It was an arm of what is now the Arctic Ocean, and extended through what is now western Canada into the central western United States. The sea receded when highlands to the west began to rise.

The _____ did not occur at a single time; geological evidence suggests that the Sea was actually a series of five successive marine transgressions--each separated by an erosional hiatus--which advanced and receded from the middle Jurassic onward.

a. Superocean
c. Piemont-Liguria Ocean
b. Sundance Sea
d. Pan-African Ocean

26. _____ is located in Glacier National Park, Montana, United States. It is a hydrologic apex of the North American continent (the other is Snow Dome in Jasper National Park, on the border between Alberta and British Columbia, Canada.) The Continental (Great) Divide and the Laurentian Divide meet at the summit of the peak, and all water that falls at this point can flow to the Pacific and Atlantic Oceans and to Hudson Bay, which opens into the North Atlantic to the north of Labrador.

a. 1509 Istanbul earthquake
c. 1703 Genroku earthquake
b. 1700 Cascadia earthquake
d. Triple Divide Peak

Chapter 11. Test Preparation Part 11

27. An _____ is the result of a sudden release of energy in the Earth's crust that creates seismic waves. They are recorded with a seismometer or the related and mostly obsolete Richter magnitude, with a magnitude 3 or lower _____ being mostly imperceptible and magnitude 7 causing serious damage over large areas.
   a. Earthquake
   b. AASHTO Soil Classification System
   c. AL 333
   d. AL 129-1

28. _____ are clouds claimed to be signs of imminent earthquakes. The analyses of _____ as a form of earthquake prediction are generally not accepted by seismologists and other scientists.

In chapter 32 of his work Brihat Samhita, Indian scholar Varahamihira (505 - 587) discussed a number of signs warning of earthquakes: Unusual animal behavior, astrological influences, underground movements of water, and extraordinary clouds occurring a week before the earthquake.

   a. AASHTO Soil Classification System
   b. AL 129-1
   c. AL 333
   d. Earthquake clouds

29. An _____ is an alleged unusual luminous aerial phenomenon, similar in appearance to the aurora borealis, that supposedly appears in the sky at or near areas of tectonic stress, seismic activity or volcanic eruptions. Scientific evidence for the presence of lights is unreliable, given that there are few references documenting the phenomenon. The sky in New Mexico a few days before the 2008 Sichuan Earthquake

The lights are most evident while an earthquake is occurring, although there are reports of lights occurring before or after the earthquake, such as before the 1976 Tangshan earthquake.

   a. AASHTO Soil Classification System
   b. AL 333
   c. AL 129-1
   d. Earthquake light

30. _____ is a planning tool to determine the appropriate emergency responses or building systems in seismic risk areas. It uses the basics of seismic hazard studies, but usually places a set earthquake on a specific fault, most likely near a high-population area. Most scenarios relate directly to urban seismic risk, and seismic risk in general.
   a. Earthquake storm
   b. AL 129-1
   c. AASHTO Soil Classification System
   d. Earthquake scenario

31. An _____ is a recently proposed theory about earthquakes, where one triggers a series of other large earthquakes-- within the same tectonic plate--as the stress transfers along the fault. This is similar to the idea of aftershocks, with the exception that they take place years apart. These series of earthquakes can devastate entire countries or geographical regions.
   a. Earthquake storm
   b. ICEARRAY
   c. AL 129-1
   d. AASHTO Soil Classification System

32. _____ is an abbreviation for Icelandic Strong-motion Array. The _____ network is a seismic array of 14 strong-motion stations located within the South Iceland Seismic Zone. Each station consists of a seismograph situated in a protective housing.
   a. Earthquake storm
   b. AL 129-1
   c. AASHTO Soil Classification System
   d. ICEARRAY

33. _____ is an important factor in earthquake engineering and construction in earthquake-prone areas. The destabilizing action of an earthquake on constructions may be direct (seismic motion of the ground) or indirect (earthquake-induced landslides, liquefaction of the foundation soils and waves of tsunami.)

Knowledge of local amplification of the seismic motion from the bedrock is very important in order to choose the suitable design solutions.

a. Riprap
b. Geologic preliminary investigation
c. Sediment trap
d. Mitigation of seismic motion

34. When building a house, regional _____ maps are used to find the best (or the worst) place to locate for earthquake shaking. Although greatly confused with its sister, seismic risk, _____ is the study of expected earthquake ground motions at any point on the earth. Surface motion map for a hypothetical earthquake on the northern portion of the Hayward Fault Zone and its presumed northern extension, the Rodgers Creek Fault Zone

The calculations for _____ can be quite complex.

a. 1509 Istanbul earthquake
b. 1700 Cascadia earthquake
c. Seismic risk
d. Seismic hazard

35. _____ is defined as the process of subdividing a potential seismic or earthquake prone area into zones with respect to some geological and geophysical characteristics of the sites such as ground shaking, liquefaction susceptibility, landslide and rock fall hazard, earthquake-related flooding, so that seismic hazards at different locations within the area can correctly be identified. Microzonation provides the basis for site-specific risk analysis, which can assist in the mitigation of earthquake damages. In most general terms, _____ is the process of estimating the response of soil layers under earthquake excitations and thus the variation of earthquake characteristics on the ground surface.

a. 1700 Cascadia earthquake
b. Seismic risk
c. 1509 Istanbul earthquake
d. Seismic microzonation

36. _____ uses the results of a seismic hazard analysis, and includes both consequence and probability. _____ has been defined, for most management purposes, as the potential economic, social and environmental consequences of hazardous events that may occur in a specified period of time. A building located in a region of high seismic hazard is at lower risk if it is built to sound seismic engineering principles.

a. Seismic microzonation
b. 1700 Cascadia earthquake
c. 1509 Istanbul earthquake
d. Seismic risk

37. _____ also known as Stellar seismology is the science that studies the internal structure of pulsating stars by the interpretation of their frequency spectra. Different oscillation modes penetrate to different depths inside the star. These oscillations provide information about the otherwise unobservable interiors of stars in a manner similar to how seismologists study the interior of Earth and other solid planets through the use of earthquake oscillations.

a. AL 129-1
b. AASHTO Soil Classification System
c. AL 333
d. Asteroseismology

Chapter 11. Test Preparation Part 11

38. In geology, a _____ or _____ line is a planar fracture in rock in which the rock on one side of the fracture has moved with respect to the rock on the other side. Large faults within the Earth's crust are the result of differential or shear motion and active _____ zones are the causal locations of most earthquakes. Earthquakes are caused by energy release during rapid slippage along a _____.
    a. 1509 Istanbul earthquake
    b. Fault
    c. 1703 Genroku earthquake
    d. 1700 Cascadia earthquake

39. _____ is a field of study that investigates the behavior of geologic faults.

Behind every good earthquake is some weak rock. Whether the rock remains weak becomes an important point in determining the potential for bigger earthquakes.

    a. 1509 Istanbul earthquake
    b. 1703 Genroku earthquake
    c. 1700 Cascadia earthquake
    d. Fault mechanics

40. _____ is the study of the propagation of pressure waves in the Sun. Unlike seismic waves on Earth, solar waves have practically no shear component (s-waves.) Solar pressure waves are generated by the turbulence in the convection zone, near the surface of the sun, and certain frequencies are amplified by constructive interference.
    a. 1509 Istanbul earthquake
    b. Helioseismology
    c. 1700 Cascadia earthquake
    d. 1703 Genroku earthquake

41. _____ looks at geologic sediments and rocks, for signs of ancient earthquakes. It is used to supplement seismic monitoring, for the calculation of seismic hazard. _____ is usually restricted to geologic regimes that have undergone continuous sediment creation for the last few thousand years, such as swamps, lakes, river beds and shorelines.
    a. Tejas sequence
    b. Geological history
    c. First appearance datum
    d. Paleoseismology

42. The _____ is a mountain range which extends along the southern margin of Eurasia. Stretching from Java to Sumatra through the Himalayas, the Mediterranean, and out into the Atlantic, it includes the Alps, the Carpathians, the mountains of Asia Minor and Iran, the Hindu Kush, the Himalayas, and the mountains of Southeast Asia. It is the second most seismic region in the world.
    a. Obduction
    b. East Pacific Rise
    c. Elastic rebound theory
    d. Alpide belt

43. The _____ is a volcanic hotspot in central British Columbia, Canada. It is situated on the Interior Plateau, a large region that lies between the Cariboo and Monashee Mountains to the east, and the Hazelton Mountains, Coast Mountains and Cascade Range to the west. As a geologic hotspot, it is a place that has experienced active volcanism over a long period of time.
    a. AL 129-1
    b. AL 333
    c. AASHTO Soil Classification System
    d. Anahim hotspot

44. The _____ is a seismic wave anomaly in the Earth's mantle, from ~700-1400 km depth, characterized by relatively high attenuation and decreased sound speed. It is centered beneath northern China, just northwest of Beijing.

The seismic properties of the anomaly are similar to those of the asthenosphere, which contains water absorbed from subducting slabs.

a. 1700 Cascadia earthquake
b. 1509 Istanbul earthquake
c. Seismogenic layer
d. Beijing Anomaly

45. The _____ is a major, active left lateral-moving transform fault which cuts across Guatemala. It forms part of the tectonic boundary between the North American Plate and the Caribbean Plate. It is considered the onshore continuation of the Cayman Trench which runs under the Caribbean Sea.
   a. Gorda Ridge
   b. Panthalassa
   c. Continental crust
   d. Motagua Fault

46. The _____ is a geological fault line that runs through eastern New Orleans. The _____ is the subject of extensive scientific inquiry into why Louisiana is losing vast tracts of land.

Subsurface mapping identified the _____, on the basis of well cutoffs and seismic surveys. Sedimentary growth implies that movement along the _____ has been intermittent since Oligocene time.

   a. Tectonites
   b. Sag pond
   c. Crenulation
   d. Michoud fault

47. The _____ is a major seismic zone in the Southern and Midwestern United States stretching to the southwest from New Madrid, Missouri.

The _____ is made up of reactivated faults that formed when North America began to split or rift apart during the breakup of the supercontinent Rodinia in the Neoproterozoic Era (about 750 million years ago). The resulting rift system failed but remained as an aulacogen (a scar or zone of weakness). The area was then flooded by an ancient ocean, depositing layers of sediment on the rift.

   a. 1509 Istanbul earthquake
   b. 1703 Genroku earthquake
   c. 1700 Cascadia earthquake
   d. New Madrid Seismic Zone

48. The _____ is an area where large numbers of earthquakes and volcanic eruptions occur in the basin of the Pacific Ocean. In a 40,000 km horseshoe shape, it is associated with a nearly continuous series of oceanic trenches, volcanic arcs, and volcanic belts and/or plate movements. The _____ has 452 volcanoes and is home to over 75% of the world's active and dormant volcanoes.
   a. 1703 Genroku earthquake
   b. 1509 Istanbul earthquake
   c. 1700 Cascadia earthquake
   d. Pacific Ring of Fire

49. The _____ is a major geologic fault which runs eastward from the eastern end of the Terceira Rift in the Azores, extending through the Strait of Gibraltar and into the Mediterranean Sea. It forms part of the tectonic boundary between the Eurasian Plate and the African Plate. The extension east of the Strait of Gibraltar is poorly understood and is currently regarded as a 'diffuse' boundary.
   a. Obduction
   b. East Pacific Rise
   c. Elastic rebound theory
   d. Azores-Gibraltar Transform Fault

50. The _____ is one of the longest and most significant faults in Australia, exposed for over 1000 km in a north-south orientation near the west coast of southern Western Australia. It is a major geological boundary separating the Archaean Yilgarn Craton in the east from the younger Pinjarra Orogen and overlying Phanerozoic Perth Basin to the west. The fault is very ancient and initially formed during the Precambrian Era.
   a. Darling Fault
   b. 1703 Genroku earthquake
   c. 1700 Cascadia earthquake
   d. 1509 Istanbul earthquake

51. The _____ fault system, also sometimes referred to as the Dead Sea Rift, is a geologic fault which extends through the Jordan River Valley in the Middle East. It runs along the boundary of two tectonic plates, the African Plate on the west and the Arabian Plate on the east. It is a left lateral transform fault, signifying the relative motions of the two plates.
   a. 1700 Cascadia earthquake
   b. 1703 Genroku earthquake
   c. 1509 Istanbul earthquake
   d. Dead Sea Transform

52. The _____ is a major geologic fault in eastern Turkey. It runs along the tectonic boundary between the Anatolian Plate and the northward-moving Arabian Plate. The difference in the relative motions of the two plates is manifest in the left lateral motion along the fault.
   a. AL 333
   b. AL 129-1
   c. AASHTO Soil Classification System
   d. East Anatolian Fault

53. A _____ is the topographic expression of faulting attributed to the displacement of the land surface by movement along the fault. It can be caused by differential erosion along an old inactive geologic fault (a sort of old rupture) with hard and weak rock, or by a movement on an active fault. In many cases, bluffs form from the upthrown block and can be very steep.
   a. Toreva block
   b. Shutter ridge
   c. Rejuvenated
   d. Fault scarp

54. A _____ is the intersection of a geological fault with the ground surface, leaving a visible mark. The term also applies to a line plotted on a geological map to represent a fault.
   a. Fault trace
   b. Sonoma orogeny
   c. Rivera Plate
   d. Cocos Plate

55. The Indonesian island of Sumatra is located in a highly seismic area of the world. In addition to the subduction zone and the associated Sunda Arc off the west coast of the island, Sumatra also has a large strike-slip fault, the so-called _____, running the entire length of the island. This fault zone accommodates most of the strike-slip motion associated with the oblique convergence between the Indo-Australian and Eurasian plates.
   a. Great Sumatran fault
   b. Magallanes-Fagnano Fault
   c. Sorong Fault
   d. Macquarie Fault Zone

56. The _____ is a geologic fault that traverses Scotland from Arran and Helensburgh on the west coast to Stonehaven in the east. It separates two distinctly different physiographic regions: the Highlands from the Lowlands, but in most places it is only recognisable as a change in topography.
   a. 1703 Genroku earthquake
   b. 1509 Istanbul earthquake
   c. Highland Boundary Fault
   d. 1700 Cascadia earthquake

57. The _____ is a right-lateral oblique slip fault in the South Island of New Zealand. It extends northeast from the Alpine Fault on the West Coast to the Pacific Ocean near Kaikoura on the islands East Coast.

The last rupture of the _____ was in 1888 when an earthquake of estimated magnitude 7-7.3 displaced the fault horizontally by approximately 2.5m.

   a. 1700 Cascadia earthquake   b. 1703 Genroku earthquake
   c. 1509 Istanbul earthquake   d. Hope Fault

58. _____ is a major fault that runs from the city of Itoigawa, Niigata Prefecture, through Lake Suwa to the city of Shizuoka in Shizuoka Prefecture. .

   a. AASHTO Soil Classification System   b. AL 129-1
   c. AL 333   d. Itoigawa-Shizuoka Tectonic Line

59. _____ , also Median Tectonic Line (MTL), is Japan's longest fault line system. It connects with the Itoigawa-Shizuoka Tectonic Line , the left blue line on the map, and the Fossa Magna, the pink shaded region.

The _____ begins near Ibaraki Prefecture, runs through central Honshu to near Nagoya, passing through Mikawa Bay, then through the Inland Sea from the Kii Channel and Naruto Strait to Shikoku along the Sadamisaki Peninsula and the Bungo Channel and Hōyo Strait to Kyūshū.

   a. 1703 Genroku earthquake   b. Japan Median Tectonic Line
   c. 1509 Istanbul earthquake   d. 1700 Cascadia earthquake

60. The _____ is a thrust fault which runs along the base of the Longmenshan Mountains in Sichuan province in southwestern China. The strike of the fault plane is approximately NE. Motion on this fault is responsible for the uplift of the mountains relative to the lowlands of the Sichuan Basin to the east.

   a. 1700 Cascadia earthquake   b. 1509 Istanbul earthquake
   c. 1703 Genroku earthquake   d. Longmenshan Fault

61. _____ is a large river on southern Vancouver Island, British Columbia, Canada.

The creek runs east-west from north of River Jordan, British Columbia to Sombrio Beach. It is geologically very interesting since the creek follows the Leech River major thrust fault and forms a distinct border between two different terranes: In the south the Crescent Terrane, an ancient volcanic island, and in the north the Pacific Rim Terrane, composed of gneiss and schist.

   a. 1700 Cascadia earthquake   b. 1703 Genroku earthquake
   c. 1509 Istanbul earthquake   d. Loss Creek

62. The _____ is a major right lateral-moving transform fault along the seafloor of the south Pacific Ocean which runs from New Zealand southwestward to the Macquarie Triple Junction. It is also the tectonic plate boundary between the Indo-Australian Plate to the northwest and the Pacific Plate to the southeast.

The _____ includes a component of convergence which increases as it approaches the South Island of New Zealand.

a. Ross Lake Fault
c. Magallanes-Fagnano Fault

b. Macquarie Fault Zone
d. Sorong Fault

63. The _____ is a continental transform fault. The fault marks a transform boundary between the Scotia Plate and the South American Plate, cutting across continental crust. It runs under the Strait of Magellan's western arm, Almirantazgo Sound and Fagnano Lake.

a. Ross Lake Fault
c. Magallanes-Fagnano Fault

b. Macquarie Fault Zone
d. Sorong Fault

64. The _____ is a major active right lateral-moving geologic fault in northern Anatolia which runs along the tectonic boundary between the Eurasian Plate and the Anatolian Plate. The fault extends westward from a junction with the East Anatolian Fault at the Karliova Triple Junction in eastern Turkey, across northern Turkey and into the Aegean Sea. It runs about 20 km south of Istanbul.

a. 1509 Istanbul earthquake
c. 1700 Cascadia earthquake

b. 1703 Genroku earthquake
d. North Anatolian Fault

65. The Upper Rhine valley (Oberrheinische Tiefebene) describes the Upper Rhine area on the earth's surface, while the Upper _____ is the geological formation below.

The _____ is a striking reminder of the tectonic plates that created Europe. Rift valleys are usually formed when two plates pull apart, thus causing land to collapse into the gap.

a. 1700 Cascadia earthquake
c. 1509 Istanbul earthquake

b. 1703 Genroku earthquake
d. Rhine rift

66. The 10-km-wide _____ system is part of a 500-km-long zone of high-angle faults in the northern Cordillera. The _____ System consists of two major sets of faults. The eastern set of the Hozameen and Slate Creek faults and more southerly North Creek fault form the western boundary of the Jura-Cretaceous Methow basin and in part separate it from metamorphic equivalents of Methow strata.

a. Macquarie Fault Zone
c. Ross Lake Fault

b. Magallanes-Fagnano Fault
d. Sorong Fault

67. A _____ is used to measure and compare the severity of earthquakes.

Two fundamentally different but equally important types of scales are commonly used by seismologists to describe earthquakes. The original force or energy of an earthquake is measured on a magnitude scale, while the intensity of shaking occurring at any given point on the Earth's surface is measured on an intensity scale.

a. Surface wave magnitude
c. Seismic scale

b. Moment magnitude scale
d. China Seismic Intensity Scale

68. _____ is a way of determining the size of an earthquake, using the amplitude of the initial P-wave to calculate the magnitude. The P-wave is a type of body wave that is capable of traveling through the earth at a velocity of around 5 to 8 km/s, and is the first wave from an earthquake to reach a seismometer. Because of this, calculating the _____ can be the quickest method of determining the size of an earthquake that is of a large distance from the seismometer.

a. Surface wave magnitude
b. Richter magnitude scale
c. Rossi-Forel scale
d. Body wave magnitude

69. The _____ is a national standard in the People's Republic of China used to measure seismic intensity. Similar to EMS-92 on which _____ drew reference, seismic impacts are classified into 12 degrees of intensity, or liedu in Roman numerals from I for insensible to XII for landscape reshaping.

The scale was initially formalized by the China Earthquake Administration in 1980, therefore often referred to by its original title as '_____'.

a. China Seismic Intensity Scale
b. Richter magnitude scale
c. Surface wave magnitude
d. Moment magnitude scale

70. The _____ is a macroseismic intensity scale used to evaluate the severity of ground shaking on the basis of observed effects in an area of the earthquake occurrence.

The scale was first proposed by Sergei Medvedev, Wilhelm Sponheuer , and V>ít K>árn>ík in 1964. It was based on the experiences being available in the early 1960s from the application of the Modified Mercalli scale and the 1953 version of the Medvedev scale, known also as the GEOFIAN scale.

a. Moment magnitude scale
b. Rossi-Forel scale
c. Mercalli intensity scale
d. Medvedev-Sponheuer-Karnik scale

71. The _____ is a scale used for measuring the intensity of an earthquake. The scale quantifies the effects of an earthquake on the Earth's surface, humans, objects of nature, and man-made structures on a scale of I through XII, with I denoting not felt, and XII one that causes almost complete destruction. The values will differ based on the distance to the earthquake, with the highest intensities being around the epicentral area.

a. Surface wave magnitude
b. Mercalli intensity scale
c. Medvedev-Sponheuer-Karnik scale
d. Seismic scale

72. The _____ is used by seismologists to measure the size of earthquakes in terms of the energy released. The magnitude is based on the moment of the earthquake, which is equal to the rigidity of the Earth multiplied by the average amount of slip on the fault and the size of the area that slipped. The scale was developed in the 1970s to succeed the 1930s-era Richter magnitude scale, M_L.

a. Rossi-Forel scale
b. Moment magnitude scale
c. China Seismic Intensity Scale
d. Mercalli intensity scale

73. The _____, also known as the local magnitude (M_L) scale, assigns a single number to quantify the amount of seismic energy released by an earthquake. It is a base-10 logarithmic scale obtained by calculating the logarithm of the combined horizontal amplitude of the largest displacement from zero on a Wood-Anderson torsion seismometer output. So, for example, an earthquake that measures 5.0 on the Richter scale has a shaking amplitude 10 times larger than one that measures 4.0.

a. Surface wave magnitude
b. Richter magnitude scale
c. Mercalli intensity scale
d. Medvedev-Sponheuer-Karnik scale

74. The _____ was one of the first seismic scales to reflect earthquake intensities. Developed by Michele Stefano Conte de Rossi of Italy and Fran>çois-Alphonse Forel of Switzerland in the 1800s, it was used for about two decades until the introduction of the Mercalli intensity scale in 1902.

This system is still being used by some countries, including the Philippines.

a. Rossi-Forel scale
b. China Seismic Intensity Scale
c. Seismic scale
d. Surface wave magnitude

75. In physics, a _____ is a mechanical wave that propagates along the interface between differing media, usually two fluids with different densities. A _____ can also be an electromagnetic wave guided by a refractive index gradient. In radio transmission, a ground wave is a _____ that propagates close to the surface of the Earth.

a. Surface wave
b. 1703 Genroku earthquake
c. 1700 Cascadia earthquake
d. 1509 Istanbul earthquake

76. The _____ scale is one of the magnitude scales used in seismology to describe the size of an earthquake. It is based on measurements in Rayleigh surface waves that travel primarily along the uppermost layers of the earth. It is currently used in People's Republic of China as a national standard (GB 17740-1999) for categorising earthquakes.

a. Moment magnitude scale
b. China Seismic Intensity Scale
c. Surface wave magnitude
d. Richter magnitude scale

77. An _____ is a fault which has had displacement or seismic activity during the geologically recent period. In the United States, an _____ is generally defined as a fault which displaced earth materials during the Holocene Epoch (during the last 11,000 or so years before present.) Active faults are the most common sources of earthquakes and tectonic movements.

a. AL 333
b. AL 129-1
c. Active fault
d. AASHTO Soil Classification System

78. An _____ is an earthquake that occurs after a previous earthquake (the main shock.) An _____ is in the same region of the main shock but is always of smaller magnitude strength. If an _____ is larger than the main shock, the _____ is redesignated as the main shock and the original main shock is redesignated as a foreshock.

a. Aftershock
b. AL 333
c. AL 129-1
d. AASHTO Soil Classification System

79. In geology, _____ is measurable surface displacement along a fault in the absence of notable earthquakes.

An example is along the Calaveras fault in Hollister, California. Streets crossing the fault in Hollister show significant offset and several houses sitting atop the fault are notably twisted (yet habitable.)

a. Aseismic creep
b. AL 129-1
c. AL 333
d. AASHTO Soil Classification System

80. _____ is the gradual uplift (positive _____) or descent (negative _____) of part of the Earth's surface caused by the filling or emptying of an underground magma chamber and/or hydrothermal activity, particularly in volcanic calderas. It can persist for millennia in between eruptions and is normally accompanied by thousands of small tremors and sometimes larger earthquakes.

a. Gravitational erosion
b. Rejuvenated
c. Bradyseism
d. Shutter ridge

81. The _____ is the strongest part of the Earth's crust. For quartz and feldspar rich rocks in continental crust this occurs at an approximate depth of 13-18 km (roughly equivalent to temperatures in the range 250-400>°C.) At this depth rock becomes less likely to fracture, and more likely to deform ductilely by creep.
   a. 1700 Cascadia earthquake
   b. 1509 Istanbul earthquake
   c. Brittle-ductile transition zone
   d. Seismogenic layer

82. A _____ is a term used to describe a seismic jolt occurring within a mine. The term refers to the explosive collapse of a wall or one or more support pillars, sometimes called a rock burst. These pillars are left in place during room and pillar mining, where an original narrow passage is dug and then substantially widened as ore is removed, creating open rooms with support pillars left in place.
   a. 1703 Genroku earthquake
   b. Coal mine bump
   c. 1509 Istanbul earthquake
   d. 1700 Cascadia earthquake

83. A _____ is a continuous release of seismic energy typically associated with the underground movement of magma. It contrasts distinctly with the sudden release and rapid decrease of seismic energy associated with the more common type of earthquake caused by slippage along a geological fault.
   a. Teleseism
   b. Seismic gap
   c. Shadow zone
   d. Continuous Tremor Signal

84. A _____ known as a frost quake may be caused by a sudden cracking action in frozen soil or rock saturated with water or ice. As water seeps down into the rock, it freezes and expands, putting stress on surrounding rock. This builds up until it is relieved explosively in a _____.
   a. Geohazard
   b. Sturzstrom
   c. Cryoseism
   d. Debris flow

85. The _____ or epicentre is the point on the Earth's surface that is directly above the hypocenter or focus, the point where an earthquake or underground explosion originates.

The _____ is usually the location of greatest damage. However, in some cases the _____ is above the start of a much larger event.

   a. AL 129-1
   b. Epicenter
   c. AASHTO Soil Classification System
   d. AL 333

86. _____ is a phenonemon recently observed in seismology describing a particular type of tremor pattern observed in regions of convergent plate boundaries. These are characterised by non-earthquake like tremors, accompanied by aseismic slip in the same region of the local megathrust. For some GPS stations around the _____, there is an apparent slipping back or reversal of direction of the normal tectonic plate movement, although the fault motion remains consistent with subduction.
   a. AL 333
   b. AL 129-1
   c. AASHTO Soil Classification System
   d. Episodic tremor and slip

Chapter 11. Test Preparation Part 11

87. _____ describes the relation of friction to fault mechanics. Rock failure and associated earthquakes are very much a fractal operation The process remains scale-invariant down to the smallest crystal.
   a. Receiver function
   b. Tornillo event
   c. Fault friction
   d. Meizoseismal area

88. _____ describes a long-duration release of seismic energy with distinct spectral (harmonic) lines that and often precedes or accompanies volcanic eruptions. More generally, volcanic tremor, is a sustained signal that may or may not possess these harmonic spectral features.

   _____ is a sustained release of seismic and/or infrasonic energy typically associated with the underground movement or venting of magma and/or volcanic gases.
   a. Rayleigh waves
   b. Seismic waves
   c. Shadow zone
   d. Harmonic tremor

89. The _____, refers to the site of an earthquake or to that of a nuclear explosion. In the former, it is a synonym of the focus; in the latter, of ground zero.

   The location of an earthquake's _____ is the position where the energy stored in the strain in the rock is released, which occurs at the focal depth below the epicentre. The focal depth can be calculated from measurements based on seismic wave phenomena.
   a. Meizoseismal area
   b. Seismic shadowing
   c. Shadow zone
   d. Hypocenter

90. In seismology _____ refers to typically minor earthquakes and tremors that are caused by human activity that alters the stresses and strains on the Earth's crust. Most _____ is of an extremely low magnitude, and in many cases, human activity is merely the trigger for an earthquake that would have occurred naturally in any case.

   There are a number of ways in which _____ has been seen to occur:

   The mass of water in a reservoir alters the pressure in the rock below, which can trigger earthquakes.
   a. Induced seismicity
   b. AL 333
   c. AASHTO Soil Classification System
   d. AL 129-1

91. _____ is sound that is lower in frequency than 20 cycles per second, the normal limit of human hearing. Hearing becomes gradually less sensitive as frequency decreases, so for humans to perceive _____, the sound pressure must be sufficiently high. The ear is the primary organ for sensing _____, but at higher levels it is possible to feel _____ vibrations in various parts of the body. This frequency range is utilized for monitoring earthquakes, charting rock and petroleum formations below the earth.
   a. AL 333
   b. AASHTO Soil Classification System
   c. AL 129-1
   d. Infrasound

92. _____ is a geological term that refers to the collapse of a (usually high-altitude) lake. High-altitude lakes tend to form in volcanic craters - where they are called crater lakes - or in valleys dammed as the result of earthquakes or glacial or volcanic deposition. Lake breakouts are most common a few weeks or months after a volcanic eruption as a river becomes blocked by volcanic debris.
   a. 1509 Istanbul earthquake
   b. 1703 Genroku earthquake
   c. 1700 Cascadia earthquake
   d. Lake breakout

93. In seismology, _____ are surface seismic waves that cause horizontal shifting of the earth during an earthquake. A.E.H. Love predicted the existence of _____ mathematically in 1911. They form a distinct class, different from other types of seismic waves, such as P-waves and S-waves (both body waves), or Rayleigh waves (another type of surface wave). _____ travel with a slower velocity than P- or S- waves, but faster than Rayleigh waves.
   a. 1509 Istanbul earthquake
   b. Seismic refraction
   c. Love waves
   d. Strainmeter

Chapter 12. Test Preparation Part 12

1. An important parameter in the calculation of seismic hazard, _____ is also one of the more contentious. The choice of the value can greatly influence the final outcome of the results, yet this is most likely a size of earthquake that has not yet occurred in the region under study. Frequency-magnitude plot

    The seismic hazard calculation involves a double integration (integral) over the region, combined with the expected number (earthquake frequency) of earthquakes, from the smallest to the largest.

    a. Seismic gap
    b. Shadow zone
    c. Teleseism
    d. Maximum magnitude

2. The _____ in an earthquake is the area of maximum damage. For example, in the Charleston, South Carolina, earthquake of 1886, the _____ was an area about twenty by thirty miles stretching northeast between Charleston and Jedburg and incorporating Summerville. The estimated epicenter was near Middleton Place.

    a. Teleseism
    b. Meizoseismal area
    c. Strong ground motion
    d. Seismic waves

3. _____ are type of elastic wave, also called seismic waves, that can travel through gases, elastic solids and liquids, including the Earth. _____ can be produced by earthquakes and recorded by seismometers.

    a. 1509 Istanbul earthquake
    b. 1700 Cascadia earthquake
    c. P-waves
    d. 1703 Genroku earthquake

4. _____ is the term used to describe liquefaction features attributed to seismic events occurring before measurements or detailed records were kept of earthquakes. The study of these features can tell us a great deal about the seismicity of regions where large earthquakes happen infrequently. This is a subset of the broader field of paleoseismology.

    a. Receiver function
    b. Meizoseismal area
    c. Maximum magnitude
    d. Paleoliquefaction

5. _____ is a measure of earthquake acceleration on the ground and an important input parameter for earthquake engineering.

    Unlike the Richter magnitude scale, it is not a measure of the total size of the earthquake, but rather how hard the earth shakes in a given geographic area.

    Unlike the Mercalli intensity scale, it is measured by instruments, not from personal reports, although it generally correlates well with the Mercalli scale.

    a. 1700 Cascadia earthquake
    b. 1703 Genroku earthquake
    c. 1509 Istanbul earthquake
    d. Peak ground acceleration

6. _____ are a type of elastic surface wave that travel on solids. They are produced on the Earth by earthquakes, in which case they are also known as 'ground roll', or by other sources of seismic energy such as an explosion or even a sledgehammer impact. They are also produced in materials by acoustic transducers, and are used in non-destructive testing for detecting defects.

    a. Maximum magnitude
    b. Seismic shadowing
    c. Hypocenter
    d. Rayleigh waves

7. A _____ technique is a way to model the structure of the Earth by using the information from teleseismic earthquakes recorded at a three component seismograph.

A teleseismic P-wave will generate P to S conversions at crustal boundaries beneath the seismograph. The difference in travel time between the generated S-wave and P-wave contains information about the distance to the boundary and if further reverberations are included more detailed structure can be resolved.

   a. Tornillo event
   c. Meizoseismal area
   b. Paleoliquefaction
   d. Receiver function

8. A type of seismic wave, the _____, secondary wave or shear wave (sometimes called an elastic _____) is one of the two main types of elastic body waves, so named because they move through the body of an object, unlike surface waves.

The _____ move as a shear or transverse wave, so motion is perpendicular to the direction of wave propagation: S-waves, like waves in a rope, as opposed to waves moving through a slinky, the P-wave. The wave moves through elastic media, and the main restoring force comes from shear effects.

   a. 1700 Cascadia earthquake
   c. 1509 Istanbul earthquake
   b. 1703 Genroku earthquake
   d. S-wave

9. A _____ is a body of water, which forms as water collects in the lowest parts of the depression that forms between two strands of an active strike-slip fault . The relative motion of the two fault strands results in a stretching of the land between them, causing the land between them to sink.
   a. Michoud fault
   c. Shear
   b. Petermann Orogeny
   d. Sag pond

10. _____ is a naturally occurring granular material composed of finely divided rock and mineral particles.

As the term is used by geologists, _____ particles range in diameter from 0.0625 (or $>^1\!\!>\!\!/_{16}$ mm, or 62.5 micrometers) to 2 millimeters. An individual particle in this range size is termed a _____ grain.

   a. 1509 Istanbul earthquake
   c. 1703 Genroku earthquake
   b. Sand
   d. 1700 Cascadia earthquake

11. A _____ or sand blow is a cone of sand formed by the ejection of sand onto a surface from a central point. The sand builds up as a cone with slopes at the sand's angle of repose. A crater is commonly seen at the summit. The cone looks like a small volcanic cone and can range in size from millimetres to metres in diameter.
   a. 1703 Genroku earthquake
   c. Sand volcano
   b. 1509 Istanbul earthquake
   d. 1700 Cascadia earthquake

12. A _____ is an opening in a planet's surface or crust, which allows hot, molten rock, ash, and gases to escape from below the surface. Volcanic activity involving the extrusion of rock tends to form mountains or features like mountains over a period of time.

Chapter 12. Test Preparation Part 12

 a. 1509 Istanbul earthquake
 c. 1703 Genroku earthquake
 b. Volcano
 d. 1700 Cascadia earthquake

13. A _____ is a segment of an active fault that has not slipped in an unusually long time when compared with other segments along the same structure. _____ hypothesis/theory states that, over long periods of time, the displacement on any segment must be equal to that experienced by all the other parts of the fault. Any large and longstanding gap is therefore considered to be the fault segment most likely to suffer future earthquakes.
 a. Paleoliquefaction
 c. Seismic gap
 b. Strong ground motion
 d. Maximum magnitude

14. _____ is a geophysical principle governed by Snell's Law. Used in the fields of engineering geology, geotechnical engineering and exploration geophysics, _____ traverses (seismic lines) are performed using a seismograph(s) and/or geophone(s), in an array and an energy source. The _____ method utilizes the refraction of seismic waves on geologic layers and rock/soil units in order to characterize the subsurface geologic conditions and geologic structure.
 a. Mazuku
 c. 1509 Istanbul earthquake
 b. Seismic refraction
 d. Strainmeter

15. _____ is a global effect of an earthquake. The seismic waves generated by an earthquake pass through the body of the Earth, but between 104° and 140° from the focus of an earthquake, little or no seismic waves can be detected. This is because primary waves (P-waves) are refracted by the Earth's core and secondary waves (S-waves) are stopped by the core.
 a. Shadow zone
 c. Strong ground motion
 b. Teleseism
 d. Seismic shadowing

16. _____ are waves that travel through the Earth or other elastic body, for example as the result of an earthquake, explosion, or some other process that imparts forces to the body. _____ are also continually excited on Earth by the incessant pounding of ocean waves (referred to as the microseism) and the wind. _____ are studied by seismologists, and measured by a seismograph, which records the output of a seismometer, or geophone.
 a. Seismic waves
 c. Hypocenter
 b. Shadow zone
 d. Strong ground motion

17. The _____ is the range of depths within the crust or lithosphere over which most earthquakes are initiated. Typically in continental crust this is in the uppermost 15 km. The base of this layer represents the downwards change in deformation mechanism from elastic and frictional processes associated with brittle faulting to a generally aseismic zone where ductile creep becomes the dominant process.
 a. 1509 Istanbul earthquake
 c. Brittle-ductile transition zone
 b. 1700 Cascadia earthquake
 d. Seismogenic layer

18. A _____ is an area in which an S-Wave (secondary seismic wave) is not detected due to it not being able to pass through the outer core of the earth due to it being liquid. When an earthquake occurs, seismographs near the epicenter, out to about 90° distance, are able to record both Primary and Secondary waves, but those at a greater distance no longer detect the S-wave. This is because shear waves cannot pass through liquids.
 a. Harmonic tremor
 c. Rayleigh waves
 b. Shadow zone
 d. Seismic gap

19. A _____ is a ridge which has moved along a fault line, blocking or diverting drainage. Typically, a _____ creates a valley corresponding to the alignment of the fault that produces it.

a. Toreva block
b. Rejuvenated
c. Gravitational erosion
d. Shutter ridge

20. _____ describes the behavior of soils that, when loaded, suddenly go from a solid state to a liquefied state, or having the consistency of a heavy liquid. Liquefaction is more likely to occur in loose to moderate saturated granular soils with poor drainage, such as silty sands or sands and gravels capped or containing seams of impermeable sediments . During loading, usually cyclic undrained loading, e.g. earthquake loading, loose sands tend to decrease in volume, which produces an increase in their porewater pressures and consequently a decrease in shear strength, i.e. reduction in effective stress.
a. 1509 Istanbul earthquake
b. 1700 Cascadia earthquake
c. 1703 Genroku earthquake
d. Soil liquefaction

21. Seismologists usually define _____ as the strong earthquake shaking that occurs close to (less than about 50 km from) a causative fault. The strength of the shaking involved in _____ usually overwhelms a seismometer, forcing the use of accelerographs (or _____ accelerometers) for recording.

As seismic instruments (and accelerometers in particular) become more common, it becomes necessary to correlate expected damage with instrument-readings.

a. Teleseism
b. Seismic gap
c. Hypocenter
d. Strong ground motion

22. In physics, a _____ is a mechanical wave that propagates along the interface between differing media, usually two fluids with different densities. A _____ can also be an electromagnetic wave guided by a refractive index gradient. In radio transmission, a ground wave is a _____ that propagates close to the surface of the Earth.
a. 1700 Cascadia earthquake
b. 1509 Istanbul earthquake
c. 1703 Genroku earthquake
d. Surface wave

23. A _____ is the tremor caused by an earthquake that is very far away, often picked up only by seismometers that are in low background noise locations. Generally, a tremor from a magnitude 5.3 earthquake can be seen anywhere in the world with modern seismic instruments.
a. Seismic waves
b. Seismic shadowing
c. Meizoseismal area
d. Teleseism

24. A _____ is a type of fault in which rocks of lower stratigraphic position are pushed up and over higher strata. They are often recognized because they place older rocks above younger. Thrust faults are the result of compressional forces.
a. Thrust fault
b. Panthalassa
c. Juan de Fuca Ridge
d. Gorda Ridge

25. In geology, a _____ or _____ line is a planar fracture in rock in which the rock on one side of the fracture has moved with respect to the rock on the other side. Large faults within the Earth's crust are the result of differential or shear motion and active _____ zones are the causal locations of most earthquakes. Earthquakes are caused by energy release during rapid slippage along a _____.
a. 1509 Istanbul earthquake
b. Fault
c. 1703 Genroku earthquake
d. 1700 Cascadia earthquake

Chapter 12. Test Preparation Part 12

26. A _____ is a low-frequency seismic event associated with volcanoes. The term, which means 'screw' in Spanish, was coined in the mid-1990s at the Observatorio Vulcanológico y Sismológico de Pasto in Pasto, Colombia to describe seismic events seen at the Galeras volcano.

A tornillo has the following characteristics that distinguish it from other seismic events:

- very limited distribution of frequencies (monochromatic)
- a long coda that decays slowly
- small amplitude

Like volcanic tremor, tornillos are thought to be caused by magma moving at depth.

a. Teleseism
c. Fault friction

b. Tornillo event
d. Meizoseismal area

27. An _____ can be referred to as a strong motion seismograph, or simply as an earthquake accelerometer. They are usually constructed as a self-contained box, more commonly now being connected directly to the Internet.

Accelerographs are useful for when the earthquake ground motion is so strong that it causes the more sensitive seismometers to go off-scale.

a. AL 129-1
c. Accelerograph

b. AASHTO Soil Classification System
d. AL 333

28. In geophysics, _____ is a variation in seismic reflection amplitude with change in distance between shotpoint and receiver. It is also referred as AVA (amplitude variation with angle.) As _____ studies are being done on CMP data, the offset increases with the angle.

a. AASHTO Soil Classification System
c. Amplitude versus offset

b. AL 333
d. AL 129-1

29. The _____ is a model in Seismic tomography that describes the shape of the Fresnel zone along the entire ray path. This theory suggests that the area that influences the ray velocity is the surrounding material and not the infinitesimally small ray path. This surrounding material forms a tube enclosing the ray but does not incorporate the ray path itself.

a. Coulomb stress transfer
c. Gutenberg-Richter law

b. Passive seismic
d. Banana Doughnut theory

30. _____ is an interaction criterion that promises a deeper understanding of earthquake occurrence, and a better description of probabilistic hazard.

When an earthquake reduces the average value of the shear stress on the fault that slipped, shear stress rises at sites in addition to the fault tips. This discovery lay in waiting for 20 years, when lobes of off-fault aftershocks were seen to correspond to small calculated increases in shear or Coulomb stress.

a. Frequency separation
c. Reflection seismology

b. Coulomb stress transfer
d. Plus minus methos

31. _____ is an important step of the seismic reflection method, which converts the acoustic wave travel time to actual depth, based on the acoustic velocity of subsurface medium (sediments, rocks, water.)

_____ integrates several sources of information about the subsurface velocity to derive a three dimensional velocity model:

- 'Well tops', i.e., depth of geological layers encountered in oil and gas wells
- Velocity measurements made in oil and gas wells
- Empirical knowledge about the velocities of the rocks in the area investigated
- Root Mean Square (RMS) stacking velocities which are derived from the processing of the seismic reflection data

This conversion permits to produce depth and thickness maps of subsurface layers interpreted on seismic reflection data. These maps are crucial in hydrocarbon exploration because they permit the volumetric evaluation of gas or oil in place. In the example subsurface map presented below, depth increases from red to blue.

a. Frequency separation
c. Swell filter
b. Depth conversion
d. Gutenberg-Richter law

32. An _____ is the result of a sudden release of energy in the Earth's crust that creates seismic waves. They are recorded with a seismometer or the related and mostly obsolete Richter magnitude, with a magnitude 3 or lower _____ being mostly imperceptible and magnitude 7 causing serious damage over large areas.
a. Earthquake
c. AL 333
b. AASHTO Soil Classification System
d. AL 129-1

33. _____ is a term used in Helio and Asteroseismology for the spacing in frequency between adjacent modes of oscillation having the same angular degree (l) but different radial order (n.)

For a sun-like star the frequency can be further described using the 'large frequency spacing' between modes of different radial order (136 µHz in the sun), and the 'small frequency spacing' between modes of even and odd angular degree within the same radial order (68 µHz in the sun.) The period corresponding to the large frequency spacing can be shown to be approximately the same as the time required for a sound wave to travel to the centre of the sun and return, confirming the global nature of the oscillations seen.

a. Seismic moment
c. Reflection seismology
b. Gutenberg-Richter law
d. Frequency separation

34.

A _____ is a device which converts ground movement into voltage, which may be recorded at a recording station. The deviation of this measured voltage from the base line is called the seismic response and is analyzed for structure of the earth.

a. Geophone
c. Passive seismic

b. Frequency separation
d. Gutenberg-Richter law

35. In seismology, the _____ expresses the relationship between the magnitude and total number of earthquakes in any given region and time period of at least that magnitude.

$$\log N = A - bM$$

or

$$N = 10^{A-bM}$$

Where:

- N is the number of events in a given magnitude range
- M is a magnitude minimum
- A and b are constants

The relationship was first proposed by Charles Francis Richter and Beno Gutenberg. The relationship is surprisingly robust and does not vary significantly from region to region or over time.

The constant b is typically equal to 1.0. This means that for every magnitude 4.0 event there will be 10 magnitude 3.0 quakes and 100 magnitude 2.0 quakes.

a. Seismic moment
c. Gutenberg-Richter law

b. Passive seismic
d. Depth conversion

36. In physics, in the area of dynamical systems, the _____ is an earthquake model conjectured to be an example of self-organized criticality where local exchange dynamics are not conservative.

The system behaviour reproduces some empirical laws that earthquakes follow (such as the Gutenberg-Richter law and the Omori law)

The model is a simplification of the Burridge-Knopoff model, where the blocks move instantly to their balanced positions when submitted to a force greater than their friction.

Let S be a square lattice with L x L sites and let $K_{mn} \geq 0$ be the tension at site (m,n.)

a. AL 333
c. AASHTO Soil Classification System

b. AL 129-1
d. Olami-Feder-Christensen model

37. _____ is the detection of natural low frequency earth movements, usually with the purpose of discerning geological structure and locate underground oil, gas, or other resources. Usually the data listening is done in multiple measurement points that are separated by several hundred meters, over periods of several hours to several days, using portable seismometers. The conclusions about the geological structure are based on the spectral analysis or on the mathematical reconstruction of the propagation and possible sources of the observed seismic waves

_____ usually focuses on a low frequency signals (0 to 10 Hz) and is sometimes called the 'low frequency' seismology.

a. Frequency separation
b. Passive seismic
c. Swell filter
d. Seismic moment

38. _____ is a method of exploration geophysics that uses the principles of seismology to estimate the properties of the Earth's subsurface from reflected seismic waves. The method requires a controlled seismic source of energy, such as dynamite/Tovex, a specialized air gun or vibrators, commonly known by their trademark name Vibroseis. By noting the time it takes for a reflection to arrive at a receiver, it is possible to estimate the depth of the feature that generated the reflection.

a. Seismic moment
b. Geophone
c. Frequency separation
d. Reflection seismology

39. _____ is the scientific study of earthquakes and the propagation of elastic waves through the Earth. The field also includes studies of earthquake effects, such as tsunamis as well as diverse seismic sources such as volcanic, tectonic, oceanic, atmospheric, and artificial processes . A related field that uses geology to infer information regarding past earthquakes is paleoseismology.

a. 1703 Genroku earthquake
b. 1700 Cascadia earthquake
c. Seismology
d. 1509 Istanbul earthquake

40. A _____ is simply a plot of the peak or steady-state response (displacement, velocity or acceleration) of a series of oscillators of varying natural frequency, that are forced into motion by the same base vibration or shock. The resulting plot can then be used to pick off the response of any linear system, given its natural frequency of oscillation. One such use is in assessing the peak response of buildings to earthquakes.

a. 1703 Genroku earthquake
b. Response spectrum
c. 1509 Istanbul earthquake
d. 1700 Cascadia earthquake

41. _____ is a quantity used by earthquake seismologists to measure the size of an earthquake. The scalar _____ M_0 is defined by the equation $M_0 = >\mu A u$, where

- $>\mu$ is the shear modulus of the rocks involved in the earthquake, typically 30 gigapascals
- A is the area of the rupture along the geologic fault where the earthquake occurred, and
- u is the average displacement on A.

The _____ of an earthquake is typically estimated using whatever information is available to constrain its factors. For modern earthquakes, moment is usually estimated from ground motion recordings of earthquakes known as seismograms. For earthquakes that occurred in times before modern instruments were available, moment may be estimated from geologic estimates of the size of the fault rupture and the displacement.

a. Seismic moment
c. Plus minus methos
b. Gutenberg-Richter law
d. Depth conversion

42. _____ are instruments that measure and record motions of the ground, including those of seismic waves generated by earthquakes, nuclear explosions, and other seismic sources. Records of seismic waves allow seismologists to map the interior of the Earth, and locate and measure the size of these different sources. Seismograph is another Greek term from seismós and γρῐ́φω, gráphō, to draw.
   a. 1509 Istanbul earthquake
   b. Seismometers
   c. 1703 Genroku earthquake
   d. 1700 Cascadia earthquake

43. A _____ is an instrument used by geophysicists to measure the deformation of the Earth. A linear _____ measures the changes in the distance between two points, using either a solid piece of material (over a short distance) or a laser interferometer (over a long distance, up to several hundred meters.) The type using a solid length standard was invented by Benioff in 1932, using an iron pipe; later instruments used rods made of fused quartz.
   a. Mazuku
   b. Strainmeter
   c. 1509 Istanbul earthquake
   d. Seismic refraction

44. The term _____ in high resolution seismics (reflection seismology) or sub bottom profiling refers to the static correction that restores the coherence of a high resolution seismic profile. The coherence of the image got lost because of the relative movement (a function of the wavelength of the signal and the swell) of the source and receiver during the recording. In normal seismic recordings, the term _____ refers to filtering the acoustic noise, created by waves, out of the seismic recording.
   a. Seismic moment
   b. Gutenberg-Richter law
   c. Swell filter
   d. Frequency separation

45. A _____ is an instrument designed to measure very small changes from the horizontal level, either on the ground or in structures. A similar term, in less common usage, is the inclinometer. They are used extensively for monitoring volcanos, the response of dams to filling, the small movements of potential landslides, the orientation and volume of hydraulic fractures, and the response of structures to various influences such as loading and foundation settlement.
   a. 1700 Cascadia earthquake
   b. 1509 Istanbul earthquake
   c. 1703 Genroku earthquake
   d. Tiltmeter

46. The _____ is a diatreme in the Northwest Territories, Canada, located about 100 km (62 mi) east of Yellowknife. It is thought to have formed about 1850 million years ago with the eruption of pyroclastic breccia.
   a. AL 333
   b. AL 129-1
   c. Aristifats Diatreme
   d. AASHTO Soil Classification System

47. The _____ is a mafic volcanic belt and large igneous province located at the northern margin of the Trans-Hudson orogeny on central Baffin Island, Nunavut, Canada. It is exposed along a nearly continuous east-west passage for 120 km (75 mi) and changes in stratigraphic thickness from 1 to 2.5 kilometers. The formation is a rare alkaline-suite that formed as a result of submarine rifting during the Paleoproterozoic period.
   a. Bravo Lake Formation
   b. 1509 Istanbul earthquake
   c. 1700 Cascadia earthquake
   d. Mountain Lake cluster

48. _____ is a bay at the extreme east of Lake Nipissing in Ontario, Canada. It is 3 km in diameter and the main community of Callander is located just east of _____.

_____ is an eroded Proterozoic volcanic pipe formed by the violent, supersonic eruption of a deep-origin volcano.

a. Callander Bay
b. 1703 Genroku earthquake
c. 1509 Istanbul earthquake
d. 1700 Cascadia earthquake

49. The _____ is a greenstone belt located in the northern part of the Fennoscandian Shield. The region belongs to Lapland, northern Finland. The _____ is part of a much larger belt of Paleoproterozoic greenstones, a cover of metamorphosed volcanic and sedimentary rocks that cover the Archean basement, the latter which is representative of the Archaean Karelian craton.

a. 1509 Istanbul earthquake
b. Central Lapland Greenstone Belt
c. 1703 Genroku earthquake
d. 1700 Cascadia earthquake

50. _____ - also known as greenstone - is a general field petrologic term applied to metamorphic and/or altered mafic volcanic rock. The green is due to abundant green chlorite, actinolite and epidote minerals that dominate the rock. However, basalts may remain quite black if primary pyroxene does not revert to chlorite or actinolite.

a. Hornfels
b. Greenschist
c. Mylonite
d. Granoblastic

51. _____ are zones of variably metamorphosed mafic to ultramafic volcanic sequences with associated sedimentary rocks that occur within Archaean and Proterozoic cratons between granite and gneiss bodies.

The name comes from the green hue imparted by the colour of the metamorphic minerals within the mafic rocks. Chlorite, actinolite and other green amphiboles are the typical green minerals.

a. Metasomatism
b. Granoblastic
c. Greenstone belts
d. Foliation

52. The _____ is a 1884-1864 million year old large igneous province surrounding much of the Superior craton in Canada. It extends from the Labrador Trough in Labrador and northeastern Quebec though the Cape Smith Belt in northern Quebec, the Belcher Islands in southern Nunavut, the Fox River and Thompson belts in northern Manitoba, the Winnipegosis komatiite belt in central Manitoba, and on the southern side of the Superior craton in the Animikie Basin of northwestern Ontario.

a. Kerguelen Plateau
b. High Arctic Large Igneous Province
c. North Atlantic Igneous Province
d. Circum-Superior Belt

53. The _____ is a large circular gabbro and syenite intrusion within the Earth's crust. Located on the North Shore of Lake Superior in northwestern Ontario, Canada, it is the largest alkaline igneous intrusion in North America with a diameter of 25 km (16 mi.)

Like the steep cliffs of Lake Superior, the _____ has its origins in the Midcontinent Rift System about 1,100 million years ago.

a. Charnockite
b. Great Dyke
c. Coldwell Complex
d. Litchfieldite

54. The _____ is a diatreme complex in northwestern Ontario, Canada, located approximately 25 km (16 mi) west of Marathon. It is thought to have formed by the Midcontinent Rift System, a 2,000 km (1,243 mi) long rift in the center of the North American continent that was active in the Mesoproterozoic.
   a. Deadhorse Creek diatreme complex
   b. 1509 Istanbul earthquake
   c. 1703 Genroku earthquake
   d. 1700 Cascadia earthquake

55. The _____, also referred to as the Flin Flon-Snow Lake greenstone belt, is a Precambrian greenstone belt located in the central area of Manitoba and east-central Saskatchewan, Canada. It lies in the central portion of the Trans-Hudson orogeny and was formed by arc volcanism during the Paleoproterozoic period. The _____ is 250 km long by 75 km wide and is exposed just north of McClarty Lake.
   a. 1509 Istanbul earthquake
   b. 1700 Cascadia earthquake
   c. 1703 Genroku earthquake
   d. Flin Flon greenstone belt

56. The _____ is a 2.04 billion year old dike swarm located in the Kangerlussuaq region of western Greenland. The dikes cut archaen orthogneisses and are exposed along approximately 150 km (93 mi) of the coast and a similar distance up to the inland ice to the east, covering an area of about 18,000 km². To the north it is bounded by the paleoproterozoic Ikert>ôq shear zone and to the south the boundary is gradational with a gradual reduction in the density of dikes.
   a. 1703 Genroku earthquake
   b. 1509 Istanbul earthquake
   c. 1700 Cascadia earthquake
   d. Kangamiut dike swarm

57. A _____ or dyke in geology is a type of sheet intrusion referring to any geologic body that cuts discordantly across

   - planar wall rock structures, such as bedding or foliation
   - massive rock formations, like igneous/magmatic intrusions and salt diapirs.

They can therefore be either intrusive or sedimentary in origin.

An intrusive _____ is an igneous body with a very high aspect ratio, which means that its thickness is usually much smaller than the other two dimensions. Thickness can vary from sub-centimeter scale to many meters and the lateral dimensions can extend over many kilometers. A _____ is an intrusion into an opening cross-cutting fissure, shouldering aside other pre-existing layers or bodies of rock; this implies that a _____ is always younger than the rocks that contain it.

   a. Pneumatolysis
   b. Duricrust
   c. Detritus
   d. Dike

58. The _____ form a large igneous province in the western Canadian Shield of Canada. It is one of more than three dozen dike swarms in various parts of the Canadian Shield and is the largest dike swarm known on Earth, more than 500 kilometers wide and 3,000 kilometers long, extending in a northwesterly direction across the whole of Canada from the Arctic to the Great Lakes. The mafic dikes cut Archean and Proterozoic rocks, including those in the Athabasca Basin in Saskatchewan, Thelon Basin in Nunavut and the Baker Lake Basin in the Northwest Territories.

a. 1700 Cascadia earthquake
b. 1703 Genroku earthquake
c. 1509 Istanbul earthquake
d. Mackenzie dike swarm

59. _____ was an early Miocene shield volcano in northeastern New South Wales, Australia. In the course of about three million years, _____ was formed over the East Australia hotspot when this part of the continent passed over it around 23 million years ago. Mount Warning, Lamington Plateau and the Border Ranges between New South Wales and Queensland are among the remnants of this volcano that was originally over 100 km in diameter and nearly twice the height of Mount Warning today (1,156 m.)
a. 1703 Genroku earthquake
b. 1509 Istanbul earthquake
c. 1700 Cascadia earthquake
d. Tweed Volcano

60. The _____ age is a period of geologic time (23.8--20 Ma) within the Miocene used more specifically with European Land Mammal Ages. It follows the Orleanian age and overlaps the Aquitanian and Burdigalian ages. .
a. Agenian
b. AL 129-1
c. AASHTO Soil Classification System
d. Early Miocene

61. In the geologic timescale, the _____ is the lower age of the Middle Triassic epoch and lasted from 245 million years ago until 237 million years ago, approximately. The _____ age succeeds the Olenekian age of the Lower Triassic epoch and precedes the Ladinian age of the Middle Triassic epoch.

The earliest potential dinosaur fossil to date is a partial pubis from _____-age rocks of the Moenkopi Formation, Arizona.

a. Olenekian
b. AASHTO Soil Classification System
c. Induan
d. Anisian

62. _____ stage is a faunal stage of the Early Cretaceous epoch in the geologic timescale, that extends from 125.0 >± 1.0 Ma to 112.0 >± 1.0 Ma (million years ago), approximately. The _____ stage succeeds the Barremian stage and precedes the Albian stage, all in the same epoch.

- Pictetia
- Eogaudryceras
- Georgioceras
- Lithancylus
- Salfeldiella
- Zuercherella

- Eotetragonites
- Pseudosaynella
- Roloboceras
- Helicancylus
- Procheloniceras
- Prodeshayesites
- Shastoceras
- Ammonitoceras
- Australiceras
- Cheloniceras
- Cicatrites
- Colombiceras
- Dufrenoya
- Melchiorites
- Parahoplites

Tropaeum imperator

- Hypacanthoplites
- Sinzovia
- Trochleiceras
- Mathoceratites
- Metahamites
- Neosilesites
- Protanisoceras
- Ammonoceratites
- Beudanticeras
- Gyaloceras
- Hulenites
- Knemiceras
- Uhligella
- Acanthohoplites
- Acanthoplites
- Argonauticeras
- Burckhardites
- Cloioceras
- Diadochoceras
- Diodochoceras
- Eodouvilleiceras
- Epancyloceras
- Epicheloniceras

- Gargasiceras
- Jauberticeras
- Kazanskyella
- Mathoceras
- Megatyloceras
- Miyakoceras
- Nodosohoplites
- Nolaniceras
- Protacanthoplites
- Somalites
- Theganoceras
- Tropaeum
- Gabbioceras
- Tetragonites
- Desmoceras
- Hamites

- Vectibelus
- Conoteuthis

- Tetrabelus
- Peratobelus
- Parahibolites

- Heminautilus
- Carinonautilus

- Zhuralevia

- Euphylloceras

- Adygeya
- Naefia

- Boluochia zhengi
- Chaoyangia beishanensis
- Confuciusornis sanctus
- Cuspirostrisornis houi
- Jeholornis prima
- Jixiangornis orientalis
- Largirostrornis sexdentoris
- Longchengornis sanyanensis
- Longipteryx chaoyangensis
- Sapeornis chaoyangensis
- Sinornis santensis/Cathayornis yandica
- Songlingornis linghensis
- Yanornis martini
- Yixianornis grabaui

- Sarcosuchus

- Hybodus
- Jinanichthys longicephalus
- Lycoptera davidi
- Lycoptera muroii
- Peipiaosteus pani

- Protosephurus liui
- Sinamia zdanskyi

- Anhanguera
- Araripedactylus dehmi
- Araripesaurus castilhoi
- Arthurdactylus conandoylei
- Boreopterus cuiae
- Brasileodactylus araripensis
- Cearadactylus atrox
- Chaoyangopterus zhangi
- Dsungaripterus weii
- Dsungaripterus brancai
- Eoazhdarcho liaoxiensis
- Eopteranodon lii
- Gegepterus changi
- Haopterus gracilis
- Hongshanopterus lacustris
- Huaxiapterus benxiensis
- Huaxiapterus corollatus
- Huaxiapterus jii
- Istiodactylus latidens
- Istiodactylus sinensis
- Jidapterus edentus
- Liaoningopterus gui
- Liaoxipterus brachyognathus
- Lonchodectes
- Longchengpterus zhaoi
- Ludodactylus sibbicki
- Nemicolopterus crypticus
- Nurhachius ignaciobritoi
- Ornithocheirus simus
- Ornithocheirus mesembrinus
- Pricesaurus megalodon
- Santanadactylus
- Sinopterus dongi
- Sinopterus gui
- Tapejara navigans
- Tapejara wellnhoferi
- Thalassodromeus sethi
- Tropeognathus mesembrinus
- Tropeognathus robustus
- Tupandactylus imperator

Antlers Formation, Cedar Mountain Formation, Cloverly Formation, Elrhaz Formation, Jiufotang Formation, Little Atherfield, Mazong Shan, Potomac Formation, Santana Formation, Twin Mountains Formation, Xinminbao Group, Yixian Formation

   a. AASHTO Soil Classification System   b. Early Cretaceous
   c. AL 129-1   d. Aptian

63. The _____ was an extinction event of the early Cretaceous Period. It is dated to c. 116 or 117 million years ago, in the middle of the Aptian stage of the geological time scale, and has sometimes been termed the mid-_____ event as a result.

It is classified as a minor extinction event, rather than a major event like the famous Cretaceous-Tertiary extinction event that brought about the end of the 'age of dinosaurs' and the Mesozoic Era. The Aptian event is most readily detected among marine rather than terrestrial fossil deposits.

   a. Aptian extinction   b. AL 333
   c. AL 129-1   d. AASHTO Soil Classification System

64. The _____ age is a period of geologic time (48.6--37.2 Ma) within the Early Eocene epoch of the Paleogene used more specifically with Asian Land Mammal Ages. It follows the Bumbanian age and precedes the Irdinmanhan age.

The upper boundary layer of the _____ can be the lower boundary of the Priabonian

   a. Irdinmanhan   b. Ergilian
   c. Ulangochuian   d. Arshantan

65. The _____ age age is a period of geologic time (16.0--11.6 Ma), equivalent with the Middle Miocene and used more specifically with European Land Mammal Ages. It precedes the Vallesian age and follows the Orleanian age. The _____ overlaps the Langhian and Serravallian ages.

   a. Astaracian   b. AL 333
   c. AASHTO Soil Classification System   d. AL 129-1

66. _____ refers to 9 informal subdivisions of the lunar Pre-Nectarian geologic period.

The motivation for creating the _____ subdivisions was to place 30 pre-Nectarian impact basins into 9 relative age groups. The relative age of the first basin in each group is based on crater densities and superposition relationships, whereas the other basins are included based on weaker grounds.

   a. Basin Groups   b. Calymmian
   c. Stenian   d. Siderian

67. In the geologic timescale, _____ is a stage of the Early Cretaceous epoch, and the first of the entire Cretaceous period. It spanned between 145.5 >± 4.0 Ma and 140.2 >± 3.0 Ma (million years ago.) The _____ stage succeeds the Tithonian stage of the Late Jurassic epoch and precedes the Valanginian stage of the Early Cretaceous epoch.

a. Berriasian
b. Santonian
c. Campanian
d. Hauterivian

68. The _____ age is a period of geologic time (55.8--46.8 Ma) within the Paleogene and is the equivalent to the Early Eocene and Ypresian age. The _____ is used more specifically with Asian Land Mammal Ages. It follows the Gashatan age and precedes the Arshantan age.
   a. Houldjinian
   b. Mustersan
   c. Divisaderan
   d. Bumbanian

69. _____ is a age of the early Miocene Epoch. It spans the time between 20.43 ± 0.05 Ma and 15.97 ± 0.05 Ma (million years ago).
   a. Tortonian
   b. Serravallian
   c. Sinemurian
   d. Burdigalian

70. _____ is a geological term relating to strata at the base of the Carboniferous formation, below the entire sequence of coal measures. This term may be unique to the UK.

Typically this part of the geological sequence, as in the Touch Hills and Fintry Hills to the west of Stirling tends to contain a mixture of lavas and sedimentary rocks, including sandstone and mudstone, and lies unconformably on top of older Devonian strata.

   a. Mississippian
   b. Pennsylvanian
   c. Dinantian
   d. Calciferous sandstone

71. The _____ is the first geologic period in the Mesoproterozoic Era and lasted from 1600 Ma to 1400 Ma (million years ago.) Instead of being based on stratigraphy, these dates are defined chronometrically.

The period is characterised by expansion of existing platform covers, or by new platforms on recently cratonized basements.

   a. Cryptic era
   b. Mesoarchean
   c. Calymmian
   d. Marine Isotopic Stage 11

72. The _____ is a stage on the geologic time scale occurring from 83.5 ± 0.7 Ma to 70.6 ± 0.6 Ma (million years ago).

It is the middle stage of the Late Cretaceous Epoch.

   a. Campanian
   b. Hauterivian
   c. Santonian
   d. Berriasian

73. The _____ age is a period of geologic time (54.0--48.0 Ma) within the Eocene epoch of the Paleogene used more specifically with South American Land Mammal Ages. It follows the Riochican and precedes the Mustersan age.
   a. Hsandagolian
   b. Tiupampan
   c. Tinguiririican
   d. Casamayoran

74. The _____ age is a period of geologic time (4.0--3.0 Ma) within the Pliocene epoch of the Neogene used more specifically with South American Land Mammal Ages. It follows the _____ and precedes the Uquian age.
   a. Friasian
   b. Huayquerian
   c. Montehermosan
   d. Laventan

75. The _____ is the second and final of two stages of the Oligocene Epoch. It spans the time between 28.4 ± 0.1 Ma and 23.03 ± 0.05 Ma

During the _____ the largest known single-event volcanic eruption occurred: the Fish Canyon eruption of La Garita with a magnitude of 9.2.

   a. 1703 Genroku earthquake
   b. 1509 Istanbul earthquake
   c. Chattian
   d. 1700 Cascadia earthquake

76. The _____ age is a period of geologic time (21.0--17.5 Ma) within the Miocene epoch of the Neogene used more specifically with South American Land Mammal Ages. It follows the Deseadan and precedes the Santacrucian age.
   a. Lujanian
   b. Mayoan
   c. Huayquerian
   d. Colhuehuapian

77. The _____ age is a period of geologic time (15.5--13.8 Ma) within the Miocene epoch of the Neogene used more specifically with South American Land Mammal Ages. It follows the Friasian and precedes the Laventan age.
   a. Colloncuran
   b. Friasian
   c. Santacrucian
   d. Mayoan

78. The _____ is a stage of the Late Cretaceous Epoch. It spans the time between 89.3 ± 1 Ma and 85.8 ± 0.7 Ma (million years ago).
   a. Valanginian
   b. Campanian
   c. Santonian
   d. Coniacian

79. The _____ is an informal term that refers to the earliest geologic evolution of the Earth and Moon. It is the oldest era of the (informal) Hadean eon, and it is commonly accepted to have begun close to 4567.17 million (about 4.6 billion) years ago when the Earth and Moon formed. No samples exist to date the transition between the _____ and the following Basin Groups era for the Moon, though sometimes it is stated that this era ended 4150 million years ago for one or both of these bodies.
   a. Permo-Carboniferous
   b. Marine isotope stages
   c. Mesoarchean
   d. Cryptic era

80. The _____ is the first stage of the Paleocene Epoch, making up the Early Paleocene sub-epoch. The beginning of the stage is defined by the Cretaceous-Tertiary extinction event 65.5 ± 0.3 Ma The stage ended 61.7 ± 0.2 Ma.
   a. 1700 Cascadia earthquake
   b. 1703 Genroku earthquake
   c. 1509 Istanbul earthquake
   d. Danian

81. The _____ age is a period of geologic time (29.0--21.0 Ma) within the Oligocene epoch of the Paleogene used more specifically with South American Land Mammal Ages. It follows the Tinguirirican and precedes the Colhuehuapian age.

a. Peligran
b. Mustersan
c. Tiupampan
d. Deseadan

82. _____ is the name of a series or epoch from the Lower Carboniferous system in Europe. It can stand for a series of rocks in Europe or the time span in which they were deposited.

The _____ is equal to the lower part of the Mississippian series in the international geologic timescale of the ICS.

a. Pennsylvanian
b. Mississippian
c. Calciferous sandstone
d. Dinantian

83. The _____ age is a period of geologic time (42.0--36.0 Ma) within the Eocene epoch of the Paleogene used more specifically with South American Land Mammal Ages. It follows the Mustersan and precedes the Tinguirirican age.

a. Sharamurunian
b. Divisaderan
c. Mustersan
d. Tabenbulakian

84. The _____ , usually abbreviated K for its German translation Kreide, is a geologic period and system from circa >145.5 >± 4 to >65.5 >± 0.3 million years ago . In the geologic timescale, the _____ follows on the Jurassic period and is followed by the Paleogene period. It is the youngest period of the Mesozoic era, and at 80 million years long, the longest period of the Phanerozoic eon. The end of the _____ defines the boundary between the Mesozoic and Cenozoic eras.

a. Hauterivian
b. Coniacian
c. Santonian
d. Cretaceous

85. The _____ or the Lower Cretaceous (logstratigraphic name), is the earlier of the two major divisions of the Cretaceous Period. It is usually considered to stretch from 146 million years ago to 100 mya.

During this time many new types of dinosaurs appeared or came into prominence, including psittacosaurs, spinosaurs and coelurosaurs, while other survivors from the Late Jurassic continued.

a. AL 129-1
b. Aptian
c. AASHTO Soil Classification System
d. Early Cretaceous

86. The '_____' is a term usually defined as Earth's first billion years, or gigayear. On the geologic time scale, the '_____' comprises all of the Hadean eon (itself unofficially defined), as well as the Eoarchean and part of the Paleoarchean eras of the Archean eon.

This period of Earth's history, being its earliest, involved the planet's condensation from a solar nebula and accretion from meteorites, as well as the formation of the earliest atmosphere and hydrosphere.

a. AL 129-1
b. AL 333
c. AASHTO Soil Classification System
d. Early Earth

87. The _____ is a sub-epoch of the Miocene Epoch made up of two stages: the Aquitanian and Burdigalian stages.

The sub-epoch lasted from 23.03 ± 0.05 mya to 15.97 ± 0.05 mya It was preceded by the Oligocene epoch.

a. AL 129-1
b. Aquitanian
c. Early Miocene
d. AASHTO Soil Classification System

88. The _____ is the first of three epochs of the Triassic period. It spans the time between 251 ± 0.4 Ma and 245 ± 1.5 Ma The Permian-Triassic extinction event spawned the Triassic period.
   a. AASHTO Soil Classification System
   b. Olenekian
   c. Induan
   d. Early Triassic

89. The _____ is the second geologic period in the Mesoproterozoic era and lasted from 1400 Ma ago to 1200 Ma (million years ago.) Instead of being based on stratigraphy, these dates are defined chronometrically.

Evidence of a eukaryotic red algae, Bangiomorpha pubescens, has been identified from ca. 1200 Ma old rocks in the Hunting Formation (Somerset Island, Canada).

   a. AASHTO Soil Classification System
   b. AL 129-1
   c. AL 333
   d. Ectasian

90. The _____ age is a period of geologic time (1.2--0.8 Ma) within the Early Pleistocene epoch of the Neogene used more specifically with South American Land Mammal Ages. It follows the _____ and precedes the Lujanian age.
   a. AL 129-1
   b. Uquian
   c. AASHTO Soil Classification System
   d. AL 333

91. In the geologic record the _____ erathem and the _____ era in the geologic timescale correspond to one another in the dual system of classification of rock strata laid down beginning 4000 Ma to 3600 Ma (million years ago.)

It was formerly officially unnamed and usually referred to as the first part of the Early Archean (now an obsolescent name) together with the later Paleoarchean era. It is the first part of the Archaean Eon, preceded by the 'informal' Hadean eon, during which the Earth was considered to be essentially molten.

   a. AASHTO Soil Classification System
   b. AL 129-1
   c. AL 333
   d. Eoarchean

92. In stratigraphy and geology, an _____ is the totality of rock strata laid down in the stratigraphic record deposited during a certain eon of the continuous geologic timescale. The _____ is not to be confused with the eon itself, which is a corresponding division of geologic time spanning a specific amount of (millions of) years, during which rocks were formed that are classified within the _____.
   a. Eonothem
   b. AASHTO Soil Classification System
   c. AL 333
   d. AL 129-1

93. In stratigraphy, paleontology, geology, and geobiology an _____ is the total stratigraphic record deposited during a certain corresponding span of time, an era in the geologic timescale.

It can therefore be used as a chronostratigraphic unit of time which delineates a large span of years -- less than an geological eon, but greater than its successively smaller and more refined subdivisions (geologic periods, epochs, and geologic ages.) By 3,500 Million years ago (Mya) simple life had developed on earth (the oldest known microbial fossils in Australia are dated to this figure.

a. Erathem
b. AL 129-1
c. AASHTO Soil Classification System
d. AL 333

94. The _____ age is a period of geologic time (37.2--33.9 Ma) within the Late Eocene epoch of the Paleogene used more specifically with Asian Land Mammal Ages. It follows the Ulangochuian and precedes the Houldjinian age.

The _____'s lower boundary is the approximate base of the Priabonian age and approximate upper base of the Rupelian age.

a. Itaboraian
b. Irdinmanhan
c. Ulangochuian
d. Ergilian

95. The _____ age is a period of geologic time (16.3--15.5 Ma) within the Miocene epoch of the Neogene used more specifically with South American Land Mammal Ages. It follows the Santacrucian and precedes the Colloncuran age.
a. Mayoan
b. Huayquerian
c. Montehermosan
d. Friasian

96. The _____ age is a period of geologic time (58.7--55.8 Ma) within the Late Paleocene epoch of the Paleogene used more specifically with Asian Land Mammal Ages. It precedes the Bumbanian age. .
a. Hsandagolian
b. Gashatan
c. Casamayoran
d. Divisaderan

97. The _____ is a stage whose belonging to either the Pliocene or the Pleistocene Epochs is currently discussed. It spans the time between 2.588 ± 0.005 mya (million years ago) and 1.806 ± 0.005 mya.. The _____ correlates with the period covering the deposition of the Red Crag of Butley and Newbourn and the Norwich and Weybourn Crags, all from East Anglia (England.)
a. Ruscian
b. Gelasian
c. Vallesian
d. Piacenzian

98. The _____ is a stage of the Early Cretaceous Epoch. It spans the time between 136.4 >± 2 Ma and 130 >± 1.5 Ma (million years ago.)
a. Coniacian
b. Cretaceous
c. Hauterivian
d. Campanian

99. _____ may refer to the traditional uranium-thorium dating or uranium-thorium/_____.

A relatively new dating method, tritium-_____ has been developed for determining rates of oxygen utilization in the ocean.

a. Helium dating
b. 1509 Istanbul earthquake
c. 1703 Genroku earthquake
d. 1700 Cascadia earthquake

100. The _____ is the first stage of the Early Jurassic Epoch. It spans the time between 199.6 >± 0.6 Ma and 196.5 >± 1 Ma (million years ago.) The stage follows the Rhaetian Stage of the Triassic Period.

a. Bathonian
b. Toarcian
c. La Voulte-sur-Rhone
d. Hettangian

101. The _____ age is a period of geologic time (37.2--33.9 Ma) within the Late Eocene epoch of the Paleogene used more specifically with Asian Land Mammal Ages. It follows the Ergilian and precedes the Kekeamuan age.

The _____'s lower boundary is the approximate base of the Priabonian age.

a. Houldjinian
b. Tinguiririran
c. Paleogene
d. Riochican

102. The _____ age is a period of geologic time (33.9--23.03 Ma) within the Oligocene epoch of the Paleogene used more specifically with Asian Land Mammal Ages. It follows the Kekeamuan and precedes the Tabenbulakian age.

The Ulangochuian's lower boundary is the approximate base of the Rupelian age and upper boundary is the approximate upper base of the Aquitanian.

a. Houldjinian
b. Hsandagolian
c. Tabenbulakian
d. Kekeamuan

103. The _____ age is a period of geologic time (9.0--6.8 Ma) within the Miocene epoch of the Neogene used more specifically with South American Land Mammal Ages. It follows the Mayoan and precedes the Montehermosan age.

a. Friasian
b. Huayquerian
c. Mayoan
d. Santacrucian

104. The _____ is the first stage of the Early Triassic epoch. It spans the time between 251 ± 0.4 Ma and 249.7 ± 0.7 Ma This stage follows the mass extinction event of the late Permian period.

a. AASHTO Soil Classification System
b. Induan
c. Early Triassic
d. Olenekian

105. The _____ age is a period of geologic time (48.6--37.2 Ma) within the Middle Eocene epoch of the Paleogene used more specifically with Asian Land Mammal Ages. It follows the Arshantan and precedes the Sharamurunian age.

The _____'s lower boundary is the approximate base of the Lutetian age and upper base of the Priabonian age.

a. Ulangochuian
b. Ergilian
c. Itaboraian
d. Irdinmanhan

106. The _____ age is a period of geologic time (59.0--57.0 Ma) within the Paleocene epoch of the Paleogene used more specifically with South American Land Mammal Ages. It follows the Peligran and precedes the Riochican age.

This age is named after Itaborai, in the state Rio de Janeiro in Brazil.

a. Ulangochuian
b. Ergilian
c. Irdinmanhan
d. Itaboraian

107. The _____ age is a period of geologic time (33.9--28.4 Ma) within the Early Oligocene epoch of the Paleogene used more specifically with Asian Land Mammal Ages. It follows the Houldjinian and precedes the Hsandagolian age.

The _____'s upper boundary is the approximate base of the Chattian age.

a. Deseadan
b. Tinguirirican
c. Paleogene
d. Kekeamuan

108. The _____ is a stage of the Middle Triassic epoch. It spans the time between 237 ± 2 Ma and 228 ± 2 Ma The _____ was preceded by the Anisian Stage and succeeded by the Carnian Stage of the Late Triassic Period.

a. Selandian
b. Sinemurian
c. Late Miocene
d. Ladinian

109. _____ is the older ICS age of the Middle Miocene epoch. It spans the time between 15.97 >± 0.05 Ma and 13.65 >± 0.05 Ma (million years ago.) Defined by M. F. Pareto in 1864, it was originally based on evidence from the Langhe area north of Ceva in northern Italy, hence the name. The _____ is preceded by the Early Miocene Burdigalian and followed by the Middle Miocene Serravallian stage.

a. Statherian
b. Pliensbachian
c. Sinemurian
d. Langhian

110. The _____ is a sub-epoch of the Miocene Epoch made up of two stages. The Tortonian and Messinian stages comprise the _____ sub-epoch.

The sub-epoch lasted from 11.608 >± 0.005 mya to 5.332 >± 0.005 Mya.

a. Serravallian
b. Statherian
c. Late Miocene
d. Thermochronology

111. The _____ is a stage of the Pleistocene Epoch. The beginning of the stage is defined by the base of Eemian interglacial phase before final glacial episode of Pleistocene 126,000 ± 5,000 years ago. The end of the stage is defined exactly at 10,000 Carbon-14 years BP

a. Pleistocene
b. Sicilian Stage
c. Tyrrhenian
d. Late Pleistocene

112. The _____ is the epoch from 1.8 million to 11550 years BP covering the world's recent period of repeated glaciations. The _____ epoch follows the Pliocene epoch and is followed by the Holocene epoch. The _____ is the third epoch of the Neogene period or 6th epoch of the Cenozoic Era. The end of the _____ corresponds with the retreat of the last continental glacier. It also corresponds with the end of the Paleolithic age used in archaeology.

a. Pleistocene
b. Late Pleistocene
c. Sicilian Stage
d. Tyrrhenian

113. The _____ age is a period of geologic time (13.8--11.8 Ma) within the Miocene epoch of the Neogene used more specifically with South American Land Mammal Ages. It follows the Colloncuran and precedes the Mayoan age.

a. Santacrucian
b. Laventan
c. Lujanian
d. Friasian

114. The _____ age is a period of geologic time (0.8--0.011 Ma or 800--11 Tya) within the Pleistocene and Holocene epochs of the Neogene used more specifically with South American Land Mammal Ages. It follows the Ensenadan.
a. Montehermosan
b. Friasian
c. Mayoan
d. Lujanian

115. The _____ is a stage of the Eocene Epoch. It spans the time between 48.6 >± 0.2 Ma and 40.4 >± 0.2 Ma (million years ago.)

It is usually united with the Bartonian to form the Middle Eocene subepoch.

a. Ypresian
b. 1509 Istanbul earthquake
c. Priabonian
d. Lutetian

116. The _____ age is a period of geologic time (10--9 Ma) within the Miocene epoch of the Neogene used more specifically with South American Land Mammal Ages. It follows the _____ and precedes the Huayquerian age.
a. Colloncuran
b. Santacrucian
c. Friasian
d. Mayoan

117. The _____ is a geologic era within the Archean, spanning 3200 Mya to 2800 Mya (million years ago.) The period is defined chronometrically and is not referenced to a specific level in a rock section on Earth. Fossils from Australia show that stromatolites have lived on Earth since the _____.
a. Marine isotope stages
b. Siderian
c. Mesoarchean
d. Tonian

118. The _____ Era is a geologic era that occurred between 1600 Ma and 1000 Ma (million years ago.)

The major events of this era are the formation of the Rodinia supercontinent, the breakup of the Columbia supercontinent, and the evolution of sexual reproduction.

a. 1703 Genroku earthquake
b. 1700 Cascadia earthquake
c. 1509 Istanbul earthquake
d. Mesoproterozoic

119. _____ is the last age of the Miocene epoch. It spans the time between 7.246 ± 0.005 Ma and 5.332 ± 0.005 Ma (million years ago.) It is named after the _____ evaporite deposit, which was named after Messina in Sicily.
a. 1700 Cascadia earthquake
b. 1509 Istanbul earthquake
c. 1703 Genroku earthquake
d. Messinian

120. The _____ is a sub-epoch of the Miocene Epoch made up of two stages: the Langhian and Serravallian stages. The _____ is followed by the Early Miocene.

The sub-epoch lasted from 15.97 >± 0.05 mya to 11.608 >± 0.005 Mya (million years ago.)

a. Thermochronology
b. Statherian
c. Langhian
d. Middle Miocene

121. The term _____, alternatively the Middle Miocene extinction or Middle Miocene extinction peak, refers to a wave of extinctions of terrestrial and aquatic life forms that occurred around the middle of the Miocene Epoch, c. 14.8 to 14.5 million years ago, during the Langhian stage of the Miocene.

Researchers dispute the full extent of the extinctions in the middle Miocene; the most extreme estimates assert that 30% of the mammalian genera of the early Miocene epoch went extinct in the disruption -- though other scientists rate the event much less severe.

a. 1509 Istanbul earthquake
b. Toarcian turnover
c. Permian-Triassic extinction event
d. Middle Miocene disruption

122. The _____ is the second of three epochs of the Triassic period. It spans the time between 245 ± 1.5 Ma and 228 ± 2 Ma The _____ is divided into the Anisian and Ladinian faunal stages.
a. 1509 Istanbul earthquake
b. 1700 Cascadia earthquake
c. 1703 Genroku earthquake
d. Middle Triassic

123. The _____ is a geologic subperiod and stratigraphic subsystem of the Carboniferous Period. It is the earliest/lowermost of two divisions of the Carboniferous, lasting from roughly 359 to 318 Ma (million years ago.) As with most other geochronologic units, the rock beds that define the _____ are well identified, but the exact start and end dates are uncertain by a few million years.
a. Pennsylvanian
b. Calciferous sandstone
c. Dinantian
d. Mississippian

124. The _____ age is a period of geologic time (48.0--42.0 Ma) within the Eocene epoch of the Paleogene used more specifically with South American Land Mammal Ages. It follows the Casamayoran and precedes the Divisaderan age.
a. Mustersan
b. Gashatan
c. Houldjinian
d. Riochican

125. The _____ is a geologic era within the Archaean. It spans the period of time from 2,800 to 2,500 million years ago-- the period being defined chronometrically and not referenced to a specific level in a rock section on Earth. Oxygenic photosynthesis first evolved in this era and was accountable for the oxygen catastrophe which was to happen later in the paleoproterozoic from a poisonous buildup of oxygen in the atmosphere, produced by these oxygen producing photoautotrophs, which evolved earlier in the _____.
a. Cryptic era
b. Neoarchean
c. Stenian
d. Geon

126. The _____ is a stage in the Permian stratigraphy (and an age in the geologic timescale) of North America. The _____ age is roughly simultaneous with the Changhsingian age in the timescale of the ICS. This post-Guadalupian stage is known for high levels of evaporite deposits.
a. AL 333
b. AL 129-1
c. AASHTO Soil Classification System
d. Ochoan

127. The _____ is a stage of the Early Triassic epoch. It spans the time between 249.7 >± 0.7 Ma and 245 >± 0.7 Ma. The _____ is divided into the Smithian and the Spathian age. It is defined as starting near the lowest occurrence of Hedenstroemia or Meekoceras gracilitatis ammonites, and of the conodont Neospathodus waageni. It is defined as ending near the lowest occurrences of genera Japonites, Paradanubites, and Paracrochordiceras; and of the conodont Chiosella timorensis. Archosaurs -- a group encompassing crocodiles, pterosaurs, dinosaurs, and ultimately birds -- are diapsid reptiles that first evolved from Archosauriform ancestors during the _____.
  a. Early Triassic
  b. AASHTO Soil Classification System
  c. Induan
  d. Olenekian

128. The _____ was the diversification of animal life at the start of the Ordovician period, just 40 million years after the Cambrian explosion. It followed a series of extinction events at the Cambrian-Ordovician boundary, and the resulting fauna went on to dominate the Palaeozoic relatively unchanged.. Marine diversity to levels typical of the Palaeozoic, and disparity was similar to today's.

The causes of the explosion are complex, and probably varied for different localities. Possible causes include changes in palaeogeography or tectonic activity, as well as a modified nutrient supply.

  a. AL 129-1
  b. AASHTO Soil Classification System
  c. AL 333
  d. Ordovician radiation

129. The _____ age is a period of geologic time (20.0--16.0 Ma), within the Miocene and used more specifically with European Land Mammal Ages. It precedes the Astaracian age and follows the Agenian age. .
  a. AASHTO Soil Classification System
  b. AL 333
  c. AL 129-1
  d. Orleanian

130. The _____ is the third geologic period in the Paleoproterozoic Era and lasted from 2050 Ma to 1800 Ma (million years ago.) Instead of being based on stratigraphy, these dates are defined chronometrically.

Latter half of the period was an episode of intensive orogeny on virtually all continents.

  a. AL 333
  b. AL 129-1
  c. Orosirian
  d. AASHTO Soil Classification System

Chapter 13. Test Preparation Part 13

1. The _____ is the first stage of the Late Jurassic Epoch. It spans the time between 161.2 >± 4 Ma and 155.7 >± 4 Ma (million years ago).
   a. AASHTO Soil Classification System
   b. AL 129-1
   c. Oxfordian stage
   d. AL 333

2. In chronostratigraphy, a _____ is a succession of rock strata laid down in an single age on the geologic timescale, which usually represents millions of years of deposition. A given _____ of rock and the corresponding age of time will by convention have the same name, and the same boundaries.
   a. Paleomagnetism
   b. Chronozone
   c. Global Standard Stratigraphic Age
   d. Stage

3. The _____ is a geologic era within the Archaean. It spans the period of time 3600 Ma to 3200 Ma (million years ago)-- the period being defined chronometrically and not referenced to a specific level in a rock section on Earth. The oldest ascertained life form (Well-preserved bacteria older than 3.46 billion years found in Western Australia) is from this era.
   a. Marine Isotopic Stage 11
   b. Paleoarchean
   c. Geon
   d. Neoarchean

4. The _____ is the first of the three sub-divisions of the Proterozoic occurring between >1,600 to 2,500 million years ago. This is when the continents first stabilized. This is also when Cyanobacteria evolved, a type of bacteria which uses the biochemical process of photosynthesis to produce energy and oxygen.

During this era the earliest surviving mountain belt appears, in the Wopmay Fault Zone of Canada (West of Hudson Bay, 2100-1800 million years ago).

   a. 1700 Cascadia earthquake
   b. 1509 Istanbul earthquake
   c. 1703 Genroku earthquake
   d. Paleoproterozoic

5. The _____ age is a period of geologic time (62.5--59.0 Ma) within the Paleocene epoch of the Paleogene used more specifically with South American Land Mammal Ages. It follows the Tiupampan and precedes the Itaboraian age. .
   a. Kekeamuan
   b. Mustersan
   c. Sharamurunian
   d. Peligran

6. The _____ is a geologic subperiod and stratigraphic subsystem of the Carboniferous Period. It is the later subperiod of the Carboniferous, lasting from roughly 318.1>± 1.3 to 299>± 0.8 Ma (million years ago.) As with most other geochronologic units, the rock beds that define the _____ are well identified, but the exact date of the start and end are uncertain by a few million years.
   a. Calciferous sandstone
   b. Mississippian
   c. Dinantian
   d. Pennsylvanian

7. The _____ refers to the time period including the latter parts of the Carboniferous and early part of the Permian period. _____ rocks are in places not differentiated because of the presence of transitional fossils, and also where no conspicuous stratigraphic break is present.

_____ time, about 300 million years ago, was a period of great glaciation. The widespread distribution of _____ glacial sediments in South America, Africa, Madagascar, Arabia, India, Antarctica and Australia was one of the major pieces of evidence for the theory of continental drift, and led ultimately to the concept of a supercontinent, Pangea.

a. Marine Isotopic Stage 11
b. Neoarchean
c. Siderian
d. Permo-Carboniferous

8. _____ is a age of the Pliocene Epoch. It spans the time between 3.6 >± 0.005 Ma and 2.588 >± 0.005 Ma

It is usually referred to as the Early Late Pliocene, and sometimes, unofficially, as the Middle Pliocene.

a. Piacenzian
b. Ruscian
c. Villanyian
d. Turolian

9. The _____ is a stage of the Early Jurassic Epoch. It spans the time between 189.6 >± 1.5 Ma and 183 >± 1.5 Ma

The stage takes its name from the town of Pliensbach, some 30 km east of Stuttgart in Germany.

a. Thermochronology
b. Thanetian
c. Selandian
d. Pliensbachian

10. The _____ is an archaeological term that is coming into increasing use to describe a long and continuous run of dated sedimentary layers in Jakarta, East Africa. This archaeological pseudo-period dates from about 2.5 MYA to 1.5 MYA, straddling the boundary between the Pliocene and Pleistocene. The contents of its layers give a clear view of the continuous development of recent vertebrates, especially hominins.

a. Ruscian
b. Villanyian
c. Turolian
d. Plio-Pleistocene

11. The _____ is the final stage of the Eocene Epoch. It spans the time between 37.2 >± 0.1 Ma and 33.9 >± 0.1 Ma
a. Lutetian
b. Ypresian
c. 1509 Istanbul earthquake
d. Priabonian

12. The _____ Stage is the final stage of the Late Triassic Period. It lasted from 203.6 >± 1.5 to 199.6 >± 0.6 million years ago. It was preceded by the Norian Stage of the Triassic Period and succeeded by the Hettangian Stage of the Jurassic Period.
a. 1700 Cascadia earthquake
b. 1509 Istanbul earthquake
c. 1703 Genroku earthquake
d. Rhaetian

13. The _____ is the second geologic period in the Paleoproterozoic Era and lasted from 2300 Ma to 2050 Ma (million years ago.) Instead of being based on stratigraphy, these dates are defined chronometrically.

The Bushveld Complex and other similar intrusions formed during this period.

a. Marine isotope stages
b. Rhyacian
c. Permo-Carboniferous
d. Neoarchean

14. The _____ age is a period of geologic time (57.0--54.0 Ma) within the Paleocene epoch of the Paleogene used more specifically with South American Land Mammal Ages. It follows the Itaboraian and precedes the Casamayoran age.

a. Mustersan
b. Tabenbulakian
c. Riochican
d. Hsandagolian

15. The _____ stage is an age of the geologic timescale from >1,400 to 800 million years ago. The name _____ was used in a number of older geologic timescales but is in the most recent timescales of the ICS replaced by the Stenian, Ectasian and Tonian periods of the Neo- and Mesoproterozoic eras.
   a. Cryptic era
   b. Geon
   c. Mesoarchean
   d. Riphean

16. The _____ is the first of two stages of the Oligocene Epoch. It spans the time between 33.9 >± 0.1 Ma and 28.4 >± 0.1 Ma.
   a. 1703 Genroku earthquake
   b. 1700 Cascadia earthquake
   c. 1509 Istanbul earthquake
   d. Rupelian

17. In the new science of tephrochronology, _____ are volcanic ejecta that form an ash layer that is useful in dating Northern European sediment layers that were laid down during the Boreal period, the warm climate phase that followed the cold snap of the Younger Dryas as the earth made the transition from the last Pleistocene glaciation to the current interglacial, or Holocene. This was a period of rapid climatic transitions around the North Atlantic, some of which took place during a matter of decades. Similar effects are evident in independent palaeoclimatic reconstructions obtained from pollen zones, marine and ice-core records, but these sequences cannot be reliably calibrated with one another.
   a. 1700 Cascadia earthquake
   b. Saksunarvatn tephra
   c. 1509 Istanbul earthquake
   d. 1703 Genroku earthquake

18. The _____ age is a period of geologic time (17.5--16.3 Ma) within the Miocene epoch of the Neogene used more specifically with South American Land Mammal Ages. It follows the Colhuehuapian and precedes the Friasian age.
   a. Mayoan
   b. Huayquerian
   c. Friasian
   d. Santacrucian

19. The _____ is an age in the geologic timescale or chronostratigraphic stage, part of the Late Cretaceous epoch. It spans the time between 85.8 ± 0.7 mya (million years ago) and 83.5 ± 0.7 mya.

According to the ICS, its start is defied by the appearance of the inoceramid bivalve Cladoceramus undulatoplicatus.

   a. Campanian
   b. Coniacian
   c. Valanginian
   d. Santonian

20. _____ or Middle Paleocene is a stage of the Paleocene Epoch. It spans the time between 61.7 ± 0.2 Ma and 58.7 ± 0.2 Ma (million years ago.) It is usually considered preceded by the Danian and followed by the Thanetian.
   a. Late Miocene
   b. Sinemurian
   c. Selandian
   d. Thanetian

21. _____ is a age of the middle Miocene epoch that spans the time between 13.65 >± 0.05 Ma and 11.608 >± 0.005 Ma (million years ago.)

a. Thermochronology
b. Late Miocene
c. Selandian
d. Serravallian

22. The _____ age is a period of geologic time (48.6--37.2 Ma) within the Middle Eocene epoch of the Paleogene used more specifically with Asian Land Mammal Ages. It follows the Irdinmanhan age and precedes the Ulangochuian age.

The upper boundary layer of the _____ can be the approximate lower base of the Lutetian age.

a. Sharamurunian
b. Hsandagolian
c. Riochican
d. Gashatan

23. The Sicilian European Stage is a European faunal stage in the period of geological time between 0.781 +/- 0.005 Ma and 0.26 Ma (million years ago.) It is considered to be in the middle of the Pleistocene epoch.

The _____ starts with the Brunhes-Matuyama magnetic reversal at the end of the Calabrian.

a. Pleistocene
b. Tyrrhenian
c. Late Pleistocene
d. Sicilian Stage

24. The _____ is the first geologic period in the Paleoproterozoic Era and lasted from 2500 Ma to 2300 Ma (million years ago.) Instead of being based on stratigraphy, these dates are defined chronometrically.

Abundance of banded iron formations (BIFs) peaked early this period.

a. Riphean
b. Calymmian
c. Neoarchean
d. Siderian

25. The _____ is a stage of the Early Jurassic Epoch. It spans the time between 196.5 ± 2 Ma and 189.6 ± 1.5 Ma (million years ago.)

The stage takes its name from the town of Semur-en-Brionnais, near Sancerre in the upper Loire Valley.

a. Middle Miocene
b. Serravallian
c. Late Miocene
d. Sinemurian

26. The _____ is the final geologic period in the Paleoproterozoic Era and lasted from 1800 Ma to 1600 Ma (million years ago.) Instead of being based on stratigraphy, these dates are defined chronometrically.

During this period the first complex single-celled life appeared.

a. Serravallian
b. Pliensbachian
c. Thermochronology
d. Statherian

27. The _____ is the final geologic period in the Mesoproterozoic Era and lasted from 1200 Ma to 1000 Ma (million years ago.) Instead of being based on stratigraphy, these dates are defined chronometrically.

Name derives from narrow polymetamorphic belts formed over this period.

a. Tonian
b. Stenian
c. Geon
d. Rhyacian

28. The _____ age is a period of geologic time (28.4--23.03 Ma) within the Oligocene epoch of the Paleogene used more specifically with Asian Land Mammal Ages. It follows the Ulangochuian age.

The _____ age's lower boundary is the approximate base of the Chattian age and upper boundary is the approximate base of the Aquitanian age.

a. Tabenbulakian
b. Peligran
c. Tinguiririean
d. Hsandagolian

29. The _____ is the last stage of the Paleocene Epoch, corresponding to the Late Paleocene sub-epoch. It spans the time between 58.7 ± 0.2 Ma and 55.8 ± 0.2 Ma The name derives from the Thanet Beds, the oldest Paleocene deposits in the London Basin.

a. Ladinian
b. Tortonian
c. Statherian
d. Thanetian

30. _____ is the use of radiometric dating along with the closure temperatures that represent the temperature of the mineral being studied at the time given by the date recorded, to understand the thermal history of a specific rock, mineral, or geologic unit. It is a subfield within geology, and is closely associated with geochronology.

a. Middle Miocene
b. Selandian
c. Thanetian
d. Thermochronology

31. The _____ age is a period of geologic time (36.0--29.0 Ma) within the Oligocene epoch of the Paleogene used more specifically with South American Land Mammal Ages. It follows the Divisaderan and precedes the Deseadan age.

a. Tiupampan
b. Deseadan
c. Tinguiririean
d. Gashatan

32. The _____ age is a period of geologic time (64.5--62.5 Ma) within the Paleocene epoch of the Paleogene used more specifically with South American Land Mammal Ages. It precedes the Peligran age. .

a. Deseadan
b. Sharamurunian
c. Tinguiririean
d. Tiupampan

33. The _____ Stage was the last faunal stage of the Early Jurassic period. It is usually used to cover the period from 183 Ma to 175 Ma (million years ago.)

The _____ stage began with the _____ turnover, the extinction event that set it apart from the previous Pliensbachian stage.

a. La Voulte-sur-Rhone
b. Bathonian
c. Toarcian
d. Hettangian

34. The term _____, alternatively the Toarcian extinction, the Pliensbachian-Toarcian extinction or the Early Jurassic extinction refers to the wave of extinctions that marked the end of the Pliensbachian stage and the start of the Toarcian stage of the Early Jurassic period, c. 183 million years ago.

The _____ was most strongly manifested in aquatic lifeforms, notably in mollusk groups like ammonites; its reach was global in extent, as evidenced by research in Japanese waters, the Andean basin, and the floor of the former Tethys Sea.

a. Permian-Triassic extinction event
b. 1509 Istanbul earthquake
c. Middle Miocene disruption
d. Toarcian turnover

35. The _____ is the first geologic period in the Neoproterozoic Era and lasted from 1000 Ma to 850 Ma (million years ago.) Instead of being based on stratigraphy, these dates are defined by the ICS based on radiometric chronometry.

Events leading to the breakup of supercontinent Rodinia started in this period.

a. Cryptic era
b. Siderian
c. Permo-Carboniferous
d. Tonian

36. _____ is a age of the late Miocene epoch that spans the time between 11.608 ± 0.005 Ma and 7.246 ± 0.005 Ma (million years ago.)

a. Thermochronology
b. Turonian
c. Tortonian
d. Langhian

37. The _____ age is a period of geologic time (9.0--5.3 Ma) within the Pliocene used more specifically with European Land Mammal Ages. It precedes the Ruscinian age and follows the Vallesian age. The _____ overlaps the Tortonian and Messinian ages.

a. Turolian
b. Villanyian
c. Ruscan
d. Vallesian

38. The _____ is a stage of the Late Cretaceous Epoch. It spans the time between 93.5 >± 0.8 Ma and 89.3 >± 1 Ma (million years ago.)

The _____ was definied by the French paleontologist Alcide d'Orbigny , who named it after the city of Tours in the French department of Indre-et-Loire.

a. Pliensbachian
b. Tortonian
c. Ladinian
d. Turonian

39. The _____ Stage is the last faunal stage of the Pleistocene in Europe. It runs from 0.26 million (260,000) to 0.01143 million (11,430) years ago. It overlaps with the end of the Middle Pleistocene and all of the Late Pleistocene.

a. Sicilian Stage
b. Late Pleistocene
c. Tyrrhenian
d. Pleistocene

40. The _____ age is a period of geologic time (37.2--33.9 Ma) within the Late Eocene epoch of the Paleogene used more specifically with Asian Land Mammal Ages. It follows the Sharamurunian and precedes the Ergilian age.

The _____'s upper boundary is the approximate base of the Rupelian age.

   a. Ulangochuian
   c. Ergilian
   b. Irdinmanhan
   d. Itaboraian

41. The _____ age is a period of geologic time (1.2--0.8 Ma) within the Early Pleistocene epoch of the Neogene used more specifically with South American Land Mammal Ages. It follows the _____ and precedes the Lujanian age.
   a. AL 129-1
   c. AL 333
   b. AASHTO Soil Classification System
   d. Uquian

42. In the geologic timescale, _____ is a stage of the Early Cretaceous epoch. It spanned between 140.2 ± 3.0 Ma and 136.4 ± 2.0 Ma (million years ago.) The _____ stage succeeds the Berriasian stage of the Early Cretaceous and precedes the Hauterivian stage of the Early Cretaceous.
   a. Campanian
   c. Coniacian
   b. Hauterivian
   d. Valanginian

43. The _____ age is a period of geologic time (11.6--9.0 Ma) within the Miocene used more specifically with European Land Mammal Ages. It precedes the Turolian age and follows the Astaracian age. The Turolian overlaps the Tortonian and Messinian ages.
   a. Turolian
   c. Piacenzian
   b. Villanyian
   d. Vallesian

44. _____ age is a period of geologic time (3.4--1.8 Ma) within the Pliocene used more specifically with European Land Mammal Ages. It precedes the Ruscinian age and overlaps the early Piacenzian and Zanclean ages. .
   a. Piacenzian
   c. Plio-Pleistocene
   b. Vallesian
   d. Villanyian

45. The _____ is the first stage of the Eocene Epoch and usually corresponds to the Early Eocene subepoch, though sometimes the Lutetian is included therein.

It spans the time between 55.8 ± 0.2 Ma and 48.6 ± 0.2 Ma (million years ago.) The stage is named after Ypres, Belgium.

   a. Priabonian
   c. 1509 Istanbul earthquake
   b. Lutetian
   d. Ypresian

46. The _____ divides the history of Earth's Moon into five generally recognized periods: the Copernican, Eratosthenian, Imbrian (Late and Early epochs), Nectarian, and Pre-Nectarian. The boundaries of this time scale are related to large impact events that have modified the lunar surface, changes in crater morphology that occur through time, and the size-frequency distribution of craters superposed on geological units. The absolute ages for these periods have been constrained by radiometric dating of samples obtained from the lunar surface.
   a. 1703 Genroku earthquake
   c. Lunar geological timescale
   b. 1509 Istanbul earthquake
   d. 1700 Cascadia earthquake

47. The _____ is a chronologic schema (or idealized model) relating stratigraphy to time that is used by geologists, paleontologists and other earth scientists to describe the timing and relationships between events that have occurred during the history of the Earth. The table of geologic time spans presented here agrees with the dates and nomenclature proposed by the International Commission on Stratigraphy, and uses the standard color codes of the United States Geological Survey.

Evidence from radiometric dating indicates that the Earth is about 4.570 billion years old.

    a. 1700 Cascadia earthquake   b. 1509 Istanbul earthquake
    c. 1703 Genroku earthquake   d. Geologic time scale

48. _____ refers to 9 informal subdivisions of the lunar Pre-Nectarian geologic period.

The motivation for creating the _____ subdivisions was to place 30 pre-Nectarian impact basins into 9 relative age groups. The relative age of the first basin in each group is based on crater densities and superposition relationships, whereas the other basins are included based on weaker grounds.

    a. Stenian   b. Basin Groups
    c. Siderian   d. Calymmian

49. The _____ in the lunar geologic timescale runs from approximately 1100 million years ago to the present day. The base of the _____ is defined by impact craters that possess bright optically immature ray systems. The crater Copernicus is a prominent example of rayed crater, but it does not mark the base of the _____.

    a. Copernican period   b. 1509 Istanbul earthquake
    c. Late Imbrian   d. 1700 Cascadia earthquake

50. In the lunar geologic timescale, the _____ epoch occurred between 3850 million years ago to about 3800 million years ago. It overlaps the end of the Late Heavy Bombardment of the inner solar system. The impact which created the huge Mare Imbrium basin occurred at the start of the epoch.

    a. AASHTO Soil Classification System   b. Early Imbrian
    c. AL 333   d. AL 129-1

51. The _____ period in the lunar geologic timescale runs from 3,200 million years ago to 1,100 million years ago. It is named after the crater Eratosthenes, whose formation marks the beginning of this period. The formation of the crater Copernicus marks its end, and the beginning of the subsequent Copernician Period.

    a. AASHTO Soil Classification System   b. AL 333
    c. Eratosthenian   d. AL 129-1

52. In the Lunar geologic timescale, the _____ epoch occurred between 3800 million years ago to about 3200 million years ago. It was the epoch during which the mantle below the lunar basins partially melted and filled them with basalt. The melting is thought to have occurred because the impacts thinned the overlying rock - either causing the mantle to rise because of the reduced pressure on it, bringing molten material closer to the surface; or the top melting as heat flowed upwards through the mantle because of reduced overlying thermal insulation.

    a. 1509 Istanbul earthquake   b. 1700 Cascadia earthquake
    c. Nectarian   d. Late Imbrian

53. The _____ Period of the lunar geologic timescale runs from 3920 million years ago to 3850 million years ago. It is the period during which the Nectaris Basin and other major basins were formed by large impact events. Ejecta from Nectaris forms the upper part of the densely cratered terrain found in lunar highlands.
   a. Nectarian
   b. 1509 Istanbul earthquake
   c. Late Imbrian
   d. 1700 Cascadia earthquake

54. The _____ Eon is the current eon in the geologic timescale, and the one during which abundant animal life has existed. It covers roughly 545 million years and goes back to the time when diverse hard-shelled animals first appeared.
   a. Phanerozoic
   b. 1509 Istanbul earthquake
   c. 1703 Genroku earthquake
   d. 1700 Cascadia earthquake

55. _____ is the branch of stratigraphy which focuses on correlating and assigning relative ages of rock strata by using the fossil assemblages contained within them. Usually the aim is correlation, demonstrating that a particular horizon in one geological section represents the same period of time as another horizon at some other section. The fossils are useful because sediments of the same age can look completely different because of local variations in the sedimentary environment.
   a. Biostratigraphy
   b. 1700 Cascadia earthquake
   c. 1703 Genroku earthquake
   d. 1509 Istanbul earthquake

56. _____ is the branch of geology that deals with traces of organismal behavior. It is generally considered as a branch of paleontology; however, only one division of _____, paleoichnology, deals with trace fossils, while neoichnology is the study of modern traces. Parallels can often be drawn between modern traces and trace fossils, helping scientists to decode the possible behavior and anatomy of the trace-making organisms even if no body fossils can be found.
   a. AL 333
   b. AL 129-1
   c. Ichnology
   d. AASHTO Soil Classification System

57. An _____ is an animal lacking a vertebral column. The group includes 98% of all animal species -- all animals except those in the Chordate subphylum Vertebrata (fish, reptiles, amphibians, birds, and mammals.)

Carolus Linnaeus' Systema Naturae divided these animals into only two groups, the Insecta and the now-obsolete vermes (worms.)

   a. Invertebrate
   b. AL 129-1
   c. AL 333
   d. AASHTO Soil Classification System

58. _____ is sometimes described as Invertebrate paleozoology and/or Invertebrate paleobiology. Whether it is considered to be a subfield of paleontology, paleozoology, and/or paleobiology, this discipline is the scientific study of prehistoric invertebrates by analyzing invertebrate fossils in the geologic record.

By invertebrates are meant the non-vertebrate creatures of the kingdom Animalia (or Metazoa+b vmbnParazoa) in the biotic domain of Eukaryota.

   a. Index fossils
   b. Indian bead
   c. Allotrioceras
   d. Invertebrate paleontology

59. _____ is the study of fossil wood. In the fossil record, wood is more often and better preserved than any other plant parts. Fossil wood may be petrified, but this is not necessarily the case.
   a. Paleotempestology
   b. Amblypoda
   c. Ambulocetus
   d. Palaeoxylology

60. _____ is a growing and comparatively new discipline which combines the methods and findings of the natural science biology with the methods and findings of the earth science paleontology. It is occasionally referred to as 'geobiology.'

Paleobiological research uses biological field research of current biota and of fossils millions of years old to answer questions about the molecular evolution and the evolutionary history of life. In this scientific quest, macrofossils, microfossils and trace fossils are typically analyzed.

   a. 1700 Cascadia earthquake
   b. Petrifaction
   c. Paleobiology
   d. 1509 Istanbul earthquake

61. _____ uses data from fossils and subfossils to reconstruct the ecosystems of the past. It includes the study of fossil organisms and their bromalites and other trace fossils in terms of their life cycle, their living interactions, their natural environment, their manner of death and burial. _____'s aim is therefore to build the most detailed model possible of the life environment of those living organisms found today as fossils; such reconstruction work involves complex interactions among environmental factors (temperature, food supplies, degree of solar illumination, etc.).
   a. Paleotempestology
   b. Amblypoda
   c. Ambulocetus
   d. Paleoecology

62. _____ is the study of past tropical cyclone activity by means of geological proxies as well as historical documentary records. The term was coined by Kerry Emanuel.

Examples of proxies include overwash deposits preserved in the sediments of coastal lakes and marshes, microfossils such as foraminifera, pollen, diatoms, dinoflagellates, phytoliths contained in coastal sediments, wave-generated or flood-generated sedimentary structures or deposits (called tempestites) in marine or lagoonal sediments, storm wave deposited coral shingle, shell, sand and shell and pure sand shore parallel ridges.

   a. Ambulocetus
   b. Paleotempestology
   c. Amblypoda
   d. Paleoecology

63. _____ is the study of decaying organisms over time and how they become fossilized (if they do.) The term _____, , was introduced to paleontology in 1940 by Russian scientist, Ivan Efremov, to describe the study of the transition of remains, parts from the biosphere, to the lithosphere, i.e. the creation of fossil assemblages.

Taphonomists study such phenomena as biostratinomy, decomposition, diagenesis, and encrustation and bioerosion by sclerobionts.

   a. Amblypoda
   b. Ambulocetus
   c. Taphonomy
   d. Andrija Mohorovičić

64. The _____ claims that the mass extinction of the dinosaurs and many other living things was caused by the impact of a large asteroid on the Earth sixty-five million years ago, called the Cretaceous-Tertiary extinction event. Evidence indicates that the asteroid fell in the Yucatán Peninsula, Mexico.
   a. Ecological extinction
   b. Extinction vortices
   c. AASHTO Soil Classification System
   d. Alvarez hypothesis

65. _____ refers to the standard rate of extinction in earth's geological and biological history before humans became a primary contributor to extinctions. This is primarily the pre-human extinction rates during periods in between major extinction events.

Extinctions are normally occurring in nature, and the _____ is a measurement of how often they naturally occur.

   a. Habitat fragmentation
   b. Dead Clade Walking
   c. Signor-Lipps effect
   d. Background extinction rate

66. _____ can be described as either a natural or a human attempt to assemble or re-assemble the genes of an extinct subspecies or of a domesticated breed, which may still be present in the larger gene pool of the overall species or other interbreedable species.

In Domestic animals _____ has occurred with the Utonagan and the Northern Inuit dogs in an attempt to recreate the 'wolf-look' without actually cross breeding with wolves. Other selectively bred examples of _____ include that of the aurochs, the extinct forerunner of domestic cattle.

   a. 1703 Genroku earthquake
   b. 1700 Cascadia earthquake
   c. 1509 Istanbul earthquake
   d. Breeding back

67. The phrase _____ refers to the fact that some clades (groups) of organisms which survive mass extinctions either become extinct a few million years after the mass extinction or fail to recover in numbers and diversity.
   a. Habitat fragmentation
   b. Dead Clade Walking
   c. Local extinction
   d. Signor-Lipps effect

68. In population dynamics, _____ is the effect on a population (or stock) whereby, due to certain causes, a decrease in the breeding population (mature individuals) leads to reduced survival and production of eggs or offspring. The cause may be either:

- predation levels rising per offspring (given the same level of overall predator pressure), or
- the allee effect, which is the reduced likelihood of finding a mate.

Although _____ is often considered in relation to the population being harvested (especially fish), the actual level of harvesting, by definition, is not part of _____.

When the level of _____ is high enough that the population is no longer able to sustain itself, it is said to be a critical _____. This occurs when the population size has a tendency to decline when the population drops below a certain level (known as the 'Critical _____ level'.)

a. 1703 Genroku earthquake
c. 1509 Istanbul earthquake
b. 1700 Cascadia earthquake
d. Depensation

69. _____ is defined as 'the reduction of a species to such low abundance that, although it is still present in the community, it no longer interacts significantly with other species.'

_____ stands out because it is the interaction ecology of a species that is important for conservation work. They state that 'unless the species interacts significantly with other species in the community (e.g. it is an important predator, competitor, symbiont, mutualist, or prey) its loss may result in little to no adjustment to the abundance and population structure of other species.'

This view stems from the neutral model of communities that assumes there is little to no interaction within species unless otherwise proven.

a. Extinction threshold
c. Extinction vortices
b. AASHTO Soil Classification System
d. Ecological extinction

70. _____ is a term used in conservation biology to explain the point at which a species, population or metapopulation, experiences an abrupt change in density or number because of an important parameter, such as habitat loss. It is at this critical value below which a species, population, or metapopulation, will go extinct.

Extinction Thresholds are important to conservation biologists when studying a species in a population or metapopulation context because the colonization rate must be larger than then extinction rate, otherwise the entire entity will go extinct once it reaches the threshold.

a. Ecological extinction
c. Extinction vortices
b. Extinction threshold
d. AASHTO Soil Classification System

71. In paleontology, a _____ is the occurrence of abundant fern spores in the fossil record, usually immediately (in a geological sense) after an extinction event. The spikes are believed to represent a large, temporary increase in the number of ferns relative to other terrestrial plants after the extinction or thinning of the latter, probably because fern dispersal is more rapid over large geographic areas, since single-celled fern spores are more easily distributed by the wind than are seeds. Fern spikes are most associated with the Cretaceous-Tertiary extinction event, although they have been found at other events such as at the Triassic-Jurassic boundary.

a. Petrifaction
c. Fern spike
b. 1509 Istanbul earthquake
d. 1700 Cascadia earthquake

72. The _____ hypothesis describes a model in which extinction is non-selective and occurs randomly. The metaphor of the _____ suggest that species are simply out in a field and 'bullets' are hitting them at random, thus there extinction is due only to stochastic effects. The _____ operates without relation to the organisms' adaptability, or fitness of specific animals.

a. Dead Clade Walking
c. Local extinction
b. Signor-Lipps effect
d. Field of Bullets

Chapter 13. Test Preparation Part 13

73. _____ is the extinction of a species or other taxon such that:

   1. it disappears from the fossil record, or historic reports of its existence cease;
   2. the reduced population no longer plays a significant role in ecosystem function; or
   3. the population is no longer viable. There are no individuals able to reproduce, or the small population of breeding individuals will not be able to sustain itself due to inbreeding depression and genetic drift, which leads to a loss of fitness.

In plant populations, self-incompatibility mechanisms may cause related plant specimens to be incompatible, which may lead to _____ if an entire population becomes self incompatible. This does not occur in larger populations.

In polygynous populations, where only a few males leave offspring, there is a much smaller reproducing population than if all viable males were considered. Furthermore, the successful males act as a genetic bottleneck, leading to more rapid genetic drift or inbreeding problems in small populations.

   a. Pseudoextinction
   b. Dead Clade Walking
   c. Local extinction
   d. Functional extinction

74. _____ is a process of environmental change important in evolution and conservation biology. As the name implies, it describes the emergence of discontinuities (fragmentation) in an organism's preferred environment (habitat.) _____ can be caused by geological processes that slowly alter the layout of the physical environment or by human activity such as land conversion, which can alter the environment on a much faster time scale.
   a. Habitat fragmentation
   b. Functional extinction
   c. Local extinction
   d. Pseudoextinction

75. In paleontology, a _____ is a taxon that disappears from one or more periods of the fossil record, only to appear again later. _____ are observational artifacts that appear to occur either because of (local) extinction, later resupplied, or as a sampling artifact.
   a. 1703 Genroku earthquake
   b. 1509 Istanbul earthquake
   c. Lazarus taxon
   d. 1700 Cascadia earthquake

76. _____ is an informal term for any living species (or clade) of organism which appears to be the same as a species otherwise only known from fossils and which has no close living relatives. These species have all survived major extinction events, and generally retain low taxonomic diversities. A species which successfully radiates (forming many new species after a possible genetic bottleneck) has become too successful to be considered a '_____'.
   a. 1703 Genroku earthquake
   b. 1700 Cascadia earthquake
   c. 1509 Istanbul earthquake
   d. Living fossil

77. _____ are the preserved remains or traces of animals, plants, and other organisms from the remote past. The totality of _____, both discovered and undiscovered, and their placement in fossiliferous rock formations and sedimentary layers (strata) is known as the fossil record. The study of _____ across geological time, how they were formed, and the evolutionary relationships between taxa (phylogeny) are some of the most important functions of the science of paleontology.

a. Fossils
b. 1509 Istanbul earthquake
c. 1703 Genroku earthquake
d. 1700 Cascadia earthquake

78. _____ is where a species (or other taxon) ceases to exist in the chosen area of study, but still exists elsewhere. This phenomenon is also known as extirpation. Local extinctions are contrasted with global extinctions.
a. Local extinction
b. Pseudoextinction
c. Habitat fragmentation
d. Field of Bullets

79. _____ of a species occurs where there are no more living members of that species, but members of a daughter species or subspecies remain alive. As all species must have an ancestor of a previous species, much of evolution is believed to occur through _____. However, it is difficult to prove that any particular fossil species is pseudoextinct unless genetic information has been preserved.
a. Functional extinction
b. Local extinction
c. Field of Bullets
d. Pseudoextinction

80. The _____ is a paleontological principle proposed by Philip W. Signor and Jere H. Lipps which states that, since the fossil record of organisms is never complete, neither the first nor the last organism in a given taxon will be recorded as a fossil.

The most spectacular example is the coelacanth, which was thought to have become extinct in the very late Cretaceous - until a live specimen was caught in 1938.

But the _____ is more important for the difficulties it raises in paleontology:

- It makes it very difficult to be confident about the timing and speed of mass extinctions, and this makes it difficult to test theories about the causes of mass extinctions. For example the extinction of the dinosaurs was long thought to be a gradual process, but evidence collected since the late 1980s suggests it was abrupt, which is consistent with the idea that an asteroid impact caused it.
- The uncertainty about when a taxon first appeared makes it difficult to be confident about the ancestry of specific genera. For example if the earliest known fossil of genus X is much earlier than the earliest known fossil of genus Y and genus Y has all the features of genus X plus a few of its own, it is natural to suppose that X is an ancestor of Y. But this hypothesis could be called into question at any time by the finding of a fossil of Y that is earlier than any known fossil of X - unless an even older fossil of genus X is found, and so on.

a. Field of Bullets
b. Pseudoextinction
c. Signor-Lipps effect
d. Local extinction

81. The _____ or Clovis comet hypothesis refers to the hypothesized large air burst or earth impact of an object or objects from outer space that initiated the Younger Dryas cold spell about 10,900 BP uncalibrated (12,900 BP calibrated.) The theory proposes that an air burst and/or earth impact with a rare swarm of carbonaceous chondrites or comets set vast areas of the North American continent on fire, causing the extinction of most of the large animals in North America and the demise of the North American Clovis culture at the end of the last glacial period. This swarm would have exploded above or even into the Laurentide Ice Sheet north of the Great Lakes.

a. 1509 Istanbul earthquake
b. 1703 Genroku earthquake
c. Younger Dryas impact event
d. 1700 Cascadia earthquake

82. _____, commonly referred to as the 'First Family', is a collection of prehistoric hominid teeth and bones. Discovered in 1975 by Donald Johanson's team in Hadar, Ethiopia, the 'First Family' is estimated to be about 3.2 million years old and consists of the remains of at least thirteen individuals. They are generally thought to be members of the species Australopithecus afarensis.
   a. Index fossils
   b. Invertebrate paleontology
   c. Indian bead
   d. AL 333

83. An _____ is a small organic fossil, present from approximately >2,500 million years ago to the present. Their diversity reflects major ecological events such as the appearance of predation and the Cambrian explosion.

In general, any small, non-acid soluble (i.e. non-carbonate, non-siliceous) organic structure that can not otherwise be accounted for is classified as an _____.

   a. AL 333
   b. AASHTO Soil Classification System
   c. AL 129-1
   d. Acritarch

84. _____ is a tubular fossil from the middle Chazyan (Mid Ordovician) of New York state, collected by Rousseau Flower and included by him in the Endocerida and placed in a new family the Allotrioceratidae. (Flower 1955.) _____ is characterized by a lateral pair of subequal endocones separated by a straight partition that extends more than half way across from either the dorsal or vental side, as perceived, and runs along the length.
   a. Allotrioceras
   b. Invertebrate paleontology
   c. Indian bead
   d. Index fossils

85. _____ are an extinct group of marine animals of the subclass Ammonoidea in the class Cephalopoda, phylum Mollusca. They are excellent index fossils, and it is often possible to link the rock layer in which they are found to specific geological time periods.

_____' closest living relative is probably not the modern Nautilus (which they outwardly resemble), but rather the subclass Coleoidea (octopus, squid, and cuttlefish.)

   a. AASHTO Soil Classification System
   b. AL 333
   c. AL 129-1
   d. Ammonites

86. _____ is an extinct group of marine animals, commonly called Ammonites, of the order Ammonitida in the class Cephalopoda, phylum Mollusca. They are excellent index fossils, and it is often possible to link the rock layer in which they are found to specific geological time periods.

Ammonites' closest living relative is probably not the modern Nautilus (which they outwardly resemble), but rather the subclass Coleoidea (octopus, squid, and cuttlefish.)

   a. AL 333
   b. Ammonitina
   c. AASHTO Soil Classification System
   d. AL 129-1

87. The _____ constitute a subclass of extinct cephalopods found in marine sediments from the Early Devonian through the Cretaceous. Baring an external shell, ammonoids superficially resemble nautiloids, such as the modern Nautilus, however, based on similarity of the radulas, they are more closely related to modern coleoids, squid, octopus, and cuttlefish.
   a. AASHTO Soil Classification System
   b. Ammonoidea
   c. AL 333
   d. AL 129-1

88. _____ are a group of very early marine animals known from fossils found in Cambrian deposits in China, USA, Canada, Poland and Australia. They were long thought to be restricted to this range, but the discovery of the Devonian Schinderhannes extended their record by some hundred million years - their non-mineralised nature means they are absent from the intermediate fossil record. Anomalocarids are the largest Cambrian animals known - some Chinese forms may have reached 2 m in length - and most of them were probably active carnivores.
   a. AASHTO Soil Classification System
   b. AL 129-1
   c. Orthrozanclus
   d. Anomalocaridids

89. A _____ is any geological stratum or deposit that contains bones of whatever kind. Inevitably, such deposits are sedimentary in nature. Not a formal term, it tends to be used more to describe especially dense collections. It is also applied to brecciated and stalagmitic deposits on the floor of caves, which frequently contain osseous remains.
   a. Derived fossil
   b. Fossil wood
   c. Copalite
   d. Bone bed

90. Characteristic of the Neoproterozoic and Cambrian epochs, the heterogeneous group called _____ are calcareous colonial microfossils, which include many morphologically dissimilar organisms, whose effect in massive aggregations, in association with shelly metazoans, was to lay down the earliest recognizable reef systems: compare Archaeocyathids. The earliest recognizable patch reefs date to the Tommotian. Individual _____ laid down calcium carbonate in tubules, threads, chambered structures and other forms.
   a. Stegocephalia
   b. Cambrian explosion
   c. Bromalites
   d. Calcimicrobes

91. The _____ or Cambrian radiation was the seemingly rapid appearance of most major groups of complex animals around 530 million years ago, as evidenced by the fossil record. This was accompanied by a major diversification of other organisms, including animals, phytoplankton, and calcimicrobes. Before about 580 million years ago, most organisms were simple, composed of individual cells occasionally organized into colonies.
   a. Conodont Alteration Index
   b. Romer's Gap
   c. Labyrinthodont
   d. Cambrian explosion

92. A _____ is an organism outline of a fossil. It is a type of fossil found in any rock when organic material is compressed, leaving a thick carbon film.

When an organism is buried under many layers of sediment, pressure and heat may build up, leaving this thin film of carbon residue on rock surfaces.

   a. Copalite
   b. Compression fossil
   c. Derived fossil
   d. Carbonaceous film

93. In geology, _____ is a fossilized fruit, nut, or seed.

a. Turgai Sea
b. Choia
c. Carpolite
d. Xanioascus

94. In geology the term _____ refers to the system of forces that tend to decrease the volume of or shorten rocks. Compressive strength refers to the maximum compressive stress that can be applied to a material before failure occurs. In tectonics, plates are always subjected to compressive stress.
   a. Compression
   b. Seismic to simulation
   c. Geodiversity
   d. Leaverite

95. A _____ is a fossil preserved in sedimentary rock that has undergone physical compression. While it is uncommon to find animals preserved as good compression fossils, it is very common to find plants preserved this way. The reason for this is that physical compression of the rock often leads to distortion of the fossil.
   a. Copalite
   b. Derived fossil
   c. Fossil wood
   d. Compression fossil

96. _____, also termed fossil resin and Highgate resin, is a naturally occurring organic substance found as irregular pieces of pale-yellow colour in the London Clay at Highgate Hill. It has a resinous aromatic odour when freshly broken, volatilizes at a moderate temperature, and burns readily with a yellow, smoky flame, leaving scarcely any ash.
   a. Derived fossil
   b. Copalite
   c. Fossil wood
   d. Compression fossil

97. _____ are fossilised primitive plant spores that first appear in the fossil record during the late Ordovician to early Silurian period.

_____ are generally found in non-marine rocks and decrease in abundance with distance offshore. This suggests that any _____ found in the marine environment were transported there by the wind from the land, rather than originating from the marine environment.
   a. Petrified wood
   b. Cryptospores
   c. 1700 Cascadia earthquake
   d. 1509 Istanbul earthquake

98. A _____ is a fossil found in rock made later than when the fossilized animal or plant died: it happens when a hard fossil is freed from a soft rock formation by erosion and redeposited in a currently forming sediment deposit.
   a. Derived fossil
   b. Carbonaceous film
   c. Fossil wood
   d. Compression fossil

99. _____ - also known as diatomite, diahydro, kieselguhr, kieselgur or celite - is a naturally occurring, soft, chalk-like sedimentary rock that is easily crumbled into a fine white to off-white powder. This powder has an abrasive feel, similar to pumice powder, and is very light, due to its high porosity. The typical chemical composition of _____ is 86% silica, 5% sodium, 3% magnesium and 2% iron. _____ consists of fossilized remains of diatoms, a type of hard-shelled algae.
   a. Jasperoid
   b. Keystone
   c. Porcellanite
   d. Diatomaceous earth

100. _____ is a fossil swallowtail butterfly in the subfamily Parnassiinae. The genus and its sole species was described from the Miocene of Tuscany, Italy.

a. Doritites bosniackii
b. 1703 Genroku earthquake
c. 1509 Istanbul earthquake
d. 1700 Cascadia earthquake

101. The _____ are ancient life-forms of the Ediacaran Period, which represent the earliest known complex multicellular organisms. They appeared soon after the Earth thawed from the Cryogenian period's extensive glaciers, and largely disappeared soon before the rapid appearance of biodiversity known as the Cambrian explosion, which saw the first appearance in the fossil record of the basic patterns and body-plans that would go on to form the basis of modern animals. Little of the diversity of the _____ would be incorporated in this new scheme, with a distinct Cambrian biota arising and usurping the organisms that dominated the Ediacaran fossil record.

a. Ediacara biota
b. AASHTO Soil Classification System
c. AL 333
d. AL 129-1

102. _____ is the archaeological or paleontological term for a group of associated animal fossils found together in a given stratum.

The principle of faunal succession is used in biostratigraphy to determine each biostratigraphic unit, or biozone. The biostratigraphic unit being a section of geological strata that is defined on the basis of its characteristic fossil taxa or _____.

a. 1700 Cascadia earthquake
b. 1509 Istanbul earthquake
c. 1703 Genroku earthquake
d. Faunal assemblage

Chapter 14. Test Preparation Part 14

1. _____ is wood that is preserved in the fossil record. Over time the wood will usually be the part of a plant that is best preserved (and most easily found.) _____ may or may not be petrified.
   a. Carbonaceous film
   b. Fossil wood
   c. Copalite
   d. Derived fossil

2. The _____ in stratigraphy, Chronostratigraphy, paleontology and other natural sciences refers to the entirety of the layers of rock strata -- depositions laid down in volcanism or by weathering detritus (clays, sands etc.) including all its fossil content and the information it yields about the history of the Earth: its past climate, geography, geology and the evolution of life on its surface. According to the Law of Superposition (first proposed in the mid-seventeenth century by the Danish naturalist Nicolas Steno) sedimentary and volcanic rocklayers are deposited on top of each other.
   a. Global Standard Stratigraphic Age
   b. Law of superposition
   c. Global Boundary Stratotype Section and Point
   d. Geologic record

3. _____ is a genus of fossil marine Hydrozoan from the Upper Triassic. They are mostly discoid or spherical and some forms found in the Karakorum mountains are called Karakorum stones. They vary in diameter from 1 to 35 cm and appear to follow Cope's rule for the prehistoric climate.
   a. Heterastridium
   b. Transitional fossils
   c. Macrofossils
   d. Submerged forest

4. _____ are fossil termite mounds occurring widely in the south-western Cape of South Africa. _____ can sometimes be recognised as large mounds above or near the surface of the landscape. There are two conflicting interpretations as to the origins of _____, the one view maintaining that _____ were built by the harvester termite Microhodotermes viator while other researchers maintain that _____ were built by a now possibly extinct termite species.
   a. Megabalanus
   b. Macrofossils
   c. Heuweltjies
   d. Transitional fossils

5. An _____ is an animal lacking a vertebral column. The group includes 98% of all animal species -- all animals except those in the Chordate subphylum Vertebrata (fish, reptiles, amphibians, birds, and mammals.)

Carolus Linnaeus' Systema Naturae divided these animals into only two groups, the Insecta and the now-obsolete vermes (worms.)

   a. AASHTO Soil Classification System
   b. AL 129-1
   c. AL 333
   d. Invertebrate

6. _____ victoria is an extinct species of anomalocaridid that lived 500 million years ago during the Cambrian era. It is part of the ancestral lineage that led to Arthropods and is related to Anomalocaris.

_____ was one of the largest organisms in the Cambrian oceans, reaching approximately 50 cm (1.5 feet) in length.

   a. Sanctacaris
   b. 1509 Istanbul earthquake
   c. Marrella
   d. Hurdia

7. An _____ is any disarticulated remains of a fish found in the fossil record, most often a scale, denticle or tooth.

a. AASHTO Soil Classification System
b. AL 333
c. AL 129-1
d. Ichthyolith

8. _____ are fossils used to define and identify geologic periods They work on the premise that, although different sediments may look different depending on the conditions under which they were laid down, they may include the remains of the same species of fossil. If the species concerned were short-lived, then it is certain that the sediments in question were deposited within that narrow time period.
   a. Invertebrate paleontology
   b. Indian bead
   c. Allotrioceras
   d. Index fossils

9. _____ are the preserved remains or traces of animals, plants, and other organisms from the remote past. The totality of _____, both discovered and undiscovered, and their placement in fossiliferous rock formations and sedimentary layers (strata) is known as the fossil record. The study of _____ across geological time, how they were formed, and the evolutionary relationships between taxa (phylogeny) are some of the most important functions of the science of paleontology.
   a. 1509 Istanbul earthquake
   b. 1703 Genroku earthquake
   c. Fossils
   d. 1700 Cascadia earthquake

10. _____ is a colloquial term for the fossilized stem segments of columnal crinoids, marine echinoderms of the class Crinoidea. The fossils, generally a centimeter or less in diameter, tend to be cylindrical with a small hole (either open or filled) through the axis and can resemble unstrung beads. The fossils are relatively abundant in certain areas, including parts of the American Midwest where they're present in gravel.
    a. Invertebrate paleontology
    b. Allotrioceras
    c. Index fossils
    d. Indian bead

11. _____ is sometimes described as Invertebrate paleozoology and/or Invertebrate paleobiology. Whether it is considered to be a subfield of paleontology, paleozoology, and/or paleobiology, this discipline is the scientific study of prehistoric invertebrates by analyzing invertebrate fossils in the geologic record.

By invertebrates are meant the non-vertebrate creatures of the kingdom Animalia (or Metazoa+b vmbnParazoa) in the biotic domain of Eukaryota.

   a. Index fossils
   b. Invertebrate paleontology
   c. Allotrioceras
   d. Indian bead

12. _____ is an informal term for any living species (or clade) of organism which appears to be the same as a species otherwise only known from fossils and which has no close living relatives. These species have all survived major extinction events, and generally retain low taxonomic diversities. A species which successfully radiates (forming many new species after a possible genetic bottleneck) has become too successful to be considered a '_____'.
    a. 1509 Istanbul earthquake
    b. 1703 Genroku earthquake
    c. 1700 Cascadia earthquake
    d. Living fossil

13. _____ are a group of armoured, segmented annelid worms, known from the Early Ordovician (Late Tremadoc) to Carboniferous. The group consist of three distinct families: the plumulitids, turrilepadids and lepidocoleids.

Only the calcitic scleretomes ('armour plates') of these worms tend to be preserved in the fossil record.

Chapter 14. Test Preparation Part 14

a. Paracrinoids
c. Submerged forest
b. Heuweltjies
d. Machaeridians

14. _____ are preserved organic remains large enough to be visible without a microscope.
a. Machaeridians
c. Paracrinoids
b. Macrofossils
d. Heuweltjies

15. _____ is a genus of barnacle. It grows to centimetres in length, and inhabits the lower intertidal zone.

_____ is an acorn barnacle comprising an organism dwelling in a calcium carbonate shell consisting of five plates.

a. Paracrinoids
c. Heuweltjies
b. Phosphatic fossilization
d. Megabalanus

16. A _____ is a large lenticular fossil, characterized by its numerous coils, subdivided by septa into chambers. They are the shells of the fossil and present-day marine protozoan Nummulites, a type of foraminiferan. Nummulites commonly reach 6 cm (2.4 inches) in diameter, and are common in Tertiary marine rocks, particularly around the Mediterranean (e.g. Eocene limestones from Egypt.)
a. 1703 Genroku earthquake
c. 1700 Cascadia earthquake
b. 1509 Istanbul earthquake
d. Nummulite

17. _____ is a growing and comparatively new discipline which combines the methods and findings of the natural science biology with the methods and findings of the earth science paleontology. It is occasionally referred to as 'geobiology.'

Paleobiological research uses biological field research of current biota and of fossils millions of years old to answer questions about the molecular evolution and the evolutionary history of life. In this scientific quest, macrofossils, microfossils and trace fossils are typically analyzed.

a. Petrifaction
c. 1700 Cascadia earthquake
b. 1509 Istanbul earthquake
d. Paleobiology

18. _____ studies examine the preservation of particulate organic matter and palynomorphs to provide information on the depositional environment of sediments and depositional palaeoenvironments of sedimentary rocks. The term _____ was introduced by the French geologist Combaz in 1964. _____ studies are often linked to investigations of the palynology and organic geochemistry of sedimentary rocks.
a. Cambrian explosion
c. Labyrinthodont
b. Palynofacies
d. Conodont Alteration Index

19. _____, are extinct marine animals that make up the class Paracrinoidea of the echinoderms (phylum Echinodermata), and are closely related to crinoids. They lived in shallow seas during the Early Ordovician through the Early Silurian.

_____ are characterized by a mouth with two to five feeding arms arranged asymmetrically.

a. Heuweltjies
b. Paracrinoids
c. Phosphatic fossilization
d. Macrofossils

20. In geology, _____, is the process by which organic material is converted into stone by impregnation with silica. It is a rare form of fossilization. Petrified wood is the most well known result of this process, but all organisms from bacteria to vertebrates can be petrified.
a. Petrifaction
b. 1700 Cascadia earthquake
c. Paleobiology
d. 1509 Istanbul earthquake

21. A _____ is a forest in which tree trunks have fossilized. That is, the wood in the trunks have turned into petrified wood, where organic cells have decomposed and are replaced by minerals, while preserving the structure of the wood.
a. 1703 Genroku earthquake
b. Petrified forest
c. 1509 Istanbul earthquake
d. 1700 Cascadia earthquake

22. _____ is a type of fossil: it consists of fossil wood where all the organic materials have been replaced with minerals , while retaining the original structure of the wood. The petrifaction process occurs underground, when wood becomes buried under sediment and is initially preserved due to a lack of oxygen. Mineral-rich water flowing through the sediment deposits minerals in the plant's cells and as the plant's lignin and cellulose decay away, a stone mould forms in its place.
a. 1509 Istanbul earthquake
b. Pteridospermatophyta
c. 1700 Cascadia earthquake
d. Petrified wood

23. _____ has occurred in unusual circumstances to preserve some extremely high-resolution microfossils in which careful preparation can even reveal preserved cellular structures. Such microscopic fossils are only visible under the scanning electron microscope.

Soft-tissue fossils themselves are rare. Its Cambrian soft animals, preserved in oxygen-free mud, made the Burgess shale familiar to every fossil buff. In phosphatic fossils, the preservation is so fine that even some cellular structure has been preserved.

a. Machaeridians
b. Transitional fossils
c. Megabalanus
d. Phosphatic fossilization

24. _____ are various groups of insects that lived before recorded history. Insects inhabited Earth since before the time of the dinosaurs. Many modern insects had already evolved to very similar forms even before the dawning of the dinosaur and lived alongside them and beyond up to the present day.
a. Calcimicrobes
b. Prehistoric insects
c. Trackway
d. Coracoid tubercle

25. The _____ is the posterior body part or shield of crustaceans and some arthropods, such as insects and the extinct trilobites. It contains the anus and, in females, the ovipositor. It is composed of fused body segments, sometimes with a tail, and separated from thoracic segments by an articulation.
a. 1509 Istanbul earthquake
b. 1703 Genroku earthquake
c. 1700 Cascadia earthquake
d. Pygidium

Chapter 14. Test Preparation Part 14

26. Before the advent of absolute dating in the 20th century, archaeologists and geologists were largely limited to the use of the _____ techniques. It estimates the order of prehistoric and geological events determined by using basic stratigraphic rules, and by observing where fossil organisms lay in the geological record, often in horizontal, stratified bands of rocks present throughout the world.

Though _____ can determine the sequential order in which a series of events occurred, not when they occur, it is in no way inferior to radiometric dating; in fact, _____ by biostratigraphy is the preferred method in paleontology, and is in some respects more accurate (Stanley, 167-9.)

a. Paleomagnetism
b. Relative dating
c. Global Boundary Stratotype Section and Point
d. Chronozone

27. A _____ is the jaw of a polychaete annelid, a common type of fossil-producing segmented worm useful in invertebrate paleontology. Scolecodonts are common and diverse microfossils, which range from the Cambrian period (around half a billion years ago at the start of the Paleozoic era) to the present. However, scolecodonts are reported most commonly from Ordovician, Silurian and Devonian marine deposits of the Paleozoic era.

a. 1703 Genroku earthquake
b. Scolecodont
c. 1700 Cascadia earthquake
d. 1509 Istanbul earthquake

28. The _____ is a paleontological principle proposed by Philip W. Signor and Jere H. Lipps which states that, since the fossil record of organisms is never complete, neither the first nor the last organism in a given taxon will be recorded as a fossil.

The most spectacular example is the coelacanth, which was thought to have become extinct in the very late Cretaceous - until a live specimen was caught in 1938.

But the _____ is more important for the difficulties it raises in paleontology:

- It makes it very difficult to be confident about the timing and speed of mass extinctions, and this makes it difficult to test theories about the causes of mass extinctions. For example the extinction of the dinosaurs was long thought to be a gradual process, but evidence collected since the late 1980s suggests it was abrupt, which is consistent with the idea that an asteroid impact caused it.
- The uncertainty about when a taxon first appeared makes it difficult to be confident about the ancestry of specific genera. For example if the earliest known fossil of genus X is much earlier than the earliest known fossil of genus Y and genus Y has all the features of genus X plus a few of its own, it is natural to suppose that X is an ancestor of Y. But this hypothesis could be called into question at any time by the finding of a fossil of Y that is earlier than any known fossil of X - unless an even older fossil of genus X is found, and so on.

a. Pseudoextinction
b. Field of Bullets
c. Local extinction
d. Signor-Lipps effect

29. The _____ are mineralized fossils, many only a few millimetres long, with a nearly continuous record from the latest stages of the Ediacaran to the end of the Early Cambrian period. They are very diverse, and there is no formal definition of '_____' or 'small shelly fossils'. Almost all are from earlier rocks than more familiar fossils such as trilobites.
  a. 1700 Cascadia earthquake
  b. 1509 Istanbul earthquake
  c. 1703 Genroku earthquake
  d. Small shelly fauna

30. _____ is an old term for early (generally large) amphibians, comprising all pre-Jurassic and some later extinct large amphibians of more or less salamander-like build. The term was coined in 1868 by American palaentologist Edward Drinker Cope and comes from Greek stego cephalia - 'roofed head', and refer to the copious amounts of dermal armour some of the larger forms evidently had. Originally, the term was used as a systematic unit at the rank of order.
  a. Stegocephalia
  b. Cambrian explosion
  c. Prehistoric insects
  d. Conodont Alteration Index

31. _____ refers to remains whose fossilization process is not complete, either for lack of time or because the condition in which they were buried were not optimal for fossilization.

_____ remains that date back into the Mesozoic are exceptionally rare, usually in an advanced state of decay and consequently much disputed. The vast bulk of the material comes from Quaternary deposits.

  a. Cap carbonates
  b. Subfossil
  c. Sclavia craton
  d. Planar deformation features

32. _____ is a term used to describe the remains of trees (especially tree stumps) which have been submerged by marine transgression, i.e. sea level rise. Examples can be found at low tide around the coast of England and Wales, and off the coast of Denmark. These remains have usually been buried in mud, peat or sand for several thousand years before being uncovered by sea level change and erosion.
  a. Transitional fossils
  b. Megabalanus
  c. Machaeridians
  d. Submerged forest

33. _____ are the fossilized remains of intermediary forms of life that illustrate an evolutionary transition. They can be identified by their retention of certain primitive (plesiomorphic) traits in comparison with their more derived relatives, as they are defined in the study of cladistics. 'Missing link' is a popular term for transitional forms.
  a. Machaeridians
  b. Megabalanus
  c. Submerged forest
  d. Transitional fossils

34. In the natural sciences, _____ is the study of how life on Earth could have arisen from inanimate matter. It should not be confused with evolution, which is the study of how groups of living things change over time. Amino acids, often called 'the building blocks of life', occur naturally, due to chemical reactions unrelated to life.
  a. AASHTO Soil Classification System
  b. Abiogenesis
  c. AL 129-1
  d. AL 333

35. _____ Island is an island in southwestern Greenland, about 22 kilometers south of Nuuk. _____ is the location of a rock formation that has been proposed to contain the oldest known sedimentary rocks on Earth, and perhaps the oldest evidence of life on Earth.

The rocks in question are part of a metamorphosed supracrustal sequence located at the south-western tip of the island.

   a. AASHTO Soil Classification System
   b. AL 333
   c. Akilia
   d. AL 129-1

36. _____ is the process of lifeforms producing other lifeforms, e.g. a spider lays eggs, which develop into spiders. It may also refer to biochemical processes of production in living organisms.
   a. Bugonia
   b. Miller-Urey experiment
   c. Biogenesis
   d. Primordial sandwich

37. The word _____ is Greek in origin, meaning 'ox birth'. It denotes the mythical practice by which bees are produced from the carcasses of dead oxen- a misunderstanding similar to the notion of 'spontaneous generation'. The process is most clearly described by Virgil in the fourth book of the Georgics, but had been rendered in literature by Varro Reatinus before Virgil.
   a. PAH world hypothesis
   b. Primordial sandwich
   c. Miller-Urey experiment
   d. Bugonia

38. The _____ was an experiment that simulated hypothetical conditions thought at the time to be present on the early Earth, and tested for the occurrence of chemical evolution. Specifically, the experiment tested Soviet scientist Alexander Oparin's and J. B. S. Haldane's hypothesis that conditions on the primitive Earth favored chemical reactions that synthesized organic compounds from inorganic precursors.
   a. PAH world hypothesis
   b. Bugonia
   c. Miller-Urey experiment
   d. Primordial sandwich

39. The _____ meteorite is named after _____, Victoria, in Australia. It is one of the most studied meteorites due to its large mass (>100 kg), the fact that it was an observed fall, and it belongs to a group of meteorites rich in organic compounds.
   a. 1700 Cascadia earthquake
   b. 1703 Genroku earthquake
   c. Murchison
   d. 1509 Istanbul earthquake

40. The _____ is a biological hypothesis that proposes that the use of polycyclic aromatic hydrocarbons (PAH) was a means for a pre-RNA World basis for the origin of life. As yet it is untested, though in 2007 Cassini spacecraft found the presence of heavy negative ions of tholin in the upper regions of Titan's atmosphere.

Experiments such as the Miller experiment and others allow the simple construction of primitive organic molecules including amino acids.

   a. Primordial sandwich
   b. PAH world hypothesis
   c. Miller-Urey experiment
   d. Bugonia

41. _____ is the hypothesis that 'seeds' of life exist already all over the Universe, that life on Earth may have originated through these 'seeds', and that they may deliver or have delivered life to other habitable bodies.

The related but distinct idea of exogenesis is a more limited hypothesis that proposes life on Earth was transferred from elsewhere in the Universe but makes no prediction about how widespread it is. Because the term '_____' is more well-known, it tends to be used in reference to what should strictly speaking be called exogenesis.

a. 1703 Genroku earthquake
b. 1700 Cascadia earthquake
c. 1509 Istanbul earthquake
d. Panspermia

42. The concept of the _____ was proposed by the chemist G>ünter W>ächtersh>äuser to describe the possible origins of the first cell membranes, and, therefore, the first cell.

According to the two main models of abiogenesis, RNA world and iron-sulfur world, prebiotic processes existed before the development of the cell membrane. The difficulty with this idea, however, is that it is almost impossible to create a complex molecule such as RNA (or even its molecular precursor, pre-RNA) directly from simple organic molecules dissolved in a global ocean (Joyce, 1991), because without some mechanism to concentrate these organic molecules, they would be too dilute to generate the necessary chemical reactions to transform them from simple organic molecules into genuine prebiotic molecules.

a. Bugonia
b. Primordial sandwich
c. Miller-Urey experiment
d. PAH world hypothesis

43. In planetary astronomy and astrobiology, the _____ argues that the emergence of complex multicellular life (metazoa) on Earth required an improbable combination of astrophysical and geological events and circumstances.

a. 1703 Genroku earthquake
b. 1700 Cascadia earthquake
c. 1509 Istanbul earthquake
d. Rare Earth hypothesis

44. Thioesters are compounds resulting from the bonding of sulfur with an acyl group with the general formula R-S-CO-R'. They are the product of esterification between a carboxylic acid and a thiol (as opposed to an alcohol in regular esters.)

In biochemistry a _____ connects the acetyl groups in acetyl-CoA and malonyl-CoA. Some biochemists believe that the _____ bond was critical for the origin of life.

a. Thioester
b. 1703 Genroku earthquake
c. 1509 Istanbul earthquake
d. 1700 Cascadia earthquake

45. _____, is a heteropolymer molecule formed by solar ultraviolet irradiation of simple organic compounds such as methane or ethane. They do not form naturally on modern-day Earth, but are found in great abundance on the surface of icy bodies in the outer solar system. They usually have a reddish-brown appearance.

a. 1703 Genroku earthquake
b. 1509 Istanbul earthquake
c. 1700 Cascadia earthquake
d. Tholin

46. The _____ Fossil Beds are an important paleontological site located on _____ Station in Central Australia, 200km north-east of Alice Springs. It is notable for the occurrence of well-preserved, rare, Tertiary vertebrate fossils, which provide evidence of the evolution of the Northern Territorye;s fauna and climate. The _____ Fossil Beds are also significant as a research and teaching site for palaeontology students.

a. AASHTO Soil Classification System
c. AL 333
b. AL 129-1
d. Alcoota

47. The _____ of Antelope County in northeastern Nebraska are among the rare preservation sites called lagerstätten, which preserve ecological 'snapshots' from a brief moment in time, due to extraordinary local conditions that have preserved a range of fossilized organisms undisturbed.

The _____ are especially famous for fossils of mammals from the middle Miocene geologic epoch. The _____ are stratigraphically part of the Serravallian-age Ogallala Group.

a. AL 129-1
c. AASHTO Soil Classification System
b. AL 333
d. Ashfall Fossil Beds

48. The _____ is an ancient karstic region of Spain, near the town of the same name and Ibeas de Juarros, containing several caves, where fossils and stone tools of the earliest known Hominians in West Europe have been found.

a. AL 129-1
c. AL 333
b. AASHTO Soil Classification System
d. Atapuerca Mountains

49. The sedimentary deposits in eroded badlands at _____ in the Patagonian province of Neuquen, Argentina, are among the paleontologist's rare lagerst>ätten, the undisturbed strata that give glimpses of a range of ecology at a given moment in the Earth's history. The sedimentary layers at _____ were laid down 80 million years before present and offer an unequalled view of a fossilized titanosaurid sauropod hatchery.

At _____ dinosaur eggs containing identifiable embryonic remains have been the most spectacular discoveries.

a. Auca Mahuevo
c. AL 129-1
b. AASHTO Soil Classification System
d. AL 333

50. The _____ is an impressive six-cave complex known as a living site of stone-age man. It lies about 3 km northeast of Tugh village in southern Karabakh, an area legally within the Fizuli district of Azerbaijan but now under de-facto self rule by the ethnic Armenian population of Nagorno-Karabakh since the war of the early 1990s.

Extensively examined by archaeologists in the 1960s, the cave is considered to be the site of one of the most ancient proto-human habitations in Eurasia.

a. AASHTO Soil Classification System
c. AL 129-1
b. AL 333
d. Azykh Cave

51. _____ is a lower Cretaceous locality in Siberia, on the left bank of the Vitim River. The Zaza Formation sediments exposed at _____ are represented mostly by sandstones, siltstones, marls and bituminous shales. The total thickness if the section is about 80 m.

a. Neocomian
c. Thrace Basin
b. Baissa
d. Juan Fernandez hotspot

52. _____ were anatomically modern humans who first appeared in Sri Lanka about 34,000 _____.

There is evidence of Paleolithic (Homo Erectus) people in Sri Lanka about 300,000 _____ and possibly even as early as 500,000 _____. By about 125,000 _____ if is certain that there were prehistoric settlements in Sri Lanka.

a. Wavula Pane
b. 1509 Istanbul earthquake
c. Balangoda people
d. Batadombalena

53. _____ is fossil tree resin, which is appreciated for its color and beauty. Good quality _____ is used for the manufacture of ornamental objects and jewelry. Although not mineralized, it is often classified as a gemstone.

A common misconception is that _____ is made of tree sap; it is not. Sap is the fluid that circulates through a plant's vascular system, while resin is the semi-solid amorphous organic substance secreted in pockets and canals through epithelial cells of the plant.

a. AL 333
b. Amber
c. AASHTO Soil Classification System
d. AL 129-1

54. _____ is one of world historic archeological site with evidence of 28,000 BC over, Balangoda People. Located 85 km from Colombo in Sri Lanka, a two hour drive from Colombo.

_____ is one of the archeological sites located in Sri Lanka, to prove clearly said by Professor Paul Mellars, a Cambridge University archaeologist. He has revealed remarkable cultural and technological similarities that suggest a common origin.

a. Belilena
b. Wavula Pane
c. 1509 Istanbul earthquake
d. Batadombalena

55. The _____ in Montana is a fossiliferous lagerstätte, a limestone layer laid down in the Mississippian epoch of the Carboniferous period, about 318 mya. This lens of limestone was laid down in a surrounding matrix that indicates a landscape of mudflats and braided channels (linear sandstone seams) in fresh and brackish water, in an arid climate (gypsum formation.) Magnetic orientation of particles relative to the bedding planes of the strata suggest a latitude of about 12°N, a tropical siting.

a. Bear Gulch Limestone
b. Calciferous sandstone
c. Mississippian
d. Dinantian

56. The _____ is the third of the main subdivisions of the Karoo Supergroup of geological strata in Southern Africa. It follows conformably after the Ecca Group and consists essentially of sandstones and shales, deposited in the Karoo Basin from the Middle Permian to the early part of the Middle Triassic Periods.

Fossils of tetrapods, especially therapsids, are common, and the vertebrate biostratigraphy has been mapped out in detail, beginning with the work of Robert Broom at the start of the 20th century and developed and revised a number of times since.

a. 1700 Cascadia earthquake
b. 1703 Genroku earthquake
c. 1509 Istanbul earthquake
d. Beaufort Group

57. _____ is the famous largest cave in Sri Lanka. It is located eight km from the town of Kitulgala. It holds evidence of a lost generation of Sri Lanka 12,000 years old; then this cave belonged to the Balangoda People, described as Homo sapiens balangodensis by Paul E. P. Deraniyagala who found here ten skeletons of these people, who lived 2000 feet above the sea level.
   a. Wavula Pane
   b. Batadombalena
   c. 1509 Istanbul earthquake
   d. Belilena

58. The _____ is a stratum of limestone of the Bathonian stage, found in the Jurassic ridge which extends north and south through England. It was laid down in the shallows of the Jurassic sea and is part of the more widely defined Great Oölite Series. It is also known as the Great Oolite Limestone.
   a. Sanga da Alemoa
   b. La Venta
   c. Blisworth Limestone
   d. Le Moustier

59. _____ is a village in the Veneto, on the southern margin of the Italian Alps. It is a frazione of the comune of Vestenanova, in the province of Verona. The area is famous for the marine fossils from the lagerstätte of Monte _____. It was one of the first fossil sites with high quality preservation known to Europeans, and is still an important source of fossils from the Eocene.
   a. 1509 Istanbul earthquake
   b. Bolca
   c. 1703 Genroku earthquake
   d. 1700 Cascadia earthquake

60. _____ lies approximately fifteen miles north of Laramie, Wyoming near historic Como Bluff. During the summer of 1897 Walter W. Granger, a paleontologist from the American Museum of Natural History, came upon a hillside littered with Jurassic period dinosaur bone fragments. Nearby was a sheepherder's cabin built entirely out of fossil bones, hence the name '_____.' It is possible, although unverifiable, that the _____ was originally discovered by Frank Williston, the brother of Samuel Wendell Williston, an assistant to Othniel Charles Marsh.
   a. 1703 Genroku earthquake
   b. 1509 Istanbul earthquake
   c. Bone Cabin Quarry
   d. 1700 Cascadia earthquake

61. _____ are a range of hills in eastern Balochistan, Pakistan. It includes the tribal tract called Bugti country.

30 million years ago the Haplorrhinies: Bugtipithecus inexpectans, Phileosimias kamali and Phileosimias brahuiorum, similar to today's lemurs, lived in rainforests on the _____ of central Pakistan.

   a. 1700 Cascadia earthquake
   b. 1509 Istanbul earthquake
   c. 1703 Genroku earthquake
   d. Bugti Hills

62. The _____ Fossil site is one of three known vertebrate fossil sites in the Australia's Northern Territory, along with the Alcoota Fossil Beds on Alcoota Station and the Kangaroo Well site on Deep Well Station. It is located about 550km south-southeast of Darwin, on Camfield Station.

The _____ Fossil Site is part of the Camfield Fossil Beds which outcrop in a narrow belt about 50km long.

a. Fur Formation
b. Gunflint Chert
c. Bullock Creek
d. Hell Creek Formation

63. The _____ Formation is one of the world's most celebrated fossil localities, and is famous for the exceptional preservation of the fossils found within it, in which the soft parts are preserved. It is 505 million years (Middle Cambrian) in age, making it one of the earliest fossil beds to preserve the soft parts of animals. The pre-Cambrian fossil record of animals is sparse and ambiguous.
   a. 1703 Genroku earthquake
   b. Burgess Shale
   c. 1509 Istanbul earthquake
   d. 1700 Cascadia earthquake

64. The _____ is a Miocene lagerstätte located near Clarkia, Idaho.

The fossil beds were laid down in a lake roughly 15 million years ago, when a drainage basin was dammed by the flood basalts of the Columbia River Plateau. Narrow and deep, the lake's cold, anoxic water and rapid sedimentation created perfect fossil conditions.

   a. Turritellenplatte
   b. Milk River Formation
   c. Clarkia fossil beds
   d. La Venta

65. The _____ National Natural Landmark, located near Cleveland, Utah contains the densest concentration of Jurassic dinosaur fossils ever found, Well over 15,000 bones have been excavated from this Jurassic 'predator trap' and there are many thousands more awaiting excavation and study. It was designated a National Natural Landmark in October 1965.
   a. 1703 Genroku earthquake
   b. 1509 Istanbul earthquake
   c. 1700 Cascadia earthquake
   d. Cleveland Lloyd Dinosaur Quarry

66. The _____ is a geologic formation located in western Tennessee and extreme northeast Mississippi. It is a sedimentary sandy marl deposit, Late Cretaceous (Maastrichtian) in age, about 73 million years old. The formation is known for producing mosasaurs and plesiosaurs.
   a. 1509 Istanbul earthquake
   b. Tumblagooda sandstone
   c. Jiufotang Formation
   d. Coon Creek Formation

67. Located near the southern end of New Zealand's South Island, _____ is best known as the site of a petrified forest some 180 million years old.

The now petrified logs, from ancient conifers closely related to modern Kauri and Norfolk Pine, were buried by volcanic mud flows and gradually replaced by silica to produce the fossils now exposed by the sea.

   a. Sanga da Alemoa
   b. Bushveld Sandstone Formation
   c. Fur Formation
   d. Curio Bay

68. _____ is part of the Morrison Fossil Area National Natural Landmark located in Morrison, Colorado, just west of Denver.

The _____ area is one of the world's most famous dinosaur fossil localities. In 1877, some of the best-known dinosaurs were found here, including Apatosaurus, Diplodocus, Stegosaurus, and Allosaurus.

a. 1700 Cascadia earthquake
b. 1703 Genroku earthquake
c. 1509 Istanbul earthquake
d. Dinosaur Ridge

69. _____ is amber from the Dominican Republic. Resin from the extinct species Hymenaea protera is the source of _____ and probably of most amber found in the tropics.

_____ differentiates itself from Baltic amber by being nearly always transparent, and it has a higher number of fossil inclusions.

a. 1509 Istanbul earthquake
b. Dominican amber
c. 1700 Cascadia earthquake
d. 1703 Genroku earthquake

70. The _____ is a lagerst>ätte in Guizhou Province, China that is notable for being one of the oldest fossil beds to contain highly preserved fossils. The formation is of particular interest because it appears to cover the boundary between the problematic organisms of the Ediacaran geological period and the more famous Cambrian explosion. Taken as a whole, the _____ ranges from about 590 Ma at its base to about 565 Ma at its top, predating by perhaps five million years the earliest of the 'classical' Ediacaran faunas from Mistaken Point, Newfoundland, and recording conditions a good forty to fifty million years before the Cambrian explosion.
   a. Milk River Formation
   b. Doushantuo Formation
   c. Naturita Formation
   d. Bushveld Sandstone Formation

71. _____ are a range of low hills in the northern part of the Flinders Ranges of South Australia, around 650 km north of Adelaide. The area has many old copper and silver mines from mining activity in the late 19th century. The hills also contain fossils of early life forms, the Ediacaran biota (lagerst>ätte), and have given their name to the Ediacaran geological period.
   a. AL 129-1
   b. Ediacara Hills
   c. AL 333
   d. AASHTO Soil Classification System

72. The _____ is a geological formation in Emu Bay, South Australia, containing a major Konservat-Lagerst>ätten (fossil beds with soft tissue preservation.) It is one of two in the world containing Redlichiidan trilobites.

Its mode of preservation is the same as the Burgess shale, but the larger grain size of the Emu Bay rock means that the quality of preservation is lower.

   a. AASHTO Soil Classification System
   b. AL 129-1
   c. AL 333
   d. Emu Bay shale

73. _____ is a cave in the district of Kalutara, Western Province, Sri Lanka. The cave is important for the Late Pleistocene human skeletal remains discovered there in the 1960s and 1980s.

The first human burials in the cave were uncovered in 1968 by Dr Siran U. Deraniyagala (the Sri Lankan government department of archaeology), and he returned with an assistant, W. H. Wijepala, in 1988. The main finds consisted of microliths, the remains of ancient fires, and the remains of plants and human beings. Radiocarbon dating indicated that the cave had been occupied from about 33,000 to 4,750 years ago.

a. 1703 Genroku earthquake
c. 1509 Istanbul earthquake
b. Fa Hien Cave
d. 1700 Cascadia earthquake

74. The _____ is a division of Upper Cretaceous rocks found in Saskatchewan, Canada. More accurately described as Late Maastrichtian, these rocks contain the youngest of dinosaur genera, much like the Hell Creek Formation in the United States.
   a. Frenchman Formation
   b. Le Moustier
   c. Turritellenplatte
   d. Curio Bay

75. The _____ is a marine deposit approximately 60 meters thick consisting of diatoms and clay minerals (Mo-clay.) It is known for its abundant fossil fish, insects, reptiles, birds and plants. The _____ was deposited just above the Palaeocene-Eocene boundary, about 54-55 million years ago, and its tropical or sub-tropical flora indicate that the climate after the Paleocene-Eocene Thermal Maximum was moderately warm (approximately 4-8 degrees warmer then today.)
   a. Gilboa fossil forest
   b. Turritellenplatte
   c. Fur Formation
   d. Kaili Formation

76. _____ is a site in the Tenere desert of Niger known for its extensive fossil graveyard, where remains of Sarcosuchus imperator, popularly known as SuperCroc, have been found (by Paul Sereno in 1997, for example), including vertebrae, limb bones, armor plates, jaws, and a nearly complete 6-foot (1.8 m) skull.

_____ is very hot and dry. However, it is supposed that millions of years ago, _____ had trees, plants and wide rivers. The river covered the remains of dead animals, the fossilized remains of which were protected by the drying rivers over the centuries.

   a. 1703 Genroku earthquake
   b. 1700 Cascadia earthquake
   c. 1509 Istanbul earthquake
   d. Gadoufaoua

77. _____, New York is cited as home to the Earth's oldest forest. Located near the Gilboa Dam in Schoharie County, New York, the region is home to tree trunks from the Devonian Period, roughly 380 million years old. The fossils, some of the only survivors of their type in the world, are remnants of the Earth's earliest forests.
   a. Doushantuo Formation
   b. Kaili Formation
   c. Nacimiento Formation
   d. Gilboa fossil forest

78. The _____ is a Late Miocene-epoch assemblage of fossils located near the unincorporated town of Gray in Washington County, Northeast Tennessee, and dates back 4.5 to 7 million years BCE). The _____ was discovered by geologists in May 2000. They were investigating unusual clay deposits turned up during the course of a Tennessee Department of Transportation highway project to widen State Route 75 south of its intersection with Interstate 26.
   a. 1509 Istanbul earthquake
   b. 1700 Cascadia earthquake
   c. 1703 Genroku earthquake
   d. Gray Fossil Site

79. The _____ is an Eocene geologic formation that records the sedimentation in a series of intermountain lakes. The sedimentary layers were formed in a large area of interconnecting lakes a tributary of the Colorado River. The area of the formation exists as three separate basins around the Uinta Mountains of northeastern Utah: an area in northwestern Colorado east of the Uintas, a larger area in the southwest corner of Wyoming just north of the Uintas known as Lake Gosiute, and the largest area, which lies in northeastern Utah and western Colorado south of the Uintas, known as Lake Uinta.

a. Green River Formation	b. 1700 Cascadia earthquake
c. 1509 Istanbul earthquake	d. 1703 Genroku earthquake

80. _____ is a disused coal mine that contains a diverse array of fossil animals and plants from the Upper Jurassic, Kimmeridgian period. It is located in central Portugal, near the town of Leiria.

The locality was extensively worked by paleontologists from the Free University of Berlin, but this activity stopped in 1982.

a. 1700 Cascadia earthquake	b. 1703 Genroku earthquake
c. Guimarota	d. 1509 Istanbul earthquake

81. _____ is a fine-grained silica-rich microcrystalline, cryptocrystalline or microfibrous sedimentary rock that may contain small fossils. It varies greatly in color (from white to black), but most often manifests as gray, brown, grayish brown and light green to rusty red; its color is an expression of trace elements present in the rock, and both red and green are most often related to traces of iron (in its oxidized and reduced forms respectively.)

_____ occurs as oval to irregular nodules in greensand, limestone, chalk, and dolostone formations as a replacement mineral, where it is formed as a result of some type of diagenesis.

a. 1700 Cascadia earthquake	b. 1509 Istanbul earthquake
c. 1703 Genroku earthquake	d. Chert

82. The _____ is a sequence of banded iron formation rocks that are exposed in the Gunflint Range of northern Minnesota and western Ontario along the north shore of Lake Superior. The black layers in the sequence contain microfossils that are 1.9 to 2.3 billion years in age. Stromatolite colonies of cyanobacteria that have been converted to jasper are found in Ontario.

a. Lancefield Swamp	b. Sanga da Alemoa
c. Gunflint Chert	d. La Venta

83. _____ is a fossil lagerstätte near Hamilton, Kansas, United States. It has a diverse assemblage of unusually well-preserved marine, euryhaline, freshwater, flying, and terrestrial fossils (invertebrates, vertebrates, and plants.) This extraordinary mix of fossils has led to the interpretation of an estuarine environment.

a. Clarkia fossil beds	b. Hell Creek Formation
c. Le Moustier	d. Hamilton Quarry

84. _____ is the name given a paleontological excavation site approximately 150 feet (46 m) wide by 600 feet (180 m) long near Hanksville, Utah where scientists have found a large mix of remains of sauropods, trees, freshwater clams, and other species dating between 145 million years ago to 150 million years ago. The mixed assortment of remains deposited in this one location provide a unique opportunity to scientists to study the paleoecology of the area in the late Jurassic period.

In June 2008 following three weeks of excavation, paleontologists from the Burpee Museum of Natural History announced major recent discoveries made at the site, including a probable Stegosaurus, four sauropods, and at least two carnivorous dinosaurs.

a. 1703 Genroku earthquake
b. 1700 Cascadia earthquake
c. 1509 Istanbul earthquake
d. Hanksville-Burpee Quarry

85. The _____ is an intensely-studied division of Upper Cretaceous to lower Paleocene rocks in North America near Jordan, Montana.

The _____ occurs in Montana and portions of North Dakota, South Dakota, and Wyoming. In Montana, the _____ overlies the Fox Hills Formation and is the uppermost formation of the Cretaceous period.

a. Bullock Creek
b. Lancefield Swamp
c. Wheeler Shale
d. Hell Creek Formation

86. The _____ site is located in the Oglala National Grassland of western Nebraska northwest of Crawford. It was originally excavated by Dr. Larry Agenbroad in the 1970's. The excavation was over 400 square meters and it was considered the largest Alberta Culture bison kill site ever discovered.

a. Hudson-Meng Bison Kill
b. 1509 Istanbul earthquake
c. 1700 Cascadia earthquake
d. 1703 Genroku earthquake

87. _____ is a fine-grained, foliated, homogeneous metamorphic rock derived from an original shale-type sedimentary rock composed of clay or volcanic ash through low grade regional metamorphism. The result is a foliated rock in which the foliation may not correspond to the original sedimentary layering. _____ is frequently grey in colour especially when seen en masse covering roofs.

a. Cataclasite
b. Geothermobarometry
c. Slate
d. Mylonite

Chapter 15. Test Preparation Part 15

1. The _____ is an Early Cretaceous geological formation in Chaoyang, Liaoning which has yielded fossils of feathered dinosaurs, primitive birds, pterosaurs, and other organisms. It is a member of the Jehol group. The exact age of the Jiufotang has been debated for years, with estimates ranging from the Late Jurassic to the Early Cretaceous.
   a. Maevarano Formation
   b. Tumblagooda sandstone
   c. 1509 Istanbul earthquake
   d. Jiufotang Formation

2. _____ are the preserved remains or traces of animals, plants, and other organisms from the remote past. The totality of _____, both discovered and undiscovered, and their placement in fossiliferous rock formations and sedimentary layers (strata) is known as the fossil record. The study of _____ across geological time, how they were formed, and the evolutionary relationships between taxa (phylogeny) are some of the most important functions of the science of paleontology.
   a. 1509 Istanbul earthquake
   b. 1700 Cascadia earthquake
   c. 1703 Genroku earthquake
   d. Fossils

3. The _____, ranging from the late Lower Cambrian to early Middle Cambrian, contains an early Middle Cambrian Konservat Lagerstätte with many well-preserved fossils known collectively as the Kaili Biota. The _____ is more than 200 meters thick with boundaries dated from the early to the early-middle Cambrian (513 to 501 million years ago.) This age places it between the two most important and famous Cambrian Lagerstätten: the Burgess Shale and the Maotianshan Shale (containing the Chengjiang Biota).
   a. Clarkia fossil beds
   b. Milk River Formation
   c. Naturita Formation
   d. Kaili Formation

4. The _____ is the largest stratigraphic unit in Southern Africa, covering almost two thirds of the present land surface, including central Cape Province, almost all of Orange Free State, western Natal, much of south-east Transvaal, Zambia, Zimbabwe and Malawi.

Its strata, mostly shales and sandstones (Hamilton ' Finlay 1928), record an almost continuous sequence of marine glacial to terrestrial deposition from the Late Carboniferous to the Early Jurassic, a period of about a hundred million years. These accumulated in a retroarc foreland basin called the Karoo Basin.

   a. 1700 Cascadia earthquake
   b. Karoo Supergroup
   c. 1703 Genroku earthquake
   d. 1509 Istanbul earthquake

5. _____ is an anthropological and an archaeological site located in southern Borkou-Ennedi-Tibesti Region in Chad. It is known for the discovery of the Australopithecus bahrelghazali fossil hominin that was first discovered in January 1995.
   a. 1509 Istanbul earthquake
   b. Koro Toro
   c. 1703 Genroku earthquake
   d. 1700 Cascadia earthquake

6. _____ is a fossil-bearing breccia filled cave located about 2km east of the well known South African hominid-bearing site of Sterkfontein and about 45km Northwest of the City of Johannesburg, South Africa. It is situated within the Cradle of Humankind World Heritage Site.

In 1938 The site was brought to the attention of Robert Broom by a local schoolboy named Gert Terrblanche who had discovered several hominin teeth.

a. Kromdraai
b. 1509 Istanbul earthquake
c. 1700 Cascadia earthquake
d. 1703 Genroku earthquake

7. _____ is a settlement in Tolima Department, Colombia. Nearby, one of the richest Neogene fossil assemblages in the whole of South America is known. It provides a fascinating glimpse of how life in the region was like before the main wave of the Great American Interchange.
   a. La Venta
   b. Gunflint Chert
   c. Lancefield Swamp
   d. Frenchman Formation

8. The late mid-Jurassic lagerstätte at _____, in the Ardèche region of southwestern France, offers paleontologists an outstanding view of an undisturbed paleoecosystem that was preserved in fine detail as organisms died at the site and settled to the bottom of a shallow epicontinental sea, with a folded floor that in places exceeded 200 m at this site. The site preserves a marine system of the Lower Callovian stage, a little over 160 mya. Some soft parts of organisms are preserved as phosphatised concretions, in exceptional cases down to cellular details.
   a. Bathonian
   b. La Voulte-sur-Rhone
   c. Toarcian
   d. Hettangian

9. _____ is a site in Tanzania, dated to the Plio-Pleistocene and famous for its hominin footprints, preserved in volcanic ash (Site G.) The site of the _____ footprints is located 45 km south of Olduvai gorge. Professor Terry Harrison, a physical anthropologist at New York University, has continued research at the site since the late 1990s.
   a. 1700 Cascadia earthquake
   b. 1509 Istanbul earthquake
   c. 1703 Genroku earthquake
   d. Laetoli

10. The _____ is a sequence of rocks from the Barremian (early Cretaceous) epoch from Western North America.

Life forms recovered include the ornithopod dinosaurs Iguanodon lakotaensis and Camptosaurus depressus, and the ankylosaur Hoplitosaurus marshi.

   a. Fur Formation
   b. Bullock Creek
   c. Lancefield Swamp
   d. Lakota Formation

11. The _____ is a rich fossil deposit from the Pleistocene epoch was discovered in the 19th century near Lancefield, Victoria.

The site consists of a bone bed lying directly atop a layer of fluvial gravel between layers of clay (Gillespie et al 1978.) The layer of bones is estimated to contain the remains of perhaps 10,000 individual Pleistocene animals(Gillespie 1978.)

   a. Bullock Creek
   b. Naturita Formation
   c. Wheeler Shale
   d. Lancefield Swamp

12. _____ is an archeological site consisting of two rock shelters in Peyzac-le-Moustier, Dordogne, France. It is known for a fossilized skull of the species Homo neanderthalensis that was discovered in 1909. The Mousterian tool culture is named after _____.

a. Le Moustier
b. Nacimiento Formation
c. Wessex Formation
d. Turritellenplatte

13. _____ is a naturally occurring material composed primarily of fine-grained minerals, which show plasticity through a variable range of water content, and which can be hardened when dried and/or fired. _____ deposits are mostly composed of _____ minerals (phyllosilicate minerals), minerals which impart plasticity and harden when fired and/or dried, and variable amounts of water trapped in the mineral structure by polar attraction. Organic materials which do not impart plasticity may also be a part of _____ deposits.
 a. 1703 Genroku earthquake
 b. Clay
 c. 1700 Cascadia earthquake
 d. 1509 Istanbul earthquake

14. The _____ is an Upper Cretaceous sedimentary rock formation found in the Mahajanga Province of northwestern Madagascar. It is most likely Maastrichtian in age, and records a seasonal, semiarid environment with rivers that had greatly varying discharges. Notable animal fossils recovered include the theropod dinosaur Majungasaurus and the early birds Rahonavis and Vorona, the titanosaurian sauropod Rapetosaurus, and the giant frog Beelzebufo.
 a. Maevarano Formation
 b. 1509 Istanbul earthquake
 c. Tumblagooda sandstone
 d. Jiufotang Formation

15. _____ is an archaeological and paleontological site in Imperial, Missouri, containing the Kimmswick Bone Bed. Bones of mastodons and other now-extinct animals were first found here in the early 1800s. The area gained fame as one of the most extensive Pleistocene ice age deposits in the country and attracted scientific interest worldwide.
 a. 1700 Cascadia earthquake
 b. 1703 Genroku earthquake
 c. 1509 Istanbul earthquake
 d. Mastodon State Historic Site

16. A _____ is any geological stratum or deposit that contains bones of whatever kind. Inevitably, such deposits are sedimentary in nature. Not a formal term, it tends to be used more to describe especially dense collections. It is also applied to brecciated and stalagmitic deposits on the floor of caves, which frequently contain osseous remains.
 a. Fossil wood
 b. Derived fossil
 c. Bone Bed
 d. Copalite

17. _____ is a paleontological site located at Crane Creek in Melbourne, Florida. This site contains fossils from 20,000 to 10,000 years before present in the Pleistocene period. The fossils include extinct animals such as varieties of Camels, Giant Armadillos, Giant Beavers, Giant Bison, Giant Ground Sloths, Mammoths, Mastodons, Saber-toothed cats and Tapirs.
 a. 1700 Cascadia earthquake
 b. Melbourne Bone Bed
 c. 1703 Genroku earthquake
 d. 1509 Istanbul earthquake

18. The _____ is a near- shore to terrestrial sedimentary unit deposited during the Late Cretaceous (late Santonian to early Campanian) in southern Alberta. It is equivalent to the marine Lea Park Formation of eastern Alberta, and the Eagle and Telegraph Creek Formations of north-central Montana, and to the upper part of the Niobrara Formation in Kansas.

In Alberta, the _____ is subdivided into the Telegraph Creek, Virgelle, and Deadhorse Coulee Members.

 a. Lakota Formation
 b. Bullock Creek
 c. Turritellenplatte
 d. Milk River Formation

19. The _____ is a sedimentary rock formation found in the San Juan Basin of western New Mexico (United States) and named for the Nacimiento Mountains. It is a heterogeneous nonmarine formation composed of shale, siltstone, and sandstone, deposited in floodplain, fluvial and lacustrine settings, and made up of sediment shed from the San Juan uplift to the north and the Brazos-Sangre de Cristo uplift to the east. It was deposited mostly between ~64.5 and ~61 million years ago, during the early and middle Paleocene.
   a. Hamilton Quarry
   b. Nacimiento Formation
   c. Kaili Formation
   d. Naturita Formation

20. The _____ was named by Robert G. Young (1960, 1965) for Cretaceous sedimentary rocks exposed near Naturita, Colorado.

The formation lies between the Cedar Mountain Formation (sometimes called the Burro Canyon Formation in Colorado) and Mancos Shale, thus occupies the position for sedimentary strata that have historically been called the Dakota Formation. However, as Witzke and Ludvigson (1994) noted, the term cannot be used for Cretaceous strata that were deposited on the western side of the Cretaceous Seaway.

   a. Turritellenplatte
   b. Hell Creek Formation
   c. Clarkia fossil beds
   d. Naturita Formation

21. _____ is one of the most important prehistoric sites in the world and has been instrumental in furthering understanding of early human evolution. Excavation work there was pioneered by Louis and Mary Leakey in the 1950s and continued into the twenty first century by Professor Fidelis Masao of the Open University of Tanzania supported by Earthwatch; there have also been teams from Rutgers University. Millions of years ago, the site was that of a large lake, the shores of which were covered with successive deposits of volcanic ash. Around 500,000 years ago seismic activity diverted a nearby stream which began to cut down into the sediments, revealing seven main layers in the walls of the gorge.
   a. AL 129-1
   b. AL 333
   c. Olduvai Gorge
   d. AASHTO Soil Classification System

22. _____ is a geological formation in East Africa containing a group of Lower Paleolithic archaeological sites. It is on the floor of the Eastern Rift Valley in southern Kenya, 40 miles (64 km) southwest of Nairobi along the road to Lake Magadi. _____ is noted for the large number of Acheulean hand axes, associated with animal butchering, discovered there.
   a. AASHTO Soil Classification System
   b. AL 129-1
   c. Olorgesailie
   d. AL 333

23. The _____ are a series of lakes which existed during the Devonian period in the region which is now northern Scotland, Orkney and Shetland. The sedimentary rocks they left behind have been studied since the 1830's. They contain a huge variety of very well preserved fish fossils, which give a notable insight into the evolution of fish during this period.
   a. AL 333
   b. AL 129-1
   c. AASHTO Soil Classification System
   d. Orcadian Lakes

24. The Upper Cambrian _____ fauna includes fossilized organisms preserved in _____ lagerst>ätten, notably at Kinnekulle and on the island of >Öland, all in Sweden.

The initial site, discovered in 1975 by Klaus M>üller and his assistants, exceptionally preserves soft-bodied organisms, and their larvae, who are preserved uncompacted in three dimensions. The fossils are phosphatized and silicified, thus the delicate chitinous cuticle and soft parts are not affected by acids, which act upon the limestone nodules within which the fossils have survived.

a. Orsten
b. AL 333
c. AASHTO Soil Classification System
d. AL 129-1

25. _____ is a Jurassic marine sedimentary rock underlying much of South East England, from as far west as Dorset and as far north as Yorkshire. The _____ is argillaceous (consists of clay) and is of Callovian to lower Oxfordian age.

_____ appears at the surface around Oxford, Peterborough and Weymouth and is exposed in many quarries around these areas.

a. AASHTO Soil Classification System
b. AL 129-1
c. AL 333
d. Oxford Clay

26. The _____ is a deep hole in the bed of the Aucilla River (between Jefferson and Taylor Counties in the Big Bend region of Florida) that has stratified deposits of late Pleistocene and early Holocene animal bones and human artifacts reaching back to about 14,500 to 12,500 years before the present. The earliest dates for artifacts recovered from the site are between 1,000 and 1,500 years before the advent of the Clovis culture.

At the height of the last ice age (the Wisconsin glaciation), the sea level was up to 100 meters lower than at present.

a. 1509 Istanbul earthquake
b. 1700 Cascadia earthquake
c. 1703 Genroku earthquake
d. Page-Ladson prehistory site

27. _____, is a geopark located in the center of the state of the Rio Grande do Sul in Brazil, along which are found Triassic rocks and fossils, from a time when there was only the continent Pangaea.

The route is located within a vast area that belongs to the period called the Triassic and Late Permian ages and which have varied between 210 and 270 million years ago. The Geopark has several palaeontological sites, which belongs to rock formation Santa Maria, Caturrita, Sanga do Cabral, Rio do Rastro and Irati.

a. 1509 Istanbul earthquake
b. 1700 Cascadia earthquake
c. Paleorrota
d. Thirtynine Mile volcanic field

28. _____ near Swayzee in Grant County, Indiana, is one of the most important paleontological sites in the interior of the eastern half of North America. Uncovered in 1996 by workers at the Pipe Creek Junior limestone quarry, the sinkhole has yielded a diverse array of fossils from the Pliocene epoch dating back five million years. Discoveries have been made there of the remains of camelids, bears, beavers, frogs, snakes, turtles and several previously unknown species of rodents.

a. 1509 Istanbul earthquake
b. 1700 Cascadia earthquake
c. 1703 Genroku earthquake
d. Pipe Creek Sinkhole

29. The _____ consists of Lower Cretaceous to Upper Cretaceous strata located in Delaware, Maryland, and New Jersey, in the eastern United States.

Flora found include large cycads.

a. 1700 Cascadia earthquake
b. 1509 Istanbul earthquake
c. Dakota Sandstone
d. Potomac Formation

30. _____ is a limestone rock formation near Waikari in the North Canterbury region of New Zealand. It is lying 80 km north-west of Christchurch. On the foot of that valley is a swamp which became notable in 1939 as New Zealand's largest paleontological site for moa fossils.
a. Pyramid Valley
b. 1509 Istanbul earthquake
c. 1700 Cascadia earthquake
d. 1703 Genroku earthquake

31. _____ is a fine-grained silica-rich microcrystalline, cryptocrystalline or microfibrous sedimentary rock that may contain small fossils. It varies greatly in color (from white to black), but most often manifests as gray, brown, grayish brown and light green to rusty red; its color is an expression of trace elements present in the rock, and both red and green are most often related to traces of iron (in its oxidized and reduced forms respectively.)

_____ occurs as oval to irregular nodules in greensand, limestone, chalk, and dolostone formations as a replacement mineral, where it is formed as a result of some type of diagenesis.

a. 1703 Genroku earthquake
b. 1700 Cascadia earthquake
c. Chert
d. 1509 Istanbul earthquake

32. _____, in North West Queensland, is Australia's most famous fossil site. The 100 km² area has fossil remains of ancient mammals, birds and reptiles of Oligocene and Miocene age. The site was inscribed as a World Heritage site in 1994 and is an extension of the Lawn Hill National Park.
a. 1700 Cascadia earthquake
b. Riversleigh
c. 1509 Istanbul earthquake
d. 1703 Genroku earthquake

33. _____, with an elongated shape approx. 10 miles (16 km) from end to end and 3 miles (5 km) at its widest point, lies in the eastern part of Lake Victoria at the mouth of the Winam Gulf.

_____ is widely known for its extraordinarily rich and important fossil beds of extinct Miocene mammals, dated to 18 million years. The island had been only cursorily explored until the Leakey expedition of 1947-1948 began systematic searches and excavations, which have continued sporadically since then.

a. 1700 Cascadia earthquake
b. 1703 Genroku earthquake
c. 1509 Istanbul earthquake
d. Rusinga Island

Chapter 15. Test Preparation Part 15

34. The _____ paleontological site is located in the city of Santa Maria, Rio Grande do Sul, in Brazil. It belongs to the Caturrita Formation and the Santa Maria Formation. It is located in the neighborhood of Castelinho. The early sauropodomorph dinosaur Saturnalia was discovered at this site, along with rhynchosaurs and many other fossil specimens.

The first terrestrial reptile fossil discovered in South America came from this site in 1902.

a. Hamilton Quarry
c. Gunflint Chert
b. Lakota Formation
d. Sanga da Alemoa

35. The _____ of Ermingen is a type of very rich fossil-bearing rock which is of particular interest to geologists and paleontologists. It occurs in a very restricted outcrop and is protected in its entirety as a natural monument.

This outcrop of these marine sedimentary rocks is situated in the northern part of the North Alpine Foreland Basin and it is famous for a superabundance of the shells of Turritella turris, a marine gastropod mollusk in the family Turritellidae.

a. Sanga da Alemoa
c. Turritellenplatte
b. Lancefield Swamp
d. Doushantuo Formation

36. _____ is a cave located in Bulutota Rakwana range, northwest of Embilipitiya one of the archeological site located in Sri Lanka. The cave is located in the Ratnapura District, in the Kolonne Korale, about 278 m (912 feet) above sea level. The meaning of Wavul Pane (Sinhalese name) is Cave of Bats.

a. Wavula Pane
c. Belilena
b. 1509 Istanbul earthquake
d. Batadombalena

37. The _____ is an English fossil site and geological formation that dates back to the Barremian stage of the Early Cretaceous. It is part of the Wealden Group and underlies the younger Vectis Formation.

Invertebrates are commonly preserved in the _____. Freshwater bivalves can be found including unionoids such as Margaritifera, Nippononaia, and Unio. These bivalves are helpful in reconstructing what the freshwater paleoenvironment may have been like during the formation's deposition.

a. Wessex Formation
c. Curio Bay
b. Turritellenplatte
d. Hamilton Quarry

38. The _____ is a Cambrian (c.507 Ma) fossil locality world famous for prolific agnostid and Elrathia kingii trilobite remains (even though many areas are barren of fossils) and represents a Konzentrat-Lagerstätten. Varied soft bodied organisms are locally preserved, a fauna (e.g. Naraoia, Wiwaxia ' Hallucigenia) and preservation style (carbonaceous film) normally associated with the more famous Burgess Shale. As such, the _____ also represents a Konservat-Lagerstätten.

a. Milk River Formation
c. Turritellenplatte
b. Bullock Creek
d. Wheeler Shale

39. The _____ is a geological formation located at Qujing, Yunnan, South China. _____ has remains of petalichthyid and galeaspid fish and it represents the Early Devonian period (Early Lochkovian) of China.

a. 1700 Cascadia earthquake
c. Xitun Formation
b. 1509 Istanbul earthquake
d. Xishancun Formation

40. The _____ is a palaeontological formation which named after the Xitun, a location in South China. This formation it includes many remains of fossilized fish of Early Devonian period (Late Lochkovian.)
   a. 1700 Cascadia earthquake
   b. Xitun Formation
   c. Xishancun Formation
   d. 1509 Istanbul earthquake

41. The _____ is a palaeontological formation located at Qujing, Yunnan, South China. The formation represents the Late Silurian period (Pridoli) of China.
   a. Yulongsi Formation
   b. 1700 Cascadia earthquake
   c. 1509 Istanbul earthquake
   d. 1703 Genroku earthquake

42. The _____ is a unit of sedimentary rock layers of Middle to Late Permian age located in the European Permian Basin which stretches from the east coast of England to northern Poland. The name _____ was formerly also used as a unit of time in the geologic timescale, but nowadays it is only used for the corresponding sedimentary deposits in Europe.

The _____ lies on top of the Rotliegend; on top of the _____ is the Buntsandstein or Bunter.

   a. Tidal scour
   b. Bediasite
   c. Subfossil
   d. Zechstein

43. _____ is a deeply eroded impact crater in the Gawler Ranges of South Australia. Its location is marked by Lake Acraman, a circular ephemeral playa lake about 20 km in diameter.

The discovery of the crater and independent discovery of its ejecta were first reported in the journal Science in 1986.

   a. AL 129-1
   b. AASHTO Soil Classification System
   c. AL 333
   d. Acraman crater

44. _____ is a meteorite crater in Algeria.

It is 450 m in diameter and the age is estimated to be less than 100,000 years and is probably Pleistocene. The crater is exposed at the surface.

   a. Arkenu craters
   b. Amguid
   c. Aouelloul
   d. Aorounga

45. _____ is an eroded meteorite impact crater in Chad, Africa. The exposed remnant of the crater is 12.6 km in diameter and its age is estimated to be less than 345 million years (Carboniferous or younger).
   a. Aouelloul
   b. Arkenu craters
   c. Obolon' crater
   d. Aorounga

46. _____ is an impact crater in Mauritania.

It is 390 metres wide and the age is estimated to be 3.0 >± 0.3 million years (Pliocene.) The crater is exposed at the surface.

   a. Obolon' crater
   b. Aorounga
   c. Aouelloul
   d. Arkenu craters

47. The _____ are a pair of eroded impact craters in Libya. They are 10 km and 6.8 km in diameter. The craters are believed to have formed simultaneously as a double impact event less than 140 million years ago (Jurassic or younger.).
   a. Aorounga
   b. Aouelloul
   c. Obolon' crater
   d. Arkenu craters

48. _____ is a geological and geophysical feature centered about 250 km off the northwestern coast of Australia in the Canning and overlying Roebuck basins. Although not obvious from sea floor topography, it is a roughly circular area about 30 km in diameter where older rocks have been uplifted as much as 4 km towards the surface. The _____ High was penetrated by two petroleum exploration wells (_____-1, Lagrange-1) in the 1970s and 1980s.

In 1996 Australian geologist John Gorter first suggested that the _____ High might mark the centre of a very large buried impact crater up to 250 km in diameter, based mainly on its internal geological structure as revealed on a single seismic survey line, and suggested that it may be of near end Permian age, based on the reported age of volcanic rocks in Lagrange-1.

   a. 1509 Istanbul earthquake
   b. 1700 Cascadia earthquake
   c. 1703 Genroku earthquake
   d. Bedout

49. The _____ is an impact crater in the Kirovohrad Oblast province of Ukraine. The crater is 24 km in diameter and its age of 65.17 ± 0.64 million years, based on argon dating techniques, is within error of that of Chicxulub Crater in Mexico, and the KT boundary. The Chicxulub impact is believed to have caused the mass extinction at the end of the Cretaceous era, which included the extinction of the dinosaurs.
   a. Shiva crater
   b. 1509 Istanbul earthquake
   c. 1700 Cascadia earthquake
   d. Boltysh crater

50. The _____ crater field is a group of at least 22 meteorite impact craters situated on the border between the provinces of Chaco and Santiago del Estero, 1000 kilometres northwest of Buenos Aires, Argentina. The largest and best known crater, located near the village of Gancedo, is 50 meters in diameter. The age is estimated to be around 4,000 years (Holocene.)It was reported in 1576, but well known before by the original inhabitants.
   a. Kebira Crater
   b. Deep Bay
   c. Kursk
   d. Campo del Cielo

51. The _____ is a large eroded meteorite impact crater in Quebec, Canada. Only part of the crater is exposed at the surface, the rest being covered by the Saint Lawrence River. The original crater is estimated to have been 54 km in diameter and the age is estimated to be 342 ± 15 million years (Mississippian). The projectile was probably a stony asteroid, at least two kilometres in diameter, and weighing an estimated 15 billion tonnes.
   a. Sudbury Basin
   b. Chesapeake Bay impact crater
   c. Manson crater
   d. Charlevoix crater

52. The _____ was formed by a bolide that impacted the eastern shore of North America about 35.5 million years ago, in the late Eocene epoch. It is one of the best-preserved 'wet-target' or marine impact craters, and the largest impact crater in the U.S. Continued slumping of sediments over the rubble of the crater have helped shape Chesapeake Bay.
   a. Vredefort crater
   b. Chesapeake Bay impact crater
   c. Tookoonooka
   d. Santa Fe impact structure

53. In the broadest sense, the term _____ can be applied to any depression, natural or manmade, resulting from the high velocity impact of a projectile with larger body. In most common usage, the term is used for the approximately circular depression in the surface of a planet, moon or other solid body in the Solar System, formed by the hyper-velocity impact of a smaller body with the surface. This is in contrast to the pit crater which results from an internal collapse.
   a. AASHTO Soil Classification System
   b. AL 333
   c. AL 129-1
   d. Impact crater

54. The _____ is an ancient impact crater buried underneath the Yucatán Peninsula in Mexico. The crater is more than 180 kilometers (110 mi) in diameter, making the feature one of the largest confirmed impact structures in the world; the impacting bolide that formed the crater was at least 10 km (6 mi) in diameter.
   a. 1700 Cascadia earthquake
   b. 1509 Istanbul earthquake
   c. 1703 Genroku earthquake
   d. Chicxulub crater

55. The _____ , are a pair of circular lakes on the Canadian Shield in Quebec, Canada, near Hudson Bay.

The lakes are actually a single body of water with a sprinkling of islands forming a 'dotted line' between the eastern and western parts. The name is due to the clear water it holds.

The lakes fill circular depressions that are interpreted as paired impact craters (astroblemes). The eastern and western craters are 26 km and 36 km in diameter, respectively. Each crater has the same age, 290 >± 20 million years (Permian), and it is believed that they formed simultaneously.

   a. Chesapeake Bay impact crater
   b. Manson crater
   c. Tookoonooka
   d. Clearwater Lakes

56. The _____, also referred to as the Decaturville Dome, is an impact crater in Missouri, United States, and is one of the 38th parallel structures.

It is 6 km in diameter and the age is estimated to be less than 300 million years (Permian or younger.) The crater is exposed at the surface.

   a. Kebira Crater
   b. Decaturville crater
   c. Dobele crater
   d. Kalkkop

57. _____ is a bay near the south-western tip of Reindeer Lake in Saskatchewan, Canada. The bay is strikingly circular and very deep (220 m) in an otherwise irregular and shallow lake.

The bay was formed in a 13 km wide impact crater.

a. Decaturville crater
b. Kebira Crater
c. Foelsche
d. Deep Bay

58. _____ is an impact crater in central Latvia. The town of Dobele is built over the site of the crater.

It is 4.5 km in diameter and the age is estimated to be 290 ± 35 million years (Cisuralian epoch of the Permian period.)

a. Foelsche
b. Dobele crater
c. Wilkes Land crater
d. Kalkkop

59. _____ is a partly buried impact structure (or astrobleme), the eroded remnant of a former impact crater. It is situated at latitude 16>° 40' S and longitude 136>° 47' E in the Northern Territory, Australia, and named after the nearby _____ River. Although little of it is exposed at the surface, and no crater shaped topography is evident, the circular nature of the feature is obvious on aeromagnetic images, a factor that led to its discovery.

a. Dobele crater
b. Kebira Crater
c. Foelsche
d. Deep Bay

60. _____ is an impact crater which can be found on a private farm 50 kilometres south of the town of Graaff Reinet, in the Eastern Cape Province of South Africa.

The meteorite impact occurred about 250,000 years ago (Pleistocene) on what is now the flat Karoo landscape. It left a crater 640 metres in diameter and a few hundred metres deep.

a. Foelsche
b. Kalkkop
c. Wilkes Land crater
d. Deep Bay

61. _____ is the name that has recently been proposed for a circular topographic feature in the Sahara desert. The center of the feature lies in Libya, but the eastern edge extends into Egypt. Its discovery from satellite images was announced in March 2006 by researchers Dr. Farouk El-Baz and Dr. Eman Ghoneim from the Center for Remote Sensing at Boston University, who propose that it may be an eroded impact crater.

The feature has two rings, the outer of which is 31 kilometres (19 mi) in diameter. If it is an impact crater, it is bigger than the largest confirmed impact crater in the region, the Oasis crater in Libya, which is approximately half the size, with a diameter of approximately 18 kilometres (11 mi).

a. Kebira Crater
b. Pingualuit crater
c. Foelsche
d. Decaturville crater

62. _____ is a meteor crater in Russia.

It is 6 km in diameter and the age is estimated to be 250 ± 80 million years old (Late Permian or Early Triassic.) The crater is not exposed to the surface.

a. Kebira Crater
b. Kalkkop
c. Pingualuit crater
d. Kursk

63. The _____ is near the site of Manson, Iowa where an asteroid or comet nucleus struck the Earth during the Cretaceous Period, 74 million years ago. It was one of the largest impacts by an object from outer space to have happened in North America and was previously thought to have led to the extinction of the dinosaurs until isotopic ages proved that it was too old.

No surface evidence exists due to coverage by glacial till and the site where the crater lies buried is now a flat landscape.

a. Manson crater
b. Meteor Crater
c. Clearwater Lakes
d. Tookoonooka

64. _____ is a subterranean meteorite crater in Saskatchewan, Canada. It is 6 km in diameter and the age is estimated to be less than 75 million years (Cretaceous or later.) The crater is buried beneath younger sediments and cannot be seen at the surface.

a. 1700 Cascadia earthquake
b. 1509 Istanbul earthquake
c. 1703 Genroku earthquake
d. Maple Creek

65. _____ is a meteorite impact crater located approximately 43 miles (69 km) east of Flagstaff, near Winslow in the northern Arizona desert of the United States. The site was formerly known as the Canyon Diablo Crater, and scientists generally refer to it as Barringer Crater in honor of Daniel Barringer who was first to suggest that it was produced by meteorite impact.

The crater was created about 50,000 years ago during the Pleistocene epoch when the local climate on the Colorado Plateau was much cooler and damper. At the time, the area was an open grassland dotted with woodlands inhabited by woolly mammoths, giant ground sloths, and camels.

a. Sudbury Basin
b. Vredefort crater
c. Meteor Crater
d. Tookoonooka

66. The New Quebec Crater (previously known as Chubb Crater), now known as _____, is a young meteorite crater, by geological standards, located in the Ungava Peninsula of Quebec, Canada. It is 3.44 km (2.14 mi) in diameter, and is estimated to be 1.4 >± 0.1 million years old (Pleistocene.)

The crater is exposed to the surface, rising 160 m (520 ft) above the surrounding tundra and is 400 m (1,300 ft) deep.

a. Deep Bay
b. Pingualuit crater
c. Kalkkop
d. Foelsche

67. _____ is an impact crater in France.

The crater diameter is still under debate but expected to be about 21 km (13 mi) and its current age estimate is given as 214 ± 8 million years, placing it in the Upper Triassic period. Since then the crater has been deeply eroded, and no trace of its original surface morphology is visible anymore.

The _____ was the first crater proven by the determination of the impact effects on the rocks, without any circular topographic feature visible.

- a. Rochechouart crater
- b. 1509 Istanbul earthquake
- c. 1703 Genroku earthquake
- d. 1700 Cascadia earthquake

1. The _____ is an eroded remnant of a bolide impact crater in the Sangre de Cristo Mountains northeast of Santa Fe, New Mexico. The discovery was made in 2005 by a geologist who noticed shatter cones in the rocks in a decades-old road cut on New Mexico State Highway 475 between Santa Fe and Hyde Memorial State Park. Shatter cones are a definitive indicator that the rocks had been exposed to a shock of pressures only possible in a meteor impact or a nuclear explosion.

   a. Santa Fe impact structure
   b. Clearwater Lakes
   c. Manson crater
   d. Vredefort crater

2. The term _____ is closely related to the terms impact crater or meteorite impact crater, and is used in cases where erosion or burial have destroyed or masked the original topographic feature with which we normally associate the term crater. This is the fate of almost all old impact craters on Earth, unlike the ancient pristine craters preserved on the Moon and most other rocky bodies in the Solar System. _____ is synonymous with the less commonly used term astrobleme meaning 'star wound'.

   a. AL 129-1
   b. AL 333
   c. AASHTO Soil Classification System
   d. Impact structure

3. The _____ is a sea floor structure located beneath the Indian Ocean, west of Mumbai, India.

   Its age is estimated to around 65 million years ago, at about the same time as a number of other impact craters and the Cretaceous-Tertiary extinction event (K-T boundary). Although the site has shifted since its formation because of sea floor spreading, the formation is approximately 600 kilometers long by 400 km wide. It is estimated that a crater of that size would have been made by an asteroid or comet approximately 40 km in diameter. The _____ adds weight to the theory that the K-T extinction was caused by a massive asteroid fragmenting and hitting the Earth in several locations, known as the 'Multiple impact theory.'

   a. K-T boundary
   b. 1700 Cascadia earthquake
   c. 1509 Istanbul earthquake
   d. Shiva crater

4. The _____ is the second largest known impact crater or astrobleme on Earth, and a major geologic structure in Ontario, Canada.

   The full extent of the _____ is 62 km long, 30 km wide and 15 km deep, although the modern ground surface is much shallower. It was created as the result of a 10 km meteorite impact that occurred 1.85 billion years ago in the Paleoproterozoic era. Debris was scattered over an area of 1.6 million square kilometers and travelled over 800 kilometers away -- rock fragments ejected by the impact have been found as far as Minnesota. Its present size is believed to be a smaller portion of a 250 km round crater that the bolide originally created.

   a. Tookoonooka
   b. Sudbury Basin
   c. Manson crater
   d. Clearwater Lakes

5. The _____ is the site where one or more objects from space struck the Atlantic continental shelf, about 160 km (100 mi) east of Atlantic City, New Jersey.

   The crater dates to the late Eocene geological time period (about 35 million years ago), and may have been formed by the same event as the larger Chesapeake Bay impact crater, 320 km (200 mi) to the southwest at the mouth of Chesapeake Bay, and also dating to the late Eocene.

Seismic reflection profiles, studied by USGS scientists, show that the crater was formed by an object or objects which struck from the southwest at a glancing angle and formed a long, oval crater.

  a. 1703 Genroku earthquake
  c. 1509 Istanbul earthquake
  b. 1700 Cascadia earthquake
  d. Toms Canyon impact crater

6. In the broadest sense, the term _____ can be applied to any depression, natural or manmade, resulting from the high velocity impact of a projectile with larger body. In most common usage, the term is used for the approximately circular depression in the surface of a planet, moon or other solid body in the Solar System, formed by the hyper-velocity impact of a smaller body with the surface. This is in contrast to the pit crater which results from an internal collapse.
  a. AASHTO Soil Classification System
  c. AL 333
  b. AL 129-1
  d. Impact crater

7. _____ is a large meteorite impact crater (astrobleme) situated in southwestern Queensland, Australia. It lies deeply buried within Mesozoic sedimentary rocks of the Eromanga Basin and is not visible at the surface.

_____ was discovered using seismic data collected during routine petroleum exploration and first reported in a publication in 1989, with proof of the impact theory coming from the discovery of shocked quartz in drill core.

  a. Sudbury Basin
  c. Tookoonooka
  b. Manson crater
  d. Meteor Crater

8. _____ is a meteorite crater in South Africa. This astrobleme is 1.13 km in diameter and 100 m deep and the age is estimated to be 220,000 >± 52,000 years (Pleistocene.) The impactor is believed to have been a chondrite or stony meteorite some 30 to 50 m in diameter that was vaporized during the impact event.
  a. 1703 Genroku earthquake
  c. 1509 Istanbul earthquake
  b. 1700 Cascadia earthquake
  d. Tswaing

9. Evidence for a _____ was published by a combined team of scientists from the University of Oxford and the University of Aberdeen, in March 2008. The evidence is centred on Ullapool, a harbour town on Loch Broom in the Ross and Cromarty district of the Highland council area of northwest Scotland. This suggests it was the largest bolide impact ever to strike what are now the British Isles. The impact, about 1.2 billion years ago, melted rock at the site and left parallel shock fractures in quartz and biotite and a tell-tale trace of iridium. Centered on the impact crater, a wide ejecta field has been traced, some 50 km across.
  a. Campo Del Cielo
  c. Decaturville crater
  b. Bolide impact centered on Ullapool
  d. Foelsche

10. _____ is the largest verified impact crater on Earth.

The asteroid that hit Vredefort is one of the largest to ever impact Earth, estimated at over 10 km (6 miles) wide. The crater has a diameter of roughly 250 - 300 km (155 - 186 miles), larger than the 200 km (124 miles) Sudbury Basin, and the 170 km (106 miles) Chicxulub crater. This makes Vredefort the largest known impact structure on Earth (though the Wilkes Land crater in Antarctica, if confirmed to have been the result of an impact event, is even larger at 500 kilometers across).

a. Tookoonooka
b. Clearwater Lakes
c. Vredefort crater
d. Meteor Crater

11. _____ is an informal term that may apply to two separate cases of conjectured giant impact craters hidden beneath the ice cap of Wilkes Land, East Antarctica. These are separated below under the heading Wilkes Land anomaly and Wilkes Land mascon (mass concentration), based on terms used in their principal published reference sources.

A hypothetical giant impact crater beneath the Wilkes Land ice sheet was first proposed by RA Schmidt in 1962, based on geophysical data.

a. Kalkkop
b. Deep Bay
c. Kebira Crater
d. Wilkes Land crater

12. A _____ is a line of craters along the surface of an astronomical body. The descriptor term for crater chains is catena (plural catenae), as specified by the International Astronomical Union's rules on planetary nomenclature.

These chains are thought to be made by the impact of a body that was broken up by tidal forces into a string of smaller objects following roughly the same orbit or by volcanic rift activity.

a. Ray system
b. 1700 Cascadia earthquake
c. 1509 Istanbul earthquake
d. Crater chain

13. _____ refers to a method for estimating the age of a planet's surface. The method is based upon the hypothesis that a new surface forms with zero impact craters, and that impact craters accumulate at some known, roughly constant, rate. The method has been calibrated using the ages of samples returned from the Moon.

a. 1509 Istanbul earthquake
b. 1700 Cascadia earthquake
c. 1703 Genroku earthquake
d. Crater counting

14. The term _____ structure (or cryptovolcanic structure) is now largely obsolete, but was once commonly used to describe sites where there was geological evidence of a large scale explosion within the Earth's crust, but no definitive evidence for the cause such as normal volcanic rocks or meteorite fragments. These sites are usually circular with signs of anomalous rock deformation contrasting with the surrounding region, and often showing evidence that crustal material had been uplifted and/or 'blown' outwards. It was once commonly assumed that some unusual form of volcanism, or a gas explosion originating within the crust, was to blame.

a. Cryptoexplosion
b. 1509 Istanbul earthquake
c. 1700 Cascadia earthquake
d. Ray system

Chapter 16. Test Preparation Part 16

15. _____ can mean:

- In volcanology, particles that came out of a volcanic vent, traveled through the air or under water, and fell back on the ground surface or on the ocean floor. _____ can consist of:
    1. Juvenile particles - (fragmented magma and free crystals)
    2. Cognate or accessory particles - older volcanic rocks from the same volcano
    3. Accidental particles - derived from the rocks under the volcano.
- In planetary geology, the debris that is ejected during the formation of an impact crater.
- In astrophysics, material expelled in a stellar explosion.
- In firearms ballistics, everything expelled from a gun, including the bullet, propellant, sabot, wad, etc.

a. Ejecta
b. AL 333
c. AL 129-1
d. AASHTO Soil Classification System

16. An _____ is a generally symmetrical apron of ejecta that surrounds a crater; it is layered thickly at the cratere;s rim and thin to discontinuous at the blankete;s outer edge.

After an impact event, the falling debris forms an _____ surrounding the crater. Approximately half the volume of ejecta falls within 1 crater radius of the rim, or 2 radii from the center of the crater.

a. AASHTO Soil Classification System
b. AL 129-1
c. AL 333
d. Ejecta blanket

17. In planetary geology, a _____ is a crater with its ejecta sitting above the surrounding terrain and thereby forming a raised platform. They form when an impact crater ejects material which forms an erosion resistant layer, thus causing the immediate area to erode more slowly than the rest of the region. Some pedestals have been accurately measured to be hundreds of meters above the surrounding area.
   a. 1703 Genroku earthquake
   b. 1509 Istanbul earthquake
   c. 1700 Cascadia earthquake
   d. Pedestal crater

18. A _____ is a depression formed by a sinking of the ground surface lying above a void or empty chamber, rather than by the eruption of a volcano or lava vent. It is often found in chains or troughs, which may merge into a linear alignment and usually lack an elevated rim. They also lack ejected deposits and the lava flows that are associated with impact craters.
   a. 1700 Cascadia earthquake
   b. 1509 Istanbul earthquake
   c. Supervolcano
   d. Pit crater

19. A _____ comprises radial streaks of fine ejecta thrown out during the formation of an impact crater, looking a bit like many thin spokes coming from the hub of a wheel. The rays can extend for lengths up to several times the diameter of their originating crater, and are often accompanied by small secondary craters formed by larger chunks of ejecta. Ray systems have been identified on the Moon, Mercury, and some moons of the outer planets.
   a. Cryptoexplosion
   b. Ray system
   c. 1700 Cascadia earthquake
   d. 1509 Istanbul earthquake

20. _____ are impact craters formed by the ejecta that was thrown out of a larger crater. They sometimes form radial crater chains.

a. 1700 Cascadia earthquake
c. 1703 Genroku earthquake
b. 1509 Istanbul earthquake
d. Secondary craters

21. _____ are rare geological features that are only known to form in the bedrock beneath meteorite impact craters or underground nuclear explosions. They are evidence that the rock has been subjected to a shock with pressures in the range of 2-30 GPa.

_____ have a distinctively conical shape that radiates from the top of the cones repeating cone-on-cone in large and small scales in the same sample.

a. 1700 Cascadia earthquake
c. 1703 Genroku earthquake
b. Shatter cones
d. 1509 Istanbul earthquake

22. In geology, engineering, and surveying, _____ is the motion of a surface (usually, the Earth's surface) as it shifts downward relative to a datum such as sea-level. The opposite of _____ is uplift, which results in an increase in elevation. There are several types of _____.
a. 1703 Genroku earthquake
c. 1509 Istanbul earthquake
b. 1700 Cascadia earthquake
d. Subsidence

23. A _____ is a hole or depression left on the surface of an area which has had an underground (usually nuclear) explosion. Many such craters are present at the Nevada Test Site, which is no longer in use for nuclear testing.

Subsidence craters are created as the roof of the cavity caused by the explosion collapses.

a. 1509 Istanbul earthquake
c. 1700 Cascadia earthquake
b. 1703 Genroku earthquake
d. Subsidence crater

24. _____ crater is a crater on Mars's moon Deimos. It is about 3km in diameter. _____ crater is named after Jonathan _____, who predicted the existence of the moons of Mars.
a. 1703 Genroku earthquake
c. Swift
b. 1700 Cascadia earthquake
d. 1509 Istanbul earthquake

25. _____ is a rock composed of angular fragments of minerals or rocks in a matrix (cementing material), that may be similar or different in composition to the fragments. A _____ may have a variety of different origins, as indicated by the named types including sedimentary _____, tectonic _____, igneous _____, impact _____ and hydrothermal _____.

Sedimentary breccias are a type of clastic sedimentary rock which are composed of angular to subangular, randomly oriented clasts of other sedimentary rocks.

a. 1700 Cascadia earthquake
c. 1509 Istanbul earthquake
b. Breccia
d. Coprolite

26. In geology, a _____ or _____ line is a planar fracture in rock in which the rock on one side of the fracture has moved with respect to the rock on the other side. Large faults within the Earth's crust are the result of differential or shear motion and active _____ zones are the causal locations of most earthquakes. Earthquakes are caused by energy release during rapid slippage along a _____.
   a. 1703 Genroku earthquake
   b. 1700 Cascadia earthquake
   c. 1509 Istanbul earthquake
   d. Fault

27. _____, or tectonic breccia is a breccia (a rock type consisting of angular clasts) that was formed by tectonic forces. _____ has no cohesion, it is normally an unconsolidated rock type, unless cementation took place at a later stage. Sometimes a distinction is made between fault gouge and _____, the first has a smaller grain size.
   a. Coprolite
   b. Fault breccia
   c. 1509 Istanbul earthquake
   d. 1700 Cascadia earthquake

28. _____ is the name that has recently been proposed for a circular topographic feature in the Sahara desert. The center of the feature lies in Libya, but the eastern edge extends into Egypt. Its discovery from satellite images was announced in March 2006 by researchers Dr. Farouk El-Baz and Dr. Eman Ghoneim from the Center for Remote Sensing at Boston University, who propose that it may be an eroded impact crater.

The feature has two rings, the outer of which is 31 kilometres (19 mi) in diameter. If it is an impact crater, it is bigger than the largest confirmed impact crater in the region, the Oasis crater in Libya, which is approximately half the size, with a diameter of approximately 18 kilometres (11 mi).

   a. Foelsche
   b. Kebira Crater
   c. Pingualuit crater
   d. Decaturville crater

29. _____ refers to a variety of sedimentary rocks deposited on the Precambrian basement in the eastern Sahara, north-east Africa and Arabia. It consist of continental sandstones with thin beds of marine limestones, and marls. _____ was deposited between the Lower Paleozoic and Upper Cretaceous, with marine beds dating from the Carboniferous to Lower Cretaceous.
   a. 1509 Istanbul earthquake
   b. 1700 Cascadia earthquake
   c. 1703 Genroku earthquake
   d. Nubian Sandstone

30. The _____ is a volcanic hotspot located at the Azores in the northern Atlantic Ocean. It has interactions with the Mid-Atlantic Ridge which lies just west of the hotspot.
   a. Azores hotspot
   b. AL 333
   c. AASHTO Soil Classification System
   d. AL 129-1

31. The _____ is the supposed 'hotspot' (or mantle plume)proposed to explain the Bermuda Rise (a cluster of extinct volcanoes in the Atlantic Ocean, including the island of Bermuda), and also invoked by Cox and Van Arsdale to explain the origin of the Mississippi Embayment and by Nunn to explain the Sabine Uplift (southwest of the Mississippi Embayment.)

A hotspot origin for the Bermuda Rise has never been strongly supported, and has been largely shut out by a detailed and tightly argued paper by Vogt and Jung.

Evidence cited against a hotspot origin include: 1) Lack of a chain of age-progressive seamounts, such as with the Hawaiian-Emperor or Great Meteor seamount chains.

a. New England hotspot
b. Canary hotspot
c. 1509 Istanbul earthquake
d. Bermuda hotspot

32. The _____ is a volcanic hotspot believed to be located at the Canary Islands off the north-western coast of Africa, although alternative theories to explain the volcanism there exist. The _____ is believed to be underlain by a mantle plume that is relatively deep. It is believed to have first appeared about 60 million years ago.
a. New England hotspot
b. 1509 Istanbul earthquake
c. Jan Mayen hotspot
d. Canary hotspot

33. The _____ is a hotspot which is partly responsible for the high volcanic activity which has formed the island of Iceland.

Iceland is one of the most active volcanic regions in the world, with eruptions occurring on average roughly every five years. About a third of the basaltic lavas erupted in recorded history have been produced by Icelandic eruptions.

a. Iceland hotspot
b. AL 129-1
c. AL 333
d. AASHTO Soil Classification System

34. The _____ is a volcanic hotspot responsible for the volcanic activity that has formed the island of Jan Mayen in the northern Atlantic Ocean.
a. New England hotspot
b. Canary hotspot
c. 1509 Istanbul earthquake
d. Jan Mayen hotspot

35. The _____, also referred to as the Great Meteor hotspot, is a long-lived volcanic hotspot in the Atlantic Ocean. The hotspot's most recent eruptive center is the Great Meteor Seamount and probably created a short line of mid to late-Tertiary age seamounts on the African Plate but appears to be currently inactive.

The _____ track is used to estimate the movement of the North American Plate away from the African Plate from early Cretaceous period to the present.

a. 1509 Istanbul earthquake
b. Canary hotspot
c. Jan Mayen hotspot
d. New England hotspot

36. The _____ is a volcanic hotspot located in the southern Atlantic Ocean. It is responsible for the island of St. Helena and the St. Helena Seamount chain. It is one the oldest known hotspots on Earth, which began to produce basaltic lava about 145 million years ago.
a. Messinian evaporite
b. Saint Helena hotspot
c. Mediterranean Ridge
d. Messinian salinity crisis

37. The _____ is a tectonic spreading center between the South American Plate and the Antarctic Plate. It runs along the seafloor from the Bouvet Triple Junction in the South Atlantic Ocean southwestward to a major transform fault boundary east of the South Sandwich Islands.
a. AASHTO Soil Classification System
b. AL 333
c. American-Antarctic Ridge
d. AL 129-1

38. The _____ is a mid-ocean ridge, a divergent tectonic plate boundary located along the floor of the Atlantic Ocean, and the longest mountain range in the world. It separates the Eurasian Plate and North American Plate in the North Atlantic, and the African Plate from the South American Plate in the South Atlantic. The MAR extends from a junction with the Gakkel Ridge (Mid-Arctic Ridge) northeast of Greenland southward to the Bouvet Triple Junction in the South Atlantic.
   a. 1700 Cascadia earthquake
   b. Mid-Atlantic Ridge
   c. 1703 Genroku earthquake
   d. 1509 Istanbul earthquake

39. _____ is an ocean ridge in the southern Atlantic Ocean, extending for thousands of miles, off the coast of southwest Africa. Both it and the Rio Grande Rise originated from hotspot volcanism now occurring at the islands of Tristan da Cunha (the Tristan hotspot), 300 kilometres east of the crest of the Mid-Atlantic Ridge. The eastern section of the ridge is thought to have been created in the Middle Cretaceous period, between 120 and 80 million years ago.
   a. 1700 Cascadia earthquake
   b. Walvis Ridge
   c. 1509 Istanbul earthquake
   d. 1703 Genroku earthquake

40. The _____ is a major volcanic ridge under the Arctic Ocean between the Canada Basin (off Ellesmere Island) and the Lomonosov Ridge. It was active during the formation of the Amerasian Basin. It was discovered in 1963.
   a. AASHTO Soil Classification System
   b. AL 129-1
   c. AL 333
   d. Alpha Ridge

41. The _____ is a tectonic plate which includes most of the continent of Eurasia (a landmass consisting of the traditional continents of Europe and Asia), with the notable exceptions of the Indian subcontinent, the Arabian subcontinent, and the area east of the Chersky Range in East Siberia. It also includes oceanic crust extending westward to the Mid-Atlantic Ridge and northward to the Gakkel Ridge.

The easterly side is a boundary with the North American Plate to the north and a boundary with the Philippine Mobile Belt and the Philippine Sea Plate to the south, and possibly with the Okhotsk Plate and the Amurian Plate.

   a. Arabian Plate
   b. Antarctic Plate
   c. Intermontane Plate
   d. Eurasian Plate

42. The Adriatic or _____ is a small tectonic plate carrying primarily continental crust that broke away from the African plate along a large transform fault in the Cretaceous period. The name Adriatic Plate is usually used when referring to the northern part of the plate. This part of the plate was deformed during the Alpine orogeny, when the Adriatic/_____ collided with the Eurasian plate.
   a. AASHTO Soil Classification System
   b. AL 129-1
   c. AL 333
   d. Apulian Plate

43. An _____ is the result of a sudden release of energy in the Earth's crust that creates seismic waves. They are recorded with a seismometer or the related and mostly obsolete Richter magnitude, with a magnitude 3 or lower _____ being mostly imperceptible and magnitude 7 causing serious damage over large areas.
   a. AASHTO Soil Classification System
   b. AL 333
   c. AL 129-1
   d. Earthquake

44. _____ is made up of a sequence of sedimentary rocks of a Silurian age, dipping to the south-east. The main Silurian succession of limestones and shales comprises thirteen units spanning 200-500 m of stratigraphic thickness, being thickest in the south, and overlies a 75-125 m thick Ordovician sequence. It was deposited in a shallow, hot and salty sea, on the edge of an equatorial continent.
   a. 1703 Genroku earthquake
   b. 1700 Cascadia earthquake
   c. 1509 Istanbul earthquake
   d. Gotland

45. The _____ is the large central basin in the Baltic Sea between Sweden and the Baltic countries. It is subdivided into the Gdansk Deep (or Gdansk Basin), the Western _____ and the Eastern _____. Within the Eastern _____ is the Gotland Deep (249 meters deep) which is an anoxic basin.

The sediments in the _____ are important for studying the climate changes in northern Europe over the past 5,000 years.

   a. 1700 Cascadia earthquake
   b. 1703 Genroku earthquake
   c. 1509 Istanbul earthquake
   d. Gotland Basin

46. The _____ is a geological syncline in southern England underlying parts of Hampshire, the Isle of Wight, Dorset, and Sussex. Like the London Basin to the northeast, it consists of an area of sands and clays of Paleocene and younger age surrounded by a broken rim of chalk hills of Cretaceous age.

The _____ is the traditional name for the landward section of a basin underlying the northern English Channel and much of central southern England, known more fully as the Hampshire-Dieppe Basin.

   a. Hampshire Basin
   b. 1509 Istanbul earthquake
   c. 1703 Genroku earthquake
   d. 1700 Cascadia earthquake

47. The _____ is a sedimentary basin, located off the west coast of Ireland. It lies between the Hatton and Edoras Banks to the west and the Rockall Bank to the east. The age of the basin fill is uncertain, as its relationship to the Rockall Basin.
   a. 1509 Istanbul earthquake
   b. 1703 Genroku earthquake
   c. 1700 Cascadia earthquake
   d. Hatton Basin

48. The _____ or Carpathian Basin is a large basin in Central Europe. The basin forms a topographically discrete unit set in the European landscape, surrounded by imposing geographic boundaries that have created a fairly unified cultural area that looks more towards the south and east than to the north and west. The rivers Danube and Tisza divide the basin roughly in half.
   a. Pannonian Basin
   b. 1703 Genroku earthquake
   c. 1509 Istanbul earthquake
   d. 1700 Cascadia earthquake

49. The _____ is one of the major geological regions of France having developed since the Triassic on a basement formed by the Variscan orogeny.

It is a geological basin of sedimentary rocks. It overlies geological strata disturbed by the Variscan orogeny and forms a broad shallow bowl in which successive marine deposits from throughout periods from the Triassic to the Pliocene were laid down: their extent generally diminishing with time.

a. 1703 Genroku earthquake
c. 1509 Istanbul earthquake
b. Paris Basin
d. 1700 Cascadia earthquake

50. _____ is a small, uninhabited, rocky islet in the north Atlantic Ocean. It gives its name to one of the sea areas named in the Shipping Forecast, provided by the British Meteorological Office. It could be, in James Fisher's words, 'the most isolated small rock in the oceans of the world'.

_____ is made of a type of granite that is relatively rich in sodium and potassium. Within this granite are darker bands richer in the alkali pyroxene mineral aegirine and the alkali amphibole mineral riebeckite. The dark bands are a type of granite that geologists have named 'rockallite', although use of this term is now discouraged. In 1975, a new mineral was discovered on _____. The mineral is called bazirite, (chemical composition $BaZrSi_3O_9$), named after the elements barium and zirconium. _____ was formed approximately 55 million years ago, when the ancient continent of Laurasia was split apart by plate tectonics.

a. Rockall
c. 1509 Istanbul earthquake
b. Logarithmic Spiral Beach
d. Historical geology

51. The _____ is a large (ca. 800 km by 150 km) sedimentary basin that lies to the west of Ireland and the United Kingdom beneath the major deepwater area known as the Rockall Trough.

The nature of the crust beneath the Rockall Trough has long been a matter of debate. Originally thought to be oceanic crust it is now generally considered to be highly stretched continental crust, although some groups of researchers continue to favour either oceanic or transitional style crust, particularly at the southern end of the basin.

a. Rockall Basin
c. Skarn
b. Slyne-Erris Trough
d. Diapir

52. The _____ is a geological basin off the west coast of Donegal, Ireland.

In recent years it has been shown to be prospective for hydrocarbons, hosting Shell's Corrib gas field (discovered by Enterprise Oil, bought by Shell), and several other prospects being evaluated by a number of other oil companies.

Structurally, the trough is a series of NNE-SSW trending half-grabens.

a. Rockall Basin
c. Skarn
b. Diapir
d. Slyne-Erris Trough

53. The _____ is a volcanic hotspot at the Kerguelen Plateau in the Southern Indian Ocean. The _____ has produced basaltic lava for about 130 million years and has also produced the Kerguelen Islands, Heard Island and the McDonald Islands.

a. Neocomian
c. Kerguelen hotspot
b. Tristan hotspot
d. Mediterranean Ridge

54. The _____ is a major geological province in central South Australia. It stretches from the northernmost parts of the Flinders Ranges, narrowing at the Fleurieu Peninsula and extending into Kangaroo Island, and composes the two major mountain ranges of the State: the Flinders Ranges and the Mount Lofty Ranges. The sediments in the rift complex were deposited between about 870 Ma to ~500 Ma.

Fossils are to be found in the Geosyncline; those discovered in the Ediacara Hills of the northern Flinders in 1946 are of worldwide significance for being some of the oldest examples of fossilised animal life ever found. They date from the very end of the Neoproterozoic, and in 2004 the location gave its name to the last geological period of the era, the Ediacaran.

  a. AL 129-1
  b. AL 333
  c. AASHTO Soil Classification System
  d. Adelaide Geosyncline

55. _____ theory is an obsolete concept involving vertical crustal movement that has been replaced by plate tectonics to explain crustal movement and geologic features. _____ is a term still occasionally used for a subsiding linear trough that was caused by the accumulation of sedimentary rock strata deposited in a basin and subsequently compressed, deformed, and uplifted into a mountain range, with attendant volcanism and plutonism. The filling of a _____ with tons of sediment is accompanied in the late stages of deposition by folding, crumpling, and faulting of the deposits.

  a. Storegga Slides
  b. Geosyncline
  c. Tejas sequence
  d. Paleogeology

56. The _____ was a major tectonic (mountain building) episode in central Australia responsible for the formation of a series of large mountain ranges. The episode started at about 450 million years ago and concluded about 300 million years ago. The orogeny was centred in an area that had previously been a marine sedimentary basin, and involved the thrusting up of the underlying metamorphic and igneous rocks of Proterozoic age.

  a. Alpine orogeny
  b. Alleghenian orogeny
  c. AASHTO Soil Classification System
  d. Alice Springs Orogeny

57. _____ refers to natural mountain building, and may be studied as a tectonic structural event, (b) as a geographical event, and (c) a chronological event. Orogenic events (a) cause distinctive structural phenomena and related tectonic activity, (b) affect certain regions of rocks and crust, and (c) happen within a specific period of time.

  a. Alleghenian orogeny
  b. Orogeny
  c. AASHTO Soil Classification System
  d. Alpine orogeny

58. The _____ is a large (ca. 170,000 km^2) intracratonic sedimentary basin in central Australia, lying mostly within the southern Northern Territory, but extending into the state of Western Australia. Deposition of locally up to 14 km of marine and non-marine sedimentary rocks took place from the Neoproterozoic to the late Paleozoic.

  a. AASHTO Soil Classification System
  b. AL 129-1
  c. AL 333
  d. Amadeus Basin

59. The _____, covering at least one-tenth of the Earth's surface, is the largest and the youngest of the tektite strewnfields. The 800,000 year-old strewnfield includes most of Southeast Asia (Vietnam, Thailand, Southern China, Laos and Cambodia.) The material from the impact stretches across the ocean to include the islands of the Philippines, Indonesia, Malaysia and Java and reaches far out into the Indian Ocean and south to the western side of Australia.

a. Australasian strewnfield
c. AL 333

b. AASHTO Soil Classification System
d. AL 129-1

60. The _____ occupies more than half of the continent of Australia. It occupies the portion of Australia west of a line running north-south roughly from the eastern shore of Arnhem Land on the Bay or Gulf of Carpentaria to the Eyre Peninsula in the state of South Australia, and skirting to the west of the Simpson Desert in the interior. The plateau has an average elevation of between 305 and 460 m. The shield is fractured into a number of distinct blocks, including the Pilbara craton in the North and the Yilgarn craton in the Southwest. Some of these blocks have been raised to form uplands; others have been depressed, forming lowlands and basins.

a. AL 333
c. AASHTO Soil Classification System

b. AL 129-1
d. Australian Shield

61. The _____ is a term for a large intracratonic sedimentary basin which is interpreted to have occupied a large area of central, southern and western Australia during much of the Neoproterozoic (~830-540 Ma.) This superbasin was disrupted by two periods of uplift and mountain building, the latest Neoproterozoic Petermann Orogeny and Palaeozoic Alice Springs Orogeny, to leave remnants including the Amadeus, Georgina, Ngalia, and Officer basins.

a. Hunter-Bowen orogeny
c. Centralian Superbasin

b. Wianamatta shale
d. Lachlan Fold Belt

62. The _____ is a volcanic hotspot that takes advantage of weak spots in the Indo-Australian Plate to feed magma to the volcanoes of Eastern Australia. It does not produce a single chain of volcanoes like the Hawaiian Islands. Tweed Volcano in New South Wales is a large shield volcano that was formed by the hotspot about 23 million years ago and has one of the biggest erosion calderas in the world.

a. AL 333
c. AASHTO Soil Classification System

b. East Australia hotspot
d. AL 129-1

63. The _____ covers approximately 440,000 square kilometres of central South Australia. Its Precambrian crystalline basement crustal block was cratonised ca. 1550-1450 Ma. Prior to 1550 Ma the craton comprised a number of active Proterozoic orogenic belts extending back in time to at least 2450 Ma.

The Craton can be subdivided into a number of tectonic subdomains on the basis of structure and tectonostratigraphic history.

The _____, is a distinct physiographic province of the larger West Australian Shield division. It includes the smaller Stuart Range Basin and Pimba Platform physiographic sections.

a. Canadian Shield
c. Great Artesian Basin

b. Sahara pump theory
d. Gawler craton

64. A _____ is an old and stable part of the continental crust that has survived the merging and splitting of continents and supercontinents for at least 500 million years. Some are over two billion years old. They are generally found in the interiors of continents and are characteristically composed of ancient crystalline basement crust of lightweight felsic igneous rock such as granite.

a. Superior craton
c. Kalahari craton

b. Craton
d. Sebakwe proto-craton

65. The _____ in the Kimberley region of Western Australia is a world famous Lagerstätte that exhibits exceptional preservation of a Devonian reef community.

Unweathered sections of the _____ are comprised of siltstone, shale and calcarenite with numerous limestone concretions. These concretions are resistant to weathering, producing extensive nodule fields on the ground in areas where the surrounding rock has eroded away.

   a. Gogo Formation
   c. 1700 Cascadia earthquake
   b. Xitun Formation
   d. 1509 Istanbul earthquake

66. _____ , originally Gondwanaland is the name given to a southern precursor-supercontinent and then as a remnant separated from Laurasia 180->200 million years ago during the breakup of the Pangaea supercontinent that existed about 500 to 200 Ma ago into two large segments. While the corresponding northern hemisphere continent Laurasia moved further north, the nearly equal in area _____ included most of the landmasses in today's southern hemisphere, including Antarctica, South America, Africa, Madagascar, Australia-New Guinea, and New Zealand, as well as Arabia and the Indian subcontinent, which have now moved into the Northern Hemisphere.

   a. 1700 Cascadia earthquake
   c. 1703 Genroku earthquake
   b. 1509 Istanbul earthquake
   d. Gondwana

67. The _____ provides the only reliable source of water through much of inland Australia. The basin is the largest and deepest artesian basin in the world, covering a total of 1,711,000 square kilometres (661,000 sq mi).

The water of the _____ is held in a sandstone layer laid down by continental erosion of higher ground during the Triassic, Jurassic, and early Cretaceous periods. During a time when much of what is now inland Australia was below sea level, the sandstone was then covered by a layer of marine sedimentary rock shortly afterwards, which formed a confining layer - thus trapping water in the sandstone aquifer.

   a. Great Artesian Basin
   c. Quaternary
   b. Canadian Shield
   d. Sahara pump theory

68. _____ is a type of sandstone prevalent in the Sydney region of New South Wales, Australia. It dates from the Triassic Period. Well known for its durable quality, it is the reason many Aboriginal rock carvings and drawings in the area still exist.

   a. Narooma Terrane
   c. Widgiemooltha Komatiite
   b. Lachlan Fold Belt
   d. Hawkesbury sandstone

69. The _____ was a significant arc accretion event in the Permian and Triassic periods affecting approximately 2,500 km of the Australian continental margin.

The _____ occurred in two main phases, a Permian accretion of previously formed passive-marginal Devonian and Carboniferous sediments in the Hunter region and mid-west region of what is now New South Wales, separated by rifting, back-arc volcanism and a later Permian to Triassic event resulting in arc accretion and metamorphism during a subduction event.

The _____ has resulted in the New England Fold Belt, a tectonic accretion of metamorphic terranes and mid-crustal granitoid intrusions, flanked by Permian to Triassic sedimentary basins which were formed distally to the now-eroded orogenic mountain belt.

a. Hawkesbury sandstone
b. Surat Basin
c. Wianamatta shale
d. Hunter-Bowen orogeny

70. The _____ is a major tectonic plate that includes the continent of Australia and surrounding ocean, and extends northwest to include the Indian subcontinent and adjacent waters. Recent studies suggest that the _____ may be in the process of breaking up into two separate plates due primarily to stresses induced by the collision of the _____ with Eurasia along the Himalayas. The two protoplates or subplates are generally referred to as the Indian Plate and the Australian Plate.

a. AL 333
b. Indo-Australian Plate
c. AASHTO Soil Classification System
d. AL 129-1

71. The term _____ is used in geology when one or a stack of originally flat and planar surfaces, such as sedimentary strata, are bent or curved as a result of plastic (i.e. permanent) deformation. Synsedimentary folds are those due to slumping of sedimentary material before it is lithified. Folds in rocks vary in size from microscopic crinkles to mountain-sized folds.

a. 1509 Istanbul earthquake
b. 1703 Genroku earthquake
c. 1700 Cascadia earthquake
d. Fold

72. The _____ or Lachlan Orogen is a geological subdivision of the east part of Australia. It is a zone of folded and faulted rocks of similar age. It dominates New South Wales and Victoria, also extending into Tasmania, the Australian Capital Territory and Queensland.

a. Wianamatta shale
b. Hunter-Bowen orogeny
c. Lachlan Fold Belt
d. Narooma Terrane

73. A _____ is a forest in which tree trunks have fossilized. That is, the wood in the trunks have turned into petrified wood, where organic cells have decomposed and are replaced by minerals, while preserving the structure of the wood.

a. 1703 Genroku earthquake
b. 1509 Istanbul earthquake
c. 1700 Cascadia earthquake
d. Petrified Forest

74. The _____ meteorite is named after _____, Victoria, in Australia. It is one of the most studied meteorites due to its large mass (>100 kg), the fact that it was an observed fall, and it belongs to a group of meteorites rich in organic compounds.

a. 1509 Istanbul earthquake
b. 1700 Cascadia earthquake
c. 1703 Genroku earthquake
d. Murchison

75. The _____ is an east-west trending belt of Proterozoic granulite-gneiss basement rocks approximately 500km long. The _____ extends from western South Australia into Western Australia. The _____ is primarily exposed through the actions of the Petermann Orogeny at c. 535-550 Ma, which exhumed the orogenic belt along the Woodroffe Thrust.

a. Gawler craton
b. Quaternary
c. Musgrave Block
d. Canadian Shield

76. The Narooma Accretionary Complex or _____ is a geological structural region on the south coast of New South Wales, Australia that is the remains of a subduction zone or an oceanic terrane. It can be found on the surface around Narooma, Batemans Bay and down south into Victoria near Mallacoota. It has attached itself to the Lachlan Fold Belt and has been considered as either an exotic terrane or as a part of the fold belt.
   a. Hawkesbury sandstone
   b. Surat Basin
   c. Narooma Terrane
   d. Lachlan Fold Belt

77. The _____ is a part of the Great Artesian Basin of Australia. The _____ extends across an area of 27,000 square kilometres and the southern third of the basin occupies a large part of northern New South Wales, the remainder is in Queensland. It comprises Jurassic through to Cretaceous aged sediments derived from Triassic and Permian arc rocks of the Hunter-Bowen orogeny.
   a. Narooma Terrane
   b. Hunter-Bowen orogeny
   c. Surat Basin
   d. Wianamatta shale

78. _____ are the fragments of a larger meteorite that fell in 1879 in a remote area of Australia near the Tenham station, South Gregory, in western Queensland. Although the fall was seen by a number of people its exact date has not been established. Bright meteors were seen to be moving roughly from west to east.

Because the Tenham meterites were recovered quite soon after they fell, from a remote and dry region in which weathering and other alterations had not set in, they have been invaluable for scientific study of meteorites and their mineral contents.

   a. Tenham Meteorites
   b. 1703 Genroku earthquake
   c. 1700 Cascadia earthquake
   d. 1509 Istanbul earthquake

79. The _____ is a geological formation deposited during the Silurian or Ordovician periods, around four to five hundred million years ago, and is now exposed on the west coast of Australia, straddling the boundary of the Carnarvon and Perth basins. Visible trackways may prove to be the earliest evidence of terrestrial animals.

The _____ is over 1,400 m (4,500 ft) deep: the bottom has never been found, but seismic data suggests it unconformably overlies a Proterozoic basement.

   a. 1509 Istanbul earthquake
   b. Jiufotang Formation
   c. Maevarano Formation
   d. Tumblagooda sandstone

80. _____ is a type of shale prevalent in the Sydney region of New South Wales, Australia. It dates from the Triassic Period. It produces a rich clayey soil, often with poor drainage, such as that in the Cumberland Plain.
   a. Wianamatta shale
   b. Hunter-Bowen orogeny
   c. Hawkesbury sandstone
   d. Surat Basin

81. _____ are ultramafic mantle-derived volcanic rocks. They have low SiO_2, low K_2O, low Al_2O_3, and high to extremely high MgO. They were named for their type locality along the Komati River in South Africa.

True _____ are very rare and essentially restricted to rocks of Archaean age, with few Proterozoic or Phanerozoic _____ known (although high-magnesian lamprophyres are known from the Mesozoic). This restriction in age is thought to be due to secular cooling of the mantle, which may have been up to 500 >°C hotter during the early to middle Archaean (4.5 to 2.6 Ga).

   a. 1509 Istanbul earthquake   b. Komatiites
   c. 1703 Genroku earthquake   d. 1700 Cascadia earthquake

82. The _____ is a formation of komatiite in the Yilgarn Craton of Western Australia.

The stratigraphy of the _____ is well known to be part of the regional komatiite magmatic event also seen at the Kambalda Dome, 50 km to the north. There are comparisons which place the _____ as equivalent to the Silver Lake Komatiite.

   a. Hunter-Bowen orogeny   b. Surat Basin
   c. Hawkesbury sandstone   d. Widgiemooltha Komatiite

83. The _____ is an oceanic ridge, a tectonic divergent plate boundary between the Nazca and Antarctic Plates. Its eastern end is the Chile Triple Junction where the _____ is being subducted below the South American Plate in the Peru-Chile Trench. It runs westward to a triple point south of the Juan Fern>ández Microplate where it intersects the East Pacific Rise.

   a. 1703 Genroku earthquake   b. Chile Rise
   c. 1700 Cascadia earthquake   d. 1509 Istanbul earthquake

84. The _____ is a mid-oceanic ridge, a divergent tectonic plate boundary located along the floor of the Pacific Ocean. It separates the Pacific Plate to the west from (north to south) the North American Plate, the Rivera Plate, the Cocos Plate, the Nazca Plate, and the Antarctic Plate. It runs from an undefined point near Antarctica in the south northward to its termination at the northern end of the Gulf of California in the Salton Sea basin in southern California.

   a. Elastic rebound theory   b. Azores-Gibraltar Transform Fault
   c. Obduction   d. East Pacific Rise

85. The _____ is a mid-ocean ridge, a divergent tectonic plate boundary located about 241 km (150 mi) west of Vancouver Island, British Columbia, Canada. It lies at the northern extremity of the Pacific spreading axis. To its east is the Explorer Plate, which together with the Juan de Fuca Plate and the Gorda Plate to its south, is what remains of the once-vast Farallon Plate which has been largely subducted under the North American Plate.

   a. Explorer Ridge   b. AL 129-1
   c. AL 333   d. AASHTO Soil Classification System

86. The _____ is a divergent boundary located between the South American coast and the triple junction of the Nazca Plate, the Cocos Plate, and the Pacific Plate. The volcanically active Galapagos Islands exist on the Galápagos hotspot above the _____. The Galapagos Microplate is a small separate plate on the rise just to the southeast of the triple junction.

   a. Pacific-Antarctic Ridge   b. Nazca Ridge
   c. Pacific-Kula Ridge   d. Galapagos Rise

87. The _____ is a tectonic spreading center located off the coast of Oregon and northern California north of Cape Mendocino. It runs from a triple junction with the San Andreas Fault and the Mendocino Fracture Zone northward to another transform boundary, the Blanco Fracture Zone. To its east is the Gorda Plate, which together with the Juan de Fuca Plate to its north, is what remains of the once-vast Farallon Plate which has been largely subducted under the North American Plate.
   a. Gorda Ridge
   b. Motagua Fault
   c. Juan de Fuca Ridge
   d. Mirovia

88. The _____ is a tectonic spreading center located off the coasts of the state of Washington in the United States and the province of British Columbia in Canada. It runs northward from a transform boundary, the Blanco Fracture Zone, to a triple junction with the Nootka Fault and the Sovanco Fracture Zone. To its east is the Juan de Fuca Plate, which together with the Gorda Plate to its south and the Explorer Plate to its north, is what remains of the once-vast Farallon Plate which has been largely subducted under the North American Plate.
   a. Copperbelt Province
   b. Convergent boundary
   c. Juan de Fuca Ridge
   d. Thrust fault

89. The _____ was an ancient mid-ocean ridge that existed between the Kula and Farallon plates in the Pacific Ocean during the Jurassic period. There was a small piece of this ridge off the Pacific Northwest 43 million years ago. The rest of the ridge has since been subducted beneath Alaska.
   a. Nazca Ridge
   b. Pacific-Farallon Ridge
   c. Pacific-Antarctic Ridge
   d. Kula-Farallon Ridge

90. The _____ is an underwater plateau that extends from southwest of New Caledonia to the Challenger Plateau, west of New Zealand. To its west is the Tasman Basin and to the east is the New Caledonia Basin. _____ has a total area of about 1,500,000 square km, and generally lies about 1500 to 2500 metres under water. It is part of Zealandia, a much larger continent that is now mostly submerged, and so is composed of continental crust. It was rifted away from Eastern Australia by a mid-ocean ridge that was active from 80 to 60 million years ago, and now lies 800 kilometres offshore from mainland Australia.
   a. 1509 Istanbul earthquake
   b. 1703 Genroku earthquake
   c. 1700 Cascadia earthquake
   d. Lord Howe Rise

91. The _____ is a major right lateral-moving transform fault along the seafloor of the south Pacific Ocean which runs from New Zealand southwestward to the Macquarie Triple Junction. It is also the tectonic plate boundary between the Indo-Australian Plate to the northwest and the Pacific Plate to the southeast.

The _____ includes a component of convergence which increases as it approaches the South Island of New Zealand.

   a. Macquarie Fault Zone
   b. Sorong Fault
   c. Ross Lake Fault
   d. Magallanes-Fagnano Fault

92. The _____ is an ocean ridge in the southern Pacific Ocean. It lies on the Nazca Plate and is being subducted in the Peru-Chile Trench under the South American Plate by ongoing plate motion.
   a. Pacific-Kula Ridge
   b. Pacific-Farallon Ridge
   c. Pacific-Antarctic Ridge
   d. Nazca Ridge

Chapter 16. Test Preparation Part 16

93. The _____ is a long submarine ridge running between New Caledonia and New Zealand, about 1300 km off the east-coast of Australia. Little is known about the _____; however, it generally lies about 2000 m below sea level and consists of Late Cretaceous continental crust. It is part of Zealandia, a submerged continent that sank 60-85 million years ago.
   a. 1700 Cascadia earthquake
   b. 1703 Genroku earthquake
   c. 1509 Istanbul earthquake
   d. Norfolk Ridge

94. The _____ is a divergent tectonic plate boundary located on the seafloor of the South Pacific Ocean, separating the Pacific Plate from the Antarctic Plate. It is regarded as the southern section of the East Pacific Rise in some usages, generally south of the Challenger Fracture Zone and stretching to the Macquarie Triple Junction south of New Zealand.

Stretching north-west from the _____ is a long line of seamounts called the Louisville seamount chain which is thought to have formed from the Pacific Plate sliding over a long-lived center of upwelling magma called the Louisville hotspot.

   a. Pacific-Kula Ridge
   b. Pacific-Farallon Ridge
   c. Nazca Ridge
   d. Pacific-Antarctic Ridge

95. The _____ is a former mid-ocean ridge that existed between the Pacific and Farallon plates in the Pacific Ocean during the Tertiary period. Its appearance was in a north-south direction. About 60 million years ago, it might have extended at least 10,000 km (6,214 mi). Remnants of the _____ include the Explorer, Gorda, Juan de Fuca and the East Pacific ridges.
   a. Pacific-Antarctic Ridge
   b. Nazca Ridge
   c. Pacific-Kula Ridge
   d. Pacific-Farallon Ridge

96. The _____ is a former mid-ocean ridge that existed between the Pacific and Kula plates in the Pacific Ocean during the early Tertiary period. Its appearance was in an east-west direction and the Hawaiian-Emperor seamount chain had its attribution with the ridge. The Kula-Farallon Ridge lay south of the Hawaii hotspot around 80 million years ago, moving northward relative to the hotspot.
   a. Pacific-Kula Ridge
   b. Pacific-Antarctic Ridge
   c. Nazca Ridge
   d. Pacific-Farallon Ridge

97. _____ is a small, soft-bodied invertebrate of unknown affinity known from fossils of the Middle Cambrian Lagerst>ätten both in the Burgess shale formation in British Columbia and the Maotianshan shales of Yunnan Province, China.

Very few specimens of this organism have been found, only five in the Burgess shale -- which may be a reflection of its genuine rarity, but is more likely to be due to taphonomic (preservational) or behavioural factors. The fossils reach 25 mm (1 in) in length.

   a. Amiskwia
   b. AASHTO Soil Classification System
   c. AL 333
   d. AL 129-1

98. _____ are a group of very early marine animals known from fossils found in Cambrian deposits in China, USA, Canada, Poland and Australia. They were long thought to be restricted to this range, but the discovery of the Devonian Schinderhannes extended their record by some hundred million years - their non-mineralised nature means they are absent from the intermediate fossil record. Anomalocarids are the largest Cambrian animals known - some Chinese forms may have reached 2 m in length - and most of them were probably active carnivores.
   a. Orthrozanclus
   b. AASHTO Soil Classification System
   c. AL 129-1
   d. Anomalocaridids

99. _____ is an extinct genus of anomalocaridid, which are, in turn, thought to be closely related to the arthropods. The first fossils of _____ were discovered in the Ogygopsis shale by Joseph Frederick Whiteaves, with more examples found by Charles Doolittle Walcott in the famed Burgess Shale. Originally several fossilized parts discovered separately (the mouth, feeding appendages and tail) were thought to be three separate creatures, a misapprehension corrected by Harry B. Whittington and Derek Briggs in a 1985 journal article.
   a. AL 333
   b. AL 129-1
   c. Anomalocaris
   d. AASHTO Soil Classification System

100. _____ was a genus of soft-bodied, caterpillar-shaped organisms average body length of 1-6 cm. The genus name commemorates a mountain peak named 'Ashea' due north of the Waptia Glacier. They are known from fossils found in the middle Cambrian Burgess shale of British Columbia, and from the Wheeler Formation in Utah.
   a. AASHTO Soil Classification System
   b. AL 129-1
   c. Aysheaia
   d. AL 333

101. _____ is a genus of animals described from Early Cambrian fossils. The genus was named after Banff, Alberta, near where the first fossil specimens were discovered. Its placement in higher taxa is controversial.
   a. Vetulicola
   b. Banffia
   c. Nectocaris
   d. Vetulicolia

102. The _____ Formation is one of the world's most celebrated fossil localities, and is famous for the exceptional preservation of the fossils found within it, in which the soft parts are preserved. It is 505 million years (Middle Cambrian) in age, making it one of the earliest fossil beds to preserve the soft parts of animals. The pre-Cambrian fossil record of animals is sparse and ambiguous.
   a. 1703 Genroku earthquake
   b. Burgess Shale
   c. 1509 Istanbul earthquake
   d. 1700 Cascadia earthquake

103. A number of assemblages bear fossil assemblages similar in character to that of the Burgess shale. While many are also preserved in a similar fashion to the Burgess shale, the term '_____' covers assemblages based on taxonomic criteria only.

The fauna of the middle Cambrian has a cosmopolitan range..

   a. Thaumaptilon
   b. Leanchoilia
   c. Burgess shale type fauna
   d. Dinomischus

104. _____ is a fossil demosponge from the Cambrian period. It was unusual because it was not attached to the sea bed, and radiated spines from the edge of its flattish, conical body, producing an appearance not unlike that of the peak of a big top, with guy lines. Water entered the sponge parallel to the spines, being expelled, presumbaly, from a central opening.

a. Xanioascus
c. Choia

b. Carpolite
d. Turgai Sea

1. _____ is a proposed extinct taxon of fossil arthropod-like marine animals found in the early and middle Cambrian. It is subdivided into the anomalocarids and the opabinids. The name of this group comes from Greek, 'deinos' and 'caris,' meaning 'terror shrimp' or 'terror crab,' due to their crustacean-like appearance and the hypotheses suggesting that members of this class were the apex predators of their time.

   a. Dinomischus
   b. Wiwaxia
   c. Leanchoilia
   d. Dinocaridida

2. _____ is a rare fossil animal from the Cambrian period. It reached 100 mm in height, was attached to the sea floor by a stalk, and looked loosely like a flower. The cup-shaped body at the top of the stalk probably fed by filtering the surrounding seawater, and may have created a current to facilitate this.

   a. Wiwaxia
   b. Dinomischus
   c. Leanchoilia
   d. Halwaxiida

3. _____ vesanus is an extinct species of ctenophore, known from the Canadian Burgess Shale of British Columbia. It is about 510 to 515 million years old and belongs to middle Cambrian strata.

   The species is remarkable for its two sets of long and short comb rows, not seen in similar form elsewhere in the fossil record or among modern species.

   a. Turgai Sea
   b. Xanioascus
   c. Carpolite
   d. Fasciculus

4. _____ is an extinct genus of animal found as fossils in the Middle Cambrian-aged Burgess Shale formation of British Columbia, Canada. It was named by Simon Conway Morris when he re-examined Charles Walcott's Burgess Shale genus Canadia in 1979. Conway Morris found that what Walcott had called one genus in fact included several quite different animals.

   a. Vetulicola
   b. Nectocaris
   c. Vetulicolia
   d. Hallucigenia

5. _____ is a proposed clade loosely uniting scale-bearing Cambrian animals, which may lie in the stem group to molluscs or lohpotrochozoa. Some palaeontologists question the validity of the _____ clade.

   The name 'halwaxiid' was formed by combining the names of two members of the proposed group, Halkieria and Wiwaxia.

   a. Leanchoilia
   b. Haplophrentis
   c. Dinocaridida
   d. Halwaxiida

6. _____ was a tiny shelled mollusk which lived in the Cambrian Period. Its shell was long and conical, with the open end protected by an operculum, from which two fleshy arms called helens protruded at the sides. These arms probably acted as stabilisers, or were used for locomotion, rowing the animal across undersea mudflats.

   a. Haplophrentis
   b. Halwaxiida
   c. Dinomischus
   d. Wiwaxia

7. _____ is a four-eyed arachnomorph arthropod known from the Cambrian Burgess shale. It was about 5cm long and had long, whip-like feelers mounted on frontal arm-like appendages. Its guts are sometimes preserved in three dimensions.

a. Leanchoilia
b. Dinomischus
c. Wiwaxia
d. Thaumaptilon

8. _____ splendens is an arthropod known from the Middle Cambrian Burgess Shale of British Columbia. It is the most common fossil in the Burgess Shale.

_____ was the first fossil collected by Charles Walcott from the Burgess Shale. Walcott described _____ informally as a 'lace crab' and described it more formally as an odd trilobite.

a. Marrella
b. 1509 Istanbul earthquake
c. Sidneyia
d. Sanctacaris

9. _____ pteryx is a soft-bodied animal of unknown affinity, known from the Middle Cambrian Burgess Shale. Walcott, the discoverer of the shale, had photographed the one specimen he had collected in the 1910s, but never had time to investigate it further. It was not until 1976 that it was formally described, by Simon Conway Morris.

a. Nectocaris
b. Vetulicolia
c. Hallucigenia
d. Vetulicola

10. _____ is a genus of crustacean arthropod from the Middle Cambrian. Its fossils, which reach 15cm in length, have been found in the Burgess Shale in British Columbia, Canada.

It bore a large pair of eyes at the front of its body, and may have had two smaller eyes in between.

a. AL 333
b. Odaraia
c. AASHTO Soil Classification System
d. AL 129-1

11. _____ is a genus of soft-bodied animals known from middle Cambrian Lagerst>ätte. Reaching as much as 12.5 centimetres (4.9 in) in length, _____ is a flat, oval bilaterian which apparently had a single muscular foot, and a 'shell' on its back that was moderately rigid but of a material unsuited to fossilization.

Originally it was known from only one specimen, but 189 new finds in the years immediately preceding 2006 made a detailed description possible.

a. AL 129-1
b. AL 333
c. AASHTO Soil Classification System
d. Odontogriphus

12. _____ was a trilobite from the Cambrian period. Its fossils are found well-preserved in the Burgess Shale in Canada. It grew up to 10 cm long.

_____ followed the basic structure of all trilobites -- a cephalon (head shield), a thorax with seven jointed parts, and finally a semicircular pygidium. Its antennae were long, and curved back along its sides. Its thin legs show that it was no swimmer, instead crawling along the sea floor in search of prey. This is also evidenced by fossil tracks that have been found.

The Burgess Shale's preservative qualities have helped _____ become one of the best known of trilobites.

a. AL 129-1
b. Olenoides
c. Orthrozanclus
d. AASHTO Soil Classification System

13. _____ is an animal genus found in Cambrian fossil deposits. Its sole species, _____ regalis, is known from the Middle Cambrian Burgess Shale of British Columbia. Fewer than twenty good specimens have been found. _____ was a soft-bodied animal of modest size, and its segmented body had lobes along the sides and a fan-shaped tail. The head shows unusual features: five eyes, a mouth under the head and facing backwards, and a proboscis that probably passed food to the mouth.
   a. AL 129-1
   b. AL 333
   c. AASHTO Soil Classification System
   d. Opabinia

14. _____ reburrus ('Dawn scythe with bristling hair') is a sea creature known from the Middle Cambrian (~>505 million years ago) Burgess shale, about one centimeter long, with long spikes protruding from its armored body

The describers of this fossil animal, Simon Conway Morris and Jean-Bernard Caron, say _____ may have formed a link between the halkieriid and the wiwaxiid families, uniting them tentatively in a group called 'Halwaxiida', characterized by a similar type of body armor; these organisms might have been stem group molluscs, or fall as a stem group to the larger lophotrochozoan clade (containing molluscs, annelids and brachiopods.) However, the status of the Halwaxiid grouping is not universally accepted.

J.B. Caron and D.A. Jackson found a specimen in the Burgess Shale and in 2006 referred to it as 'scleritomorph C' without a detailed description.

   a. Olenoides
   b. AL 129-1
   c. AASHTO Soil Classification System
   d. Orthrozanclus

15. _____ is among the largest and most abundant worms found in the fossils of the Cambrian Burgess Shale formation of British Columbia. It is an early penis worm that averaged about 80mm in length. Typical of extant priapulids are the infaunal living habit and the spiny evertable proboscis.
   a. AASHTO Soil Classification System
   b. Ottoia
   c. AL 333
   d. AL 129-1

16. _____ gracilens is an extinct animal known from the Middle Cambrian fossil found near Mount Pika in the Burgess Shale of British Columbia. It was discovered by Charles Walcott and was first described by him in 1911. Based on the obvious and regular segmentation of the body, Walcott classified it as a polychaete worm.
   a. 1703 Genroku earthquake
   b. 1509 Istanbul earthquake
   c. 1700 Cascadia earthquake
   d. Pikaia

17. _____ is a Middle Cambrian arthropod from the Burgess shale of British Columbia. Specimens range from 46 to 93 mm in length. _____ was most famously regarded as primitive chelicerate arthropod, although subsequent studies of phylogeny have not always supported this conclusion.

The head of _____ bears five pairs of grasping appendages and a sixth pair of large separate appendages. The grasping appendages each bear a short antenna-like second appendage.

a. 1509 Istanbul earthquake
b. Sanctacaris
c. Sidneyia
d. Marrella

18. _____ is an extinct arthropod known from fossils found in the Cambrian-age Burgess Shale formation of British Columbia.

_____ ranged from 2 to 5 inches in length and is one of the largest arthropods found at the site. It is thought to have been a benthic carnivore that walked along the sea floor in search of hard-shelled prey.

a. Sanctacaris
b. 1509 Istanbul earthquake
c. Marrella
d. Sidneyia

19. _____ is a fossil from the middle Cambrian bearing striking resemblance to a biota that had almost disappeared at the start of the Cambrian, >542 million years ago. It was up to 20 cm long, and attached itself to the sea floor with a holdfast.

Leaf-shaped, _____ had a central axis extending to its tip, with many 'ribs' radiating from it, in a similar manner to the ribs of a leaf.

a. Wiwaxia
b. Thaumaptilon
c. Haplophrentis
d. Halwaxiida

20. _____ is a genus of small animals of uncertain affinity, known from early-Cambrian fossils known from the Chengjiang biota of China.

_____ cuneata (Hou, 1987) has a body composed of two distinct parts of approximately equal length. The front part is rectangular with a carapace-like structure of four rigid cuticular plates, with a large mouth at the front end.

a. Hallucigenia
b. Vetulicolia
c. Nectocaris
d. Vetulicola

21. _____ is an extinct phylum encompassing several Cambrian organisms. Their bodies comprise two parts; their front is voluminous and is tipped with a large 'mouth', and a row of five round to oval-shaped features on each side which have been interpreted as gills - or at least openings in the vicinity of the pharynx. Their posterior section comprises seven segments.

a. Hallucigenia
b. Vetulicola
c. Nectocaris
d. Vetulicolia

22. _____ fieldensis was a small, shrimp-like stem group crustacean. Many Cambrian crustaceomorphs such as _____ lack the mouthparts to be classified as crown group crustaceans that lived during the Middle Cambrian about 510 million years ago .

_____-like arthropods discovered in the Chengjiang form chains of up to 20 individuals, with each animal's tail nested in the carapace of the one behind.

a. 1703 Genroku earthquake
b. Waptia
c. 1700 Cascadia earthquake
d. 1509 Istanbul earthquake

23. The _____ is a Cambrian (c.507 Ma) fossil locality world famous for prolific agnostid and Elrathia kingii trilobite remains (even though many areas are barren of fossils) and represents a Konzentrat-Lagerstätten. Varied soft bodied organisms are locally preserved, a fauna (e.g. Naraoia, Wiwaxia ' Hallucigenia) and preservation style (carbonaceous film) normally associated with the more famous Burgess Shale. As such, the _____ also represents a Konservat-Lagerstätten.
  a. Wheeler Shale
  b. Turritellenplatte
  c. Bullock Creek
  d. Milk River Formation

24. _____ is a genus of soft-bodied, scale-covered animals known from Burgess shale type Lagerst>ätte dating from the Early to Middle Cambrian. The organisms are mainly known from dispersed sclerites; articulated specimens, where found, range from 3.4 millimetres (0.13 in) to a little over 5 centimetres (2.0 in) in length. The precise taxonomic affinities of the genus are a matter of ongoing debate amongst palaeontologists.
  a. Halwaxiida
  b. Wiwaxia
  c. Dinocaridida
  d. Dinomischus

25. _____ canadensis is an extinct ctenophore, known from the Canadian Burgess Shale in British Columbia. The species which is about 512 million years old had 24 comb rows - in contrast to all modern forms which have only 8.

Other important Cambrian ctenophore fossils are Fasciculus vesanus and Ctenorhabdotus capulus.

  a. Carpolite
  b. Fasciculus
  c. Choia
  d. Xanioascus

26. An _____ is the result of a sudden release of energy in the Earth's crust that creates seismic waves. They are recorded with a seismometer or the related and mostly obsolete Richter magnitude, with a magnitude 3 or lower _____ being mostly imperceptible and magnitude 7 causing serious damage over large areas.
  a. AL 333
  b. AL 129-1
  c. AASHTO Soil Classification System
  d. Earthquake

27. The _____ is a geologic fault or rift zone that extends along the border region of eastern Nigeria and western Cameroon, from Mount Cameroon on the Gulf of Guinea north and east towards Lake Chad. It contains the Mb>ér>é Rift Valley. It is characterized by a chain of mountain ranges and volcanoes known as the Cameroon Range or Cameroon Highlands.
  a. 1509 Istanbul earthquake
  b. 1703 Genroku earthquake
  c. 1700 Cascadia earthquake
  d. Cameroon line

28. The _____ with its branch the Timiskaming Graben, is an ancient rift valley in the Canadian Shield of Northeastern Ontario and Quebec, Canada. This rift valley was formed when the Earth's crust moved downward about a kilometer between two major fault zones known as the Mattawa and Petawawa faults. These ancient faults are still active and occasionally release stress in the form of earthquakes, such as the 1935 Timiskaming earthquake and the 2000 Kipawa earthquake.

a. Ottawa-Bonnechere Graben
b. AL 129-1
c. AASHTO Soil Classification System
d. AL 333

29. In geology, a _____ or _____ line is a planar fracture in rock in which the rock on one side of the fracture has moved with respect to the rock on the other side. Large faults within the Earth's crust are the result of differential or shear motion and active _____ zones are the causal locations of most earthquakes. Earthquakes are caused by energy release during rapid slippage along a _____.
   a. 1700 Cascadia earthquake
   b. 1509 Istanbul earthquake
   c. Fault
   d. 1703 Genroku earthquake

30. The _____ is an active transform fault, located between the North American Plate and the Pacific Plate, Canada's equivalent of the San Andreas Fault. The _____ forms a triple junction on its south with the Cascadia subduction zone and the Explorer Ridge (the Queen Charlotte Triple Junction.) The fault is named for Queen Charlotte Island which lies just north of the triple junction.
   a. 1700 Cascadia earthquake
   b. 1703 Genroku earthquake
   c. 1509 Istanbul earthquake
   d. Queen Charlotte Fault

31. The _____ consists of a major flood basalt, which created this large igneous province. It the source of the current large eastern Pacific oceanic plateau, of which the Caribbean-Colombian oceanic plateau is the tectonized remnant. The deeper levels of the plateau have been exposed on its margins at the North and South American plates.
   a. 1509 Istanbul earthquake
   b. 1700 Cascadia earthquake
   c. Supervolcano
   d. Caribbean large igneous province

32. _____ were originally defined by Coffin and Eldholm (1992) as areas of Earth's surface that contain very large volumes of magmatic rocks (typically basalt but including rhyolites) erupted over extremely short geological time intervals of a few million years or less. These provinces are not associated with normal plate tectonic magmatism, i. e. mid-ocean ridges and island arcs.
   a. Rock cycle
   b. Large igneous provinces
   c. Serpentinite
   d. Metamorphic zone

33. The _____ are a large igneous province located on the Deccan Plateau of west-central India (between 17-24N, 73-74E) and one of the largest volcanic features on Earth. They consist of multiple layers of solidified flood basalt that together are more than 2,000 m thick and cover an area of 500,000 km^2. The term 'trap', used in geology for such rock formations, is derived from the Swedish word for stairs (trappa, or sometimes trapp), referring to the step-like hills forming the landscape of the region.
   a. 1703 Genroku earthquake
   b. Deccan Traps
   c. 1509 Istanbul earthquake
   d. 1700 Cascadia earthquake

34. The _____ is a major Late Cretaceous large igneous province located in the Arctic. It includes the Ellesmere Island Volcanics, Strand Fiord Formation, Alpha Ridge, Franz Josef Land and Svalbard.
   a. High Arctic Large Igneous Province
   b. North Atlantic Igneous Province
   c. Circum-Superior Belt
   d. Kerguelen Plateau

35. The _____ is an underwater volcanic large igneous province in the Indian Ocean. It lies about 3,000 km to the southwest of Australia and is nearly three times the size of Japan. The plateau extends for more than 2,200 km in a northwest-southeast direction and lies in deep water.

The plateau was produced by the Kerguelen hotspot, starting with or following the breakup of Gondwanaland about 130 million years ago. There is a small portion of the plateau that breaks sea level, forming the Kerguelen Islands, Heard Island and the McDonald Islands. Intermittent volcanism continues on Heard and McDonald islands.

a. North Atlantic Igneous Province
b. Circum-Superior Belt
c. High Arctic Large Igneous Province
d. Kerguelen Plateau

36. _____ is the oldest seamount in the Hawaiian-Emperor seamount chain, with an estimated age of 82 million years. It lies at the northernmost end of the chain, and is perched at the outer slope of the Kuril-Kamchatka Trench. Like the rest of the Emperor seamounts, it was formed by the Hawaii hotspot volcanism, grew to become an island, and has since subsided to below sea level, all while being carried first north and now northwest by the motion of the Pacific Plate.

a. Meiji Seamount
b. 1700 Cascadia earthquake
c. 1509 Istanbul earthquake
d. 1703 Genroku earthquake

37. The _____ is a group of two diatremes in Northern Alberta, Canada. It formed during a period of kimberlite volcanism about 77 million years ago. Other nearby kimberlite clusters include the Birch Mountains kimberlite field and the Buffalo Head Hills kimberlite field.

a. Hope Bay greenstone belt
b. 1509 Istanbul earthquake
c. 1700 Cascadia earthquake
d. Mountain Lake cluster

38. The _____ is a huge oceanic plateau located in the Pacific Ocean, lying north of the Solomon Islands. The plateau covers an area of approximately 2,000,000 km², or roughly the size of Alaska, and it reaches a thickness of up to 30 km. The plateau is of volcanic origin, composed mostly of flood basalts. Although they are now separated by thousands of kilometres, Manihiki Plateau and Hikurangi Plateau were then part of the same large igneous province, forming the world's largest oceanic plateau. It extruded some 100 million km³ of magma, covering approximately 1% of the Earth's surface, in the largest volcanic event on Earth in at least the last 200 million years.

a. AL 129-1
b. AL 333
c. AASHTO Soil Classification System
d. Ontong Java Plateau

39. The _____ is a field of diatremes located in the James Bay lowlands, Northern Ontario, Canada. It is thought to have formed about 180 million years ago when the North American Plate moved westward over a center of upwelling magma called the New England hotspot, also referred to as the Great Meteor hotspot.

a. AASHTO Soil Classification System
b. AL 333
c. AL 129-1
d. Attawapiskat kimberlite field

40. The _____ was formed during the breakup of Pangaea during the Mesozoic Era. The initial breakup of Pangaea in early Jurassic time provided a legacy of basaltic dikes, sills, and lavas over a vast area around the present central North Atlantic Ocean.

Although some connections among these basalts had long been recognized, in 1988 they were linked as constituting a single major flood basalt province[Rampino and Stothers].

a. High Arctic Large Igneous Province
b. Kerguelen Plateau
c. North Atlantic Igneous Province
d. Central Atlantic Magmatic Province

41. A _____ or dyke in geology is a type of sheet intrusion referring to any geologic body that cuts discordantly across

- planar wall rock structures, such as bedding or foliation
- massive rock formations, like igneous/magmatic intrusions and salt diapirs.

They can therefore be either intrusive or sedimentary in origin.

An intrusive _____ is an igneous body with a very high aspect ratio, which means that its thickness is usually much smaller than the other two dimensions. Thickness can vary from sub-centimeter scale to many meters and the lateral dimensions can extend over many kilometers. A _____ is an intrusion into an opening cross-cutting fissure, shouldering aside other pre-existing layers or bodies of rock; this implies that a _____ is always younger than the rocks that contain it.

a. Pneumatolysis
b. Duricrust
c. Detritus
d. Dike

42. The _____ is a major Late Jurassic dike swarm extending over 373 miles (600 km) from the eastern Transverse Ranges northward to the east-central Sierra Nevada in southeastern California, United States. The swarm consists of hundreds of dikes, filled with mafic to felsic rocks and are individually about 10 feet (3 m) in width. These dikes may be the roots of linear-fissure-array supervolcanoes.

a. AL 333
b. Independence Dike Swarm
c. AASHTO Soil Classification System
d. AL 129-1

43. The _____ together comprise a major flood basalt province, most of which is found in South Africa and Antarctica, although parts extend into South America, India, Australia and New Zealand. It formed just prior to the breakup of Gondwana about 183 million years ago; this timing corresponds to the early Toarcian anoxic event and the Pliensbachian-Toarcian extinction. The total original volume of the flow, which extends over a distance in excess of 6000 km (4000 km in Antarctica alone), was in excess of 2.5×10^6 km³.

a. 1703 Genroku earthquake
b. 1700 Cascadia earthquake
c. 1509 Istanbul earthquake
d. Karoo and Farrar provinces

44. _____ is a narrow north-south trending volcanic mountain range on the mainland portion of southwestern Nova Scotia, stretching from Brier Island to Cape Split. It forms the northern edge of the Annapolis Valley along the shore of the Bay of Fundy.

_____ rises dramatically from the valley floor and tapers somewhat more gradually to the north and west where it meets the coast, although many parts of this coast have vertical cliffs rising higher than 30 metres, most notably at Cape Split.

The ridge traces its history to the Triassic period when this part of Nova Scotia occupied the center of the supercontinent Pangaea. It is a 201 million year old sequence of tholeiitic basalts, which contains columnar jointing.

a. 1703 Genroku earthquake
b. 1509 Istanbul earthquake
c. 1700 Cascadia earthquake
d. North Mountain

45. The _____ are a mountain range in central Oregon. The _____ form the western end of the Blue Mountains province. The mountains were formed when Permian, Triassic, and Jurassic rocks were slowly uplift by volcanic eruptions to form the Clarno Formation.

During the Eocene epoch, central Oregon volcanoes deposited layers of lava and ash up to 1,000 feet thick over the area that is now the _____. Large mudflows called lahars were also common during that period. These mudflows often covered and preserved the plants and animals, resulting in fossil beds. Today, fossils of prehistoric trees, fruits, nuts, and flowers can be found in the _____ along with fossilized animals including horses, camels, rhinoceros, and hippopotamus.

a. Ochoco Mountains
b. AL 129-1
c. AL 333
d. AASHTO Soil Classification System

46. The _____ is a huge 50 million year old extinct caldera complex that spans across the BC-Yukon border in Canada. The caldera complex is surrounded by granitic rocks containing pendants.

It is located near the eastern contact of the Coast Plutonic Complex and the Whitehorse Trough.

The _____ was formed when the ancient Kula Plate was subducting under North America during the early Eocene period. Cataclysmic eruptions from the _____ were from vents along arcuate fracture systems that spewed out about 850 km^3 (200 cu mi) of glowing avalanches of pyroclastic rock called pyroclastic flows.

a. 1509 Istanbul earthquake
b. Bennett Lake Volcanic Complex
c. 1700 Cascadia earthquake
d. 1703 Genroku earthquake

47. A _____ is a cauldron-like volcanic feature usually formed by the collapse of land following a volcanic eruption such as the one at Yellowstone National Park. They are sometimes confused with volcanic craters.
a. 1703 Genroku earthquake
b. 1700 Cascadia earthquake
c. 1509 Istanbul earthquake
d. Caldera

48. The _____ is a large dissected caldera complex in the Chilcotin Group and Anahim Volcanic Belt in central British Columbia, Canada. It has a diameter of 60 km and is comprised mainly of Eocene felsic and mafic volcanic rocks. Rocks within the caldera range in composition from basalt to rhyolite.
a. 1700 Cascadia earthquake
b. 1703 Genroku earthquake
c. 1509 Istanbul earthquake
d. Clisbako Caldera Complex

49. The _____ is an early Eocene caldera complex, located 43 km west of Carcross and 32 km northeast of Mount Porsild in the Yukon Territory, Canada. The complex composes the Skukum Group. It is a northeast-trending complex of subaerial volcanic and volcaniclastic rocks covering 140 km^2.
a. 1509 Istanbul earthquake
b. Mount Skukum Volcanic Complex
c. 1703 Genroku earthquake
d. 1700 Cascadia earthquake

Chapter 17. Test Preparation Part 17 313

50. The _____ is a large igneous province estimated to be at least 1.3 >× 10^6 km^2 in area and 6.6 >× 10^6 km^3 in volume. Geographically, the _____ makes up all of the North Atlantic Ocean as well as the Paleocene and Eocene basalts of Greenland, Iceland, the United Kingdom, Denmark, Norway and many of the islands located in the north eastern portion of the North Atlantic ocean.

Isotopic dating indicates the most active magmatic phase of the _____ was between ca. 60.5 and ca. 54.5 Ma (million years ago) (mid-Paleocene to early Eocene) - further divided into Phase 1 (pre-break-up phase) dated to ca. 62-58 Ma and Phase 2 (syn-break-up phase) dated to ca. 56-54 Ma.

   a. Kerguelen Plateau
   c. High Arctic Large Igneous Province
   b. Circum-Superior Belt
   d. North Atlantic Igneous Province

51. _____ is a small, uninhabited, rocky islet in the north Atlantic Ocean. It gives its name to one of the sea areas named in the Shipping Forecast, provided by the British Meteorological Office. It could be, in James Fisher's words, 'the most isolated small rock in the oceans of the world'.

_____ is made of a type of granite that is relatively rich in sodium and potassium. Within this granite are darker bands richer in the alkali pyroxene mineral aegirine and the alkali amphibole mineral riebeckite. The dark bands are a type of granite that geologists have named 'rockallite', although use of this term is now discouraged. In 1975, a new mineral was discovered on _____. The mineral is called bazirite, (chemical composition $BaZrSi_3O_9$), named after the elements barium and zirconium. _____ was formed approximately 55 million years ago, when the ancient continent of Laurasia was split apart by plate tectonics.

   a. Rockall
   c. 1509 Istanbul earthquake
   b. Logarithmic Spiral Beach
   d. Historical geology

52. _____ is a range of volcanic mountains in Lincoln and Otero counties of south-central New Mexico. The range is about 40 miles from north to south and 20 miles wide, and is dominated by _____ Peak, whose highest point is at 12,005 feet The peak is located 10 miles west-northwest of Ruidoso and 30 miles north-northeast of Alamogordo.

_____ is a massive complex of volcanic rocks including pyroclastic materials, lava flows, and intrusions. An ancient and heavily eroded volcanic pile, it is the largest mid-Tertiary volcanic complex east of the Rio Grande with an estimated volume of erupted products of 185 cubic miles (770 km^3).

   a. Sierra Blanca
   c. 1703 Genroku earthquake
   b. 1700 Cascadia earthquake
   d. 1509 Istanbul earthquake

53. The _____ are a rugged mass of mountains in Ethiopia, Eritrea (which is sometimes referred to as the Eritrean Highlands), and northern Somalia (Somaliland) in the Horn of Africa.

The _____ began to rise 75 million years ago, as magma from the earth's mantle uplifted a broad dome of the ancient rocks of the African Craton. The opening of the Great Rift Valley split the dome of the _____ into three parts; the mountains of the southern Arabian Peninsula are geologically part of the ancient _____, separated by the rifting which created the Red Sea and Gulf of Aden and separated Africa from Arabia.

a. AASHTO Soil Classification System
c. Ethiopian Highlands
b. AL 333
d. AL 129-1

54. _____ is a large volcanic caldera located in the San Juan volcanic field in the San Juan Mountains in southwestern Colorado, United States, to the west of the town of La Garita, Colorado. The eruption that created the _____ was, perhaps, the largest known explosive eruption in all of Earth's history.

The _____ is one of a number of calderas that formed during a massive ignimbrite flare-up in Colorado, Utah and Nevada from 40-25 million years ago, and was the site of truly enormous eruptions about 28-26 million years ago, during the Oligocene Epoch.

a. 1509 Istanbul earthquake
c. Sierra Grande
b. 1700 Cascadia earthquake
d. La Garita Caldera

55. _____, (Navajo: >Ts>é Bit'a'>í, 'rock with wings' or 'winged rock') is a rock formation rising nearly 1,800 feet (550 m) above the high-desert plain on the Navajo Nation and in San Juan County, New Mexico.

_____ is composed of fractured volcanic breccia and black dikes of igneous rock called 'minette'. It is the erosional remnant of the throat of a volcano, and the volcanic breccia formed in a diatreme. The exposed rock probably was originally formed 2,500-3000 feet (750-1,000 meters) below the earth's surface, but it was exposed after millions of years of erosion. Wall-like sheets of minette, known as dikes, radiate away from the central formation. Radiometric age determinations of the minette establish that these volcanic rocks solidified about 27 million years ago.

a. 1700 Cascadia earthquake
c. 1703 Genroku earthquake
b. 1509 Istanbul earthquake
d. Shiprock

56. _____ is an island in the outer Firth of Clyde, Scotland where granite was quarried to make curling stones.

The island is located approximately 16 km west of Girvan. 2 miles in circumference and rising to 338 metres, the island consists entirely of a volcanic plug of an extinct volcano that might have been active about 500 million years ago.

a. AL 129-1
c. AL 333
b. AASHTO Soil Classification System
d. Ailsa Craig

57. The _____ is a large and wide eroded Late Devonian caldera complex, located in the northern Appalachian Mountains of southwestern New Brunswick, Canada. It is one of few noticeable pre-Cenozoic calderas, and its formation is associated to a period of crustal thinning that followed the Acadian orogeny in the northern Appalachian Mountains. It sits relatively near to the coastline.

a. 1700 Cascadia earthquake
c. 1509 Istanbul earthquake
b. 1703 Genroku earthquake
d. Mount Pleasant Caldera

58. The _____ constitute a flood basalt volcanic province in southwestern China, centered in Sichuan province. It is sometimes referred to as the Permian Emeishan Large Igneous Province or variations of that term.

Like other volcanic provinces or 'traps,' the _____ are multiple layers of igneous rock laid down by large mantle plume volcanic eruptions.The eruptions that produced the _____ began c. 260 million years ago (Ma). In volume, the _____ are dwarfed by the massive Siberian Traps, which occurred, in terms of the geological time scale, not long after, at c. 251 Ma. Nonetheless the _____ eruptions were serious enough to have global ecological and paleontological impact. The _____ are associated with the so-called end-Guadalupian or end-Capitanian mass extinction, the extinction of animal and plant life that occurred at the end of the Capitanian stage of the Guadalupian epoch of the Permian period.

   a. AASHTO Soil Classification System
   c. AL 333
   b. AL 129-1
   d. Emeishan Traps

59. The _____ Fossil Beds are an important paleontological site located on _____ Station in Central Australia, 200km north-east of Alice Springs. It is notable for the occurrence of well-preserved, rare, Tertiary vertebrate fossils, which provide evidence of the evolution of the Northern Territorye;s fauna and climate. The _____ Fossil Beds are also significant as a research and teaching site for palaeontology students.
   a. AL 129-1
   b. AL 333
   c. AASHTO Soil Classification System
   d. Alcoota

60. The _____ is an orogenic phase in the Tertiary that formed the mountain ranges of the Alpide belt. These mountains include the Atlas, the Pyrenees, the Alps, the Dinaric Alps, the Hellenides, the Carpathians, the Balkan, the Taurus, the Caucasus, the Alborz, the Zagros, the Hindu Kush, the Pamir, the Karakoram, and the Himalayas. Sometimes other names occur to describe the formation of separate mountain ranges: for example Carpathean orogeny for the Carpathians, Hellenic orogeny for the Hellenides or the Himalayan orogeny for the Himalayas.
   a. Orogeny
   b. Alpine orogeny
   c. Alleghenian orogeny
   d. AASHTO Soil Classification System

61. _____ refers to natural mountain building, and may be studied as a tectonic structural event, (b) as a geographical event, and (c) a chronological event. Orogenic events (a) cause distinctive structural phenomena and related tectonic activity, (b) affect certain regions of rocks and crust, and (c) happen within a specific period of time.
   a. Alleghenian orogeny
   b. Orogeny
   c. Alpine orogeny
   d. AASHTO Soil Classification System

62. The _____ Era, is the most recent of the three classic geological eras and covers the period from 65.5 million years ago to the present. It is marked by the Cretaceous-Tertiary extinction event at the end of the Cretaceous that saw the demise of the last non-avian dinosaurs and the end of the Mesozoic Era. The _____ era is ongoing.
   a. 1703 Genroku earthquake
   b. 1509 Istanbul earthquake
   c. 1700 Cascadia earthquake
   d. Cenozoic

63. The _____ was a fragment of the older, Phoenix Plate. The _____ was subducting under West Antarctica. The subduction of the _____ stopped before 83 Ma, and became fused onto the Antarctic Peninsula.
   a. 1700 Cascadia earthquake
   b. 1509 Istanbul earthquake
   c. 1703 Genroku earthquake
   d. Charcot Plate

64. The _____ epoch (55.8 >± 0.2 - 33.9 >± 0.1 Ma) is a major division of the geologic timescale and the second epoch of the Palaeogene period in the Cenozoic era. The _____ spans the time from the end of the Paleocene epoch to the beginning of the Oligocene epoch. The start of the _____ is marked by the emergence of the first modern mammals.
   a. AL 333
   b. Eocene
   c. AASHTO Soil Classification System
   d. AL 129-1

65. The _____ was an ancient oceanic plate, which began subducting under the west coast of the North American Plate-- then located in modern Utah-- as Pangaea broke apart during the Jurassic period. It is named for the Farallon Islands which are located just west of San Francisco, California.

Over time the central part of the _____ was completely subducted under the southwestern part of the North American Plate. The remains of the _____ are the Juan de Fuca, Explorer and Gorda Plates, subducting under the northern part of the North American Plate, the Cocos Plate subducting under Central America and the Nazca Plate subducting under the South American Plate.

   a. Rivera Plate
   b. Fault trace
   c. Sonoma orogeny
   d. Farallon Plate

66. The _____ was an ancient oceanic trench on the west coast of North America during the Late Cretaceous period. When the trench disappeared, it turned into the San Andreas Fault. Since then, it has spread out to the north and south.
   a. 1509 Istanbul earthquake
   b. 1703 Genroku earthquake
   c. 1700 Cascadia earthquake
   d. Farallon Trench

67. The _____ was an ancient oceanic plate that began subducting under the west-coast of North America around the early Cretaceous time. The _____ had a chain of active volcanic islands that were called the Insular Islands. These volcanic Islands however collided then fused onto the west-coast of North America when the _____ jammed then shut down ending the subduction zone.
   a. AL 333
   b. Insular Plate
   c. AASHTO Soil Classification System
   d. AL 129-1

68. The _____ is a New Zealand orogeny that has given birth to the Southern Alps. It began 25 million years ago along the Alpine Fault.

In this orogeny the Southern alps are being formed because the Pacific Plate is being pushed up over the Australian Plate. As the Pacific Plate rises over the Australian Plate it gains altitude, having the effect of giving birth to the Southern Alps.

   a. Pan-African orogeny
   b. Laramide orogeny
   c. Trans-Hudson orogeny
   d. Kaikoura Orogeny

69. The _____ or Palaeocene, 'early dawn of the recent' is a geologic epoch that lasted from 65.5 >± 0.3 Ma to 55.8 >± 0.2 Ma (million years ago.) It is the first epoch of the Palaeogene Period in the modern Cenozoic era. As with most other older geologic periods, the strata that define the epoch's beginning and end are well identified but the exact date of the end is uncertain.

a. 1509 Istanbul earthquake
b. 1703 Genroku earthquake
c. 1700 Cascadia earthquake
d. Paleocene

70. The _____ is the epoch from 1.8 million to 11550 years BP covering the world's recent period of repeated glaciations. The _____ epoch follows the Pliocene epoch and is followed by the Holocene epoch. The _____ is the third epoch of the Neogene period or 6th epoch of the Cenozoic Era. The end of the _____ corresponds with the retreat of the last continental glacier. It also corresponds with the end of the Paleolithic age used in archaeology.
a. Tyrrhenian
b. Sicilian Stage
c. Late Pleistocene
d. Pleistocene

71. The _____ Period is the geologic time period after the Neogene Period, spanning 1.805 +/- 0.005 million years ago to the present. The _____ includes two geologic epochs: the Pleistocene and the Holocene Epoch.

There is an ongoing debate of the status of _____ -- a recent proposal from International Commission on Stratigraphy (ICS) was to make _____ a subperiod under Neogene, but that was retracted after criticism from International Union for _____ Research (INQUA), so instead ICS and INQUA agreed to erect _____ as an Era, above Neogene, and to place the base for _____ at 2.588 >± 3.005, the base for Gelasian Stage.

a. Musgrave Block
b. Canadian Shield
c. Gawler craton
d. Quaternary

72. The _____ Eon is the current eon in the geologic timescale, and the one during which abundant animal life has existed. It covers roughly 545 million years and goes back to the time when diverse hard-shelled animals first appeared.
a. 1703 Genroku earthquake
b. 1700 Cascadia earthquake
c. 1509 Istanbul earthquake
d. Phanerozoic

73. The _____, which occurred approximately 65.5 million years ago (Ma), was a large-scale mass extinction of animal and plant species in a geologically short period of time. Widely known as the K-T extinction event, it is associated with a geological signature known as the K-T boundary, usually a thin band of sedimentation found in various parts of the world. K is the traditional abbreviation for the Cretaceous Period derived from the German name Kreidezeit, and T is the abbreviation for the Tertiary Period .
a. 1700 Cascadia earthquake
b. 1703 Genroku earthquake
c. Cretaceous-Tertiary extinction event
d. 1509 Istanbul earthquake

74. The _____ is a geological signature, usually a thin band, dated to (65.5 ± 0.3) Ma (million years ago). The boundary marks the end of the Mesozoic era and the beginning of the Cenozoic era, and is associated with the Cretaceous-Tertiary extinction event, a mass extinction.
a. 1509 Istanbul earthquake
b. 1700 Cascadia earthquake
c. Shiva crater
d. K-T boundary

75. The _____ is an impact crater in the Kirovohrad Oblast province of Ukraine. The crater is 24 km in diameter and its age of 65.17 ± 0.64 million years, based on argon dating techniques, is within error of that of Chicxulub Crater in Mexico, and the KT boundary. The Chicxulub impact is believed to have caused the mass extinction at the end of the Cretaceous era, which included the extinction of the dinosaurs.

a. 1700 Cascadia earthquake
b. 1509 Istanbul earthquake
c. Shiva crater
d. Boltysh crater

76. The _____ is an ancient impact crater buried underneath the Yucatán Peninsula in Mexico. The crater is more than 180 kilometers (110 mi) in diameter, making the feature one of the largest confirmed impact structures in the world; the impacting bolide that formed the crater was at least 10 km (6 mi) in diameter.

a. 1703 Genroku earthquake
b. 1509 Istanbul earthquake
c. Chicxulub crater
d. 1700 Cascadia earthquake

77. The _____ is a sea floor structure located beneath the Indian Ocean, west of Mumbai, India.

Its age is estimated to around 65 million years ago, at about the same time as a number of other impact craters and the Cretaceous-Tertiary extinction event (K-T boundary). Although the site has shifted since its formation because of sea floor spreading, the formation is approximately 600 kilometers long by 400 km wide. It is estimated that a crater of that size would have been made by an asteroid or comet approximately 40 km in diameter. The _____ adds weight to the theory that the K-T extinction was caused by a massive asteroid fragmenting and hitting the Earth in several locations, known as the 'Multiple impact theory.'

a. 1700 Cascadia earthquake
b. Shiva crater
c. K-T boundary
d. 1509 Istanbul earthquake

78. The _____ Era is one of three geologic eras of the Phanerozoic eon. The division of time into eras dates back to Giovanni Arduino, in the 18th century, although his original name for the era now called the '_____' was 'Secondary' (making the modern era the 'Tertiary'.)

The _____ was a time of tectonic, climatic and evolutionary activity. The continents gradually shifted from a state of connectedness into their present configuration; the drifting provided for speciation and other important evolutionary developments.

a. 1700 Cascadia earthquake
b. Mesozoic
c. 1703 Genroku earthquake
d. 1509 Istanbul earthquake

79. _____ was an ancient microcontinent or terrane whose history formed much of the older rocks of Western Europe, Atlantic Canada, and parts of the coastal United States.

The early development of _____ is believed to have been in volcanic arcs near a subduction zone on the margin of Gondwana. Some material may have accreted from volcanic island arcs which formed further out in the ocean and later collided with Gondwana as a result of plate tectonic movements.

a. AASHTO Soil Classification System
b. AL 333
c. AL 129-1
d. Avalonia

80. _____ is a large island that existed in the area of Europe in the Mesozoic era. In later continental drift and orogeny it became most of Spain and Portugal.

a. Andrija Mohorovičić
b. Ambulocetus
c. Amblypoda
d. Cantabria

81. The _____ is an ancient tectonic plate that comprises parts of present-day Anatolia, Iran, Afghanistan, Tibet, Indochina and Malaya regions. The _____ was formerly part of the ancient supercontinent of Pangaea. Pangaea was shaped like a vast 'C', facing east, and inside of the 'C' was the Paleo-Tethys Ocean.
   a. Cimmerian Plate
   b. Solomon Sea Plate
   c. Nazca Plate
   d. Kermadec Plate

82. The _____ , usually abbreviated K for its German translation Kreide, is a geologic period and system from circa >145.5 >± 4 to >65.5 >± 0.3 million years ago . In the geologic timescale, the _____ follows on the Jurassic period and is followed by the Paleogene period. It is the youngest period of the Mesozoic era, and at 80 million years long, the longest period of the Phanerozoic eon. The end of the _____ defines the boundary between the Mesozoic and Cenozoic eras.
   a. Hauterivian
   b. Coniacian
   c. Santonian
   d. Cretaceous

83. _____ was a minor supercontinent created in the Devonian as the result of a collision between the Laurentian, Baltica and Avalonia cratons (Caledonian orogeny).

_____ became a part of the major supercontinent Pangaea in the Permian. In the Jurassic, when Pangaea rifted into two continents, Gondwana and Laurasia, _____ was a part of Laurasia.

   a. Ur
   b. Euramerica
   c. Atlantica
   d. Asiamerica

84. _____ , originally Gondwanaland is the name given to a southern precursor-supercontinent and then as a remnant separated from Laurasia 180->200 million years ago during the breakup of the Pangaea supercontinent that existed about 500 to 200 Ma ago into two large segments. While the corresponding northern hemisphere continent Laurasia moved further north, the nearly equal in area _____ included most of the landmasses in today's southern hemisphere, including Antarctica, South America, Africa, Madagascar, Australia-New Guinea, and New Zealand, as well as Arabia and the Indian subcontinent, which have now moved into the Northern Hemisphere.
   a. 1703 Genroku earthquake
   b. 1509 Istanbul earthquake
   c. 1700 Cascadia earthquake
   d. Gondwana

85. The _____ is an oceanic tectonic plate under the northern Pacific Ocean south of the Near Islands segment of the Aleutian Islands. It is subducting under the North American Plate at the Aleutian Trench and is surrounded by the Pacific Plate. There is a portion of the _____ at the surface in the southern Bering Sea.
   a. Manus Plate
   b. Conway Reef Plate
   c. North Bismarck Plate
   d. Kula Plate

86. _____ was a supercontinent that most recently existed as a part of the split of the Pangaean supercontinent in the late Mesozoic era. It included most of the landmasses which make up today's continents of the northern hemisphere, chiefly Laurentia (the name given to the North American craton), Baltica, Siberia, Kazakhstania, and the North China and East China cratons.

a. 1509 Istanbul earthquake
b. Laurasia
c. 1700 Cascadia earthquake
d. 1703 Genroku earthquake

87. _____ was a separate tectonic plate in the Mesozoic. It collided with Eurasia during Cretaceous forming the present-day southern Tibet.
   a. Conway Reef Plate
   b. Niuafo'ou Plate
   c. South Bismarck Plate
   d. Lhasa Plate

88. _____ was the vast global ocean that surrounded the supercontinent Pangaea, during the late Paleozoic and the early Mesozoic eras. It included the Pacific Ocean to the west and north and the Tethys Ocean to the southeast. It became the Pacific Ocean, following the closing of the Tethys basin and the breakup of Pangaea, which created the Atlantic, Arctic, and Indian Ocean basins.
   a. Panthalassa
   b. Mirovia
   c. Subduction
   d. Thrust fault

89. The _____ is a large northeast trending Mesozoic diabase dike in southeastern Nova Scotia, Canada. It is 140 km (87 mi) long, although some evidence suggests it extends a further 60 km (37 mi) to the northeast to Sambro Island.
   a. 1700 Cascadia earthquake
   b. 1509 Istanbul earthquake
   c. 1703 Genroku earthquake
   d. Shelburne dike

90. The _____ is the earliest of three geologic eras of the Phanerozoic eon. The _____ spanned from roughly 542 to 251 million years ago (ICS, 2004), and is subdivided into six geologic periods; from oldest to youngest they are: the Cambrian, Ordovician, Silurian, Devonian, Carboniferous, and Permian.

The _____ covers the time from the first appearance of abundant, soft-shelled fossils to the time when the continents were beginning to be dominated by large, relatively sophisticated reptiles and modern plants. The lower (oldest) boundary was classically set at the first appearance of creatures known as trilobites and archeocyathids.

   a. Paleozoic
   b. 1703 Genroku earthquake
   c. 1700 Cascadia earthquake
   d. 1509 Istanbul earthquake

91. The _____ was an ancient tectonic plate that existed from the Cambrian period to the Carboniferous period. The _____ collided against Siberia, to form the Ural Mountains about 500 million years ago. The _____, however, fused onto the Eurasian Plate when the _____ collided against Siberia when the Ural Mountains were completely formed.
   a. Baltic Plate
   b. Sonoma orogeny
   c. Farallon Plate
   d. Fault trace

92. _____ is a name applied by geologists to a late-Proterozoic, early-Palaeozoic continent that now includes the East European craton of northwestern Eurasia. _____ was created as an entity not earlier than 1.8 billion years ago. Before this time, the three segments/continents that now comprise the East European craton were in different places on the globe. _____ existed on a tectonic plate called the Baltic Plate.
   a. Cimmeria
   b. Congo craton
   c. Baltica
   d. Laurentia

93. _____ was an ancient microcontinent or terrane whose history affected many of the older rocks of central Chile and western Argentina. It was once separated by oceanic crust from the Cuyania terrane to which it accreted at ~420-390 Ma when Cuyania was already amalgamated with Gondwana.

a. 1509 Istanbul earthquake
b. Chilenia
c. 1703 Genroku earthquake
d. 1700 Cascadia earthquake

94. _____ is a small continental region in the interior of Asia. It consists of that area north and east of the Aral Sea, south of the Siberian craton and west of the Altai Mountains and Lake Balkhash. Politically, it comprises most of Kazakhstan and has a total area of around 1.3 million km^2.

It is believed that present-day _____ is chiefly a collage of early Paleozoic volcanic island arcs and some small continental terranes. These were joined together during the Ordovician to form what was at the time an isolated continent of its own.

a. 1509 Istanbul earthquake
b. 1700 Cascadia earthquake
c. Kazakhstania
d. 1703 Genroku earthquake

95. The _____ was an ancient Paleozoic ocean. It was located between the paleocontinent Gondwana and the so called Hunic terranes. These are divided into the European Hunic (today the crust under parts of Central Europe (called 'Armorica') and Iberia) and Asiatic Hunic (today the crust of China and parts of eastern Central Asia.)

a. Paleo-Tethys Ocean
b. Paratethys
c. Sundance Sea
d. Slide Mountain Ocean

96. _____, are extinct marine animals that make up the class Paracrinoidea of the echinoderms (phylum Echinodermata), and are closely related to crinoids. They lived in shallow seas during the Early Ordovician through the Early Silurian.

_____ are characterized by a mouth with two to five feeding arms arranged asymmetrically.

a. Heuweltjies
b. Macrofossils
c. Phosphatic fossilization
d. Paracrinoids

97. _____ is a taxonomic hypothesis uniting a group of extinct, herbivorous mammals. They were considered a suborder of the primitive ungulate mammals and have since been shown to represent a polyphyletic group.

The _____ take their name from their short and stumpy feet, which were furnished with five toes each and supported massive pillar-like limbs.

a. Ambulocetus
b. Amblypoda
c. Canadian
d. Andrija Mohorovičić

98. _____ was an early cetacean from Pakistan that could walk as well as swim. It lived during early Eocene some 50-49 million years ago. It is a transitional fossil that shows how whales evolved from land-living mammals.

a. Canadian
b. Andrija Mohorovičić
c. Amblypoda
d. Ambulocetus

99. _____ mongoliensis, was a basal, heavily-built, wolf-like, hoofed mammal that lived during the Eocene epoch, roughly between 45 and 36 million years ago. It walked on four short legs and had a long body, a long tail, and feet with hoofed toes. It had a long snout with large, sharp teeth and flat cheek teeth that may have been used to crush bones.
   a. AL 129-1
   b. AL 333
   c. AASHTO Soil Classification System
   d. Andrewsarchus

100. _____ is an extinct genus of an early proboscidean from the middle Eocene of the Upper Kuldana Formation of Kohat, Punjab Province, Pakistan.

The size of a small tapir, it lived in a marshy environment and fed on soft aquatic plants. It is the largest known anthracobunid.

   a. AL 129-1
   b. AASHTO Soil Classification System
   c. AL 333
   d. Anthracobune

101. _____ is a genus of extinct louvar that lived in the Tethys Ocean during the early Paleogene. The first specimens were found from the Danata Formation Lagerst>ätten, of the Thanetian epoch of Turkmenistan, where they were originally thought to be smaller or juvenile individuals of the true louvar, Luvarus necopinatus. These specimens were later reexamined, and determined to be a separate genus comprising of two different species.
   a. AL 129-1
   b. AASHTO Soil Classification System
   c. AL 333
   d. Avitoluvarus

102. _____ is a genus of cetacean that lived from 40 to 34 million years ago in the Eocene. Its fossilized remains were first discovered in the southern United States (Louisiana), and were initially believed to be some sort of reptilian sea monster, hence the suffix -'saurus', but later it was found that wasn't the case. Fossils from at least two other species of this taxon have been found in Egypt and Pakistan.
   a. Kutchicetus
   b. Himalayacetus
   c. Protocetus
   d. Basilosaurus

103. _____ is a family of extinct mammals belonging to the order Perissodactyla, the order that includes horses, rhinos, and tapirs. Superficially they looked rather like rhinoceroses, although they were not true rhinos and are probably most closely related to horses. They lived around 56-34 million years ago, throughout the entirety of the Eocene and into the very earliest part of the Oligocene.
   a. 1700 Cascadia earthquake
   b. 1509 Istanbul earthquake
   c. 1703 Genroku earthquake
   d. Brontotheriidae

104. The _____ are a taxon of extinct mammals that lived from the Cretaceous to the Eocene. They were some of the more derived members of the extinct order Multituberculata. They probably lived something of a rodent-like existence until their ecological niche was assumed by true rodents.
   a. Taeniolabidoidea
   b. Microcosmodon
   c. Parectypodus
   d. Cimolodonta

Chapter 18. Test Preparation Part 18

1. _____ is an extinct genus of mammal. It was widespread in North America between 59 and 51 million years ago. It is regarded as the ancestor of the genus Hypercoryphodon of Mid Eocene Mongolia.
   a. Coryphodon
   b. 1700 Cascadia earthquake
   c. 1509 Istanbul earthquake
   d. Hsanotherium

2. _____ is an extinct genus of early proboscidean that lived during the early Eocene (Ypresian) some 55 million yers ago of North Africa.

Remains of this animal which consist of fragments of jaws and teeth have been found in the Ouled Abdoun Basin in Morocco. Of the size of a tapir weight, 300 kilograms is the earliest large mammal known from Africa and one of the oldest known proboscidean.

   a. 1509 Istanbul earthquake
   b. Daouitherium
   c. 1700 Cascadia earthquake
   d. Numidotherium

3. _____ is the earliest known entelodont, from the Middle Eocene of China. It was a very small entelodont, about the size of a modern pig, and was slightly smaller than its North American counterpart, Brachyhyops.
   a. Eoentelodon
   b. AL 129-1
   c. AASHTO Soil Classification System
   d. AL 333

4. _____ bondei is a species of extinct bony fish once identified as being a luvar from the Fuller's Earth Ypresian formation of the Barmer District of Rajasthan, India. Later, better specimens were found, and E. bondei was reappraised as being a relative of the prehistoric spadefish, Exellia.
   a. AL 333
   b. AL 129-1
   c. AASHTO Soil Classification System
   d. Eoluvarus

5. _____ is the earliest known true (and scaled) pangolin from the Middle Eocene of Europe. Fossils collected from the Messel Pit, Germany, indicate that this 50 cm long animal was rather similar to living pangolins. However, unlike modern pangolins, its tail and legs did not bear scales.
   a. AASHTO Soil Classification System
   b. AL 333
   c. AL 129-1
   d. Eomanis

6. _____ is the genus of two known early Old World primates that was discovered in 1994 in China. These species are among the oldest known member of the Catarrhini suborder (the group that includes all of the Old World primates, including humans) to date, at about 45-42 million years old during the Eocene. Only a few specimens have been uncovered and scientists assume that _____ looks like today's marmosets from South America.
   a. AL 129-1
   b. AASHTO Soil Classification System
   c. AL 333
   d. Eosimias

7. _____ is a extinct genus of bony fish from the Eocene. It contains one species, _____ daniltshenkoi. Its fossils have been found in Turkmenistan.
   a. AL 333
   b. AASHTO Soil Classification System
   c. AL 129-1
   d. Eospinus

8. _____ is a genus of extinct spadefish that lived in the Tethys Ocean during the early Paleogene. The adult form is shaped akin to a large spadefish or a short dolphinfish, with very large pelvic fins, and a long dorsal fin starting from in front of the eyes to near the base of the caudal peduncle. The juvenile form resembles a juvenile drumfish, with the dorsal fin forming a long crest on top of the head.
   a. Exellia
   b. AL 129-1
   c. AL 333
   d. AASHTO Soil Classification System

9. _____ , formerly Diatryma, is an extinct genus of large flightless bird that lived during the late Paleocene and Eocene periods of the Cenozoic. It was named in 1855, after Gaston Plant>é, who had discovered the first fossils in Argile Plastique formation deposits at Meudon near Paris (France.) At that time, Plant>é (described as a 'studious young man full of zeal') was at the start of his academic career, and his remarkable discovery was soon to be overshadowed by his subsequent achievements in physics.
   a. 1509 Istanbul earthquake
   b. 1700 Cascadia earthquake
   c. Gastornis
   d. 1703 Genroku earthquake

10. _____ is an extinct genus of lemur-like prosimians belonging to the Adapidae family. It lived during the Eocene epoch (49 million years ago), and its fossils have been found in the Messel Pit, Germany, showing that it already exhibited hominid features that would help make the primates such a successful group. It is one of the earliest-known primates, but the origins of the group remain controversial: some claim that the oldest primate is 70 million years old, but this is based on a single fossilized tooth.
   a. 1703 Genroku earthquake
   b. 1700 Cascadia earthquake
   c. Godinotia
   d. 1509 Istanbul earthquake

11. _____ was a genus of otter-like mesonychid from the Late Paleocene to Early Eocene some 55 million years ago. Although the first fossils were found in Eocene strata of Wyoming, the genus originated in Mongolia, as the oldest species is H. dux, which was found in Late Paleocene strata in the Naran Bulak Formation The genus is suggested to be related to the Archaeoceti, such as Pakicetus, due to extreme similarities between the skull and teeth anatomies of the two genera.
   a. Mesonychidae
   b. Hapalodectes
   c. Hapalodectidae
   d. Triisodontidae

12. _____ is an extinct family of relatively small-bodied (1-8 kg) mesonychian placental mammals from the Paleocene and Eocene of North America and Asia. Hapalodectids differ from the larger and better-known mesonychids in having teeth specialized for cutting (presumably meat), while the teeth of other mesonychids, such as Mesonyx or Sinonyx, are more specialized for crushing bones. Hapalodectids were once considered a subfamily of Mesonychidae, but the discovery of a skull of Hapalodectes hetangensis showed additional differences justifying placement in a distinct family.
   a. Mesonychidae
   b. Pachyaena
   c. Triisodontidae
   d. Hapalodectidae

13. _____ is an extinct genus of a group called Archaeoceti. _____ probably still had four limbs, and could probably walk on land. However, it probably hunted in shallow waters similar to crocodiles of today.
   a. Himalayacetus
   b. Protocetus
   c. Pakicetids
   d. Pakicetus

14. _____ is an extinct genus of early proboscidean from the middle Eocene, described in 2000 in the Pondaung Formation, Myanmar.

Chapter 18. Test Preparation Part 18

It is the first anthracobunid to be discovered outside India and Pakistan and to date is the smallest member of the family.

a. Pilgrimella
b. 1700 Cascadia earthquake
c. 1509 Istanbul earthquake
d. Hsanotherium

15. _____ was a genus of pakicetid whale, closely related to Pakicetus. It lived during the Early Eocene period 50 million years ago in Pakistan.
a. AASHTO Soil Classification System
b. AL 333
c. AL 129-1
d. Ichthyolestes

16. _____ is a primitive genus of the order Stomiiformes, and is an extinct relative of marine hatchetfish and viperfish. _____'s position in the order is in doubt, however, as scientists have not studied enough fossil specimens to determine exactly which stomiiforms the genus is most closely related to.

Their fossils are found in regions in northern Africa and Eurasia that correspond to the Tethys Ocean, and range from the Cenomanian epoch of the Cretaceous to the Lower Eocene, when they disappear from the fossil record altogether.

a. Idrissia
b. AASHTO Soil Classification System
c. AL 333
d. AL 129-1

17. _____ was an early Eocene 46 Ma cetacean from Pakistan that could walk as well as swim. It is a transitional fossil that shows how whales evolved from land-living mammals. It was a small animal, no larger than a river otter.
a. Himalayacetus
b. Pakicetus
c. Pakicetids
d. Kutchicetus

18. _____ is a species of extinct louvar that lived in the Tethys Ocean during the early Paleogene. It differs from the modern species, L. imperialis, in that _____ has an oval body shape, and is around one foot in length when fully grown.

The first specimens were found from the Danata Formation Lagerst>ätten, of the Thanetian to Ypresian epochs of Turkmenistan. _____ was originally described as 'Proluvarus necopinatus,' citing several anatomical differences between Proluvarus and Luvarus. A later reexamination of the fossil specimens lead researchers to reappraise Proluvarus as a junior synonym, as well as determine that specimens of what were originally thought to be juveniles were actually two different species of a different genus of louvar, Avitoluvarus.

a. 1700 Cascadia earthquake
b. 1703 Genroku earthquake
c. 1509 Istanbul earthquake
d. Luvarus necopinatus

19. _____ is a genus of early middle Eocene (ca. 47.5 mya) cetacean from Pakistan. The genus contains a single species _____ inuus described in 2009 on the basis of two specimens, including a pregnant female and its fetus. This represents the first description of a fetal skeleton of an archaeocete. The position of the fetus (head-first) suggests that these whales gave birth on land.

a. Protocetus
b. Pakicetids
c. Himalayacetus
d. Maiacetus

20. _____ was an early primate from the early Eocene, some 54-38 million years ago. Its fossil was found by Ferdinand V. Hayden in 1870 in southwestern Wyoming. When first found, _____ was thought to be a small pachyderm due to the concentration of pachyderm fossils in the area.

However, after Walter W. Granger's discovery of a nearly complete skeleton, also in Wyoming, it was firmly established as a primate. _____ most resembles modern-day Madagascar lemurs.

a. Notharctus tenebrosus
b. 1509 Istanbul earthquake
c. 1703 Genroku earthquake
d. 1700 Cascadia earthquake

21. _____ is an extinct genus of early proboscidean discovered in 1984, that lived during the middle Eocene some 46 million years ago of North Africa, weight 200 kilograms.

The type species, N. koholense is known from an almost complete skeleton from the site of El Kohol, southern Algeria dating from the early/middle Eocene period.

a. Phosphatherium
b. Numidotherium
c. 1700 Cascadia earthquake
d. 1509 Istanbul earthquake

22. _____ was a genus of heavily built, relatively short-legged mesonychids that originated from Asia. The species ranged in size from a coyote to a bear. During the height of their influence, the species of _____, like those of Dissacus before them, ranged from Europe to North America.

a. Mesonychidae
b. Hapalodectidae
c. Triisodontidae
d. Pachyaena

23. _____ are the members of the family Pakicetidae, sometimes called the subfamily Pakicetinae, of extinct mammals that are the earliest known cetaceans. While modern-day cetaceans are all water-dwelling animals such as whales and dolphins, the _____ pre-date the transition from land. Because their fossils were found near bodies of water, they are presumed to have spent part of their life in water.

a. Himalayacetus
b. Pakicetus
c. Protocetus
d. Pakicetids

24. _____ is a genus of extinct cetaceans found in the early Eocene (55.8 >± 0.2 - 33.9 >± 0.1 Ma) of Pakistan, hence their name. The strata where the fossils were found was then part of the coast of the Tethys Sea.

The first fossil, a lone skull, was thought to be a mesonychid, but Gingerich and Russell recognized it as an early cetacean from characteristic features of the inner ear, found only in cetaceans: the large auditory bulla is formed from the ectotympanic bone only.

a. Maiacetus
b. Protocetus
c. Pakicetus
d. Pakicetids

25. _____ is an obscure genus of brontothere.

Chapter 18. Test Preparation Part 18   327

The only known species is _____ latidentatus. It is represented only by a few tooth fragments from the middle Eocene Kuldana Formation, in the Ganda Kas area of Pakistan. Because this species is known only from a few tooth fragments it is difficult to compare it to other species to determine if it is indeed a distinct species and to what other species it is mostly closely related.

   a. 1700 Cascadia earthquake
   c. 1509 Istanbul earthquake
   b. Pakotitanops
   d. 1703 Genroku earthquake

26. _____ is a genus of extinct bird from the Wasachtian horizon of lower Eocene Wyoming, USA. One species, _____ howardae has been described.

It is a paleognathous bird, turkey - like in stature and size, that probably resembled a tinamou quite closely.

   a. 1700 Cascadia earthquake
   c. 1703 Genroku earthquake
   b. 1509 Istanbul earthquake
   d. Paracathartes

27. _____ is a genus of extinct mammal that lived from the Paleocene to the Eocene of North America. Some of the known fossil material may also be from the Upper Cretaceous. It was named by G.L. Jepsen in 1930.

It was a member of the extinct order of Multituberculata, and it lies within the suborder of Cimolodonta, family Neoplagiaulacidae.

   a. Mesodma
   c. Cimolodonta
   b. Parectypodus
   d. Ptilodontoidea

28. _____ is an extinct genus of primitive proboscidean that lived during the Paleocene to early Eocene some 56 million years ago of North Africa.

Known from fragmentary dentary materials from the paleocene (Thanetian) deposits of the Ouled Abdoun Basin, Morocco, it is the smallest (about 60 cm long and weight 15 kilograms) and the oldest known member of the proboscidean order. Like its later relative, Moeritherium, the animal was probably an amphibious browser that fed on aquatic plants, akin to a dog-sized hippopotamus.

   a. Phosphatherium
   c. 1700 Cascadia earthquake
   b. Numidotherium
   d. 1509 Istanbul earthquake

29. _____ is an extinct genus (early Eocene) of anthracobunid (early proto-elephant condylarth), ground dwelling grazer with massive molar cusps aligned in two transverse ridges. Remains (teeth) of this animal have been found in the Chorlakki locality, Punjab province, Pakistan as well as in the Subathu formation in North-West India. The genus is considered by some paleontologists as a synonym of Anthracobune.

   a. Hsanotherium
   c. 1700 Cascadia earthquake
   b. 1509 Istanbul earthquake
   d. Pilgrimella

30. _____ is a genus of mammals from the extinct order Multituberculata. It lived during the Upper Paleocene and the Lower Eocene in North America. The genus was formally named by G. L. Jepsen in 1940.

   a. Pentacosmodon
   b. Mesodma
   c. Cimolomyidae
   d. Prochetodon

31. _____ atavus ('first whale') is an extinct species of primitive cetacean from Egypt. It lived during the middle Eocene period 45 million years ago.

_____ had a streamlined, whale-like body around 2.5 metres (8.2 ft) long, but was relatively primitive in many respects; it still had small hind flippers, and its front flippers had webbed toes.

   a. Pakicetus
   b. Maiacetus
   c. Pakicetids
   d. Protocetus

32. _____ is an extinct spermatophyte group of the Plantae kingdom. Members of this division were predominant at the late Devonian, declined some >250 million years ago, and mostly disappeared by the Cretaceous, though fossil evidence indicates that they survived into the Eocene in Tasmania. The _____ have not yet acquired a clear position in botanical systematics and indeed appear to be a paraphyletic form taxon.

   a. 1509 Istanbul earthquake
   b. Petrified wood
   c. 1700 Cascadia earthquake
   d. Pteridospermatophyta

33. _____ is a group of extinct mammals from the Northern Hemisphere. They were generally small, somewhat rodent-like creatures of the extinct order Multituberculata.

Some of these genera boast a great many species, though remains are generally sparse.

   a. Prochetodon
   b. Microcosmodon
   c. Taeniolabidoidea
   d. Ptilodontoidea

34. _____ is an extinct genus of taeniodont mammal, and is the best known, and last genus of taeniodonts, lived some 45 million years ago during middle Eocene in North America.

The skull suggests it had a blunt face, and a very short snout. Species ranged in size from pigs to leopards, reached a body mass of up to 80 kilograms (180 lb.)

   a. Stylinodon
   b. 1509 Istanbul earthquake
   c. 1700 Cascadia earthquake
   d. 1703 Genroku earthquake

35. _____ probably belongs to the condylarth order: this is a primitive order of mammals which are ancestral to modern ungulates. It was Australia's only placental besides bats and rodents until millions of years later the arrival of the Dingo, horse, water buffalo, and more in Australia.

Lived: 55 million years ago (early Eocene) Size: Length (head to tail): 20cm Description: _____ was a small ground-dwelling mammal that ate insects and fruit.

a. Tingamarra
b. 1700 Cascadia earthquake
c. 1509 Istanbul earthquake
d. 1703 Genroku earthquake

36. _____ is an extinct family of mesonychian placental mammals. Most triisodontid genera lived during the early Paleocene in North America, but the genus Andrewsarchus is known from the late Eocene of Asia. Triisodontids were the first relatively large predatory mammals to appear in North America following the extinction of the dinosaurs.
a. Triisodontidae
b. Pachyaena
c. Hapalodectidae
d. Mesonychidae

37. The _____ was a subspecies of the Aurochs that lived in Northern Africa. It was probably a desert animal. Light colored, fine haired, and smaller than other Aurochs, its genes provide the basis for North African cattle and probably South of the Saharan cattle.
a. AL 333
b. African Aurochs
c. AASHTO Soil Classification System
d. AL 129-1

38. _____ fontoynonti is an extinct species of Malagasy lemur that was the largest primate to evolve on Madagascar. It weighed about 200kg and measured around 1.5m in height, more than a silverback gorilla. _____ is one of five known members of the Palaeopropithecinae subfamily, a part of the Indriidae family.
a. AASHTO Soil Classification System
b. Archaeoindris
c. AL 333
d. AL 129-1

39. The _____ was endemic to the island of Gran Canaria, part of the Canary Islands, Spain.

This rodent is only known from fossil remains. At different places on the centre of the island fossil remains were found, of which the youngest were dated back from shortly before Christ.

a. 1509 Istanbul earthquake
b. 1700 Cascadia earthquake
c. 1703 Genroku earthquake
d. Canary Islands Giant Rat

40. _____ are an extinct family of flightless birds comprising the genera Aepyornis and Mullerornis.

The _____, which were giant ratites native to Madagascar, have been extinct since at least the 17th century. >Étienne de Flacourt, a French governor of Madagascar in the 1640s and 1650s, recorded frequent sightings of _____.

a. AASHTO Soil Classification System
b. AL 333
c. AL 129-1
d. Elephant Birds

41. The _____ lived on Flores Island, Indonesia. MacPhee and Flemming assessed this species to be extinct in 1996, but believed it probably died out before 1500 A.D. This specimen is only known from a few subfossil fragments. It is the only member of the genus Spelaeomys.
a. 1700 Cascadia earthquake
b. 1703 Genroku earthquake
c. 1509 Istanbul earthquake
d. Flores Cave Rat

42. The _____ are an extinct group of large rodents known from fossil and subfossil material in the West Indies. One species, Amblyrhiza inundata, is estimated to have weighed between 50 and 200 kg (110 and 440 lb), big specimens being as large as an American Black Bear. This is much larger than Capybara, the largest rodent living today, but still much smaller than Josephoartigasia monesi, the largest rodent known.
   a. 1703 Genroku earthquake
   b. 1700 Cascadia earthquake
   c. 1509 Istanbul earthquake
   d. Giant hutias

43. The _____ is an extinct bird from the genus Aplonis within the Sturnidae family. It was endemic to the Polynesian island of Huahine and therefore it had the easternmost distribution of all Aplonis species in the Pacific region. The _____ is only known by a subfossil tarsometatarsus unearthed in 1984 by American archaeologist and anthropologist Yosihiko H. Sinoto of the Bernice P. Bishop Museum in the archaeological site of Fa'ahia in the north of Huahine and scientifically described by David Steadman in 1989.
   a. Huahine Starling
   b. 1700 Cascadia earthquake
   c. 1703 Genroku earthquake
   d. 1509 Istanbul earthquake

44. The _____, Malpaisomys insularis, is an extinct endemic rodent from the Canary Islands, Spain. It is the only species in the genus Malpaisomys.

The _____ is known from Holocene and Pleistocene deposits in the eastern Canary Islands, including Fuerteventura, Lanzarote and nearby islets.

   a. 1700 Cascadia earthquake
   b. 1509 Istanbul earthquake
   c. 1703 Genroku earthquake
   d. Lava Mouse

45. The _____ is an extinct flightless species of bunting. It was distinguishable by its long legs and short wings, and it inhabited the Canary Islands. It is one of the few flightless Passerines known to science, all of which are extinct.
   a. 1509 Istanbul earthquake
   b. 1700 Cascadia earthquake
   c. 1703 Genroku earthquake
   d. Long-legged Bunting

46. The _____ was a gigantic bird of prey that inhabited Madagascar until 1500 AD. Many scientists have pointed out that the bird shows many similarities with Haast's Eagle and it probably had a similar diet, feeding on the giant Elephant birds of the time It is also likely that giant lemurs were part of its diet. It was perhaps an apex predator of the Malagasy forests along with the Giant Fossa and the two species of crocodile.
   a. Malagasy Crowned Eagle
   b. Megaladapis
   c. 1509 Istanbul earthquake
   d. 1700 Cascadia earthquake

47. The _____ is an extinct member of the genus Telespiza in the family Fringillidae. It was endemic to the Hawaiian islands of Molokai and Maui. It is only known from fossil remains and likely became extinct before the first Europeans visited Hawaii in 1778.
   a. 1509 Istanbul earthquake
   b. 1700 Cascadia earthquake
   c. 1703 Genroku earthquake
   d. Maui Nui Finch

48. _____ is the genus of three extinct species of primates that once inhabited the island of Madagascar (the largest measured between 1.3 to 1.5 m/4 to 5 ft in length.)

The closest living relatives of this genus are the sportive lemurs (genus Lepilemur), and together the two genera make up the Lepilemuridae family. However, _____ was far different from any lemur.

   a. 1509 Istanbul earthquake
   b. Megaladapis
   c. Saint Croix Macaw
   d. 1700 Cascadia earthquake

49. _____ was a subfamily of crocodiles from Australia and the South Pacific that have now become extinct. They first appear in the fossil record in the Eocene in Australia, and survived until the Pleistocene in Australia and until the arrival of humans in the Pacific islands of Fiji, New Caledonia and Vanuatu. There is however disagreement on whether or not _____ is a subfamily within Crocodylidae, or a distinct family, Mekosuchidae, on its own within the superfamily Crocodyloidea.

   a. Mekosuchinae
   b. 1509 Istanbul earthquake
   c. 1703 Genroku earthquake
   d. 1700 Cascadia earthquake

Chapter 19. Test Preparation Part 19

1. The _____, Aegotheles novazelandiae, was a large species of owlet-nightjar (family Aegothelidae) formerly endemic to the islands of New Zealand. Fossil remains (which are common in the pellets of the extinct Laughing Owl) indicate the species was once widespread across both North Island and South Island. Despite a small number of reports of small owls being found in the 19th century that may have been New Zealand Owlet-nightjars, the species is thought to have become extinct around 1200 AD.

   a. 1703 Genroku earthquake
   b. 1700 Cascadia earthquake
   c. 1509 Istanbul earthquake
   d. New Zealand Owlet-nightjar

2. The _____ was a possible subspecies of the African Bush Elephant (Loxodonta africana) that existed in North Africa until becoming extinct in Ancient Roman times. These were the famous war elephants used by Carthage in the Punic Wars, their conflict with the Roman Republic. Although the subspecies has been formally described, it has not been widely recognized by taxonomists.

   a. 1509 Istanbul earthquake
   b. 1703 Genroku earthquake
   c. 1700 Cascadia earthquake
   d. North African Elephant

3. _____ is an extinct lemur that was found in central to southwestern Madagascar and known only from subfossil remains. It may have survived in the extreme south of Madagascar until as recently as 1280-1420 CE.

   a. 1509 Istanbul earthquake
   b. Pachylemur insignis
   c. 1700 Cascadia earthquake
   d. 1703 Genroku earthquake

4. _____ was an extinct genus of African wild cattle, which first appeared in the Pliocene, 2.5 million years ago, and became extinct during the Holocene, some 4,000 years ago.

   _____ was related to the African buffalo and closely resembled it except for its long, curved horns. The bony cores of the horns were each about 1 metre (3.3 ft) long; when covered with keratin (which does not survive fossilisation) they could have been up to twice this length.

   a. Pelorovis
   b. 1700 Cascadia earthquake
   c. 1509 Istanbul earthquake
   d. 1703 Genroku earthquake

5. The _____ is an extinct species of megapode. The fossil remains were found by Jean-Christophe Balouet and Storrs L. Olson in caves on New Caledonia and Tonga.

   With a weight of 3.5 kg, Megapodius molistructor was heavier than all existing megapodes.

   a. 1700 Cascadia earthquake
   b. 1509 Istanbul earthquake
   c. 1703 Genroku earthquake
   d. Pile-builder Megapode

6. The _____ is an extinct species of bird in the parrot family which is only known from sub-fossil bones found at two archeological sites on Saint Croix, U.S. Virgin Islands and central Puerto Rico. This medium sized species is one of two confirmed and named macaw species in the Caribbean, the other being the smaller Cuban Macaw (Ara tricolor.)

   The species was originally described by Wetmore from a sub-fossil left tibiotarsus of an immature bird found in the kitchen middens (dump for domestic waste) at Concordia, near Southwest Cape.

Chapter 19. Test Preparation Part 19

a. 1700 Cascadia earthquake
c. Megaladapis
b. Saint Croix Macaw
d. 1509 Istanbul earthquake

7. _____ is an extinct genus of galliform bird containing a single species, S. neocaledoniae, or erroneously, 'New Caledonian Giant Megapode'. Technically, the latter is incorrect because it has recently been found not to be a megapode, but the sole known member of its own family, the Sylviornithidae; at the time of its description, it was believed to be a ratite.
   a. 1703 Genroku earthquake
   c. 1509 Istanbul earthquake
   b. 1700 Cascadia earthquake
   d. Sylviornis

8. _____ is a member of a diverse group of primitive proboscideans called gomphotheres, a group that also gave rise to the modern elephants and their close relative the mammoth. _____ first appeared in the Great Plains and Gulf Coast regions of North America during the late Miocene, roughly between 9 and 8 million years ago, and apparently became extinct on this continent sometime around 6 million years ago. It managed to migrate to Asia via the Bering land bridge where it has been found in a number of late Miocene sites, particularly in China.
   a. AL 129-1
   c. AASHTO Soil Classification System
   b. AL 333
   d. Amebelodon

9. The _____ are an extinct order of marine mammals which existed from the Arikareean age of the late Oligocene epoch (30.8 million years ago) to the Tortonian age of the late Miocene epoch (7.25 million years ago.) Their dental and skeletal form suggests they were amphibious herbivores dependent on littoral habitats. Their name refers to their highly distinctive molars, in which each cusp was modified into hollow columns, so that a typical molar would have resembled a cluster of pipes, or in the case of worn molars, volcanoes.
   a. Desmostylia
   c. 1509 Istanbul earthquake
   b. 1703 Genroku earthquake
   d. 1700 Cascadia earthquake

10. _____ is an extinct genus of Hyaenodonts, a group of Creodonts. Some species of this genus were amongst the largest terrestrial carnivorous mammals of their time, others were only of the size of a marten. _____ was one of the latest genera of the Hyaenodonts and is known from the Late Eocene to Early Miocene.
    a. 1703 Genroku earthquake
    c. 1509 Istanbul earthquake
    b. Hyaenodon
    d. 1700 Cascadia earthquake

11. _____ is an extinct genus of marine bears which existed from the Hemingfordian age to the Aquitanian age of the Miocene epoch, about 20 million years ago. It was described in 1960 by Ruben A. Stirton, a paleontologist at the American Museum of Natural History, from a partial skull and jaw found on the Olympic Peninsula. Stirton thought the fossil was a large marine procyonid, but a specimen found in two pieces by fossil collector Douglas Emlong near Newport, Oregon, in 1969 and 1977, proved the genus was related to ancestors of bears.
    a. 1700 Cascadia earthquake
    c. Kolponomos
    b. 1509 Istanbul earthquake
    d. 1703 Genroku earthquake

12. _____ is an extinct species of marine bear which existed from the Hemingfordian age to the Aquitanian age of the Miocene epoch, about 20 million years ago. It was described in 1994 by R. Tedford, L. Barnes and Clayton E. Ray.
    a. 1703 Genroku earthquake
    c. 1509 Istanbul earthquake
    b. Kolponomos newportensis
    d. 1700 Cascadia earthquake

13. _____, also commonly known as Indricotherium or Baluchitherium or just Indricothere, is an extinct genus of gigantic hornless rhinoceros-like mammals, belonging to the family of the Hyracodontidae. Their fossils have been found in many parts of Asia, including Kazakhstan, Pakistan, India, Mongolia, and China. It lived from the middle Oligocene to the early Miocene, roughly from 30 to 20 million years ago, when this region of Asia was covered in lush subtropical forests and woodlands.
   a. 1703 Genroku earthquake
   b. 1700 Cascadia earthquake
   c. 1509 Istanbul earthquake
   d. Paraceratherium

14. _____ ferox, the Horned Armadillo, was a species of dog-sized, armadillo-like xenarthran mammal which first inhabited Argentina during the Oligocene epoch, and became extinct sometime during the Miocene epoch. Notably, the scutes on its head were so developed that they formed horns protecting its eyes. Aside from the horned gophers of North America, it is the only known fossorial horned mammal.
   a. 1700 Cascadia earthquake
   b. 1509 Istanbul earthquake
   c. 1703 Genroku earthquake
   d. Peltephilus

15. _____ was a rodent that lived in the ancient Orinoco River delta approximately 8 million years ago. It was the second-largest of the roughly 7 species of its genus. Like many other rodents, Phoberomys was a herbivore with high-crowned premolars and molars.
   a. Phoberomys pattersoni
   b. 1703 Genroku earthquake
   c. 1509 Istanbul earthquake
   d. 1700 Cascadia earthquake

16. _____ was a genus of giant flightless predatory birds that lived in Patagonia, containing the single species _____ longissimus. Their closest living relatives are Seriema birds. It was much larger than the seriemas, however, and looked more like an ostrich in appearance.
   a. 1700 Cascadia earthquake
   b. 1509 Istanbul earthquake
   c. 1703 Genroku earthquake
   d. Phorusrhacos

17. _____ is an early representative of the family Deinotheriidae, that lived in Africa, Europe, and Asia in the early and middle Miocene. It was the size of a small elephant, about 9 feet at the shoulders, but differed from elephants in possessing a pair of downward curving tusks on the lower jaw. In appearance and many characters it was like Deinotherium (with which it is placed in the subfamily, Deinotheriinae (Sanders et al 2004), but differed in being of smaller size, having shorter forelimbs, and also in various details in the shape and form of the teeth.
   a. 1703 Genroku earthquake
   b. 1700 Cascadia earthquake
   c. 1509 Istanbul earthquake
   d. Prodeinotherium

18. _____, in North West Queensland, is Australia's most famous fossil site. The 100 km^2 area has fossil remains of ancient mammals, birds and reptiles of Oligocene and Miocene age. The site was inscribed as a World Heritage site in 1994 and is an extension of the Lawn Hill National Park.
   a. 1509 Istanbul earthquake
   b. 1700 Cascadia earthquake
   c. 1703 Genroku earthquake
   d. Riversleigh

19. _____ is an early fossil catarrhine that predates the divergence between hominoids and Old World monkeys. It is known from a single species _____ zeuxis and lived some 35-33 million years ago in the early part of the Oligocene epoch. It likely resembled modern-day New World monkeys

a. AL 129-1
b. AASHTO Soil Classification System
c. Aegyptopithecus
d. AL 333

20. The genus _____ is that of at least three extinct primates living in the early Oligocene, roughly 36 to 32 millions years ago. _____ fossils are common in the Fayoum deposits of Egypt. Fossils of the earlier species, _____ moustafai, are rare; fossils of the later species _____ phiomense are fairly common.
   a. AASHTO Soil Classification System
   b. AL 129-1
   c. AL 333
   d. Apidium

21. _____ was a family of mammals belonging to the extinct order Embrithopoda. Remains have been found in the Middle East, Africa, Asia and Romania. When alive, they would have had a great, albeit very superficial resemblance to the modern rhinoceros.
   a. AASHTO Soil Classification System
   b. AL 333
   c. AL 129-1
   d. Arsinoitheriidae

22. _____ is an extinct genus of artiodactyl ungulate, and is among the earliest known anthracotheres. The genus was extremely widespread, first being found in Asia in the middle Eocene, in Europe during the latest Eocene, and having spread to North America by the early Oligocene.

_____ was about 1.5 metres (4.9 ft) in body length, and had a long, vaguely horse-like head. Its small tusks which it used to uproot plants, and spoon-shaped incisors ideal for pulling and cropping water plants.

   a. AL 333
   b. AL 129-1
   c. AASHTO Soil Classification System
   d. Elomeryx

23. _____ was a genus of small, goat-like oreodonts with proportionally big heads found throughout North America during the Late Oligocene. Because skeletons of _____ have been found by the literal thousands (in even greater numbers than the related genus Sespia), it is often quoted as being the most numerous mammal in North America during the Late Oligocene. It had high-crowned, hypsodont teeth which were used to chew gritty vegetation.
   a. 1703 Genroku earthquake
   b. 1700 Cascadia earthquake
   c. Leptauchenia
   d. 1509 Istanbul earthquake

24. _____ is an extinct family of medium to large-sized carnivorous mammals that were closely related to artiodactyls (even-toed ungulates.) They first appeared in the Early Paleocene, undergoing numerous speciation events during the Paleocene, and Eocene. _____ faired very poorly at the close of the Eocene epoch, with only one genus, Mongolestes, survived into the Early Oligocene epoch.
   a. Pachyaena
   b. Hapalodectidae
   c. Triisodontidae
   d. Mesonychidae

25. _____ is an extinct genus of the dog family (Canidae) referrable to the extinct subfamily Borophaginae. Fossils of _____ have been collected from the Oligocene of South Dakota, Montana, Wyoming.

_____ was a small borophagine characterized by a short, broad skull, a specialized middle ear, simple, tall premolar teeth, and molars that are incipiently adapted to an omnivorous diet.

a. AL 129-1
b. AASHTO Soil Classification System
c. Otarocyon
d. AL 333

26. _____ saurognathus is an extinct mesonychid mammal known from the Paleocene of New Mexico. _____ is the largest mesonychid known from the Paleocene of North America, and it provides the best evidence for sexual dimorphism in mesonychids.

The main feature that distinguishes A. saurognathus from the ancestral Dissacus species is its size: _____ grew to be as large as a bear, as compared to the coyote or jackal-sized species of Dissacus. In fact, the only North American mesonychids that surpassed _____ in size were the larger species of the Early Eocene genus, Pachyaena, such as P. gigantea and P. ossifraga.

a. Ankalagon
b. AL 333
c. AASHTO Soil Classification System
d. AL 129-1

Chapter 20. Test Preparation Part 20

1. _____ is a genus of mammals from the extinct order of Multituberculata. It is known from the Paleocene of North America.

The genus _____ was formally named by Krause in 1987 (Krause, 1987), and has also been known as Mimetodon (partly), Neoplagiaulax (partly), and Ptilodus (partly.)

   a. Mesodma
   b. Prochetodon
   c. Cimolodontidae
   d. Baiotomeus

2. _____ is an extinct mammal, once believed to be related to the modern pangolin.

It was discovered in 1956 in Alberta, Canada. It is known primarily from fossil jaws dating back 60 million years ago, during the Palaeocene epoch.

Interestingly, the canine teeth in Bisonalveus have grooves that may have been used for delivering a venomous bite. The canines that would contain venom do not correspond with the lower jaw, rendering these teeth as deadly fangs, as in many species of poisonous snakes.

   a. 1703 Genroku earthquake
   b. 1509 Istanbul earthquake
   c. 1700 Cascadia earthquake
   d. Bisonalveus browni

3. _____ is a family of fossil mammals within the extinct order Multituberculata. Representatives are known from the Upper Cretaceous and Paleocene of North America. There is some doubt as to whether Cimolodon is within this taxon.
   a. Cimolodonta
   b. Pentacosmodon
   c. Mesodma
   d. Cimolodontidae

4. _____ is a family of fossil mammal within the extinct order Multituberculata. Representatives are known from the Upper Cretaceous and the Paleocene of North America and perhaps Mongolia. The family is part of the suborder Cimolodonta.
   a. Taeniolabidoidea
   b. Ptilodontoidea
   c. Microcosmodon
   d. Cimolomyidae

5. _____ is an extinct genus of mammal, a member of the extinct order Multituberculata within the suborder Cimolodonta, family Neoplagiaulacidae. It lived during the upper Cretaceous and Paleocene Periods of what is now North America. This genus has been the subject of much revision, and has also been known in part as Cimexomys, Cimolomys, Halodon, Parectypodus, and Ptilodon.
   a. Cimolodonta
   b. Mesodma
   c. Pentacosmodon
   d. Parectypodus

6. _____ is a mammal genus from the Paleocene of North America. It was a member of the extinct order Multituberculata, and lies within the suborder Cimolodonta and family Microcosmodontidae. The genus _____ was named by G.L. Jepsen in 1930.
   a. Microcosmodon
   b. Cimolodonta
   c. Prochetodon
   d. Xyronomys

7. _____ is a mammal genus from the Paleocene of North America, so it lived somewhat after the 'age of the dinosaurs'. It was a member of the extinct order Multituberculata. It's within the suborder Cimolodonta and family Microcosmodontidae.

a. Pentacosmodon
b. Microcosmodon
c. Prochetodon
d. Cimolomyidae

8. _____ is one of the oldest known primate-like mammal species which existed about 58-55 mya in North America and Europe. It looked a little like a squirrel. _____ still had claws and its eyes were located on each side of the head, making them faster on the ground than on the top of the trees, but they begin to spend long times on lower branches of trees, feeding on fruits and leaves.

a. 1703 Genroku earthquake
b. 1509 Istanbul earthquake
c. 1700 Cascadia earthquake
d. Plesiadapis

9. _____ is a genus of extinct mammal from the Paleocene of Central Asia. It was a relatively large member of the extinct order Multituberculata within the suborder Cimolodonta and superfamily Taeniolabidoidea. The genus was named by Matthew W.D. and Granger W.

a. Taeniolabidoidea
b. Prionessus
c. Xanclomys
d. Pentacosmodon

10. _____ is a group of extinct mammals known from North America and Asia. They were the largest members of the also extinct order Multituberculata. Lambdopsalis even provides direct fossil evidence of mammalian fur in a fairly good state of preservation for a 60-million-year-old animal.

a. Ptilodontoidea
b. Prochetodon
c. Mesodma
d. Taeniolabidoidea

11. _____ tersus is a primitive, pompano-like jack fish from what is now Turkmenistan. It lived in an ocean upwelling with its relative, Archaeus oblonga during the Thanetian epoch of the late Paleocene. Some incomplete fossil specimens were once identified as being a separate species, 'Uylyaichthys eugeniae.' .

a. 1703 Genroku earthquake
b. 1509 Istanbul earthquake
c. Trachicaranx
d. 1700 Cascadia earthquake

12. _____ finitimus is an extinct lamprid from the Danata Formation Lagerstatten, of the Upper Paleocene of Turkmenistan. It lived sympatrically with its close relative, Danatinia.

In life, T. finitimus would have resembled a spadefish with beak-like lips, or a very small opah (its closest living relative) with a bulging forehead.

a. 1703 Genroku earthquake
b. 1700 Cascadia earthquake
c. 1509 Istanbul earthquake
d. Turkmene

13. _____ is a small mammal from the Paleocene of North America. It was a genus within the extinct order Multituberculata within the suborder Cimolodonta and family Neoplagiaulacidae.

The genus _____, named by Rigby J.K. in 1980, is also known as Xancolomys The identification is based on a single species, _____ mcgrewi.

| a. Parectypodus | b. Prionessus |
| c. Xyronomys | d. Xanclomys |

14. _____ is an extinct genus of small mammals from the Paleocene of North America, with one species described and a second species is awaiting publication. The genus lies within the extinct order Multituberculata within the suborder Cimolodonta and family Neoplagiaulacidae. Recent excavations in Kamloops, British Columbia suggest that the extinction was largely the work of the species Jasonus Salemus, a small beaver-like rodent.

| a. Pentacosmodon | b. Cimolomyidae |
| c. Microcosmodon | d. Xyronomys |

15. _____ is the fossilized knee joint of the species Australopithecus afarensis. It was discovered in Hadar, Ethiopia by Donald Johanson in November 1973.

It is estimated to be 3-3.2 million years old.

| a. AL 333 | b. AL200-1 |
| c. AASHTO Soil Classification System | d. AL 129-1 |

16. _____ is the fossilized upper palate and teeth of the species Australopithecus afarensis. It was discovered in the Afar Depression in Ethiopia by Donald Johanson in 1975. It is estimated to be 3.0-3.2 million years old.

| a. AL 333 | b. AL 129-1 |
| c. AASHTO Soil Classification System | d. AL200-1 |

17. _____ is the name given to the only specimen ever discovered of Australopithecus bahrelghazali. _____ was found in January 1995 in Chad in the Kanem Region by the paleontologist Michel Brunet, who named the fossil '_____' in memory of his close friend _____ Brillanceau, who had died of malaria in 1989.

Of _____ remains only part of a jaw, which explains the little information descernable concerning its way of life.

| a. AL 333 | b. AL 129-1 |
| c. Abel | d. AASHTO Soil Classification System |

18. _____ is a fossilized skull of the species Homo sapiens. It was discovered in Les Eyzies, France by Louis Lartet in 1868.

It is estimated to be 30,000 years old.

| a. 1509 Istanbul earthquake | b. 1700 Cascadia earthquake |
| c. 1703 Genroku earthquake | d. Cro-Magnon 1 |

19. The _____ Skull is a nearly complete fossilized skull of a representative of the genus Homo which lived sometime during the Late Middle Pleistocene period. It was discovered by Shuntang Liu in 1978 in _____ County in the Shaanxi Province of China

Although dating has been a subject of debate, the fossil is estimated to be about 209,000 years old, and is considered to be the most complete skull of that time period found in China. The _____ cranium is currently housed in the Institute of Vertebrate Paleontology and Paleoanthropology in Beijing, China.

There has been considerable debate regarding how to classify the fossil in terms of species, with some anthropologists insisting it to be a regional variant of Homo heidelbergensis and others categorizing it as an early representative of Homo sapiens.

   a. Compaction
   b. Dali
   c. Submersion
   d. Combe

20. _____ are the preserved remains or traces of animals, plants, and other organisms from the remote past. The totality of _____, both discovered and undiscovered, and their placement in fossiliferous rock formations and sedimentary layers (strata) is known as the fossil record. The study of _____ across geological time, how they were formed, and the evolutionary relationships between taxa (phylogeny) are some of the most important functions of the science of paleontology.
   a. 1703 Genroku earthquake
   b. Fossils
   c. 1509 Istanbul earthquake
   d. 1700 Cascadia earthquake

21. The _____ is a hominid skull discovered on February 16, 2006 near the drainage of Gawis, a tributary of the Awash River in the Afar Depression, Ethiopia. The skull is between 200,000 and 500,000 years old and appears to be an intermediate species between Homo erectus and Homo sapiens. Scientists suspect the skull could be a transitional fossil that fills a gap in human evolutionary origins.
   a. 1509 Istanbul earthquake
   b. 1703 Genroku earthquake
   c. 1700 Cascadia earthquake
   d. Gawis cranium

22. The human fossil bones remains from the _____ dated to the age of 30,150 >± 800 years BP, and Cioclovina Cave, dated to the age of 29,000>±700 years BP are among the most ancient early modern humans from the Romanian region. On the basis of radiocarbon dating and also the analysis of the archaeological context one could advance primarily the hypothesis of the association of these bones with the Aurignacian tehnocomplex. At the same time one mentions the possibility that these findings could belong to a certain regional facies from the Southern Carpathians, from the period of the Final Middle Paleolithic and Early Upper Paleolithic, characterized by the coexistence of both final stage of the Quartzitic assemblage, and the tehnocomplex of Early Aurignacian.
   a. Muierii Cave
   b. 1509 Istanbul earthquake
   c. KNM ER 3733
   d. Lucy

23. _____ is a fossilised hominid cranium. Some paleoanthropologists (e.g. Bernard Wood) consider it the remains of the species Homo ergaster, while others consider it to be Homo erectus. It was discovered in Koobi Fora, Kenya by Bernard Ngeneo in 1975.
   a. KNM ER 3733
   b. 1509 Istanbul earthquake
   c. Muierii Cave
   d. Lucy

24. _____ or Kabwe cranium, or Broken Hill 1 is a hominin fossil that was frequently classified as belonging to Homo rhodesiensis. The cranium was found in an iron and zinc mine in Broken Hill Northern Rhodesia (now Kabwe, Zambia) in 1921 by Tom Zwiglaar, a Swiss miner. In addition to the cranium, an upper jaw from another individual, a sacrum, a tibia, and two femur fragments were also found.
   a. KNM ER 3733
   b. Lucy
   c. Kabwe skull
   d. 1509 Istanbul earthquake

25. _____ is the common name of AL 288-1, the 40% complete skeleton of an Australopithecus afarensis specimen discovered in 1974 at Hadar in the Awash Valley of Ethiopia's Afar Depression. _____ is estimated to have lived 3.2 million years ago. The discovery of this hominin was significant as the skeleton shows evidence of small skull capacity akin to that of apes and of bipedal upright walk akin to that of humans, providing further evidence that bipedalism preceded increase in brain size in human evolution.
   a. KNM ER 3733
   b. Muierii Cave
   c. 1509 Istanbul earthquake
   d. Lucy

26. _____ is the fossilized upper cranium of the species Homo erectus. It was discovered in Ngandong, Indonesia by C. ter Haar and GHR von Koenigswald in 1931-1933.
   a. STS 14
   b. NG 6
   c. Sangiran 2
   d. Trachodon mummy

27. _____ is a fossilized skull of the species Homo habilis. It was discovered in Olduvai Gorge, Tanzania by Peter Nzube in 1968. The skull was found crushed almost flat and was therefore named after the famously skinny model of the time Twiggy.
   a. AL 129-1
   b. AL 333
   c. AASHTO Soil Classification System
   d. OH 24

28. The _____ are a collection of hominid bones, discovered by Richard Leakey and others at the Omo Kibish site near the Omo River in the Omo National Park in south-western Ethiopia by the International Paleontological Research Expedition. The remains from the 2 sites, Omo Kibish 1 and 2, are the earliest known fossils of Homo sapiens. The results of Potassium-Argon dating of the tuffs were published in February 2005 attributing them to circa 195,000 years ago, and making Ethiopia the current choice for the 'e;cradle of Homo Sapiens'e;.
   a. AL 333
   b. AASHTO Soil Classification System
   c. AL 129-1
   d. Omo remains

29. _____ is an example of Homo erectus. A group of fossil specimens was discovered in 1923-27 during excavations at Zhoukoudian near Beijing, China. More recently, the finds have been dated from roughly 500 000 years ago, although a new study suggests they may be as much as 680 000-780 000 years old.
   a. 1509 Istanbul earthquake
   b. Peking Man
   c. 1703 Genroku earthquake
   d. 1700 Cascadia earthquake

30. The _____ is the fossilized lower jaw and teeth of the species Paranthropus boisei. It was discovered in Peninj, Tanzania by Richard Leakey in 1964.

It is estimated to be 1.5 million years old.

a. Peninj Mandible
b. Trachodon mummy
c. STS 14
d. Leanderthal Lady

31. _____ is the fossilized partial cranium and palate of the species Paranthropus robustus. It was discovered in Swartkrans, South Africa by Robert Broom in 1949.

It is estimated to be 1.5-2 million years old.

Its characteristics include large cheek teeth and a sagittal crest. The large teeth and crest for attaching chewing muscles indicate a diet consisting mainly of course vegetable matter.

a. STS 14
b. NG 6
c. Sangiran 2
d. SK 46

32. _____ also known as Saldanha cranium or Elandsfontein cranium are fossilized remains of a hominid species believed to be Homo heidelbergensis. The remains were found in Elandsfontein, located in the Saldanha Bay of South Africa.

a. 1700 Cascadia earthquake
b. 1703 Genroku earthquake
c. 1509 Istanbul earthquake
d. Saldanha man

33. _____ is the fossilized upper cranium of the species Homo erectus. It was discovered in Sangiran, Indonesia by GHR von Koenigswald in 1937.

It is estimated to be 0.7-1.6 million years old.

a. SK 46
b. NG 6
c. STS 14
d. Sangiran 2

34. _____ the nickname given to a fossil specimen of small tyrannosaurid dinosaur (probably a juvenile Tyrannosaurus rex, officially known as BMRP 2002.4.1, discovered in the Hell Creek Formation in southern Montana. After four years of preparation, _____ was put on display at Rockford, Illinois' Burpee Museum of Natural History as the centerpiece of an exhibit called '_____: Diary of a Dinosaur.' Paleontologists who support the theory that _____ represents a juvenile believe the tyrannosaur was approximately 11 years old at its time of death, and its fully restored skeleton measured 6.5 metres (21.5 ft) long, about half as long as the largest known complete T. rex specimen, nicknamed 'Sue,' which measures 13 m (42.6 ft) long.

a. STS 14
b. NG 6
c. Trachodon mummy
d. Jane

35. _____, discovered in January of 1983, is the name given to the skeletal remains of a prehistoric woman found at the Wilson-Leonard Brushy Creek Site (an ancient Native American campsite) in the city of Cedar Park, Texas, by the Texas Department of Transportation. The remains were also alternatively labeled 'Leanne'. Both names were inspired by the proximity of the site to the town of Leander, to the north.

Carbon dating and stratigraphic analysis showed the remains to be 10,000 to 13,000 years old. The skeleton is of a five-foot, three-inch tall female who was approximately eighteen to thirty years old at the time of death.

a. Trachodon mummy
b. Peninj Mandible
c. STS 14
d. Leanderthal Lady

36. _____ is a fossilized pelvis, vertebral column and fragmentary rib and femur of the species Australopithecus africanus. It was discovered at Sterkfontein, South Africa by Robert Broom in 1947.

It is estimated to be 2.6-2.8 million years old.

a. NG 6
b. STS 14
c. Leanderthal Lady
d. SK 46

37. The _____ is a very well-preserved fossil of Edmontosaurus annectens, a duckbilled dinosaur. It was found by Charles Hazelius Sternberg and his three sons near Lusk, Wyoming, USA in 1908. Although Sternberg was working under contract to the British Museum of Natural History, Henry Fairfield Osborn of the American Museum of Natural History managed to secure the mummy for $2,000.

a. Leanderthal Lady
b. Trachodon mummy
c. SK 46
d. STS 14

38. The _____ is a geological formation dating to roughly between 228 to 223 million years ago and covering the Carnian to Norian stages. The _____ is found in South Africa and is a member of the Stormberg Group. As its name suggests, it consists mainly of sandstone. Fossils of the prosauropod dinosaur Massospondylus have been recovered from the _____.

a. Turritellenplatte
b. Lancefield Swamp
c. Hell Creek Formation
d. Bushveld Sandstone Formation

39. The _____ is a geological formation dating to roughly between 210 to 190 million years ago and covering the Norian to Sinemurian stages. The _____ is found in South Africa and Lesotho and is a member of the Stormberg Group. It consists mainly of limestone, sandstone, and mudstone. Fossils of the prosauropod dinosaur Massospondylus have been recovered from the upper _____. The upper _____ of South Africa and Lesotho contains the world's most diverse fauna of early Jurassic ornithischian dinosaurs.

a. AL 129-1
b. AASHTO Soil Classification System
c. AL 333
d. Elliot Formation

ANSWER KEY

Chapter 1
1. d	2. d	3. d	4. d	5. a	6. c	7. d	8. c	9. d	10. b
11. d	12. d	13. a	14. a	15. d	16. a	17. c	18. d	19. d	20. a
21. d	22. d	23. d	24. d	25. c	26. a	27. b	28. d	29. c	30. d
31. c	32. d	33. d	34. d	35. b	36. a	37. a	38. d	39. b	40. d
41. d	42. d	43. a	44. b	45. d	46. d	47. d	48. a	49. d	50. d
51. a	52. c	53. d	54. d	55. b	56. b	57. c	58. c	59. d	60. c
61. d	62. d	63. d	64. c	65. d	66. c	67. c	68. d	69. a	70. d
71. d	72. d	73. b	74. b	75. d	76. d	77. d	78. b	79. d	80. a
81. d	82. a	83. d	84. d	85. a	86. b	87. b	88. c	89. d	90. c
91. d	92. a	93. b	94. b	95. d	96. d	97. b	98. c	99. c	100. d
101. b									

Chapter 2
1. d	2. d	3. d	4. a	5. d	6. c	7. d	8. d	9. a	10. d
11. a	12. b	13. c	14. b	15. b	16. d	17. d	18. a	19. d	20. d
21. d	22. a	23. c	24. d	25. d	26. d	27. b	28. d	29. b	30. d
31. c	32. d	33. a	34. a	35. d	36. a	37. d	38. b	39. b	40. d
41. b	42. b	43. d	44. d	45. d	46. c	47. d	48. d	49. d	50. d
51. d	52. b	53. c	54. b	55. d	56. b	57. c	58. b	59. d	60. c
61. a	62. c	63. d	64. a	65. d	66. a	67. d	68. c	69. b	70. b
71. d	72. d	73. c	74. d	75. d	76. d	77. c	78. b	79. d	80. b
81. d	82. c	83. d	84. b	85. c	86. d	87. b	88. d	89. a	90. b
91. d	92. d	93. b	94. d	95. c	96. b				

Chapter 3
1. d	2. a	3. b	4. d	5. c	6. d	7. c	8. d	9. c	10. a
11. d	12. b	13. d	14. d	15. d	16. d	17. b	18. d	19. a	20. b
21. d	22. d	23. c	24. d	25. a	26. d	27. b	28. d	29. b	30. b
31. b	32. c	33. d	34. d	35. d	36. a	37. b	38. d	39. a	40. d
41. b	42. d	43. b	44. a	45. d	46. d	47. d	48. d	49. d	50. c
51. a	52. d	53. b	54. b	55. d	56. a	57. c	58. c	59. c	60. d
61. c	62. a	63. c	64. d	65. d	66. d	67. d	68. d	69. d	70. d
71. c	72. b	73. a	74. a	75. d	76. b	77. b	78. d	79. a	80. d
81. d	82. a	83. c	84. d	85. b	86. d	87. b	88. a	89. a	90. d
91. b	92. a	93. a	94. d	95. d	96. d	97. a	98. c	99. d	100. c
101. d	102. d	103. b	104. b	105. d	106. a	107. d	108. d	109. d	110. a
111. d	112. d	113. d							

Chapter 4

1. d	2. d	3. c	4. d	5. d	6. a	7. d	8. d	9. b	10. d
11. d	12. a	13. d	14. c	15. d	16. b	17. d	18. d	19. a	20. b
21. d	22. d	23. d	24. d	25. c	26. b	27. a	28. a	29. d	30. b
31. c	32. a	33. d	34. d	35. c	36. a	37. d	38. d	39. d	40. d
41. d	42. b	43. b	44. d	45. b	46. b	47. d	48. c	49. d	50. a
51. d	52. d	53. c	54. d	55. d	56. b	57. d	58. c	59. d	60. b
61. d	62. d	63. d	64. d	65. d	66. d	67. d	68. b	69. c	70. d
71. c	72. d	73. c	74. d	75. a	76. c	77. d	78. d	79. b	80. a
81. d	82. c	83. d	84. d	85. a	86. b	87. d	88. d	89. d	90. d
91. a	92. d	93. d	94. b	95. d	96. a	97. c	98. d	99. b	100. c
101. d	102. b	103. a	104. c	105. d	106. a	107. d	108. d	109. d	110. d
111. d	112. d	113. c	114. a	115. a	116. d	117. b	118. b	119. b	120. d

Chapter 5

1. d	2. c	3. c	4. d	5. d	6. c	7. b	8. a	9. d	10. d
11. d	12. d	13. d	14. d	15. d	16. b	17. b	18. d	19. d	20. d
21. d	22. c	23. d	24. d	25. b	26. a	27. d	28. d	29. d	30. b
31. b	32. d	33. b	34. d	35. b	36. d	37. d	38. a	39. a	40. d
41. d	42. c	43. a	44. d	45. a	46. d	47. b	48. d	49. d	50. a
51. a	52. b	53. d	54. b	55. d	56. c	57. c	58. d	59. a	60. d
61. d	62. a	63. a	64. d	65. d	66. a	67. d	68. d	69. a	70. d
71. c	72. a	73. d	74. c	75. d	76. d	77. c	78. b	79. a	80. d
81. c	82. d	83. d	84. b	85. d	86. d	87. d	88. d	89. c	90. a
91. d	92. a	93. d	94. d	95. d	96. d	97. d	98. d	99. c	100. d
101. d	102. b	103. b	104. d	105. b	106. c				

Chapter 6

1. d	2. c	3. a	4. d	5. d	6. d	7. d	8. a	9. c	10. d
11. a	12. c	13. c	14. d	15. c	16. d	17. d	18. d	19. c	20. d
21. d	22. b	23. b	24. a	25. a	26. b	27. a	28. d	29. c	30. b
31. a	32. b	33. d	34. d	35. c	36. d	37. d	38. b	39. d	40. d
41. c	42. a	43. d	44. c	45. c	46. b	47. b	48. b	49. d	50. d
51. c	52. b	53. d	54. d	55. d	56. b	57. a	58. d	59. d	60. d
61. b	62. d	63. c							

ANSWER KEY

Chapter 7

1. d	2. c	3. d	4. d	5. d	6. d	7. a	8. d	9. a	10. a
11. d	12. d	13. d	14. c	15. d	16. c	17. d	18. d	19. b	20. d
21. d	22. d	23. d	24. b	25. d	26. d	27. d	28. d	29. d	30. d
31. d	32. b	33. d	34. d	35. c	36. c	37. d	38. d	39. d	40. d
41. d	42. b	43. d	44. a	45. d	46. d	47. d	48. d	49. b	50. d
51. c	52. d	53. b	54. d	55. d	56. a	57. c	58. d	59. c	60. b
61. c	62. b	63. a	64. b	65. b	66. a	67. a	68. b	69. d	70. b
71. c	72. d	73. d	74. a	75. b	76. d	77. a	78. d	79. d	80. a
81. d	82. d	83. d	84. d	85. d	86. a	87. a	88. d	89. b	90. d
91. a	92. b	93. b	94. a	95. b	96. d	97. c	98. b	99. a	100. b
101. d	102. d	103. a	104. c	105. d	106. d	107. d	108. d		

Chapter 8

1. a	2. d	3. a	4. d	5. d	6. a	7. d	8. d	9. d	10. c
11. d	12. c	13. b	14. d	15. b	16. d	17. c	18. d	19. b	20. a
21. d	22. d	23. a	24. d	25. b	26. d	27. c	28. d	29. d	30. d
31. d	32. d	33. d	34. d	35. c	36. d	37. d	38. d	39. d	40. d
41. d	42. d	43. a	44. a	45. d	46. d	47. d	48. a	49. a	50. d
51. d	52. d	53. d	54. a	55. d	56. d	57. d	58. d	59. a	60. d
61. d	62. d	63. c	64. d	65. c	66. d	67. a	68. d	69. d	70. a
71. a	72. c	73. c	74. b	75. d	76. a	77. b	78. d	79. b	80. c
81. a	82. d	83. c	84. c	85. d	86. d	87. d	88. d	89. d	90. d
91. a	92. a	93. a	94. c	95. b	96. a	97. c	98. a	99. b	100. d
101. b	102. b	103. b	104. a						

Chapter 9

1. b	2. a	3. c	4. a	5. a	6. b	7. d	8. d	9. d	10. c
11. d	12. a	13. a	14. c	15. a	16. c	17. b	18. b	19. d	20. a
21. d	22. d	23. d	24. d	25. d	26. d	27. d	28. a	29. a	30. d
31. b	32. d	33. d	34. a	35. d	36. b	37. b	38. d	39. c	40. b
41. d	42. d	43. d	44. c	45. b	46. d	47. d	48. a	49. d	50. d
51. c	52. c	53. d	54. d	55. b	56. d	57. d	58. d	59. d	60. d
61. d	62. d	63. b	64. d	65. c	66. b	67. d	68. d	69. d	70. d
71. c	72. d	73. d	74. d	75. b	76. d	77. d	78. c	79. d	80. d
81. d	82. d	83. d	84. c	85. d	86. d	87. c	88. b	89. d	90. d
91. a	92. a	93. c	94. d	95. d	96. d	97. d	98. c	99. b	100. d
101. d	102. b	103. c	104. c	105. d	106. d				

Chapter 10

1. b	2. d	3. d	4. c	5. d	6. d	7. d	8. c	9. c	10. d
11. d	12. d	13. b	14. d	15. c	16. d	17. a	18. c	19. c	20. a
21. d	22. c	23. d	24. d	25. d	26. a	27. d	28. c	29. a	30. d
31. d	32. d	33. d	34. d	35. d	36. d	37. c	38. b	39. a	40. d
41. b	42. d	43. c	44. b	45. c	46. b	47. d	48. a	49. a	50. d
51. d	52. d	53. b	54. d	55. a	56. d	57. d	58. b	59. d	60. d
61. d	62. a	63. c	64. d	65. a	66. d	67. b	68. a	69. b	70. b
71. a	72. d	73. a	74. a	75. c	76. d	77. d	78. b	79. a	80. a
81. b	82. d	83. c	84. d	85. b	86. d	87. c	88. c	89. c	90. a
91. d	92. a	93. d	94. d	95. d	96. d	97. c	98. a	99. d	100. d
101. d	102. d	103. d	104. c	105. d	106. d	107. d	108. d	109. d	110. d
111. d	112. c	113. c	114. d	115. b	116. b	117. d	118. d	119. a	

Chapter 11

1. d	2. c	3. d	4. c	5. b	6. d	7. d	8. d	9. d	10. d
11. d	12. d	13. a	14. b	15. d	16. c	17. c	18. a	19. c	20. a
21. d	22. d	23. a	24. d	25. b	26. d	27. a	28. d	29. d	30. d
31. a	32. d	33. d	34. d	35. d	36. d	37. d	38. b	39. d	40. b
41. d	42. d	43. d	44. d	45. d	46. d	47. d	48. d	49. d	50. a
51. d	52. d	53. d	54. a	55. a	56. c	57. d	58. d	59. b	60. d
61. d	62. b	63. c	64. d	65. d	66. c	67. c	68. d	69. a	70. d
71. b	72. b	73. b	74. a	75. a	76. c	77. c	78. a	79. a	80. c
81. c	82. b	83. d	84. c	85. b	86. d	87. c	88. d	89. d	90. a
91. d	92. d	93. c							

Chapter 12

1. d	2. b	3. c	4. d	5. d	6. d	7. d	8. d	9. d	10. b
11. c	12. b	13. c	14. b	15. d	16. a	17. d	18. b	19. d	20. d
21. d	22. d	23. d	24. a	25. b	26. b	27. c	28. c	29. d	30. b
31. b	32. a	33. d	34. a	35. c	36. d	37. b	38. d	39. c	40. b
41. a	42. b	43. b	44. c	45. d	46. c	47. a	48. a	49. b	50. b
51. c	52. d	53. c	54. a	55. d	56. d	57. d	58. d	59. d	60. a
61. d	62. d	63. a	64. d	65. a	66. a	67. a	68. d	69. d	70. d
71. c	72. a	73. d	74. c	75. c	76. d	77. a	78. d	79. d	80. d
81. d	82. d	83. b	84. d	85. d	86. d	87. c	88. d	89. d	90. b
91. d	92. a	93. a	94. d	95. d	96. b	97. b	98. c	99. a	100. d
101. a	102. b	103. b	104. b	105. d	106. d	107. d	108. d	109. d	110. c
111. d	112. a	113. b	114. d	115. d	116. d	117. c	118. d	119. d	120. d
121. d	122. d	123. d	124. a	125. b	126. d	127. d	128. d	129. d	130. c

ANSWER KEY

Chapter 13

1. c	2. d	3. b	4. d	5. d	6. d	7. d	8. a	9. d	10. d
11. d	12. d	13. b	14. c	15. d	16. d	17. b	18. d	19. d	20. c
21. d	22. a	23. d	24. d	25. d	26. d	27. b	28. a	29. d	30. d
31. c	32. d	33. c	34. d	35. d	36. c	37. a	38. d	39. c	40. a
41. d	42. d	43. d	44. d	45. d	46. c	47. d	48. b	49. a	50. b
51. c	52. d	53. a	54. a	55. a	56. c	57. a	58. d	59. d	60. c
61. d	62. b	63. c	64. d	65. d	66. d	67. b	68. d	69. d	70. b
71. c	72. d	73. d	74. a	75. c	76. d	77. a	78. a	79. d	80. c
81. c	82. d	83. d	84. a	85. d	86. b	87. b	88. d	89. d	90. d
91. d	92. d	93. c	94. a	95. d	96. b	97. b	98. a	99. d	100. a
101. a	102. d								

Chapter 14

1. b	2. d	3. a	4. c	5. d	6. d	7. d	8. d	9. c	10. d
11. b	12. d	13. d	14. b	15. d	16. d	17. d	18. b	19. b	20. a
21. b	22. d	23. d	24. b	25. d	26. b	27. b	28. d	29. d	30. a
31. b	32. d	33. d	34. b	35. c	36. c	37. d	38. c	39. c	40. b
41. d	42. b	43. d	44. a	45. d	46. d	47. d	48. d	49. a	50. d
51. b	52. c	53. b	54. d	55. a	56. d	57. d	58. c	59. b	60. c
61. d	62. c	63. b	64. c	65. d	66. d	67. d	68. d	69. b	70. b
71. b	72. d	73. b	74. a	75. c	76. d	77. d	78. d	79. a	80. c
81. d	82. c	83. d	84. d	85. d	86. a	87. c			

Chapter 15

1. d	2. d	3. d	4. b	5. b	6. a	7. a	8. b	9. d	10. d
11. d	12. a	13. b	14. a	15. d	16. c	17. b	18. d	19. b	20. d
21. c	22. c	23. d	24. a	25. d	26. d	27. c	28. d	29. d	30. a
31. c	32. b	33. d	34. d	35. c	36. a	37. a	38. d	39. d	40. b
41. a	42. d	43. d	44. b	45. d	46. c	47. d	48. d	49. d	50. d
51. d	52. b	53. d	54. d	55. d	56. b	57. d	58. b	59. c	60. b
61. a	62. d	63. a	64. d	65. c	66. b	67. a			

Chapter 16

1. a	2. d	3. d	4. b	5. d	6. d	7. c	8. d	9. b	10. c
11. d	12. d	13. d	14. a	15. a	16. d	17. d	18. d	19. b	20. d
21. b	22. d	23. d	24. c	25. b	26. d	27. b	28. b	29. d	30. a
31. d	32. d	33. a	34. d	35. d	36. b	37. c	38. b	39. b	40. d
41. d	42. d	43. d	44. d	45. d	46. a	47. d	48. a	49. b	50. a
51. a	52. d	53. c	54. d	55. b	56. d	57. b	58. d	59. a	60. d
61. c	62. b	63. d	64. b	65. a	66. d	67. a	68. d	69. d	70. b
71. d	72. c	73. d	74. d	75. c	76. c	77. c	78. a	79. d	80. a
81. b	82. d	83. b	84. d	85. a	86. d	87. a	88. c	89. d	90. d
91. a	92. d	93. d	94. d	95. d	96. a	97. a	98. d	99. c	100. c
101. b	102. b	103. c	104. c						

Chapter 17

1. d	2. b	3. d	4. d	5. d	6. a	7. a	8. a	9. a	10. b
11. d	12. b	13. d	14. d	15. b	16. d	17. b	18. d	19. b	20. d
21. d	22. b	23. a	24. b	25. d	26. d	27. d	28. a	29. c	30. d
31. d	32. b	33. b	34. a	35. d	36. a	37. d	38. d	39. d	40. d
41. d	42. b	43. d	44. d	45. a	46. b	47. d	48. d	49. b	50. d
51. a	52. a	53. c	54. d	55. d	56. d	57. d	58. d	59. d	60. b
61. b	62. d	63. d	64. b	65. d	66. d	67. b	68. d	69. d	70. d
71. d	72. d	73. c	74. d	75. d	76. c	77. b	78. b	79. d	80. d
81. a	82. d	83. b	84. d	85. d	86. b	87. d	88. a	89. d	90. a
91. a	92. c	93. b	94. c	95. a	96. d	97. b	98. d	99. d	100. d
101. d	102. d	103. d	104. d						

Chapter 18

1. a	2. b	3. a	4. d	5. d	6. d	7. d	8. a	9. c	10. c
11. b	12. d	13. a	14. d	15. d	16. a	17. d	18. d	19. d	20. a
21. b	22. d	23. d	24. c	25. b	26. d	27. b	28. a	29. d	30. d
31. d	32. d	33. d	34. a	35. a	36. a	37. b	38. b	39. d	40. d
41. d	42. d	43. a	44. d	45. d	46. a	47. d	48. b	49. a	

Chapter 19

1. d	2. d	3. b	4. a	5. d	6. b	7. d	8. d	9. a	10. b
11. c	12. b	13. d	14. d	15. a	16. d	17. d	18. d	19. c	20. d
21. d	22. d	23. c	24. d	25. c	26. a				

Chapter 20

1. d	2. d	3. d	4. d	5. b	6. a	7. a	8. d	9. b	10. d
11. c	12. d	13. d	14. d	15. d	16. d	17. c	18. d	19. b	20. b
21. d	22. a	23. a	24. c	25. d	26. b	27. d	28. d	29. b	30. a
31. d	32. d	33. d	34. d	35. d	36. b	37. b	38. d	39. d	

ANSWER KEY

Chapter 21

www.ingramcontent.com/pod-product-compliance
Lightning Source LLC
Chambersburg PA
CBHW082143230426
43672CB00015B/2837